Teaching 101

Classroom Strategies for the Beginning Teacher

Jeffrey Glanz

CORWIN PRESS
A Sage Publications Company
Thousand Oaks, California

For information:

Corwin Press
A Sage Publications Company
2455 Teller Road
Thousand Oaks, California 91320
www.corwinpress.com

Sage Publications Ltd.
6 Bonhill Street
London EC2A 4PU
United Kingdom

Sage Publications India Pvt. Ltd.
B-42, Panchsheel Enclave
Post Box 4109
New Delhi 110 017 India

Printed in the United States of America

Library of Congress Cataloging-in-Publication Data

Glanz, Jeffrey.
Teaching 101: Classroom strategies for the beginning teacher / Jeffrey Glanz.
    p. cm.
Includes bibliographical references and index.
ISBN 0-7619-3916-4 — ISBN 0-7619-3917-2 (pbk.)
   1. First year teachers—United States—Handbooks, manuals, etc.
2. Effective teaching—United States—Handbooks, manuals, etc. I. Title: Teaching one hundred one. II. Title: Teaching one hundred and one. III. Title.
LB2844.1.N4G53 2004
371.1—dc22   2003020897

This book is printed on acid-free paper.

03   04   05   06   10   9   8   7   6   5   4   3   2   1

Acquisitions Editor:	Robert D. Clouse
Editorial Assistant:	Jingle Vea
Production Editor:	Diane S. Foster
Copy Editor:	Rodney Williams
Typesetter:	C&M Digitals (P) Ltd.
Proofreader:	Taryn Bigelow
Indexer:	Teri Greenberg
Cover Designer:	Michael Dubowe
Graphic Designer:	Lisa Miller

Contents

Preface

In the opinion of fools, it is a humble task,
But, in fact, it is the noblest of occupations.

—Erasmus

On the first day of class, I tell my thirty eager prospective college students a story. After all, isn't that what good teachers do? That is, tell stories . . . This is a famous story, I tell them, told at Harvard Law School in which 175 eager, albeit anxious, first-year law students await their first professor in their first course. A middle-aged, scholarly-looking gentleman dressed in a dapper blue suit enters the huge auditorium through one of the doors adjacent to the stage. The professor walks across the stage without looking out at his audience. He places his ledger on the podium and peers out at his students and selects his victim. "You," pointing to a male student in the rear of the auditorium, "state the facts in the case before you." Nervously and hurriedly, the 175 students read the case they had only moments ago ignored. The student selected by the professor offers no response. Once again the professor repeats his request. The student again freezes. Again the request is made. "State the facts in the case before you." The student gives an inadequate answer. Stoic and silent, the professor nonchalantly reaches into his pocket and takes out a dime and says "Take this dime, call your mother (it's an old story!), and tell her to pick you up because you'll never become a lawyer." Shocked, yet thankful they weren't called upon, the 174 other students anxiously await the student's reaction. No response. "You heard what I said. Take this dime and tell your mother to pick you up." The student rises and walks slowly towards the stage. Hushed silence pervades the auditorium. Suddenly the student stops, looks up at the professor and shouts "Sir, you are a bastard." Without batting an eyelash, the professor looks up and says "Go back to your seat, you're beginning to think like a lawyer."

"This story," I inform my class, "epitomizes the purpose of law school, which is to instill habits of skepticism, verbal aggressiveness, and the readiness to challenge the authority of a lawyer." I continue by conveying my expectations and hopes for them this semester. "My purposes in teaching this course are very different from that professor at Harvard. I do, however, want to help you begin to *think and act* as a teacher . . . to respect teaching as a noble profession." That is my goal for you, too, my reader. To think, act, and be proud you are a teacher. As a new teacher, you face daunting tasks and inevitable challenges. The problems and pressures you encounter are unique. At every turn you may be belittled, criticized, and unappreciated. Those who do not teach can never really know all that you encounter and experience. As one of my non-teaching acquaintances once queried: "How tough can it be? You teach a half a year, have all holidays and summers off, and leave work when the sun is still shining?!" Go explain . . . ugh . . . Do you feel the same way? Respond to the Likert-type statements in Form P.1 to reflect upon and express your feelings about your profession and some of the reasons why you decided to teach.

If you checked Strongly Agree (SA) for most, if not all of the items, then you value your chosen profession, understand why it's so vital to society, and are upset when others misunderstand or denigrate teaching. And now for another story . . .

Many years ago when I was a fourth-grade teacher with only a few years of teaching experience, I attended a conference, unrelated to education, in Austin, Texas. Between conference sessions, I walked into a cocktail reception area and found myself in a small group with three other conference attendees. Not knowing each other, the first question one of the fellows posed was "What do you do?" An athletic, tall, tan-skinned gentleman dressed in a rather expensive black suit proclaimed proudly that he was an anesthesiologist. The next gentleman, anticipating his turn, announced boldly and arrogantly, "I am a *successful* attorney (notice the added adjective) working on Wall Street." Intent to outdo the first two contributors of this dull yet intense conversation was a short, stocky middle-aged man who stated emphatically, "Well, I own a chain of high tech companies throughout North America" (fortunately for him, this conversation took place many years prior to the recent demise of dot coms and related tech companies). Their eyes then turned towards me. I must admit I hesitated for a moment. I swallowed and looked as confident as I could saying, "I am a teacher." They stared at me in deathly silence. The seconds felt like minutes. Then, I think it was the lawyer who muttered, "uh hum. . . ." Clearing his throat nervously, he quickly changed the topic to discuss the weather. The discomfort was palpable. Although I am usually reticent in such situations, a fearless

Form P.1   Respond

RESPOND				
SA = Strongly Agree ("For the most part, yes") A = Agree ("Yes, but . . . ") D = Disagree ("No, but . . .") SD = Strongly Disagree ("For the most part, no")	*SA*	*A*	*D*	*SD*
1. I feel upset when others criticize or belittle teachers and teaching.				
2. I became a teacher and remain one because I love children (my students).				
3. I consider those who go into teaching, for the most part, committed and dedicated professionals.				
4. I would recommend that my son or daughter become a teacher if he or she is inclined to do so.				
5. I went into teaching, for the most part, because of the emotional satisfaction provided.				
6. I am disturbed when the media misrepresent teachers and teaching.				
7. I consider myself a professional on a par with lawyers and medical doctors.				
8. I am uncomfortable when I have to defend why I went into teaching.				
9. Teachers should receive more recognition and remuneration.				
10. I chose to become a teacher because I want to make a difference in the lives of my students not because I'll have summers off.				

attitude overcame me that afternoon. Perhaps it was wanting, or needing to "give it" to those snobbish, elitist "gentlemen," or perhaps I felt an obligation to the profession I loved so much. I stated loudly and clearly, "Excuse me, but may I ask how you became a lawyer?" Momentarily stunned, the fellow retorted, "Well, of course, I attended the finest law school." "And," I added, "who taught you how to conduct research, write a brief, and to do 'lawyering' in general?" "Well, my professors of course." To which I quickly responded, "Oh, you mean teachers." At that point, I placed my drink on the nearest tabletop and disdainfully walked away from the smoke-filled room with so much negative energy.

Teaching is certainly noble, as the quote by Erasmus at the beginning of the Preface indicates. Teachers have the privilege of caring for youth by helping them develop the necessary academic and social skills for successful living. As Elliot Eisner, an insightful educational critic, insightfully posits (and I'm paraphrasing), "The purpose of teaching is not to help students do well in school but, rather, to do well in life." Teachers, then, are in an optimal, influential position to make a difference in the lived experiences of their students. As such, teaching is indeed important and should receive its due recognition.

I wrote this book because I believe that teaching is a spiritual and intellectual calling. Teaching is both a science and an art. I believe that teachers are born great but I also believe that one can become a great teacher. How to do so is not as easy to answer. Many books on becoming a teacher flood the market. Many of these texts are used in college courses for preparing prospective teachers. Most, if not all, of these books are lengthy and cover many topics that are not necessarily critical for the K–12 practitioner. A new book is needed that culls the essential principles and ideas about teaching in an easy-to-read, concise yet thoughtful and still comprehensive manner. *Teaching 101* is such a text. I have tried to distill essential ideas and practices into a concise text that is reader-friendly, easy to understand, and practical.

Teaching 101 identifies, describes, and explains essential theories and practices for excellence in teaching and being a successful teacher. This book is primarily written for the new teacher, whether he or she is contemplating the career, just starting out, or within the first several years. The ideas and principles contained here are necessarily generic and relate to teachers at all levels K–12. *Teaching 101* is written in workbook format to facilitate easy reading and use. Charts, photos, blocked text, questionnaires, and practice exercises will make for easy, enjoyable, and meaningful reading.

Teaching 101 includes the following chapters:

- *Why Does Teaching Matter?* – A short and hopefully inspirational beginning to help you understand the importance of education and teaching, and the impact we have as teachers.
- *What Makes a Good Teacher?* – A practical overview of specific knowledge, skills, and dispositions that good teachers possess.
- *Who Are the Students in My Class?* – Some of the differences in student learning styles and needs of students.
- *How Should I Write Lesson Plans?* – A nuts-and-bolts approach to designing lessons from including using questions effectively.
- *Can I Effectively Manage My Classroom?* – Simple and effective suggestions and guidelines to successfully promote positive student behavior in the classroom.

- *How Can I Help My Students Learn?* – An analysis of several key metacognitive strategies that promote learning drawing on brain-based learning strategies, including study skills instruction and cooperative learning.
- *How Can I Best Incorporate State and District Curriculum Standards?* – Suggestions for teaching to the numerous statewide and local standards-based reforms while at the same time developing creative, interdisciplinary lessons.
- *How Can I Begin to Incorporate Technology into My Teaching?* – Suggestions for using technology to best promote student learning.
- *How Should I Assess and Grade My Students?* – Simple yet concise guidelines on developing a system of assessment in your classroom.
- *How Can I Build a Professional Portfolio?* – Acknowledging the complexities of effective teaching and indicating that there is much more to learn about teaching, this closing chapter guides you to develop a Mission Statement and a portfolio to record your progress as a professional educator.

Teaching 101 includes Focus Questions at the start of each chapter and Follow-up Questions/Activities that you are encouraged to answer or undertake. You will also find a number of interactive tools ("Reflect," "Respond," and "Recollection") that provide background, reinforce ideas, and/or extend practice that I hope you respond to by writing responses or thinking deeply. These interactive tools will engage and challenge you to reflect on new material and help frame your own teaching philosophy and Mission Statement (see Chapter 10) as will Appendix C. ***Teaching 101*** includes three useful appendixes: (1) contains essential readings; (2) contains key Web sites that will provide practical ideas, information, and teaching suggestions; and (3) contains a self-assessment instrument used as a reflective tool to assist you in becoming an even better teacher.

This book will acquaint you, the prospective and/or new teacher, with ideas about teaching that are essential for success. The book will also reinforce or ingrain information you might already know. ***Teaching 101*** will encourage you to develop and maintain a professional portfolio to monitor and assess your progress from a neophyte to an accomplished professional educator. Various exercises throughout the book will encourage you to develop a Mission Statement to guide your practice. To help you get started, see Respond below.

RESPOND

After you complete reading this book (see Chapter 10), I want you to develop a Mission Statement for yourself. Your Mission will include a brief statement that you can actually post on a wall or keep on your desk. This statement will be one that you can refer to daily *to inspire* you. The statement will remind you why you went into teaching in the first place and, importantly, why you remain a teacher. Now, before you do that, let's begin here in this activity to record your philosophy (beliefs) about teaching. Jot ideas below and in future activities I will guide you to more fully develop a Mission Statement.

_____

_____

_____

Acknowledgments

"I have learned much from my teachers, even more from my colleagues, but, most of all, from my students."

—Passage from the *Talmud* (ancient Hebrew text)

This work stands on the shoulders of many others that have contributed to the literature of teacher education. I owe a great debt of gratitude to my teachers. Two teachers stand out in my mind as influencing me the most during those precollege years. I thank Mrs. Barris, my Hebrew language high school teacher who taught me one of the most valuable lessons in life. One year she gave me the "Ayin Award" for highest achievement in Hebrew language. Now, you might think that I could speak Hebrew fluently. I can't now and I didn't then. In our class there were Israeli boys and girls who were fluent. Yet, she gave *me* the award. "Why?" I asked her. She responded with an invaluable lesson of life. "Jeffrey, sure they speak fluently, but you try harder and get higher marks on written tests." I learned that *effort* pays off. I have tried to instill that virtue, more than any other, in my students through my teaching. I also acknowledge Mr. Walter Benjamin, my high school geometry teacher. He was the first teacher to acknowledge my potential to succeed despite messages from other teachers to the contrary. Thanks as well to the following individuals who influenced my teaching style: Gregory Holtz, Arno Bellack, Gary Griffin, James Sanders, Carmen Benardo, Dwayne Huebner, Dorothy Hennings, and Harvey Sober.

Colleagues have perhaps inspired me even more. Their closeness and friendship meant all the difference. Deep appreciation is extended to Jeffrey Shurack, Dawn Cuccinnello, Jim Reilly, Helen Hazi, Tom Banit, Myra Weiger, Michael Andron, Susan Sullivan, Xiaobo Yu, Connie Donvito, Gerry Melnick, and Lisa Glanz, my wife and colleague.

I am most grateful to my students because it is they who challenged me, stimulated my thought, and motivated me to excel. Many, many students stand out in my mind. This book would not be possible if not for the thousands of students I have taught over the years at elementary, middle, high schools, and colleges. I'll try to mention some in fear of leaving out so many more. I apologize in advance if I left you out. Daniel, a fourth grade student in my first year of teaching, you were the first student who presented a difficult challenge. We succeeded, Daniel, and I even named my first-born after you, although you are unaware of it. Thanks to former students Tzipie Brown, Nechama Henya Kaplan, and Faigy Leffler, who worked with me on a master's degree project in 1996 to develop a guidebook for beginning teachers. I have, thanks to you, used some of that material here. Thanks to Anthony Vavallo, Erika O'Rourke, Marissa Meduri, Rivka Teitelbaum, Rachel Schwab, Moises Vazquez, Clinia Miller, Dolores Querques, Nicholas Sansone, Rivkah Dahan, Sharon Bertram, Leslie Williams-Jenkins, Gilda Spiotta, Vivian Rodriguez, Amy Quinn, Amanda Hamrah, Laura Giumarra, Shirley Nichols, Lorin Edelman, Ivonne Caceres, Nadia Wagner, Barbara Persky, and Barbara LaMort. Thanks to Randall Dancan, owner of Eden Enterprises, for some adapted material in Chapter 2.

I have unwittingly drawn on the works of many others. My notes are many and often they do not include a precise source. Nothing is new, not even the ideas in this book. Someone once said that every good teacher steals an idea or technique from someone else. That is certainly true here. I have tried to reference and acknowledge all who are deserving, but I may have inadvertently missed someone or something. If I have done so, please let me know so I can make the correction in the next edition of this work.

Many thanks to Robb Clouse, Senior Editor of Corwin Publishers, who believed in this project and my ability to make it happen. Thanks to a great graduate assistant, Melissa Dene. A great deal is owed to many other individuals who have contributed to the publication of this book. While I certainly acknowledge their contribution, any deficiencies that exist are my sole responsibility.

About the Author

 **Jeffrey Glanz** received his BA and MS from the City University of New York and an MA and EdD from Teachers College, Columbia University. He formally taught at the elementary and middle school levels for fifteen years before serving as an assistant principal in an urban elementary school. He taught at the secondary level as well as in other nonformal school settings. Dr. Glanz currently serves as Dean of Graduate Studies and Chair of Education at Wagner College in Staten Island, New York. He holds faculty status as a tenured professor in the Department of Education. Dr. Glanz was Executive Assistant to the President at Kean University and was named Graduate Teacher of the Year in 1999 by the Student Graduate Association. He was also the recipient of the Presidential Award for Outstanding Scholarship in the same year. Dr. Glanz has authored nine previous books on various educational topics, including co-authoring *Supervision That Improves Teaching* and *Supervision in Practice* with Corwin. He is also the author of Corwin's forthcoming *The Assistant Principal's Handbook: Strategies for Success* (April, 2004). He is a prominent national speaker on topics that include instructional leadership, educational supervision, and teaching strategies. You may contact him at View, his Web site at http://www. wagner.edu/faculty/users/jglanz/web/.

For my students, from whom I've learned
even more than from my colleagues or teachers

1
Why Does Teaching Matter?

A conversation between Sir Thomas More and Richard Rich, a younger associate, regarding Richard's future plans: "More: Why not be a teacher? You'd be a fine teacher. Perhaps even a great one." "Rich: And if I was, who would know it?" "More: You, your pupils, your friends, God. Not a bad public at that. . . ."

—Bolt (*A Man for All Seasons*, 1962, p. 6)

---◆---

FOCUS QUESTIONS

1. What comes to mind when you think of the word "teacher?"

2. When did you first know you wanted to become a teacher?

3. What impact can a teacher have on the life of a student?

4. Why do you think teachers are undervalued members of society? Justify a position in which teaching is as "noble" as law or medicine.

5. How can teaching serve as a spiritual endeavor or a "calling"?

Let's begin by listening to the thoughtful, poignant testimony of one of my students:

Self-exploration: Why Teaching/Why Me?

I think that I am a natural teacher. Therefore, it dumbfounds me that it took until my 37th year to realize that this was the path that I should be taking. Even as a child, I was the "teacher" when we played school . . . my blackboard was my prized possession . . .

The decision to teach came together like a puzzle. As corny as it sounds, the first glimmer that I had was when I saw a bumper sticker with the quote by the now-famous, ill-fated astronaut and teacher Christa McAuliffe, "I touch the future, I teach." I was struck by the enormity of that statement, its implications and its validity. At the time, I was unaware of my interest in this field, but I envied anyone with the gift, and the calling to choose a career that could have such an impact on our world and its inhabitants. My career choices had tended towards "flash and glitz," such as public relations and publicity. My skills as a writer, a leader, a speaker, and an enthusiastic and high-energy person worked well in these fields. These same skills, interestingly enough, are helping me in the classroom as I substitute teach.

How did I first realize that I adored children? I was blessed with my first son. Watching him grow and develop and master all of the "milestones" of those special years was unbelievable. Of course, I stayed home with him, nurtured him, and taught him, knowing that no one could do the job with the fervor and love that I could. I read with him, taught him colors and numbers, and even made trips to the grocery store educational: the produce aisle was a lesson in numbers, colors, and fruit and vegetable vocabulary words. It was at this point that people began to tell me that I had a "knack" with children and should think about teaching as a profession.

As the children grew and I participated in their school lives, as Class Mother and such, I so admired and envied those teachers. What wonderful and superior human beings they were . . . knowing so much about so many things and having the gift of imparting this information. They did it all! They managed a classroom full of children, when I felt overwhelmed by my two children. They remained cool, in control, and unbiased (mostly) toward even the obnoxious children, often seeing the specialness in the individual rather than the difficult traits . . . all this while they performed magic! They taught children to read, that most amazing skill, made sense out of math, and tried to impart humanity on children who seemed to have starred in Lord of the Flies. *Could I do this? Dare I even think about it?*

Apparently, the teachers thought that I could. When I began teaching multicultural lessons in my son's class (we were the only Jewish people in a conservative Mennonite farm town), the teachers were so impressed that the principal herself came in and asked me to present to all the other classrooms. The superintendent observed me and had me head up a committee dedicated to keeping the "Pumsy" self-esteem program intact in the district despite the rabid protests of a Fundamentalist majority. The superintendent praised me and strongly recommended that I teach. "You have a presence," he told me, "a talent for explaining things clearly and in such a way that people want to know more and become excited by what you have to say."

I know that I can motivate people. I have always had satisfaction from doing that, and it's always been noted on professional reviews and letters of recommendation. To motivate and teach at the same time, hmmmm, that is the challenge and brilliance of a teacher. When I have had a long-term substituting assignment, I have seen, through summative reviews that, yes, I did teach the class the vocabulary or the social studies lesson, and I am so proud and grateful for this ability. It is so stimulating to me, so thrilling to see the first spark of curiosity and then dawning knowledge on those faces! The feeling is certainly a powerful stimulant to refine and train teaching skills to achieve this on a consistent basis. To be honest, I love the attention of all of those faces trained on me, as I gesture, explain, question, and try to fire their interest. I am a very active person, and the nonsedentary life of a teacher works well for me.

Also, I am touched by the attention and fondness that the children generally display toward me as their teacher. This is also my weak point, however. I am aware of my intense desire to be liked by the children, thus my force as a disciplinarian is vulnerable to compromise. I do deal firmly with students and keep learning how to do this better as I observe more teachers in action and teach myself and attempt various skills that I learn in textbooks. I also observe the masters . . . those classroom teachers that do it so well.

As far as prestige, I feel that nothing (except parenting well) is as important as teaching. Christa McAuliffe's statement about touching the future is right on point. What other career impacts not only the present, but also the time that is yet to be. I feel that by teaching English/Language Arts, I will be giving my students the tools that they need to navigate through everything else that they will ever do in their lifetimes. All of my career and life experiences have convinced me that it is our language, its cadence, its literature, and the written and verbal communications that we use that determine how we will participate in the world around us. How enormously satisfying it is for me to impart something so meaningful and necessary. The students will always be judged, measured, and sized up by their communications skills. I hope to make a positive impact on them in these vital areas.

As a naturally warm person, the loving and warm feedback from the students is such a pleasure. Conversely, the catchall for my worries is, how will I deal with the student who just doesn't like me, or is always disruptive and difficult, and that frankly, I dislike. When I see a child bully another, it is hard to put my personal emotions aside and not come down unfairly on the child and say or do something demeaning to him or her. Sometimes, it helps me when I know that there is a rough family situation. My heart and desire to help and be a safe port in the storm of this youngster's life usually aids me in summoning the patience and commitment that I need to see behind the behavior and try to do something positive about it.

I am very concerned with the chronically disruptive students who make the class an arena for power struggles and discipline strategies. Will I manage and handle an entire class when I am the regular, daily teacher instead of the lenient and fun treat of being the favorite sub? I will work very hard on this aspect and hope that experience will give me confidence in this area.

As for being bored, never! I have always maintained that only boring people get bored. There is so much to teach, to learn, and so very many ways to do so that I think my teaching will always be evolving. As long as I remain a student, reading, thinking, attending conferences, seminars, and classes, I will continually be learning new and better ways to share the wonderful knowledge that the world holds.

My philosophical beliefs fit in well with teaching. Everyone has potential. It is just a matter of how to reach it, to teach it, to maximize it to its fullest. Put another way, I once heard the mother of two retarded children tell my child, when asked why her boys "couldn't talk right," that they had their own gifts, that we are all gifted, but our packages are different and may be opened at varying times and in special ways.

The above statement brought tears to my eyes and fortitude to my heart. I see some clear patterns emerging as my career gets going and I start to feel like a powerhouse of commitment instead of the shaking mess I was after my divorce. I absorb the knowledge from my courses like a sponge because I am burning with the desire to be a wonderful teacher, an important part of young peoples' lives, a positive experience in this sometimes terrible, but more often fabulous world of ours. I know that my strongest assets are my enthusiasm, dedication, people skills, and broad-based knowledge as well as the power to interest, excite, and stimulate others to listen, attend, and know more. I must conquer my all too intense desire to be liked by my students and gain their approval. Earning their respect, cooperation, and attention has to be what I strive for.

I so look forward to having my own classroom and my own students. I have much to learn myself, including how to foster independence in students. As I tell my students, "We will work well together today because this is exactly where I want to be, sharing the teaching and learning creative process with you. You can and will learn something with me today because you are bright, inquisitive, and you have the whole world in front of you. The things you get in the classroom will give you the keys to all of the doors in the future that await you." I'll succeed in teaching because I think it is more than a job, it is a calling. . . . one that I have been working toward all of my life without knowing it. The journey is and will continue to be just amazing!

Life *is* a ceaseless journey. Who we are, what we decide to do, and how we do it are influenced by a multitude of factors. We are a composite of our genetic make-up, the influence of our parents, our environment, our experiences, and even social and political forces. Our personal strengths and weaknesses, likes and dislikes, educational decisions, opportunities presented to us, help we receive from others along the way, and the many personal choices we all make influence our thoughts, speech, and actions. Why does someone go into teaching? Dan Lortie (1977), in a classic sociological study of American teachers, examined several primary reasons why people he interviewed became teachers. Aside from the more mundane explanations relating to material benefits and the desire to interact with people, Lortie and other researchers who came after him discovered that more fundamental and profound influences included the desire to engage in work that is personally and socially meaningful.

RECOLLECTION

I always wanted to become a teacher. I recall how I used to force my sister, four years my junior, to sit and take a test I prepared for her. Despite her protestations, I made her sit to take the exams. I'm not proud of what I did, but I do recall the intense joy I felt using my red pen to mark her answers wrong and to award a grade. The sense of power and authority I felt was uplifting. I regret, of course, coercing my sister in those days (happily, she has forgiven me). I matured since then, fortunately, to realize that teaching is not a matter of serving as an authority figure but, rather, helping another human being to achieve new insights and potential. I've come to realize that helping someone else is both personally and socially important.

What are your first recollections about considering teaching as your career? Why have you decided to teach? Why does teaching matter?

_____

_____

_____

Form 1.1   RESPOND

RESPOND *Is teaching for you?*	SA	A	D	SD
SA = Strongly Agree ("For the most part, yes") A = Agree ("Yes, but . . .") D = Disagree ("No, but . . .") SD = Strongly Disagree ("For the most part, no")	*SA*	*A*	*D*	*SD*
1. I get asked for help a lot, and have a hard time saying no.				
2. When I meet a person I'll give that individual the benefit of the doubt; in other words, I'll like him until he gives me a reason not to.				
3. People usually like me.				
4. I'm happiest interacting with people and aiding them in some way.				
5. People tell me I have a great sense of humor.				
6. I'm good at smoothing over others' conflicts and helping to mediate them.				
7. I believe that respect for authority is one of the cornerstones of good character.				
8. I feel I'm good at supervising a small group of people, and I enjoy doing so.				
9. I want my life to mean something.				
10. I am more spiritual than most of my friends.				

Analyzing Your Responses

Note that the items are drawn from one of my previous books (Glanz, 2002) *Finding Your Leadership Style: A Guide for Educators,* published by the Association for Supervision and Curriculum Development. For a more detailed analysis, please refer to that work. Suffice it to say here that if you answered SA or A to the items in Form 1.1 you are well suited to teaching as a career. Don't allow any one survey to sway you one way or another, but effective teachers, generally, are naturally inclined to help others, are caring, sensitive individuals, and possess a strong desire to make a difference.

Education is much more than transmitting some set of prescribed cultural, societal, or institutional values or ideas. Education is an ongoing, spirited engagement of self-understanding and discovery. Etymologically, the word "education" comes from its Latin root "educare," meaning to draw out or to lead. That is, in fact, our goal as educators—to draw out that unique latent potential within each student. As Smith (cited in Slattery, 1995, p. 73) poignantly explains, "education cannot simply tell us what we are, but what we hope to become." When we teach our students, regardless of the subject, we serve as a catalyst for them to reach their potential. A fundamental human quest is the search for meaning. The process of education becomes a lifelong journey of self-exploration, discovery, and empowerment. Teachers play a vital role in helping students attain deep understanding. As Rachel Kessler (2000) concludes in her *The Soul of Education*,

> Perhaps most important, as teachers, we can honor our students' search for what *they* believe gives meaning and integrity to their lives, and how they can connect to what is most precious for them. In the search itself, in loving the questions, in the deep yearning they let themselves feel, young people can discover what is essential in their own lives and in life itself, and what allows them to bring their own gifts to the world. (p. 171)

As educators, we affirm the possibilities for human growth and understanding. Education embodies growth and possibility, while teachers translate these ideals into action by inspiring young minds, developing capacities to wonder and become, and facilitating an environment conducive for exploring the depths of one's being. The capacity for heightened consciousness, the emphasis on human value and responsibility, and the quest of becoming are quintessential goals. Teaching thus becomes not only meaningful and important, but also exciting.

The tragic events of the atrocity that occurred on September 11th (2001) have affected all of us so very deeply—our lives are forever changed. Aside from each of our personal reactions and the ways 9/11 changed us as individuals— I am certain that we have also been affected professionally. I knew before 9/11 that my work as an educator was important. I knew at least intellectually that what I do makes a difference. Still, 9/11 has filled me with a renewed sense of determination and urgency. I know that education alone cannot put an end to hatred and I know I cannot alone change the world. Yet, I also know that in my way I can indeed raise the consciousness of others in terms of what it means to be a just, caring human being in a world filled with hate and injustice. Teaching for me, as never before, has become a moral imperative.

Extraordinary times call for extraordinary teachers. We need teachers who can challenge others to excellence; teachers who love what they do. We need teachers who help students achieve their potential; teachers who help students understand why and how to treat others with respect, dignity, and compassion.

Haim Ginott (1993) made the point that education is more than teaching knowledge and skills in dramatic fashion when he related a message sent by a principal to his teachers on the first day of school:

Dear Teacher:

I am a survivor of a concentration camp. My eyes saw what no man should witness:

Gas chambers built by *learned* engineers.

Children poisoned by *educated* physicians.

Infants killed by trained nurses.

Women and babies shot and burned by *high school* and *college* graduates.

So, I am suspicious of education.

My request is: Help your students become human. Your efforts must never produce learned monsters, skilled psychopaths, educated Eichmanns.

Reading, writing, arithmetic are important only if they serve to make our children more humane. (p. 317)

The challenges of teaching are certainly awesome. Overcrowded classrooms, lack of student interest, absenteeism, lack of preparedness, high incidence of misbehavior, lack of parental support compounded by social problems such as drugs, unstable family life, teenage pregnancy, poverty, child abuse, violence, and crime give pause to think. But think again. If not for these challenges, the rewards of teaching would not be so great. Our work matters. We make a difference. Listen to the words of praise this fourth grader has for her teacher:

Cherished Memories of Mrs. Siblo

As the flowers blossom
The weather gets warmer
And time is still passing.
June has approached quicker than ever.
Another school year is coming to an end;
And I won't have Mrs. Siblo as my teacher ever again.
I feel kind of sad to say goodbye
To the greatest teacher that once was mine.
Before I go to achieve another full year,
I want you to know that the memories
I have of you will be cherished
And remembered every year.
As we were passing through the halls of PS 42
We were, quiet and not talking,

For we knew better, Class 4–227.
You made me laugh, you made me feel bright,
You guided me to always do right.
You taught me math,
And led me down the right path.
You taught me to spell
And use vocabulary well.
You taught me punctuation and capitalization.
You taught me reading,
And that was a great feeling.
Your evil eye is sweet, and kept me on my feet.
You were not an artist,
But you sure tried your hardest.
All the good you have taught me,
All the hard work we've shared,
Mrs. Siblo, you are indeed the greatest teacher
I've once had
I sure am going to miss you, I cannot tell a lie.
I better end this poem now before I start to cry
With my heart filled with memories and gratitude,
I will always remember you.
You made an impression that will stick with me,
Even while I earn my master's degree.

Dana Criscuolo
PS 42, Eltingville
Staten Island, New York

Source: Reprinted with permission of Dana Criscuolo.

Not convinced? Listen to Dov Brezak (2002) relate the tremendous power of expressing and showing we care, and that we do make a difference:

One public school teacher in New York decided to give a tribute to all her students. She called them to the front of the class, one at a time, and told each one of them how he or she had made a difference to her and to the class. Then she presented each of them with a blue ribbon imprinted with gold letters that read, "Who I am makes a difference."

Then, as a class project, she gave each student three more of the blue ribbons, and instructed the class to use the ribbons to show similar recognition to others. Students were to report back to the class on their experiences a week later.

One of the boys in the class went to a junior executive he knew and thanked him for his help in planning his career. The boy attached a blue ribbon to the executive's shirt, and then gave him the two ribbons that were left. "We're doing a class project on recognition," he explained, "and we'd like you to find someone to honor. Present that person with a blue ribbon, and ask him or her to use the other ribbon to honor someone else as you honored him."

Later that day, the junior executive went in to his boss, who was known as a grouchy fellow. He asked his boss to sit down, and he told him that he admired him deeply. He asked if he could place the blue ribbon on his jacket. Surprised, his boss said, "Well, sure!" Then the junior executive gave his boss the extra ribbon. "Would you take this ribbon and honor someone else with it?" And he explained about his young friend's class project.

That night, the boss came home and sat with his 14-year old son. "The most incredible thing happened to me today," he told his son. "One of my junior executives came in, told me he admired me, and pinned this blue ribbon that says, 'Who I am makes a difference,' on my jacket. He gave me an extra ribbon, and told me to find someone else to honor.

"I want to honor you. My days are really hectic, and when I come home, I don't pay a lot of attention to you. Sometimes I scream at you for not getting good enough grades in school, or for the mess in your bedroom. But somehow tonight I just wanted to sit here and tell you that you make a difference to me. Besides your mother, you are the most important person in my life. You're a great kid, and I love you."

The startled boy cried and cried, his whole body shaking. Finally he looked up at his father, and through his tears he said, "I was planning on committing suicide tomorrow, Dad, because I didn't think you loved me. Now I don't need to."

Margaret Mead once said, "Never doubt that a small group of thoughtful, committed citizens can change the world, for indeed it is the only thing that ever has." It is up to each of us to change our world, touch a life, and to make a difference. We are involved in what Gary Zukav (2000) calls "sacred tasks." In his words,

Your sacred task is part of the agreement that your soul made with the Universe before you were born. When you are doing it, you are happy and fulfilled. You know that you are in a special and wonderful place . . . . When you are not doing your sacred task, you are miserable. (p. 241)

People have different sacred tasks. For some, starting a business might serve as a path for fulfillment; for others, it might be to raise a family, or cook. For us, it is teaching. Sharing, guiding, assisting, communicating, praising, encouraging . . . touching another's soul. Moving them to realization and understanding. Recognize your sacred task. Never forget why you are a teacher. Each of us entered teaching to make a difference in the lives of our students. We see the uniqueness of each child and try our utmost to light that spark of potential that lies dormant within. We realize that our task also is not just to help our students do well in school, but, more important, to succeed in life. We encourage our children by teaching them to be caring, moral, and productive members of society.

In the end, our destination is to create a vision of possibilities for our students; a journey of self-discovery. I am reminded of Robert Browning's observation that "a man's reach should exceed his grasp or what's a heaven for?" Browning gives us a moral message and serves as a moral compass. As we work against tough odds, we persevere. In doing so, we inspire our students to achieve excellence. We play a vital role. We shape lives. We touch the future. Christa McAuliffe was right.

I recently came across the Boris Pasternak poem from *Dr. Zhivago.* The poem is a fitting conclusion to this chapter. Or shall I say a beginning. A beginning of hope and possibility; of responsibility and vision.

> You in others–this is what you are.
> Your soul, your immortality, your life in others.
> And now what?
> You have always beeen in others and you remain in others.
> This will be you–the spirit that enters the future
> And becomes a part of it.

Our legacy is the future, our students. And that's why teaching matters.

*   *   *

FOLLOW-UP QUESTIONS/ACTIVITIES

1. Interview an experienced teacher and ask why he or she has remained a teacher.

2. Read some biographies of great teachers such as Anne Sullivan Macy (teacher of Helen Keller), Jaime Escalante, and so forth.

3. How are teachers portrayed in movies and television? Are these portrayals realistic? Explain. (See Bolotin & Burnaford, 2001)

4. Describe a teacher you know who personifies the ideals espoused in this chapter. What sets him or her apart from others?

5. How can the ideas and ideals discussed in this chapter assist you in developing your Mission Statement?

2
What Makes a Good Teacher?

Teaching involves much more than transmitting information. It includes representing complex knowledge in accessible ways, asking good questions, forming relationships with students and parents, collaborating with other professionals, interpreting multiple data sources, meeting the needs of students with varying abilities and backgrounds, and both posing and solving problems of practice.

—Marilyn Cochran-Smith

◆

FOCUS QUESTIONS

1. In your opinion, what makes a good teacher?

2. What are the qualities you would want a student teacher in your classroom to possess?

3. What is the one characteristic that marks a good teacher?

4. What specific skills must a good teacher possess?

5. What values, or dispositions, should teachers possess or espouse?

What are some of the important knowledge, skills, and dispositions essential to good teaching? Although the literature in teacher education attests to the various complexities and, even, difficulties in defining an effective teacher (Darling-Hammond, 2000; Good & Brophy, 1997), we have accumulated much knowledge over the years to identify common behaviors that characterize good teaching (Stronge, 2002). Drawing from this extant literature in teacher education and based on my nearly thirty years as a teacher, administrator, and teacher educator I have included in this chapter some practical ideas, strategies, and techniques.

This chapter is easy-to-read because most of the information is presented in an easy to use format. As the information is presented, try to note whether the particular item or statement refers to *knowledge,* a *skill* or a *disposition.* At the end of the chapter you will be asked to compile a list. This list will assist you in developing your Mission Statement and organizing your professional portfolio (see Chapter 10). Note that the list of twenty items included is not exhaustive but merely highlights some key areas essential to good teaching.

Let's begin this chapter on "what makes a good teacher" by challenging you to reflect on your career and what actually made you a good teacher. "But I just started teaching?" you may ask, "How can I undertake such a reflection when I have just begun?" Read on.

REFLECT

Imagine that it's your retirement dinner. For some of you that may be 30 years away, for others, less time. Still, imagine that for this celebration three former students of yours have been invited to relate what you have meant to them. What would you want them to say about you? Jot down your ideas in the space below. Read on, and we'll analyze your responses shortly.

_____

_____

_____

_____

ARE YOU A GOOD TEACHER?

We all know about the challenges of teaching. What do good teachers do to overcome these challenges? What makes a good teacher? Are you one? Do you feel you make a difference? How do you know? Here are a few guidelines that might help you evaluate yourself:

1. Good teachers take the time to reflect about what they do. They think about their failures as much as they consider their successes. They try to improve themselves by reading, attending conferences, and seeking advice from others.

2. Effective teachers are not always popular. A teacher's job is not necessarily to win a popularity contest. His or her job is to provide students with the best possible education.

3. Outstanding teachers use many different modes of teaching. The lecture method is not always in the best interest of the student.

4. Good teachers believe and feel that they can make a difference. In the words of researchers, they have "high self-efficacy." Although they may not see immediate results, they know what they do counts.

5. Teachers who show genuine and continuous interest in their students will motivate those students to higher achievement.

6. Good teachers treat all of their students alike, regardless of their academic level, ethnicity, or economic status.

7. Effective teachers can accept criticism as well as praise.

8. Good teachers can separate personal problems from their work at school.

9. Effective teachers don't give up on a child. They try and try and try.

10. Successful teachers seek input and guidance from their students, colleagues, supervisors, parents, and friends.

In summary, a good teacher is one who listens, understands, and cares about students. Respect, encouragement, and persistence are essential qualities. Take a look at what you recorded for the reflection exercise above when I asked you to imagine your retirement dinner at which three students would relate what you meant to them. I bet not one of you wrote, "he taught me the causes of the Civil War" or "she taught me how to solve algebraic equations." When we think about it, what really matters is how we affect our students as individuals, as human beings. You more likely want those students at your retirement dinner to recall how you treated them with respect, never gave up, encouraged them, or instilled values of courage or determination. These are the true reasons we go into teaching. Certainly, imparting content is important and essential. But, what matters most are those dispositions or values we impart intentionally or unintentionally. These endearing values and virtues are what good teaching is all about.

RESPOND

What are some of the major findings of the vast literature on teacher effectiveness? In your opinion, list five of the most important conclusions we can make about teacher effectiveness. (See some answers below.)

1. _____

2. _____

3. _____

4. _____

5. _____

Suggested Answers to the Previous "Respond"

Here are five of the most important conclusions I think we can make about teacher effectiveness:

1. The teacher has the greatest impact on student achievement. The teacher is the decisive element in the classroom in much the same way that a surgeon is the most critical element to the recovery of a patient in the operating room, and the mechanic in the auto shop, etc. In other words, teachers make a difference when it comes to student learning in a classroom. That's why **Teaching 101: Classroom Strategies for the Beginning Teacher** places so much emphasis on teacher self-efficacy; that is, the belief that you make a difference.

2. Our memories and experiences as students in school play an important role in terms of how we conduct ourselves in the classroom. Whether we are aware of it or not, the way we were educated and treated as students during our formative and formal years of schooling may influence our behavior and actions towards our students. For example, if you were largely taught in a deductive manner through the lecture method (i.e., teacher talks and students listen—passive learning), you are likely to teach the same way. This does not mean you will necessarily teach this way. What it does indicate is that the way you were taught may influence the way you perceive and understand teaching and learning. Remaining cognizant of such an influence while learning alternative ways of presenting information (e.g., cooperative learning, use of technology, discussion, Socratic dialogue, etc.) can go far towards thwarting such a potential negative influence. Of course, the converse may also yield positive results. The point here is that we need to carefully examine those experiences of our past in order to determine how they may or may not influence our behavior as teachers. That's why **Teaching 101** challenges you to reflect on your experiences and teachers who may have had a particularly positive or not so positive influence on you. Analyze your responses to REFLECT below. Share your responses with a colleague; keep a reflective journal. How might your recollections influence your behavior in the classroom? See RECOLLECTION (page 18).

REFLECT

These next several reflective activities are critical in building a memory bank so that you may become conscious of certain influences, good and bad, that affect your behavior in the classroom and, importantly, how you treat and teach your students.

    1. Think about your earliest recollections of your formal schooling. What do you recall? Can you recall names of teachers and significant others? What kinds of memories do you have about going to school, say from nursery through elementary school? Then, what about throughout all your formal schooling experiences through graduate school? (Write your responses, share with a colleague, and compare with the ones I discuss in this book.)

_____

_____

(Continued)

(Continued)

2. Next, recall the teachers you admire; the ones you would consider to be "good" or "great" teachers; teachers you would want to emulate. Write all you can about them. What makes them particularly memorable and admirable? From their actions, how would you describe their philosophy of teaching? What pedagogical strategies did they incorporate that were particularly successful? Why would you want to emulate their actions? How would you do so?

_____

_____

3. Next, recall the teachers you least admire; the ones you would consider "bad" or "harmful" teachers; teachers you would not want to emulate. Write all you can about them. What makes them particularly ineffective?

_____

_____

RECOLLECTION

I recall the first time I screamed at one of my children for some petty infraction I no longer remember. I do recall, however, the moments after the incident. My child walked away dejected, and I stopped in my tracks. "Oh my, I can't believe I said that to him. It's precisely the same thing my father said to me when I was growing up in his household. I had vowed never to say that to my child. . . . And I did."

How does this recollection relate to our previous discussion of the influence of our experiences on the way we may act as teachers? Share your recollections below:

_____

_____

Let's continue with three other of the most important conclusions I think we can make about teacher effectiveness:

3. Our beliefs, attitudes, and philosophies about teaching, learning, and students influence how we perform in the classroom. What we do "behind the classroom door" (Goodlad, 1970) is greatly influenced not merely by what we espouse but, rather, what we think and believe (Osterman & Kottkamp, 1993). That's why *Teaching 101* challenges you to examine your belief systems and their impact on behavior. See From 2.1, RESPOND-Beliefs Inventory.

4. Teachers who undergo intensive, long-term teacher preparation programs that include significant field experiences are better pre-pared to face the realities of teaching than those not similarly trained. For example, see Darling-Hammond, Chung, and Frelow, 2002 and Cochran-Smith, 2002. Teacher preparation does not end with student teaching. Induction programs and mentorships play a vital role in sustaining teacher effectiveness. Were you offered guidance and constructive feedback in student teaching? Are you given the emotional and technical support you need to remain successful in the classroom during your early years of teaching? If not, seek assistance. Take responsibility for your own development as a professional educator. Seek a mentor. Take a graduate course. Enroll in a master's degree program. Attend conferences, workshops, and other professional development sessions.

5. Teachers who are effective classroom managers dramatically increase their likelihood for success. How many teachers have you seen who are very knowledgeable and, even, great communicators, but simply fail because of their inability to deal appropriately with student misbehavior. The inability to deal effectively with misbehavior is the number one reason why beginning teachers leave the profession. Are you adequately prepared to deal with student misbehavior? Do you have a systematic well-thought-out discipline plan? Do you have a variety of preventive, supportive, and corrective discipline techniques at your disposal? Read Chapter 5.

Form 2.1   RESPOND - Beliefs Inventory

RESPOND
Beliefs Inventory
(These belief inventories will help you
frame your Mission Statement in Chapter 10.)

SA = Strongly Agree ("For the most part, yes") *A = Agree ("Yes, but . . .")* *D = Disagree ("No, but . . .")* *SD = Strongly Disagree ("For the most part, no")*	SA	A	D	SD
1. I really believe that all students can learn.				
2. Students can learn only at their own rate.				
3. Some students need special instructional accommodations.				
4. Male and female students are equally capable of learning mathematics.				
5. Students of all ethnic and religious groups should be afforded the same opportunities to learn.				
6. Teachers can help change a bureaucratic school or district.				
7. I am only as good as my training.				
8. I am the decisive element in the classroom.				
9. I constantly need to learn and grow to become a better teacher.				
10. I believe that students learn best by doing, active learning.				
11. I believe that good teachers encourage critical thinking.				
12. Cultural diversity and multicultural education are essential components in any good curriculum.				
13. A good teacher must care for students.				
14. Good teachers are involved in the community outside school.				

SEVEN RESEARCH-BASED FINDINGS ABOUT THE QUALITIES OF AN EFFECTIVE TEACHER

Based on the preceding information, here are seven research-based findings about the qualities of a good teacher:

1.   The single greatest influence on students in a classroom is the teacher. "Teachers have a powerful, long-lasting influence on their students" (Stronge, 2002, p. vii).

2.   Certified and experienced teachers who have specific knowledge, skills, and dispositions are more effective in terms of promoting student achievement than unlicensed and/or inexperienced teachers. "Experienced teachers differ from rookie teachers in that they have attained expertise through real-life experiences, classroom practice, and time" (Stronge, 2002, p. 9). Research demonstrates that teachers with more experience plan better, apply a range of teaching strategies, understand students' learning needs, and better organize instruction.

3.   Teachers who practice the art of reflection are more effective than those who do not. "Effective teachers continuously practice self-evaluation and self-critique as learning tools" (Stronge, 2002, p. 20). Research indicates that reflective teachers keep a journal of sorts, meet with a colleague to discuss classroom practice, and maintain high expectations for students.

4.   Teachers who possess good classroom management skills increase instructional in-class time. "An effective teacher plans and prepares for the organization of the classroom with the same care and precision used to design a high-quality lesson" (Stronge, 2002, p. 25). Research confirms that effective classroom managers minimize discipline problems, increase instructional time, maintain clear rules and procedures, and have developed a systematic class-room management plan.

5.   Teachers who carefully and methodically plan and prepare for instruc-tion are more effective than those who do not. "Organizing time and preparing materials in advance of instruction have been noted as important aspects of effective teaching" (Stronge, 2002, p. 37). Research proves that instructional planning leads to appropriate lesson objectives, use of a variety of instructional prompts (such as advance organizers, multimedia, etc.), higher level questions during a lesson, less student misbehavior, and greater student attention.

6.   Teachers who employ instructional strategies that increase time-on-task are more effective than those who do not. "Along with the importance of time allocated to instruction by the teacher, the time the students spend

'on-task,' or engaged in the teaching and learning activity, is an important contributor to classroom success" (Stronge, 2002, p. 48). Research verifies that teachers who engage learners use more positive reinforcement strategies, vary the types of questions they pose, distribute their questions to many students, tend to provide step-by-step directions to students, and come to class well prepared.

7.   Teachers who differentiate instruction by employing a variety of teaching strategies and attending to the needs of all learners are effective in promoting learning. "Effective teachers tend to recognize individual and group differences among their students and accommodate those differences in their instruction" (Stronge, 2002, p. 57). Research supports teacher use of various grouping strategies (such as cooperative learning), individualized approaches, careful monitoring and assessment of student progress, and an understanding of the specific learning needs of students.

WHAT MAKES AN EFFECTIVE TEACHER?

Some Areas of Competence: A Self-Assessment

1. *Content (subject and general knowledge)*—Are you content knowledgeable?

2. *Pedagogical (teaching theory, learning theory, curriculum theory)*—Do you possess pedagogical expertise?

3. *Self*—Do you know yourself well (e.g., your strengths, limitations, etc.)?

4. *Interpersonal (students, parents, administration, community)*—Do you relate well to others? How do you know?

5. *Questioning*—Do you pose varied, thought-provoking questions when appropriate?

6. *Planning (consequences of poor planning = behavior problems; lack of learning, monotonous presentation, lack of respect of teacher, etc.)*—Do you always plan for instruction?

7. *Classroom Management*—Are you having difficulty with classroom management and implementing an effective discipline plan?

8. *Communication*—Are you a good communicator? How do you know?

9. *Predisposition to act in a positive or negative way towards others*—4 categories:

a. *Towards self*—Assess your strengths, limitations, needs, likes/dislikes, self-esteem (feelings of adequacy). How do you know? Reflect/introspection; talk to others; keep a journal; read self-help books; field work and student teaching experiences

b. *Towards children*—Do you like kids? Do you have any biases (ethnic, religious, gender, social class, etc.)? Do you have high or low expectations for students?

c. *Towards peers*—How do you feel towards and work with colleagues, parents, administrators, custodians, and so on?

d. *Towards subject matter*—Are you enthusiastic about what you teach?

THREE APPROACHES TO TEACHING

Rather than relying on one approach, good teachers use a variety of teaching approaches. Compare and contrast the three most common approaches outlined below. How and when do good teachers use them?

1. Lecture

Purpose: To transmit or accumulate knowledge; to achieve content mastery; to present information on a subject in a direct manner within a relatively short period of time to a relatively large group of people

Process: Teacher active—talks a lot; Student passive—silent, answers/asks questions occasionally

Method of Presentation: Direct/deductive

Time Reference: Limited period of time

Quantity of Students: Large group

End Result: Exact information communicated or obtained; student accumulates a lot of knowledge, often memorized

Conclusion: Lecture is an appropriate approach to teaching, unfortunately it's overused. When would you use lecture? How would you know that lecture is inappropriate?

2. Discussion

Purpose: To give students opportunity to voice their opinions; to critically analyze a problem or issue; to give students chance to compare their views with others

Process: Teacher less active—facilitates, guides discussion, drops leading questions, ensures participation; student more active

Method of Presentation: Indirect/inductive

Time Reference: Unlimited—need a lot of time

Quantity of Students: Average group size

End Result: Non-exact (in the sense that no one answer may necessarily be best); ability to understand issue under discussion

Conclusion: Discussion is an appropriate approach to teaching when teacher wants to encourage student critical thinking. When would you use discussion? How would you encourage *all* students to participate?

3. Teacher-Directed or Socratic Teaching

Purpose: To lead student to a particular conclusion or end result through guiding, critical questions

Process: Teacher less active–drops leading questions; Student more active (seeks answers to questions)

Method of Presentation: Direct in sense that teacher directly poses questions, but indirect in the sense that teacher poses questions so facilitate student self-discovery

Time Reference: Unlimited–need a lot of time

Quantity of Students: Very small, usually one-on-one

End Result: Exact (in the sense that there is an answer, but the teacher rather than telling the students allows for self-discovery through teacher posed questions

Conclusion: Socratic Teaching is an appropriate approach to teaching when teacher wants to engage the student one-on-one to help clarify an issue or problem. When would you use Socratic Teaching?

Summary

Each of these three approaches can be used together. For instance, in a lecture, you can conduct a discussion and when a student has difficulty understanding a specific issue you can enter Socratic mode for a brief time. An effective teacher is able to use lecture, discussion, and Socratic Teaching when warranted.

THREE OF THE MOST ESSENTIAL CONCEPTS THAT AFFECT STUDENT ACHIEVEMENT

Good teachers are aware of crucial factors that promote student learning. Research into teaching effectiveness consistently points to four concepts that are critically important in promoting achievement. How do these four ideas relate to your practice as a teacher? What can you do to ensure that all of the concepts below are incorporated in your classroom?

1. Academic Allocated Time (AAT) is the amount of time you assign for various subjects, for example, reading, math, science. Research studies consistently affirm strong relationships between the amount of time you allocate for a particular subject and student achievement. Common sense dictates that if you don't spend time learning and practicing something then learning will suffer. However, merely allocated time is insufficient. What a teacher does with the time allocated for mathematics, for instance, is critical.

2. Academic Instructional Time (AIT) refers to the actual amount of time you spend in various subjects. Instructional time is influenced by external interruptions (such as excessive announcements over the school loudspeaker and constant interruptions from the main office, including monitors coming into class for attendance reports and the like). Minimizing these external interruptions goes far towards increasing the possibility for greater AIT. Internal factors are also significant. For instance, if you have difficulty controlling student behavior AIT will be negatively affected. Therefore, to increase AIT, schools must minimize classroom interruptions and you, as the teacher, should have a system of rules and procedures that deal effectively with disciplinary problems and other disruptions.

Can you think of another policy (school or classroom) that will improve AIT?
Answer: Reduce rates of tardiness and absenteeism.

3. Academic Engaged Time (AET) is the time a student actually spends attending to academic tasks. Often referred to as "time on task," this factor is most essential for promoting academic achievement. You can allocate time for, say, math and you can spend time instructing your students in the subject, but you will not see results unless they are *on-task*. According to Ornstein (1990): "Students of teachers who provide more academic engaged time (as well as actual instructional time) learn more than students of teachers who provide relatively less time" (p. 76).

4. Academic Success Time (AST) is the time students are successfully engaged in learning. You can allocate time, provide instructional time, ensure on-task behavior, but are they successfully on-task? How do good teachers ensure that students remain successfully on-task? Here are some suggestions:

a. During student independent work, you should spot check by circulating around the room providing situational assistance.
b. At times, administer a quiz.
c. Call on nonvolunteers to ascertain attention and comprehension.
d. Implement your discipline plan (see Chapter 5) with consistency.
e. Use cooperative learning grouping (see below).

   f. Group students who have specific problems in a content area.

   g. Constantly remind students to stay on-task.

   h. Reward on-task behavior.

   i. Make your lessons appealing.

   j. Meet the needs of all students by providing equal attention to all.

Can you think of other ways?

Okay, now you understand these critical concepts that "good" teachers know about. How can you actually put them into practice?

_____

_____

_____

TEN COMMANDMENTS OF HUMAN RELATIONS

1. Speak to people. There is nothing so nice as a cheerful word of greeting.

2. Smile at people. It takes 72 muscles to frown, only 14 to smile.

3. Call people by name. The sweetest music to anyone's ears is the sound of their own name.

4. Be friendly and helpful. If you want friends, you must be one.

5. Be nice. Speak and act as if everything you do is a joy to you.

6. Be genuinely interested in people. You can like almost everybody if you try.

7. Be generous with praise and cautious with criticism.

8. Be considerate with the feelings of others. There are usually three sides to a controversy: yours, the other fellow's, and the right side.

9. Be eager to lend a helping hand. Often it is appreciated more than you know. What counts most in life is what we do for others.

10. Add to this a good sense of humor, a huge dose of patience, and a dash of humility. This combination will open many doors and the rewards will be enormous.

SOURCE: Adapted from *http://www.ci.carteret.nj.us/boro/hrten.html.*

GOOD TEACHERS ALWAYS PLAN: POSITIVE FUNCTIONS OF PLANNING

- Provides an overview of instruction
- Facilitates good management and instruction
- Makes learning purposeful
- Provides for sequencing and pacing
- Ties instruction to community resources
- Reduces the impact of intrusions
- Provides for economy of time
- Aids in reteaching and measurable learner success
- Provides for variety
- Leads to higher level questioning
- Assists in ordering supplies
- Guides substitute teachers
- Provides documentation of instruction
- Aids in developing a repertoire of teaching strategies

AN IMPORTANT QUALITY OF A GOOD TEACHER

Form 2.2   RESPOND - Good Teachers Are . . . Part 1

RESPOND **Good Teachers Are . . . Part 1** (Responses are discussed after the questionnaire)				
SA = Strongly Agree ("For the most part, yes") *A = Agree ("Yes, but . . .")* *D = Disagree ("No, but . . .")* *SD = Strongly Disagree ("For the most part, no")*	*SA*	*A*	*D*	*SD*
1. I acknowledge another point of view when data indicate that the other's position is more accurate.				
2. When I make up my mind about an important educational issue or matter, I easily alter my stance if information is presented contrary to my stance.				

(Continued)

Form 2.2   (Continued)

	SA	A	D	SD
3. In making decisions, I can absorb varied positions and pieces of evidence and I usually remain neutral before I render my final decision, even in cases in which I may have vested interests.				
4. Despite natural inclinations, I would not favor someone from my ethnic group in rendering a decision about an educational matter.				
5. I am not stubbornly close-minded when I know I am right.				
6. I do not consciously make prejudgments about people.				
7. I am usually consulted because people consider me fair and nonjudgmental.				
8. I value honesty in words and action, and I have an unwavering commitment to ethical conduct.				

Good teachers are impartial. Impartiality is defined in this context as behavior that is free from prejudice and bias in which no one individual is favored over another. Bias undermines good teaching because it interferes with an impartial review of information and people. Were you the teacher's pet? Do you have a "pet?" If so, how do the other students feel? Let's examine your responses to the questionnaire above. The eight statements indicate your proclivity to act impartial as a teacher. Each of these statements clearly provides an example of an impartial leader. Analyze each statement to better understand the extent to which you possess this character trait.

   1. I acknowledge another point of view when data indicate that the other's position is more accurate.

A paradigm is a lens that affects what we perceive and how we interpret meaning. All of us view and understand the world through our lens. People in the 16th century, for instance, believed the earth was the center of the universe. They understood the world through an inaccurate paradigm. Gallileo advocated a Copernican theory that suggested that the sun, not the earth, was the center. Gallileo, as you know, was threatened with torture to change his position. Certainly, we don't confront such onerous challenges, but we too suffer from paradigm inflexibility, that is, the refusal or inability to accept alternate points of view.

2. When I make up my mind about an important educational issue or matter, I easily alter my stance if information is presented contrary to my stance.

Open-mindedness is the willingness to entertain alternate viewpoints. Can we change our minds whenever there is good reason to do so? Open-mindedness doesn't represent an "anything goes" attitude. Rather it entails the willingness to critically examine different possibilities and presupposes a measure of tolerance. An impartial leader shows intellectual respect for others and their opinions.

3. In making decisions, I can absorb varied positions and pieces of evidence and I usually remain neutral before I render my final decision, even in cases in which I may have vested interests.

Ask yourself, "What are my vested interests?" "If I had a vested interest in seeing a program implemented, for instance, could/would I remain neutral towards opposing viewpoints?" "Do I have paradigm flexibility; that is, the ability to consider multiple perspectives?"

4. Despite natural inclinations, I would not favor someone from my ethnic group in rendering a decision about an educational matter.

Feeling comfortable around those who are like us is natural. When I enter a reception area at a conference where I don't know anyone, for example, I will tend to gravitate to people most like myself (for me that's white, male, and Jewish). Such behavior is normal. However, I must remain vigilant to not favor others simply because they are very much like me. Rendering decisions as educational leaders must not entail gender, religious, sexual, social, or racial bias.

5. I am not stubbornly closed-minded when I know I am right.

Open-mindedness is easier when one is undecided or uncertain about a particular issue. Let's say you feel you are right about something. Can you still maintain an open-minded stance? An impartial educational leader can.

6. I do not consciously make prejudgments about people.

The key word is "consciously." As human beings, it is normal to prejudge people. For example, when you meet someone for the first time you will inevitably, without intenting to do so, observe their dress, manner of speech, and physical appearance. These stimuli will automatically register. Impartial leaders are aware of such reactions, acknowledge them, and purposely counter them in order to remain open-minded.

7. I am usually consulted because people consider me fair and nonjudgmental.

Do people consider you fair and nonjudgmental? Ask a colleague or two.

8. *I value honesty in words and action, and I have an unwavering commitment to ethical conduct.*

What have you done recently that would confirm such honesty and commitment to ethical conduct? Be specific. If you have difficulty coming up with an instance or two, then perhaps you are not as committed to these ideals as you might think.

Are you impartial?

ANOTHER IMPORTANT QUALITY
OF A GOOD TEACHER

Form 2.3   RESPOND - Good Teachers Are . . . Part 2

RESPOND **Good Teachers Are . . . Part 2** *(Responses are discussed after the questionnaire)*				
SA = Strongly Agree ("For the most part, yes") *A = Agree ("Yes, but . . .")* *D = Disagree ("No, but . . .")* *SD = Strongly Disagree ("For the most part, no")*	*SA*	*A*	*D*	*SD*
1. When I hear about another's suffering, I am emotionally moved.				
2. I demonstrate my compassion towards others (not part of my immediate family) by going out of my way truly offering assistance.				
3. I often think about the welfare of others and wish them the best of luck.				
4. I would give a friend the "shirt off my back" to assist him or her.				
5. I value commitment to the development of the individual within the school/district and I value treating all individuals as significant stakeholders in the organization.				
6. Others would characterize me as a person who is kind, caring, nurturing, and sensitive.				

(Continued)

Form 2.3   (Continued)

	SA	A	D	SD
7. I openly give recognition for outstanding professional performance because I sincerely want to acknowledge their contributions.				
8. I am sensitive to the social and economic conditions of students, as well as to their racial, ethnic, and cultural backgrounds.				

Good teachers are empathetic. Why is empathy such a vital virtue? If you have empathy, you have compassion for others. Caring for others communicates that they are important, worthwhile, and esteemed individuals. Treating people with such compassion will encourage them to respond in kind, to you and to others. Such behavior inspires them to do their utmost to help others. What more can a teacher hope for?

   1. When I hear about another's suffering, I am emotionally moved.

Are you so immune to others' tragedies that you no longer are emotionally concerned? Empathetic people are not merely intellectually aroused by the sufferings experienced by others. They "feel" their pain. Can you relate a time when you felt that way?

   2. I demonstrate my compassion towards others (not part of my immediate family) by truly offering assistance by going out of my way to do so.

Empathy may entail just listening to another's travail. A higher level of empathy is actually doing something to assist that person. Empathetic people don't hesitate to go out of their way to do so. When was the last time you went out of your way to help someone in a school situation?

   3. I often think about the welfare of others and wish them the best of luck.

Empathetic people don't feel pity or sorrow for someone. Sympathetic people do that. Empathetic people think and, if they are religious, pray for others.

   4. I would give a friend the "shirt off my back" to assist her or him.

Empathetic people are doers.

   5. I value commitment to the development of the individual within the school/district and I value treating all individuals as significant stakeholders in the organization.

Empathetic people are people-oriented and treat all people (custodians, teachers, students, parents, and colleagues) with kindness and benevolence.

6. *Others would characterize me as a person who is kind, caring, nurturing, and sensitive.*

This is the definition of an empathetic person.

7. *I openly give recognition for outstanding professional performance because I sincerely want to acknowledge their contributions.*

Empathetic leaders care for people by recognizing and rewarding their achievements. They do so not because it is required to do so but because they feel it is the right thing to do.

8. *I am responsive and sensitive to the social and economic conditions of students, as well as to their racial, ethnic, and cultural backgrounds.*

Empathetic leaders are concerned about all facets of peoples' lives and then conditions that affect them.

Are you empathetic?

A FINAL QUALITY OF A GOOD TEACHER

Form 2.4   RESPOND - Good Teachers Are . . . Part 3

RESPOND **Good Teachers Are . . . Part 3** *(Responses are discussed after the questionnaire)*				
SA = Strongly Agree ("For the most part, yes") *A = Agree ("Yes, but . . .")* *D = Disagree ("No, but . . .")* *SD = Strongly Disagree ("For the most part, no")*	*SA*	*A*	*D*	*SD*
1. I possess above average levels of energy in almost any endeavor I undertake.				
2. I am a highly motivated, devoted, and ardent individual.				
3. Strong values and a commitment to actualize them motivate me.				

(Continued)

Form 2.4   (Continued)

4. Although not a fanatic, I have a strong commitment to see things through to the end once I make up my mind to do something.				
5. People often tell me that I am passionate in whatever I do as opposed to someone who is usually blasé and laid-back.				
6. I dislike laziness and procrastination.				
7. I tend to see the "glass half-full" as opposed to "half-empty."				
8. Others would characterize me as resilient, alert, optimistic, and even, at times, humorous.				

Good teachers are enthusiastic. The number one quality of a good teacher is enthusiasm. Students often complain that their teacher is boring. Can you recall sitting in a class where the teacher was not enthusiastic, to say the least, about his or her work? Can you recall what a difference an enthusiastic teacher made? What about the same for teachers you've known? Enthusiasm demonstrates passion for one's work. When one is passionate one usually enjoys what he or she is doing and one usually succeeds. Moreover, such enthusiasm is inspiring. Consider some of the world's great leaders. I think you'll agree that two of the most important qualities they possess are energy and optimism. They inspire others to action.

  1. *I possess above average levels of energy in almost any endeavor I seek to undertake.*

Have you ever met someone who appears dull and disinterested most of the time? Ever meet someone who appears energetic and interested most of the time? Some people can maintain high levels of energy while undertaking almost any endeavor. Later in this chapter, I'll suggest a way to boost your energy level.

  2. *I am a highly motivated, devoted, and ardent individual.*

How do you know you are so? Are you motivated, devoted, and ardent in your current role? Why or why not? If not, what makes you certain that you would be so in another role?

  3. *Strong values and a commitment to actualize them motivate me.*

One of the important ways to engender enthusiasm is to believe in something profoundly. If you believe in something deeply, it is almost impossible not to exhibit enthusiasm when engaged in that activity.

4. *Although not a fanatic, I have a strong commitment to see things through to the end once I make up my mind to do something.*

Excessive enthusiasm can be annoying, if not dangerous. Those people who are committed to a project will eagerly pursue it vigorously.

5. *People often tell me that I am passionate in whatever I do as opposed to some-one who is usually blasé and layback.*

Do people often tell you that? If they do, you possess enthusiasm.

6. *I dislike laziness and procrastination.*

Someone who is engaged, committed, and resolute will not exhibit these negative behaviors. Have you ever engaged in a project or activity that you disliked or were not committed to? You would likely exhibit laziness and procrastination when compelled to undertake such projects or activities.

7. *I tend to see the "glass half-full" as opposed to "half-empty."*

Optimistic people are naturally enthusiastic. Working to enhance your sense of optimism will increase your enthusiasm. Of course, we cannot maintain optimism and enthusiasm in all that we do all the time. But the critical idea here is that the degree to which we can maintain a positive outlook relates to our ability to enthusiastically pursue our goals.

8. *Others would characterize me as resilient, alert, optimistic, and even, at times, humorous.*

If people do, then you are an enthusiastic leader. One of the best ways, in general, to gauge the degree to which you possess any of these virtues is to ask others to assess for their opinion.

Are you enthusiastic?

GOOD TEACHERS USE EDUCATIONAL MEDIA APPROPRIATELY

Effective teachers know that the use of various forms of educational media can enliven their classroom and promote student achievement. Here are some do's and don'ts related to the use of educational media:

It is important to ask some basic questions and evaluate educational media before using them in the classroom:

1. Does this media (e.g., film, video, CD-ROM) directly apply to the curriculum approved for the level that I teach?

2. Have I previewed it? Do I really know what is on it?

3. Is it appropriate to today's lesson, or does it relate to future lessons?

4. How will I prepare my students to make this viewing a learning experience?

5. Is showing it the best use of my instructional time?

6. How will my students actively take part in this activity?

7. How will I plan a follow-up so that I know that my students understand the content of the media?

8. Can I teach this lesson in a more active and interesting manner without using this?

9. By showing a video, for example, am I stating to my class that I am not really prepared for this lesson?

10. Am I using this video as a break?

11. Is the content of the video or CD-ROM valuable enough to my students to be worthy of school time?

12. Is the video too long for my students' attention span?

The decision to use a piece of media as instructional support should be made carefully. Be wise in selecting them for your classroom. Use them, but don't abuse them. They *should* be a valuable tool for learning!

A GOOD TEACHER MUST USE WAIT TIME EFFECTIVELY

Wait time is an instructional strategy that refers to the amount of time students have to think during questioning. Research indicates that providing between 7 and 10 seconds for students to think before the instructor answers a question or calls on someone else improves student accurate participation.

Benefits include:

1. Length of student responses increases.

2. Student initiated and appropriate responses increase.

3. Student failure to respond is reduced.

4. Student confidence in responding is increased.

5. Student speculative responses increase.

6. Student to student interactions increases, and teacher-focused instruction decreases.

7. Student evidence to support statements increases.

8. The number of student questions increases.

9. Participation of "slow" students increases.

10. The variety of student responses increases.

Here's how I use wait time: I pose a question. I do not call on anyone before about 7 seconds even if someone raises a hand immediately. I allow think time. What happens if after 7 seconds no one responds? I ask myself, "Do I need to rephrase the question?" If so, I do and start again. If not, I ask them to pair off and share thoughts about possible answers. I give them about 60 to 90 seconds. This technique always yields results. Students give their answers. Not always, however, are the answers right, but at least they had time to reflect and respond. Try it out next time.

RAISING STUDENT ACHIEVEMENT THROUGH DIRECT TEACHING: WHAT RESEARCH SAYS

1. Begin lesson with a review of relevant previous learning and a preview of upcoming lesson.

2. Present material in small steps, with clear and detailed explanations, and encourage students to practice after each step.

3. Ask questions, and check for understanding. (Don't just ask, "Do you understand?" Actually check by calling on a nonvolunteer, have class give a thumbs-up if they understand and a thumbs-down if they don't, etc.)

4. Provide systematic feedback and corrections.

5. Supervise independent practice and monitor seat-work.

6. Provide weekly/monthly review and testing.

QUESTIONING STRATEGIES

What's the difference between convergent and divergent questions? Have a colleague note the questions you ask. How many were convergent? Divergent?

Table 2.1   Convergent/Divergent Questions

Good Teachers Know the Difference Between Convergent and Divergent	
Convergent	*Divergent*
Where did the Civil War start?	Why did the Civil War start?
What are three products of India?	How does wheat production in India affect wheat export prices in our country?
Who wrote *Death of a Salesman?*	How does Miller deal with tragedy in *Death of a Salesman?*
Which planet is farthest from the sun?	How would you compare living conditions on Pluto with those on Earth?
What are the two elements of water?	How is water purified?
What is the definition of a rectangle?	How have rectangles influenced architecture?

GOOD TEACHERS INCORPORATE LITERACY STRATEGIES WHENEVER FEASIBLE: FIVE LITERACY STRATEGIES THAT WORK

(These ideas are based on the work of Fisher, Frey, and Williams, 2002.)

Read-Alouds: I believe that reading to students is not an activity reserved for the early childhood grades, but that students in all grades through high school benefit immeasurably from read-alouds or shared reading. Select a book that the students want and set aside a time each day to read to them (between 5 and 20 minutes).

1. Students can listen, read along, or respond to questions prepared in advance on a worksheet or on a chalkboard.

2. Ask questions from time to time, but avoid using this time to "test" students. Allow them the opportunity to simply "listen."

3. After each book is completed, encourage students to develop some sort of project based on the book. Allow them complete freedom to express their thoughts and ideas. If students prefer not to do anything, that's okay. Reward students who do develop projects by posting their work in appropriate settings and venues. Let students develop a project of their own.

Graphic Organizers: Graphic organizers provide students with visual information that extends class discussions or work with texts.

1. Encourage all students, especially visual learners, to demonstrate their understanding of a particular topic by visually presenting their thoughts and ideas.

2. Provide them homework and testing options to draw or depict in any way that they have learned the material.

Vocabulary Instruction: Regardless of the content taught, teach vocabulary.

1. Keep a section of the chalkboard titled, for example, "Our New Words."

2. Encourage students to record all words they do not understand. At the same time, when a new vocabulary word is encountered in class, write the word on the board.

3. Review each day the newly learned words.

4. Use role plays, storytelling, or any other nontraditional method to help students use the newly learned words in context.

5. Avoid at all costs the traditional ways of reviewing words including writing them countless times, learning to spell them, writing them in sentences devoid of context, and so on.

Writing to Learn: Encourage students to write, even in small amounts.

1. Allow class time for writing activities.

2. Encourage journal writing time.

3. Utilize "Minute Papers" in which students use class time to record, for instance, what they have just learned or questions they still have.

Reciprocal Teaching: Many forms of this very important teaching strategy can be used. I have found reciprocal teaching particularly effective during and after learning content-laden material.

1. After some time of having presented relatively difficult material, tell students to close their notebooks and texts and to find a partner to "pair and share."

2. Inform students that one of them should be designated as "Student A" and the other "Student B."

3. Let Student B tell Student A everything he or she just learned. Student A cannot ask any questions. Student A records information. As Student B

relates the information, Student A pays attention to any errors or omissions.

4. After about 5 minutes, tell Student A to tell Student B any errors or omissions. Allow about 3 minutes.

5. Tell students to now open their notebooks and texts to determine if the information they related to each other is correct.

6. Share experience with whole class.

HOW DO YOU TEACH?

1. WHAT DO YOU DO WITH YOUR HANDS? Gesture? Keep them in your pockets? Hold onto the podium? Play with the chalk? Hide them so students won't see them shake?

2. WHERE DO YOU STAND OR SIT? Behind the podium? On the table?

3. WHEN DO YOU MOVE TO A DIFFERENT LOCATION? Never? At regular ten-second intervals? When you change topics? When you need to write something on the board/overhead? When you answer a student's question? At what speed do you move? Do you talk and move at the same time?

4. WHERE DO YOU MOVE? Back behind the podium? Out to the students? To the blackboard?

5. WHERE DO YOUR EYES MOST OFTEN FOCUS? On your notes? On the board/overhead? Out the window? On a spot on the wall in the back of the classroom? On the students? Could you tell who was in class today without having taken roll?

6. WHAT DO YOU DO WHEN YOU FINISH ONE CONTENT SEGMENT AND ARE READY TO MOVE ONTO THE NEXT? Say okay? Ask if there are any student questions? Erase the board? Move to a different location? Make a verbal transition?

7. WHEN DO YOU SPEAK LOUDER/SOFTER? When the point is very important? When nobody seems to understand? When nobody seems to be listening?

8. WHEN DO YOU SPEAK FASTER/SLOWER? When an idea is important and you want to emphasize it? When you are behind where you ought to be on the content? When students are asking questions you're having trouble answering?

9. DO YOU LAUGH OR SMILE IN CLASS? When? How often?

10. HOW DO YOU USE EXAMPLES? How often do you include them? When do you include them?

11. HOW DO YOU EMPHASIZE MAIN POINTS? Write them on the board/overhead? Say them more than once? Ask the students if they understand them? Suggest ways they might be remembered?

12. WHAT DO YOU DO WHEN STUDENTS ARE INATTENTIVE? Ignore them? Stop and ask questions? Interject an anecdote? Point out the consequences of not paying attention? Move out toward them?

13. DO YOU ENCOURAGE STUDENT PARTICIPATION? How? Do you call on students by name? Do you grade it? Do you wait for answers? Do you verbally recognize quality contributions? Do you correct student answers? On a typical day, how much time is devoted to student talk?

14. HOW DO YOU BEGIN/END CLASS? With a summary and conclusion? With a preview and a review? With a gasp and a groan? With a bang and a whimper?

TEACHERS BECOME GOOD TEACHERS OVER TIME: A FEW SUGGESTIONS FOR 1ST YEAR TEACHERS

1. Be patient.

2. Don't be afraid to make a mistake.

3. Learn from your mistakes.

4. Find a mentor you admire.

5. Celebrate your successes.

6. Know that the 1st year is always the toughest.

7. Take a graduate course.

8. Smile, it'll get better.

9. Take time for yourself.

10. Don't forget to laugh.

GOOD TEACHERS ENCOURAGE "HANDS-ON" AND "MINDS-ON" LEARNING

How do people learn best? John Dewey (1899) said that people learn best "by doing." Hands-on instructional tasks encourage students to become actively involved in learning. Active learning is a pedagogically sound teaching method for any subject. Active learning increases students' interest in the material, makes the material covered more meaningful, allows students to refine their understanding of the material, and provides opportunities to relate the material to broad contexts.

More specifically, students who are encouraged to "gather, assemble, observe, construct, compose, manipulate, draw, perform, examine, interview, and collect" are likely to be engaged in meaningful learning opportunities (Davis, 1998, p. 119). Students may, for example, gather facts about the rise of Nazism in Germany by exploring the Internet and composing essays about key figures in the National Socialist Party. Students may become involved in cooperative group activities aimed at learning more about resistance efforts to Nazi oppression. Students may record their observations about reading selections and react to video segments in personal reaction journals. Students may construct posters demonstrating antisemitic propaganda, while teams of students may interview Holocaust survivors at a local senior citizen residence.

Many of us would applaud such efforts because students are actively involved in meaningful and relevant learning activities. However, as O. L. Davis, Jr. (1998) has reminded us, hands-on "activities that do not explicitly require that pupils *think* about their experience" can simply mean "minds-off" (p. 120). Davis explains further:

> Raw experiences comprise the grist for thinking. They are necessary, but not sufficient, instructional foci. For the most part, hands-on activities must include *minds-on* aspects. That is, pupils must think about their experience. They must, as Dewey noted, reflect about what they have done. Consciously, they must construct personal meanings from their active experience. (p. 120)

Constructivist learning theory that supports both "hands-on" and "minds-on" activities is essential in teaching any subject. According to constructivist theory, people learn best when they are given opportunities to construct meanings on their own. How best to accomplish this lofty goal becomes paramount. Simply leaving students "on their own" is a wholly inefficient and ineffective way of stimulating reflective thinking. Teachers *must* guide students and provide thought provoking questions or frameworks as they engage in these "hands-on" activities. Davis amplifies this key instructional component: "Indeed, for hands-on activities to qualify as educationally appropriate tasks, teachers must work with pupils before, during, and after these engagements so that pupils maintain a minds-on awareness of their unfolding experiences" (p. 120).

How can you encourage "hands-on" and "minds-on" learning? List five ways:

_____

_____

_____

_____

_____

GOOD TEACHERS EMPLOY K-W-L

Begin your class by employing the K-W-L strategy developed by Donna Sederburg Ogle (1986). K-W-L is a strategy that models active thinking needed before, during, and after learning. The letters **K**, **W**, and **L** stand for three activities students engage in when learning: recalling what they KNOW, determining what they WANT to learn, and identifying what they have LEARNED (see Form 2.5).

Teachers should encourage students to write out what they know about a given topic, what questions they want answered, and what they have learned after a particular unit of instruction. I begin a new unit by asking students to write all they know about the topic. Once students are conscious of their prior understandings, new information and meanings may replace prior knowledge that may be based on factual errors or misinterpretations. Moreover, students who realize how little they know about the topic may develop higher levels of motivation and eagerness when learning the new content. One student in my class wrote in her journal: "I never realized how little I knew about _____. I'm anxious to learn as much as I can this year."

Students then brainstorm specific topics they want to learn about and questions they want answered. Teachers who involve students in charting the nature of content to be learned are more likely to encourage attention and learning.

After each major unit and as a culminating activity of the course, the final stage of K-W-L is employed. I ask students to list what they have learned.

Students individually or in small groups record their responses and then share their information with the class.

The K-W-L activity is valuable because it activates students' own knowledge of the topic under study. Students are provided the opportunity to share in the development of topics and objectives. Finally, they are encouraged to summarize or review what they have learned.

Form 2.5   K-W-L Strategy Sheet

What I Know	What I Want To Find Out	What I Learned

GOOD TEACHERS GET PARENTS ON THEIR SIDE: 10 WAYS

1. Make a special effort at the beginning to reach out to parents.

2. Capitalize on eagerness of parents to assist in any way.

3. Make parents feel welcome and accepted.

4. Tap into diverse interests and talents of parents.

5. Give them options or ways of helping out.

6. Start a parent e-mail chat group.

7. Listen to parents.

8. Call them even when there is no trouble.

9. Ask them for assistance, be specific.

10. Give them specific instructions for assisting their child with homework and projects.

Opening the channels of communication is key!

CONCLUSION

This chapter included a number of ideas that can be categorized as essential *knowledge, skills,* and/or *dispositions.* Complete Form 2.6 by summarizing what you learned in this chapter about what makes a good teacher:

Form 2.6

Knowledge	Skills	Dispositions

The list you developed from this chapter is certainly not exhaustive. Add to your list on your own and, even, add it to your portfolio (see Chapter 10).

*   *   *

FOLLOW-UP QUESTIONS/ACTIVITIES

1. What else do you need to know about good teaching practice?

2. Interview a "good" teacher and discover what makes him or her so "good." In other words, what does the teacher attribute to his or her success?

3. Keep a journal that notes, in part, what ideas from this book you intend to try out in the classroom.

4. Interview some students to ask them what they consider makes a good teacher.

5. Take the Self-Assessment Instrument in Appendix C to assess your competence in these four areas: planning and preparation, classroom environment, instruction, and professional responsibilities. This activity will help do two things: 1) reflect on the extent to which you are engaging in meaningful teaching practice to become a "good" teacher, and 2) reflect on teaching practices that will inform your framing of a Mission Statement in Chapter 10.

3

Who Are the Students in My Class?

If students don't learn the way we teach, let us teach the way they learn.

—Motto of E. C. Lee Elementary School,
Aberdeen, South Dakota

◆

FOCUS QUESTIONS

1. Why is knowing and understanding a student's background important in helping him or her learn?

2. What would you need to know about a student in order to help him or her learn better?

3. What strategies or techniques might you employ to diagnose students' needs in your classroom?

4. How is it possible to meet the diverse needs of all your students?

5.   Would you rather teach a group of students of similar abilities as opposed to a more inclusive group? Explain why or why not.

"I gaze upon the twenty eager young faces as I stand before them on the first day of class. They look so innocent, filled with expectations and hope. They want to learn about me. Am I nice, am I fair, will I treat them with dignity? I see each face and silently wonder, 'Can I reach each one of these souls? What are their fears and hopes? What are their ambitions? What do they need? Can I really help them?' Each of my students has so much potential. I will try my best."

Indeed, each student *is* precious. Each has so much potential. That is why teaching is such an awesome responsibility. We ask ourselves, "Will I make a difference to each of them? What will they say about me at my retirement dinner? What memories will they have of me?" I know you, the reader, want to do your best (otherwise, why would you be reading this book?). You must believe you can positively affect each student you encounter even though you may feel you are not making any progress. With such a positive outlook or disposition, you are ready to get to know your students and really make a difference. This chapter reviews some of the key elements you need to keep in mind when working with your students.

WHAT DO I NEED TO KNOW ABOUT MY STUDENTS?

All students have special needs—Although we need to serve the needs of students who have been officially designated as "learning disabled," we must realize that all students have "special needs." Isn't that true? Think about your own child or neighbor's child. Each child is unique and each of them has special needs.

All students learn in different ways and at different paces—The days when teachers simply talked and students dutifully listened are over, as if they ever really listened anyway! Good teachers use multiple strategies and ways to reach students because teachers know that each student processes information differently. Some are good auditory learners while others learn best through visual stimulation. Good teachers also know that students learn at different paces. Just because Charlie "gets it" immediately doesn't mean that Sally, who doesn't immediately connect, is necessarily slower. She just may need some additional think time or special assistance.

Some students may have difficulty paying attention—Aside from those students who have serious processing problems, all students, at different times, may tune out. Think about yourself at church or at a lecture. Ask yourself, "What can I do to encourage students to attend to the tasks at hand?" You may have to gently remind Melissa, "Can you answer that question?" You may have to restate or rephrase a question for them. Rather than accusing them of daydreaming, frame your redirect in a positive way. What might you say?

All students are motivated—Ever hear someone say, "Well, he's just not motivated." That is simply not true. All students are motivated, although they may not indeed be motivated to learn what you are trying to teach them. The first step is to realize that all people are driven to act in some way and it is our task to tap into that natural motivation. How can you as their teacher use their natural energies in positive ways to connect them to the content in your class?

Who they are makes a difference—Your students' social, cultural, and ethnic backgrounds as well as gender may influence how others treat them. Can you provide instances wherein a students' social class, culture (particularly for English-language learners), ethnicity, and gender negatively affected their academic or social progress?

ALL STUDENTS HAVE FIVE BASIC NEEDS

William Glasser (1975) identifies five basic needs that we all strive to meet. As I review these needs, consider how you might take these needs into consideration in planning your classroom activities and interacting with your students:

1. Belonging—*All people have a need to belong.* That's why so many kids are involved in gang behavior. They are striving to fulfill their craving to belong. If they don't receive that sense of belonging at home or in school, they often resort to potentially negative ways to satisfy this need. Do your students feel needed? Is there a group to which they belong in class/school? How can you encourage them to feel part of the class? Can they share their ideas and feelings? Can they participate in group activities?

2. Security—*Who doesn't want to feel secure?* If you worked in a neighborhood that lacked proper security for your car could you go about your day without worry? Of course not. You'd have your car on your mind all day. Similarly, your students need to know that your classroom is a place where they can feel secure and safe. They need an environment free from ridicule and violence. Is your class a pleasant environment? Is it nicely decorated? Do you greet your students each day with a smile and pleasant countenance?

3. Power—*All of us need to feel empowered.* When a student defies your authority, for example, he or she is communicating, perhaps unconsciously, that he or she wants attention. Students have a need to feel in charge. Never take a student's verbal attack personally. Engage them in meaningful, productive activities in which they feel they are contributing to the classroom in positive ways. Selecting students as monitors is one way to empower them. Can you identify two other ways to empower your students?

4. Freedom—*Who likes to be told what to do all the time?* All of us need a sense of control over our situation. In what ways can you encourage students to feel that they have some freedom? You could, perhaps, allow them input into what gets taught for a particular lesson or allow them to develop a special assembly or project. By promoting and supporting student freedom, you will satisfy one of their innate needs.

5. Fun—*School and fun?! Isn't that an oxymoron?* How can you make your classroom a place where kids can enjoy themselves and have fun (yes, while they learn)?

Who are the students in your class? They are human beings who crave to fulfill these essential needs. Do they consider your classroom a place where they can satisfy them?

CHILDREN NEED ATTENTION AND MUCH MORE . . .

Children need ample attention and guidance from us. Each child has special needs that are unique. It is our responsibility to satisfy these needs for our students. Here is a sampling of activities that will address these needs:

- Active games—playing with family and friends
- Stories, jingles, and rhymes
- Imaginative play— "pretending to be"
- Language—listening to and talking with others
- Music—enjoying and being creative with songs and rhythms
- Tools and materials—making things of their choice

Activities that address all of their senses are as follows:

- Seeing—observing things at home, on the street, in stores, and other places

- Hearing—listening and identifying sounds at home, in nature, and other places
- Tasting—describing differences among foods
- Smelling—identifying different odors
- Touching—feeling many kinds of materials, objects, and so on

Our children have many needs that we need to pay special attention to. If a child is to develop as a healthy human being, the child needs to have more than the "basic needs." Some of these other needs are the need for love, friendship, joyfulness, flexibility, sense of humor, optimism, sensitivity, resiliency, honesty and trust, curiosity, playfulness, creativity, laughter, tears, compassion, imagination, the need to know, song, dance, the need to work, the need to learn, open-mindedness, the need to organize, the sense of wonder, explorativeness, the need to belong, and so on.

Each child is unique and each child has unique needs. We, as adults, must meet the needs of each individual child to the best of our ability. By creating an atmosphere of openness, and by listening, watching, and teaching, we must meet the needs to ensure the full growth and development of every child.

ROLE OF RACE, GENDER, SEXUAL ORIENTATION, AND SOCIAL CLASS

Asking the question, "Who are the students in my class requires us to consider the impact that race, gender, sexual orientation, and social class have on our students. Race matters, as does gender and class. Our students' backgrounds and the way they have been treated by society as a result influence their behavior. Have we as a society used race, gender, and class to classify and stigmatize our students? Find a colleague and discuss the following questions:

1. What ways might teachers overtly and, or unintentionally discriminate in their classrooms? Describe and discuss.

2. What ways might schools overtly and, or unintentionally discriminate? Describe and discuss.

3. What are some prejudices teachers might have about some people/groups and how might they affect their behavior in the classroom? Describe and discuss.

4. What groups or individuals might be targeted for discrimination? List.

5. What are some ways teachers might promote equality, opportunity, and justice? Describe and discuss.

HATRED, BIGOTRY, AND PREJUDICE

He was a 49-year-old black man living in Jasper, Texas. Three white men (John William King, Shawn Allen Berry, and Lawrence Russell Brewer) chained the man to the back of a pickup truck and dragged him behind the truck until his body came apart. The three men left the right arm and head in the ditch beside the road where they fell off, and left the remainder of the body near a black cemetery.

He was a gay University of Wyoming student who was found beaten and tied to a fence post on the Wyoming prairie.

He was a Jewish physician who performed abortions in Buffalo. He was shot with a high-powered rifle through his kitchen window in front of his wife and children.

The names of James Byrd, Matthew Shepard, and Barnett Slepian have been etched in our consciousness ever since their brutal murders several years ago. These horrific crimes are poignant reminders that hatred is ever present and, perhaps, endemic to American culture and society.

Have you ever hated someone? I think we all have felt intense anger towards someone. How did we react? Did we shout at them, hit them, plan revenge, or did we merely conjure up images of retaliation? Occasionally, our passions, our tempers get the better of us. We lose control. Yet, you may argue, you would never resort to such extreme acts of hatred as described above. Granted.

What about our tendencies towards bigotry and prejudice? If you are Christian, have you ever harbored ill will towards a Muslim? What about resentment towards Jews? If you are Israeli, have you ever thought badly about Arabs? What about intolerance and hate between Indians and Pakistanis, Asians and Westerners, Swedes and Norwegians, Hispanics and Caucasians, Caucasians and African Americans, Serbs and Kosovars.

Why is it that our fear, suspicion, and hatred of others different from us have overpowered our good sense and moral commitments to civility, goodwill, justice, and tolerance? When we think of Columbine we now know that these kids were bullied. School violence is on the rise and we as educators must consider the way students treat others who are different.

Who are the students in your class? Are they potential victims? Perpetrators? What can you do?

RECOLLECTION

Hatred

My father was a survivor of the Holocaust. He denounced hatred of all kinds. Clearly, he had his reasons.

Once he and I were traveling on the Staten Island Ferry. A Hispanic family was seated across from us. They were poorly dressed and had difficulty with the English language, a situation that was all too familiar to me since my parents were immigrants, too.

Several young, rowdy hoodlums were mocking them. My father gazed furiously at these ruffians. I observed the look and the response it elicited. These obnoxious boys timidly responded by walking away while muttering "dirty Jew bastards."

My father later told me, never to hate others for how they speak or look . . . only judge people by their actions, no matter who they are or what they look like.

It was an invaluable lesson I carry with me to this very day.

Have you encountered hate? How can you teach your students not to hate? See the story about little Keisha that follows.

_____

_____

This short, true story is told by the founder of Teaching Tolerance of the Southern Poverty Law Center. I paraphrase: I'm not a parent but through the years I've loved many children. One of them was a four-year old named Keisha, the most volatile of all four-year-olds I taught in day care. Easy to anger and slow to calm down, Keisha spent at least part of every day crying. One day I was holding her hand waiting for a class, all white, to leave the library. As our all-black class waited at the entrance, Keisha noticed the difference. "I hate white people." "My mommy hates white people and I hate white people." She spoke rather matter-of-factly without a trace of hatred. Then it dawned on her. "Teacher, are you white?" "Yes I am, do you like me?" "I love you," she said and grinned. "I love you too." For Keisha at four, it was not yet necessary to reconcile her love for her teacher and her hatred of white people.

STUDENTS WITH LEARNING DISABILITIES

You will undoubtedly encounter students who have varying degrees of difficulties with learning. Some students will have been officially designated as LD, or Learning Disabled, while others remain undiagnosed. As a classroom teacher, your responsibility is not of course to undertake the diagnosis (that should be left to specialists), rather your responsibility is to remain cognizant of potential problems and to develop ways of presenting material appropriate to the special learning needs of students. You should be aware that students with learning problems may have:

1. Difficulty paying attention

2. Poorly developed study skill strategies for learning

3. Poor motor skills

4. Difficulties in oral language skills

5. Difficulties in reading, written language, and mathematics

6. Poor time management and organizational skills

7. Problems with social behavior

8. Difficulty adjusting to change

9. Immature speech patterns and delayed speech development

10. Difficulty sounding out words

11. Difficulty remembering names of familiar things

12. Trouble listening and following directions

13. Inability to tell time or know right from left

14. Poor self-image

Any others?

For each of the problems noted above, provide a strategy or technique that you could employ that might help:

_____

_____

*   *   *

A SHORT QUIZ ON THE LEARNING DISABLED (TRUE OR FALSE)

_____1. The learning disabled student has average or above average intelligence.

_____2. The potential for a learning disabled child to succeed is present.

_____3. Ways to increase learning must be developed for the individual child.

_____4. Learning disability programs support the regular classroom and are not a replacement for the regular classroom.

_____5. Learning disabled students need to learn to function in a regular classroom setting.

_____6. A learning disabled student's self concept almost always needs to be improved.

_____7. If the problem is not recognized or diagnosed, it will not go away on its own and will continue to interfere with learning.

_____8. The learning disabled child can learn with assistance from school and home.

Answers: all true

*   *   *

WHAT ARE LEARNING DISABILITIES?

The term _learning disability_ is one of the most misunderstood in education today. It is difficult to come up with a universally accepted definition of what a learning disability is. We do know that the learning disabled child appears normal physically, is of average or above average intelligence, and is one who fails to learn at the expected rate. It is believed that one out of every fifteen school-age children in the United States has a learning disability.

A learning disability refers to one or more significant deficits in the learning process. A child with a learning disability will most likely demonstrate a discrepancy between expected and actual achievement in specific subject areas. The school and/or parent may be able to ascertain if a child has a learning disability by observing one or more of these traits:

1. Hyperactivity—The child is unable to sit still and concentrate on one thing for a period of time.

2. Distractibility—The child has a short attention span and cannot concentrate if there is noise around him or her.

3. Perception—The child has poor visual and/or auditory skills.

4. Language—The child lacks verbal skills and is unable to put ideas into complete sentences.

Once a child is identified as being learning disabled, the school can play a big part in remedying the problem. The school can provide a quality program by attending to the needs of learning disabled students. Most, if not all these students can function effectively in the regular, inclusive classroom if teachers are adequately prepared. The goals for the learning disabled student are the same as for the regular student with one exception: the method of instruction, including the rate of presentation and reinforcement techniques, will vary depending on the student and his/her assessed needs. At times, the teacher may have to form homogeneous groupings in order to provide the learning disabled child extra help and support. Still, I am not in favor of segregating these students into "special" classes because of the negative effects on the students' self-esteem that may result. Teachers, in my opinion, can utilize an array of strategies (including differentiating instruction, see discussion later in this chapter) to accommodate the learning needs of all students. If you, the reader, ask more experienced teachers if such a setting is feasible I doubt you will receive much positive feedback. Many older teachers were simply not trained to think inclusively and were certainly not given the appropriate pedagogical tools to differentiate instruction to accommodate all students' instructional and emotional needs.

The Underachiever

Have you observed a student not paying close attention in your class? Have you seen a student who does not complete assignments, is not working up to his or her potential, or is not motivated to succeed in school? One or all of the above could be symptoms of an underachieving child. There are techniques that can be used in the classroom to help the underachiever.

If a student is getting a slow start on work we can help by doing the following:

1. Keep track of how much time passes before the student starts a task. If he or she starts sooner than usual, reward them with praise.

2. When a task is assigned, use a timer and state that the task must be started before the timer goes off. Have some type of reward ready if all students start before the timer goes off.

3. Have the student work in an area where there are fewer distractions.

4. Give the student a simpler or shorter task than usual. Later, you can increase the difficulty or length of task as soon as the student progresses.

If the student is not completing any assigned tasks, consider trying one of these options:

1. Break the task down into smaller units. It is important for the student to receive some form of success.

2. Do not let the student go to another task until the first task is completed. Avoid nagging the student to finish the task.

3. Make up a daily assignment card listing all tasks assigned. Have the student check off each assignment completed. This will show him or her what progress is being made.

The goal of working with an underachiever is for the student to be able to work independently with a reasonable amount of success. It may be necessary to rearrange your schedule to fit the needs of this student, because this type of student will need more rest breaks and added personal help. Helping an underachiever can be a very rewarding experience

The Accelerated Student

Meeting the needs of all students is imperative, including the advanced, "gifted" (I hate that word because all students in my view are "gifted" in some way, see Armstrong's book in Appendix A), or accelerated learner. If a teacher is prepared to differentiate instruction to accommodate the learning needs of students, then the needs of the accelerated learner can be met. Here are a few suggestions:

1. *Utilize homogeneous grouping*—Once you have identified above average learners provide them opportunities to work with students of similar abilities on special activities and projects.

2. *Utilize their talents through peer tutoring*—Train and allow these accelerated learners to assist "slower" (different) learners in specific learning activities. Students receiving the assistance will benefit, but so too will the advanced

learners. They will benefit emotionally because they are helping fellow students. You are teaching them that all students are unique and should be valued. They, too, will learn the material better. I always say that if you want to really understand something, teach. These arguments in favor of peer tutoring can be shared with resistant parents who insist that such an activity detracts from the educational experiences of their children.

3. *Provide enrichment activities and individualized attention*—Do not ignore these accelerated learners by teaching to the "middle." Plan specific lessons for their needs. Plan on meeting and working with them individually.

The English Language Learner (ELL)

Our schools, as you very well know, are becoming more diverse than ever. The numbers of students for whom English is not the primary language is increasing. Helping second language learners is critical (Herrell & Jordan, 2004). I believe that we need to immerse these students into the mainstream as soon as possible. These students may initially need separate instruction from a licensed ELL teacher. After a short time, however, instruction should be provided in the mainstream, within the inclusive classroom. The "pull out" philosophy must be, in my view, replaced with the "push in" philosophy.

What are some teaching strategies you can employ?

1. *Total physical response*—Act out concepts and ideas by physically showing them what you mean by, for instance, "stand," "sit," or "eat." Using as much visual stimulation as possible is key.

2. *Modeling*—Do not tell them that what they said or wrote is "wrong." Rather, model for them the proper way to say something. If a child says "They was go." Say, "Oh, they were going to the park?" They'll respond, "Yes, they were going to the park." In written work, do not mark their entire composition with corrections. Focus on one or two main corrections (e.g., tense problems).

3. *Content area instruction*—ELL students generally need two years to become proficient in BICS—Basic Interpersonal Communication Skills. To develop such proficiency, they may need the help of a licensed ELL teacher, even in a pull out situation. Once, however, they pass a language proficiency exam that assesses their BICS level, they should be placed in a regular class to work on CALP–Cognitive Academic Language Proficiencies. During this time you should help the student build vocabulary much the same way you would help any other student. ELL students may, of course, need remedial work in that their vocabulary development may be several years behind their classmates.

Providing them with lower level textbooks that are age-appropriate is advisable. In sum, by building vocabulary, you will build their confidence in their language skills and, thus, have a positive impact in the content areas.

My wife, Lisa, is an ELL teacher and she related these humorous and "cute" anecdotes:

- I had just concluded teaching a unit on American idioms to fourth graders. I wasn't sure how much they really understood these "strange" sayings. A few days later the teacher next door was yelling at her class. All the children stopped to listen. Then I said, "There's no one like Mrs. K." Carlos immediately responded, "Oh, no one can fill her shoes!" I was so pleased. Thanks to Mrs. K, I knew at least one child knew how to use an idiom.
- While working on a project with first graders, I noticed that Jose looked puzzled as he started down his paper. "What's wrong Jose?" "I have a dilemma," he explained. Shocked at his use of the word, I asked "What is your *dilemma?*" Jose answered, "I don't know if I should color or cut first." Then I knew he understood the meaning of the word.
- A group of fifth graders from Albania was working on a writing assignment. One girl came over to me and told me that another girl, Olga had used a bad word. I called Olga over and asked her what word she used. She responded, "bitch." I told her that that word was not a nice word to use. She looked devastated and apologized. I asked her how she had used the word. She said, "In the summer I go to the bitch."
- The same group of students was looking at a map of the United States. One of the students suddenly exclaimed, "Oh, Oh look my country." "Where, where?" I asked. "Right there," she responded, pointing to the map. "No honey," I said trying to keep a straight face, "that's Alabama."

ARE YOU A CULTURALLY RELEVANT TEACHER?

Maria Rodriguez is a middle school teacher in an urban Los Angeles school district and Mark Ramler is a high school teacher in a suburban district in Washington, D.C. Both teachers are aware that in almost twenty years about 40 percent of the nation's school-age children will represent people of color. They also know that schools have not met the educational needs of culturally diverse students very well. Although Maria and Mark come from different cultural backgrounds, they share a common pedagogical approach that emphasizes culturally appropriate and relevant teaching strategies. Mark and Maria are sensitive to and cognizant of the extent to which a student's cultural background may influence learning and attitude towards school in general. They are responsive to their students by incorporating elements of the students' culture in their teaching.

Culturally responsive teachers (Jordan Irvine & Armento, 2003) make special efforts to get to know their students really well. Mark and Maria ask their students to share stories about their family and cultural heritage. Students are encouraged to express themselves openly about their culture. Students obtain a tremendous sense of pride and a feeling of being appreciated. Maria assigns her students a homework assignment to write a story about their family. Sensitive to the fact that "family" may mean something different to different students, Maria encourages an accepting, warm atmosphere in her class conducive to student participation. She, in fact, shares her cultural background with students, which serves to ease their apprehensions and encourages them to share as well. Mark realizes that culturally relevant teaching is much more than reviewing the contributions of Dr. Martin Luther King, Jr. on his national day of observance. His culturally responsive pedagogy is integrated in his curriculum and lessons on almost a daily basis, not just around holidays or special commemorations. He refers to King's work when, for instance, students don't appreciate a policy established by the school administration. He uses their anger as a teaching opportunity to share how Dr. King worked the system to effect the changes he desired. Then, Mark asks his students, "How might we work with administration to change that policy?"

Culturally responsive teachers know that students' culture (values, beliefs, and norms) might clash with institutional values, beliefs, and norms. Some students who do not volunteer in class, for example, might be perceived as lazy or learning disabled. Other students are taught not to look up into the eyes of an authority figure. Maria once overheard another teacher chastise an Asian girl for not looking at her when she spoke to her. The teacher said, "I know in your culture you don't look up when spoken to but you're in America now, look up at me." Culturally aware teachers take into consideration a student's cultural norms. Students feel appreciated and respected. Academic success is more likely when teachers are culturally sensitive.

Below are some suggestions for paying attention to social and cultural customs culled from Kottler and Kottler (2002, p. 20) in their *Children With Limited English: Teaching Strategies for the Regular Classroom*. Pay attention to:

- Verbal communication (pronunciation, patterns of speech, tempo of speech, etc.)
- Nonverbal communication (eye contact, meaning of gestures)
- Proxemics (spatial distance between people)
- Social values (peer group influences)
- Intellectual orientation (e.g., is frequent questioning valued or discouraged?)

Table 3.1   Culturally Relevant Versus Assimilationist Teaching Styles

Culturally Relevant	Assimilationist
Knowledge is continuously recreated, recycling, and shared by teachers and students. It is not static or unchanging.	Knowledge is static and is passed in one direction, from teacher to student.
Knowledge is viewed critically.	Knowledge is viewed as infallible.
Teacher is passionate about content.	Teacher is detached, neutral about content.
Teacher helps students develop necessary skills.	Teacher expects students to demonstrate prerequisite skills.
Teacher sees excellence as a complex standard that may involve some postulates but takes student diversity and individual differences into account.	Teacher sees excellence as a postulate that exists independently from student diversity or individual differences.

Source: From "Like Lightning in a Bottle," *International Journal of Qualitative Studies in Education, 3*(4). Reprinted with permission.

In her book, *The Dreamkeepers,* Ladson-Billings (1994) compares culturally relevant teaching with what she terms assimilationist teaching. An assimilationist believes that ethnic groups should conform to the norms, values, expectations, and behaviors of the dominant social and cultural group. Culturally relevant teachers believe that all students can learn, albeit at different paces and in different ways. Assimilationist teachers believe that failure is inevitable for some students. See Table 3.1 for a summary of the two forms of teaching and ask yourself, "Which teaching approach is better aligned with my preferred style?" Explain your response.

MISPERCEPTIONS ABOUT CULTURALLY RELEVANT PEDAGOGY

1. *Misperception:* Culturally responsive pedagogy is a new and special pedagogy that is relevant only to low-income, urban students of color.

Reality: Traditional pedagogy has always been culturally relevant. Middle-class and Euro-American students' culture is the accepted norm in most schools. Can you list some ways in which middle-class students' culture is acceptable in schools?

_____

_____

How can schools appreciate the culture of all students?

_____

_____

2. *Misperception:* In schools with diverse students, only teachers of color are capable of demonstrating culturally responsive pedagogy.

Reality: Most teachers are white. It is unrealistic and undesirable to equate culturally relevant pedagogy only with teachers of color. All teachers, regardless of their ethnic background, are capable of incorporating this kind of pedagogy. All it takes is a sensitivity and an appreciation of its importance. Are you capable of teaching in culturally relevant ways? Explain.

_____

_____

What factors might create difficulties in incorporating culturally relevant pedagogy?

_____

_____

3. *Misperception:* Cultural responsive pedagogy is primarily a teaching method.

Reality: Yes it is, but it is much more. Culturally relevant teaching is an attitude about teaching, students, the ways they can learn, and outside factors that influence successful learning. Why are you inclined or not inclined to teach this way? Explain.

_____

_____

_____

What training might you need to incorporate culturally relevant pedagogy?

_____

_____

4. *Misperception:* Culturally relevant teachers must become expert in a variety of cultures.

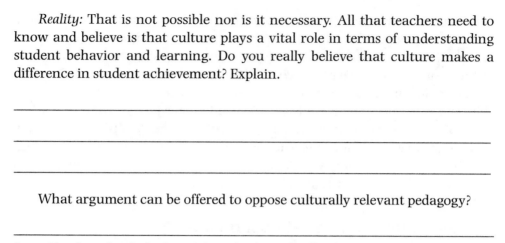

Reality: That is not possible nor is it necessary. All that teachers need to know and believe is that culture plays a vital role in terms of understanding student behavior and learning. Do you really believe that culture makes a difference in student achievement? Explain.

_____

_____

_____

What argument can be offered to oppose culturally relevant pedagogy?

_____

Source: Ideas drawn from Jordan Irvine & Armento, 2003, *Culturally Relevant Teaching*, pp. 13-14.

DIFFERENT WAYS OF LEARNING

By paying attention to the variety of ways your students learn, you can individualize instruction appropriately and thus meet their learning needs. Students will learn better when you pay attention to their learning preferences.

Sensory Modality Style

Some students learn best when you stimulate their senses—auditorily, tactily, and visually. Many students learn best when they are presented with visual stimulation. They learn best when you incorporate videos, pictures, charts, graphs, and other such material. These students learn through observation. Teachers who prepare ***advance organizers*** and use sensory aids help such students. Auditory learners prefer hearing information. They like listening to a story or a recording. You can help these students learn by, for instance, placing material on an audiotape, video, CD, and so forth. Tactile-kinesthetic learners enjoy the physical stimulation of touching things. Present information to these students through the use of manipulatives or role-playing. Using a multisensory teaching approach is very beneficial. Therefore, when you plan a lesson ask yourself, "How can I incorporate as many senses as possible to assist these learners?"

Global/Analytical Styles

These learning styles takes into consideration how your students process information. Global learners use the right hemisphere of their brain, which stresses spatial and relational processing. Global learners prefer to learn by considering the whole picture first and then breaking down the information into smaller parts. When they do so, they begin to recognize patterns and see relationships. On the other hand, analytical, learners using the left hemisphere of the brain, learn from parts to whole. When presented with new information, for example, these students seek out the details first. They are analytical thinkers. How do you prefer to learn? Do you first need to be given the context or whole picture, or do you prefer to get right into the details? Find out how many global versus analytic learners you have in class and provide for their learning preferences. How you do so is up to you. Can you think of ways to address both learning needs in a single lesson? Explain.

Field-Independent/Field-Dependent Styles

Students solve problems in different ways. Some students are able to separate information from its context or background. They are field independent in that they can work independently, are intrinsically motivated, and prefer an analytic approach to learning. Others are field dependent in that they need and prefer background information and context. They like to work with others, are extrinsically motivated and take a global approach to learning.

True or False: Field-independent students like to work alone. Teachers can assist them by assigning research projects.

True or False: Field-dependent learners prefer cooperative learning, field trips, and learning with hands-on manipulatives.

Both statements are true.

Impulsive/Reflective Styles

Some students are quick to respond to guess solutions or solve problems. They have high energy. On the other hand, others are more reflective. They take their time in responding. They are thoughtful and considerate learners. Teachers must be patient with these learners. Using wait time appropriately will help. I know someone I work with who needs a lot of time to think. I tend to move and go quickly. As I am on my fifth point, she'll comment and go back to the second point. I didn't allow her to process. What might I have done?

Teach your visual learners using pictures, videos, graphs, charts, magazines, transparencies, LCD projections, computers, diagrams, drawings, flash cards, handouts, television, and so on.

Teach your auditory learners using: tapes, videotapes, lectures, stereos, oral directions, oral review, explanations, discussion, songs, and so forth.

Teach your kinesthetic learners using: manipulatives, sense of touch, role playing, plays, demonstration, physical movement, real experiences, field trips, projects, pantomimes, and so on.

REFLECT

We've learned thus far that students have varied needs and preferences, and that teachers should be aware of the role of race, gender, sexual orientation, and social class that may impact student learning. Teachers, as culturally relevant educators, accept and consider the student's culture in developing relevant curricula. Teachers must attend to the needs of the student with learning disabilities, the English Language Learner, the underachiever, and the accelerated learner. How is it possible for a teacher to teach a class of such heterogeneous abilities? What strategies would you employ in a class of mixed abilities and needs? Jot some practical strategies below and then read on . . .

_____

_____

DIFFERENTIATING INSTRUCTION: BUT HOW CAN I MEET THE NEEDS OF ALL MY STUDENTS?

"Kids of the same age aren't all alike when it comes to learning."

—Carol Ann Tomlinson

Teachers must learn and know how to accommodate the varied and different learning abilities and styles of diverse students. Although I think schools were always diverse and the skill of differentiation (providing appropriate instruction to diverse learners in a diverse classroom) was always important, today it is even more important because students in your classroom come from many more diverse backgrounds and cultures. Differentiation is also important because today's classroom is more likely than ever to include students of varying abilities.

What Is Differentiated Instruction?

- Differentiated instruction can occur when teachers are aware and able to consider and deal with different learning needs and abilities of their students.
- Differentiated instruction is possible when teachers find opportunities for every student to succeed.

- Differentiated instruction occurs when teachers can multitask.
- Differentiated instruction occurs when teachers can manage a classroom well to allow for "structured chaos" but also know how to minimize excessive noise and disruptions.
- Differentiated instruction occurs when a range of activities is provided: whole-class instruction, small-group activities (pairs, triads, quads), individualized activities (e.g., learning centers, independent study), and student-teacher conferences (e.g., working on contracts for learning).
- Differentiated instruction occurs when teachers allow students to express themselves in diverse ways (e.g., artistically, musically, technologically, scientifically, athletically, etc.)
- Differentiated instruction allows students to express themselves in different ways (e.g., traditional compositions/essays, speeches, drama, music, building models, etc.)
- Differentiated instruction considers assessment as an ongoing, integrated process.
- Differentiated instruction can occur when a class works together to explore a particular topic or unit of study.
- Differentiated instruction occurs when students discuss ideas freely and openly, giving all students a chance to participate in the discussion.
- Differentiated instruction occurs when the whole class listens to individuals or small groups about how they plan to learn or study a particular topic.
- Differentiated instruction occurs when students work in small groups.
- Differentiated instruction occurs when the teacher works with selected students.
- Differentiated instruction occurs when teachers consider that students learn differently and must construct meaning on their own.
- Differentiated instruction occurs when teachers allow students to take responsibility for their own learning.
- Differentiated instruction occurs when teachers use peer tutoring (i.e., advanced learners on particular topics work with students not as advanced).
- Differentiated instruction occurs when teachers realize that different students have different strengths and weaknesses.
- Differentiated instruction occurs when teachers provide for flexible grouping; that is, sometimes Maria will need remediation in reading by working with the teacher in a homogeneous group but that during math she is able to work independently because her skills are average or above average.
- Differentiated instruction occurs when teachers realize students will complete work at different paces and that the teacher must plan for and provide learning activities for students who complete work before others.

- Differentiated instruction occurs when students can plan activities on their own.
- Differentiated instruction occurs when students can form their own interest groups to explore a topic of interest.
- Differentiated instruction allows for Web-questing (see Appendix B).
- Differentiated instruction incorporates cooperative learning, multiple intelligences (see below), and diverse learning styles.
- Differentiated instruction provides for literature circle opportunities (i.e., students read a common book and then form a group on their own to discuss the book and then perhaps develop a common project based on the reading).

Differentiated instruction is NOT for teachers who cannot multitask or prefer students to sit quietly and pay attention to "teacher talk."

Differentiated instruction means dividing your time among many students giving quality time to each, which reminds me of a story. There were two famous educators who attended a wedding of a common friend. One stayed for only thirty minutes, while the other stayed for several hours. When the first educator left, everyone was happy and expressed appreciation to him for having attended. Much later, when the second educator was about to leave, someone asked him, "Why are you leaving already? You just came!"

The one who stayed longer at the affair asked his colleague, "What is your secret? How is it that you come for only a short time and everyone is happy, yet I stay for a long time and no one is satisfied?"

"It's really very simple," said the other. "I spend only a half hour but during those thirty minutes my heart is totally involved in the occasion. You may stay longer, but from the moment you walk in, you can't wait to leave. It's clear that your heart isn't in it. No wonder people say you've just come—they never really felt you were present!"

How can you make your students feel that you have given them complete attention?

How many of the following points can you check off?

_____ 1. I call on students equitably.

_____ 2. I care for all students.

_____ 3. All students, regardless of ability, can learn from one another.

_____ 4. I am attuned to the different learning needs and abilities of my students.

**SCHOOL OF EDUCATION
CURRICULUM LABORATORY
UM-DEARBORN**

_____ 5. I display the work of all students, regardless of ability or achievement (which reminds me of a story, see below).

_____ 6. I help students appreciate, tolerate, and accommodate their similarities and differences in learning, culture, and interest.

_____ 7. I celebrate the successes of all students.

_____ 8. I consciously incorporate multiple intelligences whenever feasible.

_____ 9. I consciously incorporate learning styles whenever feasible.

_____ 10. I pre-assess students' knowledge prior to instruction so that I can develop appropriate lessons.

_____ 11. I use a variety of assessment strategies throughout the unit of instruction.

_____ 12. I am flexible in terms of allowing students to demonstrate different ways that they have learned the material (in other words, I give students choices about how to express their learning).

_____ 13. I offer different homework options.

_____ 14. I give different kinds of tests.

_____ 15. I grade holistically, not relying on one sole test or measure.

_____ 16. In questioning all students, I prompt and probe equitably.

_____ 17. I give the same wait time to slow learners as I do to advanced learners.

_____ 18. I use a variety of grouping procedures, including whole-class instruction and small grouping.

_____ 19. I use peer tutoring as necessary.

_____ 20. I find ways for all students to excel.

_____ 21. I use a variety of teaching strategies.

_____ 22. I take into consideration students' interests and needs in planning instruction.

_____ 23. I give students texts that are at varied levels and readability.

_____ 24. I incorporate technology into instruction wherever feasible and useful.

_____ 25. I differentiate instruction most of the time.

Now for that quick, true story: When I was an assistant principal, I entered Mrs. Smith's classroom one morning and marveled at her beautifully decorated room. I was happy to notice several bulletin boards displaying student work. On closer inspection, I saw boards entitled "Our Best Spellers," "Our Best Math Work," "Our Best Writers." I spoke with Mrs. Smith afterwards and asked if she didn't agree that all students need and should be acknowledged in some way. She agreed and asked me to return the following week, which I did. As I perused the bulletin boards again I noticed that she indeed had included *all* students' work and she removed the word "Best" from each board. She posted Sarah's score of "45" on her math test, "Renaldo's 55 in spelling, and Jean's 60 in writing!" Ugh . . .

Postscript: She later assured me that these students would do better next time!?!#

Smart teachers find ways for all students to excel and achieve in positive ways.

Using Multiple Intelligences as You Differentiate Instruction

Differentiated instruction acknowledges that each student comes to class with a variety of learning preferences or styles. Each processes information differently. Each student also has a different intelligence, according to famed Harvard researcher Howard Gardner (2000). He identifies eight different intelligences that are common to all people and which vary in degree. They include:

Verbal/Linguistic—Verbally or linguistically intelligent students make varied use of language. They are good with words. They enjoy journal writing, compositions, essays, word games, and reading. These are your future journalists, storytellers, poets, lawyers, and so on.

Logical/Mathematical—Logically or mathematically intelligent students reason well, see cause and effect relationships easily, and see numerical patterns. They enjoy experiments, number games, critical thinking, and mental calculations. These are your future mathematicians, scientists, accountants, and computer programmers.

Visual/Spatial—Visually or spatially intelligent students think in pictures and images. They have the ability to perceive, transform, and re-create different aspects of the physical world. They enjoy art activities, imagination games, maps, videos, and problem-solving. These students are your future architects, photographers, artists, pilots, and mechanical engineers.

Musical/Rhythmic—Musically or rhythmically intelligent students are sensitive to pitch, melody, rhythm, and tone. They enjoy singing, listening, musical games, audios, and musical instruments. They are your future musicians.

Interpersonal—Interpersonally intelligent students have the ability to notice and make distinctions among other people. They are people-oriented. They enjoy conversing and interacting with others. They enjoy cooperative learning, role playing, simulations, and teaching. They are your future politicians, salespeople, and teachers.

Intrapersonal—Intrapersonally intelligent students have the ability to understand themselves very well and understand others' feelings. They can "feel" the other person's needs and desires. They enjoy individualized instruction, independent study, and reflective practices. They are your future therapists, counselors, theologians, and social workers.

Bodily/Kinesthetic—Bodily kinesthetic intelligent students can handle their body and objects skillfully. They enjoy physical activities, games, drama, and manipulating objects. They are your future athletes, craftspeople, physicians, and mechanics.

Naturalist—Naturalistic intelligent students have a keen understanding of their environment. They enjoy working outdoors, in gardens, botanical gardens, with animals, and so on. They are your future gardeners, botanists, pet owners, etc.

Take this quiz and identify the correct intelligence based on the preceding list:

1. I can use both inductive and deductive reasoning to solve problems. I like to categorize information, find sequences, and determine cause and effect relationships. I love to work on projects that don't involve too much essay writing or oral speech presentations. _____

2. I work well with others in pairs or teams. _____

3. I learn best by watching first. I love art projects and to build models. I also like role-playing activities. _____

4. I am very sensitive to sounds and prefer to express myself using songs. _____

5. I like to think a lot. I need time to think and reflect about what I am doing. I like to be alone sometimes and prefer journal writing. _____

6. I love pantomime, charades, and building things. _____

7. I love to debate and argue to make my point. I enjoy reading and to teach others. _____

8. I enjoy plants and I am fascinated with natural phenomena. I have three pets. _____

Answers: 1. logical/mathematical, 2. interpersonal, 3. spatial/visual, 4. musical/rhythmic, 5. intrapersonal, 6. bodily/kinesthetic, 7. verbal/linguistic, 8. naturalist

The following story illustrates how students with different intelligences can work together well:

Sarah, Jason, Jose, and Robert were working together on a project. Sarah (verbal/linguistic intelligent) was a very serious, diligent reader who loved to write. Jason (interpersonal, intelligent), was very popular and knew how to interact well with other students. Jason was well liked by classmates. Jose (musical/rhythmic intelligent) was very artistic and loved music. Robert (logical/mathematical intelligent) was well organized and enjoyed crunching numbers. Each student worked in the group according to his or her abilities. Each offered a unique contribution. Robert planned the project and offered general oversight and direction, while Jason kept the group socially intact and happy. Jose did all the artistic work and wrote a song to introduce the project. Sarah did a considerable amount of the writing.

Can you think of ways you can integrate multiple intelligences into your lessons? How does knowledge of multiple intelligences assist in differentiating instruction? Explain by giving examples from your classroom.

THE CHALLENGE OF INCLUSION

"The ultimate rationale for inclusion is based not on law or regulations or teaching technology, but on values. What kinds of people are we and what kind of society do we wish to develop? What values do we honor?"

—A. Gartner and D. K. Lipsky

Inclusion is a belief system. It is a process of facilitating an educational environment that provides access to high quality education for all students (Allan, 1999; Barton, 1998; Capper, Frattura, & Keyes, 2000; Huber, 2002; Kochhar, West, & Taymans, 2000; McLeskey & Waldron, 2001; Wolfendale, 2000). Effective teachers believe that all children can learn together in the same schools and the same classrooms, with services and supports necessary so that they can succeed. Maintaining high expectations for all students, believing in their potential, providing needed services to fully participate are essential. No child should be demeaned or have his or her uniqueness ignored or belittled. Students with disabilities should be educated with students without disabilities as much as possible. Special classes or removal of children from the regular education environment should occur only when the nature or severity of the disability is such that education in the regular classroom cannot be achieved satisfactorily with the use of supplementary support services (Elliott & McKenney, 1998; Morse, 2002).

Practices that are inclusionary are based on democratic thought and are a hope for the future. Such hopeful thinking is reflected in the writings of Clough and Corbet, 2000; Freire, 1974/1994; Kohl, 1998; Macedo, 1994; McLaren, 1994; and Oakes and Lipton, 1999.

As a classroom teacher you are expected to develop educational programs that serve a diversity of students, including those with disabilities. Special education laws since 1975 (Public Law 94–142), including the more recent Individuals with Disabilities Education Act (IDEA) amendments, have challenged teachers to help all children learn side-by-side, although they may have varied educational needs (Kochhar, West, & Taymans, 2000). In this chapter, we have introduced some teaching strategies to assist you (e.g., differentiated instruction). Below are some suggestions for making inclusion work for you.

1. Make sure that students have not simply been "dumped" into your classroom without special services and supports provided by the administration or special education team in your school or district. Seek advice from your vice principal.

2. Make each child in your class feel special by acknowledging the good work they do and ensuring that, for instance, you post work up on classroom or hall bulletin boards from all students.

3. Focus on what a child can do rather than always on what they can't do. For example, let each student demonstrate on an occasion a special talent he or she may have (e.g., karate, art, singing, juggling, etc.).

4. Encourage and implement activities that promote the development of friendships and relationships between students with and without disabilities. For example, use cooperative learning strategies (see Chapter 6).

5. Teach all your students every day to understand and accept individual differences.

How to Develop Rapport With Your Students

A couple of simple rules: Don't be their friend (although you can be friendly). Establish rigorous standards of achievement based on their abilities and communicate high expectations for all. Respect each student as a unique individual and they, in turn, will respect you. Teach them by building on their successes and provide examples drawn from their life experiences. Can you list five other ways you can positively develop rapport with your students?

_____

_____

CONCLUSION

The students in your class are unique individuals that deserve special attention. I am certain that you must realize the awesome responsibility you face each day. Trying to understand the needs of each child can seem overwhelming, if not impossible. Don't hesitate to ask specialists, or even parents for assistance. The more information you have about a student the more likely you will best meet his or her educational needs. Don't get discouraged. Sometimes you will not see much progress or even receive acknowledgment for your efforts. Persist. You are a professional who realizes your primary task is to make each student feel accepted and special. In time, you will develop new ways of meeting each student's needs. Take time to enjoy your students. They are worth it.

* * *

FOLLOW-UP QUESTIONS/ACTIVITIES

1. Each of us is learning disabled in some way. Describe some difficulties you have or have had with learning. How can this knowledge help to deal with students you encounter who also have learning difficulties?

2. What would you do if you discovered that one of your students had difficulty paying attention (e.g., was always fidgety in class)?

3. How would you or do you foster inclusion and differentiate instruction in your classroom?

4. Make a list of each child in your present class and identify one learning weakness and one learning strength for each. Specify what new approach you may have learned in this chapter or book, thus far, to assist you in helping this child.

5. Write an essay entitled "Who Are the Students in My Class?" Share your essay with a colleague. Have this colleague describe your class to you. What additional information might your colleague need to have?

4

How Should I Write Lesson Plans?

Teacher planning is the thread that weaves the curriculum, or the what of teaching, with the instruction, or the how of teaching. The classroom is a highly interactive and demanding place. Planning provides for some measure of order in an uncertain and changing environment.

—H. Jerome Freiberg and Amy Driscoll

◆

FOCUS QUESTIONS

1. What are three reasons why lesson planning is so critical?

2. Why do experienced teachers also have to plan?

3. What are the most critical elements of a lesson?

4. Homework is a controversial topic. Some educators are in favor of homework while others are opposed. What's your stand?

5. True or False: Planning occurs before, during, and after a lesson.

Here's an evaluation letter I presented to one of the fourth grade teachers I observed when I served as assistant principal in a K–5 urban school:

> Dear Ms. Xavier,
>
> I requested to observe you teaching a lesson in Basal Reading. At our preobservation conference, you provided me with a detailed written lesson plan. Upon observing your lesson, I noted the following positive features:
>
> 1. I was impressed with this well-organized and well-planned lesson. The aim was clearly written on the board, "How do we sum up important information?" The students were reading a story titled, "Memories" in the *Over the Moon* reader. You also noted your instructional standards tied to the state learning standards.
>
> 2. You began the lesson by asking, "What are ways we sum up information?" You elicited various responses such as titles, illustrations, telegrams, headlines, graphs, and book reports. You then reviewed key vocabulary words and had students skim the story. This lesson had many good elements from silent and oral reading to good provocative questions and summaries. The lesson was quite comprehensive. The pupils were attentive and well mannered.
>
> 3. Although the lesson was fine, please consider the following few suggestions for improvement, as we discussed, in part, at our post-observation conference:
>
>   - *Utilize wait time:* Wait time is an instructional strategy that refers to the amount of time students have to think during questioning. Research indicates that providing between 7 and 10 seconds for students to think before the teacher answers a question or calls on someone else improves student accurate participation.
>   - *Check for understanding:* Although you have definitely established a warm, friendly, and supportive classroom environment conducive to eliciting student participation, research indicates that when teachers proactively check student's understanding, retention of difficult subject matter increases dramatically. Calling on students who do not volunteer a response and/or having them repeat content information in their own words to neighboring students increases the likelihood that students will really understand the material.

- *Use focused questions:* We discussed that use of one well-focused question (which you developed quite well) should suffice, under normal circumstances, to stimulate thought and participation. Use of multiple questions to get across the same idea may, at times, not be necessary.

Thank you for the wonderful opportunity to observe you teach. Please invite me again in the near future.

I am not presenting this observation/evaluation report as a model, but rather to indicate a number of issues. First, a well planned lesson is critical for effective teaching. Planning is the first stage in a three-stage process that also includes implementing the lesson and evaluating the lesson. In the case above an outside observer (i.e., supervisor) conducted the evaluation. More often, teachers themselves can determine whether or not a particular lesson was effective. Parenthetically, formal evaluation yields little change in teaching behavior in my estimation. If instructional improvement is to occur, then the evaluative mode has to be removed from the process. Evaluation, however, does have its place to ensure accountability and that the teacher in front of the class is competent. Aside from that narrow function, evaluation should give way to activities that really promote instructional improvement such as peer coaching (teachers assisting teachers) or clinical supervision (observations for feedback devoid of evaluation).

A second point to be gleaned from the report above is that lesson planning and writing are not only done when a teacher is formally observed. Lesson planning is an ongoing, introspective process that engages the teacher in selecting the most appropriate learning objectives and activities for a particular class. All teachers, regardless of experience, need to plan, and planning occurs before, during, and after instruction (so the answer to the fifth focus question is "true").

In this chapter, I will highlight important elements that go into an effective lesson. You will have an opportunity to identify and critique a lesson and I will also encourage you to have a lesson videotaped because a "picture is worth a thousand words." Sample lesson plans are also provided.

WHAT IS LESSON PLANNING?

Lesson Planning—the term suggests many different connotations. So many teachers would say it implies a necessary but unpleasant chore. Others might describe it as burdensome paperwork, an outline for instruction, or even a helpful guide. No matter whether required or not, no matter whether written elaborately or briefly, lesson plans are a part of all teachers' weekly tasks. Without a plan, instruction becomes a random assortment of activities with little rhyme or reason.

Lesson planning is usually associated with only a written design developed by the teacher. Actually, it involves two activities:

1. Mental planning

2. Keeping a written plan book

In mental planning, teachers consider questions, reflect on the topic, and envision what might occur in subsequent lessons. Mental planning is an important and legitimate prerequisite for the written plan. It takes into consideration such things as the textbook, a list of prescribed skills, and library materials. It is not unlike an athlete who mentally prepares by envisioning a successful shot. You too need to envision what your lesson will accomplish, what you want students to learn and know at the end, and how you will go about achieving your objectives.

The plan book is a shorthand outline of what will develop in the classroom based on the mental planning. The written plan serves as a reminder of topics, concepts, skills, and activities that the teacher wants to be sure to use at some point. Basically, it's the teacher's roadmap. Different schools will require different plan books and plans. This chapter merely highlights the main parts of a lesson.

Lesson plans are most effective when the interrelationships of skills are fostered. Most of us can agree with the premise that schooling should offer children opportunities to make connections, to think, and to expand learning. It is false to assume that just because students learn various skills that they will automatically know how to use them in relationships. It is also false to assume that texts make the connections for us. Some textbooks do only a fair job in structuring for continuity. Thus it becomes the teacher's responsibility to develop lessons that expand thinking and interrelate skills. For example, teachers can develop reading lessons that help students to learn that punctuation, context, and phonics clues can all be used together to interpret the written word. Subjects such as science, reading, and social studies can be interrelated. For example, a story about Columbus can be related to map reading skills taught in social studies and to navigation by constellations in science. Children need to be encouraged to make connections between various lessons, between subjects, and between in-school and out-of-school life.

Another good practice is to develop long range as well as short range goals. Having long range goals (monthly, quarterly, or yearly) helps teachers maintain an overall perspective and helps to serve as a guide for day-to-day instruction.

It is very important to use teacher judgment when writing short range objectives. Some subject objectives and daily plans, such as reading and mathematics, are greatly influenced by texts. Texts do not always provide the continuity necessary for effective learning. Also, text suggestions often need to be modified to fit individual classroom situations. Teachers should make changes in textbook guides based on criteria such as the following:

- Do these students already know this material? Does it need reviewing?
- Will this activity fit into the amount of time I have?
- How can I relate to what the students know?
- Could I do part of this activity as independent work for the group to complete while I work with another group?

When determining objectives and writing lesson plans, you should consider students' learning styles. Some students are fast, others slow; some are easily motivated, others difficult to motivate; some do well in large groups, others in small groups; some do better with written work, others with oral work. By taking such learning characteristics into consideration, you can develop strategies that are appropriate for various classes.

It is a good habit to include the method of evaluation. The primary purpose of testing is to determine the extent of student mastery of the objectives, not to determine grades. For any lesson to be productive, you must receive feedback as to how well the objectives are being met. To receive useful feedback, you should spend sufficient time incorporating good evaluation measures as part of lesson planning.

Some other helpful points for effective daily plans include:

- Estimate the time required for various activities; plan enough—don't get caught short (students are more apt to get in trouble when they have too much free time on their hands); have additional activities in reserve for those occasions when your regular lessons are completed early.
- Jot down any changes you would like to make for future use while they are fresh in your mind.
- Check off items as they are completed.
- Be flexible and make adjustments as you go. (You, as a teacher, know best how to adjust your lesson plans based on your evaluation of students progress. Sometimes you need to move slower and give more instruction before proceeding to new objectives.)

The actual format of lesson plans is not as important as the process of developing the plans. Use whatever format is most workable for you as long as it is clear and easy to follow (unless, of course, you are required to use a certain format). As implied by the points already described, consider using the following process when writing lesson plans:

1. First, analyze students' learning styles.

2. Next, specify long range goals (may be monthly, quarterly, or yearly). These long-range goals should determine your daily lesson plans.

3. Then specify objectives.

4. After objectives are stated, select or design activities and materials.

5. Include how students will be tested to determine the effectiveness of instruction.

6. After instruction, evaluate activities and make revisions as necessary.

No matter whether your planning is detailed or general, it is important. It helps you to organize your thoughts, meet objectives, coordinate materials, and be prepared for instruction. By planning properly, your teaching will be more effective.

ESSENTIAL COMPONENTS AND CRITERIA OF A SUCCESSFUL LESSON

Aims and Objectives

1. Meaningful and appropriate to the levels of students

2. Elicited from students

3. Personalized in question form

4. Definite and expressed

5. Achieved and realized

6. Written on board and in student's notebook

7. Varied use of Bloom's Taxonomy (see below)

Decide what your goals are in teaching this unit. In looking over the content that you plan to teach in a lesson, you must ask the question: "What do I want the pupils to derive from the lesson that will be meaningful and worthwhile?" The aim that you decide upon will be the backbone of the lesson. All activities should point towards the achievement of that aim. Let the student derive the aim rather than having the teacher state it at the outset. This helps the students identify with the lesson and make it their own. Your motivation should be the vehicle for revealing the aim to the class. The objectives do not necessarily have to be formally stated. Rather, they are written explicitly in your plan book. The aim is a general statement based on your objectives. Some teachers prefer to inform students about both the aim and objectives. For sample objectives, see Web site listing for Web Quest in Appendix B.

Motivation

1. Arouses interest

2. Sustains interest

3. Connects to aim of lesson

4. Challenges students

5. Relates to students' experiences

6. Easy transition to lesson

Motivation is a device to arouse student interest in the content to be taught, and also to reveal to the class the aim of the lesson. Effective motivations stimulate curiosity and utilize the experiences and the knowledge of the pupils. Some devices that can be used to motivate a lesson are: challenging statements, personal experiences, cartoons, a problem, a chart, or anecdote. Some call this stage "anticipatory sets."

Questions

1. Well phrased and understood

2. Stimulated critical thinking

3. Well distributed among students in class

4. Check for understanding

Pitfalls in Questioning

1. Calling on student first and then asking question

2. Relying only on volunteers

3. Saying "tell me" not "us"

4. Framing multiple questions

Student Responses

1. Avoid choral responses

2. Don't repeat student response

3. Use praise, prompt (student answers incorrectly), and probe (student answers correctly but lacks depth) techniques

Aside from developing your aim and learning objectives, your use of questions is the most critical part of your lesson. The success or failure of a lesson is largely determined by the questioning techniques employed, by the quality of the questions, and by the sequence in which the questions are asked. Questioning is a powerful teaching tool. Through questioning, you can develop student learning styles and habits, stimulate higher levels of thinking, foster new learning, and evaluate the progress of achievement. You actually can mold student's minds through the effective use of questions.

Unfortunately, we often do not make as effective use of questions as we could, and as we should. Research has shown that most teacher questions are on the lower levels of thinking, predominantly information and short answers, rather than on the higher levels, such as judgment, inference, application, analysis, and synthesis. This problem can be overcome by becoming familiar with the thinking hierarchy (such as Bloom's Taxonomy) and by generating questions that promote higher thinking.

Benjamin Bloom's taxonomy is one of the most important concepts in all of teaching. Basically, he asserts that learning occurs in a hierarchical manner, beginning with simple thinking processes and proceeding step-by-step through more complex processes. He classifies six major learning behaviors or ways of thinking, that translate into six types of questions you need to consider and use appropriately:

1. Knowledge—The lowest, most basic level of learning or thinking occurs when students are asked to recall or recognize bits of information. Key words here are: who, what, when, which, how many, name, identify, recall, and so on. Examples include: Who discovered the Indian Ocean? What happened to Alice in the story? Where did her mother send her? And so forth. Students merely are asked to recall bits of information. At this stage, students may merely memorize information but may not comprehend what they have learned. I once had a fourth grader who had phenomenal decoding skills who could read every word in the *New York Times*. Everyone marveled at his ability to "read." He really couldn't read because he could not understand what he had read, which brings us to Bloom's second and higher level.

2. Comprehension—This next behavior or thinking level occurs when students are able to explain or paraphrase information. Asking students to explain in their own words what a concept means or give an example may indicate that students comprehend the information. Key words here are: describe, explain, use your own words, translate, interpret, and so forth. Examples include: "What do the words ____ mean?" "Explain what ____ means," and so on. Ask a student "What is a Lut?" He doesn't know, so you tell him "A Lut is a Zut." Now, you ask him again, "Okay, what is a Lut?" He responds, "It's a Zut." Although he has some knowledge, that is, that a Lut is a Zut, he may not understand what a

Lut really is. Ask, "Okay, explain in your own words what is a Lut? Zut?" If he is able to explain correctly, you may assume he comprehends the information.

3. Application—This next higher level of thinking or behavior requires the student to use the information learned to solve a specific problem or apply it to a situation. Key words here are: solve, choose, apply, and so on. Examples include: "How might the *Roe v. Wade* decision affect human rights issues?" "How can you apply what we have learned to . . . ?" A student, for instance, may know a rule of grammar and may even understand the rule. However, can he or she apply the rule to a new situation or context, for example, using it correctly in an essay?

4. Analysis—This higher cognitive domain of learning expects students to take a situation apart and to understand the relationship between parts. For example, you may show your third-grade class a picture of three groups of animals and ask them which group does not belong. The student is required to analyze the various characteristics to arrive at an answer. Key words here are: analyze, show, how, distinguish, and so on. Examples include: "Who can distinguish between fact and opinion in the article we just read?" "Why did the balloon inflate?" "How does the use of similes convey an emotional impact to the reader?" "What is the difference between ____ and ____?"

5. Synthesis—At this higher level, students can creatively put elements or information together to form a new structure or idea. Key words here are: create, develop, devise, predict, invent, and so on. Examples include: "Given the elements of a lesson, you will develop an original lesson of your own, put together the carburetor, invent a machine that would make life easier."

6. Evaluation—This is the highest level according to Bloom. Too often, teachers ask students to make judgments about something without challenging them at the prior levels of thinking or behavior. Evaluation requires students to state their opinions, justify their points of view or answers. Key words here are: decide, judge, discuss, choose, recommend, give opinion, explain why, evaluate, and so on. Examples include: "Was the story good? Why or why not?" "Which technique would be better? Explain." "Who can tell the class what is wrong with . . ." This final level encourages critical reasoning and judgment.

Here's a little quiz for you. Identify the correct level of Bloom's Taxonomy in each of these objectives:

_____ 1. Given any art materials of your choice, you will create an oil painting using no more than four colors.

_____ 2. Given a number of objects that you have not previously seen, you will identify all those that are squares.

_____ 3. Given twenty new multiplication examples, you will solve 80% of them correctly.

_____ 4. Given eight poems written by European poets, you will determine the common theme.

_____ 5. From memory, list the nine planets in our solar system.

_____ 6. Given five master's theses, you will select the best research design.

Answers: 1. synthesis, 2. comprehension, 3. application, 4. analysis, 5. knowledge, 6. evaluation.

Mnemonic for recalling Bloom's Taxonomy: **K**eep **C**alm **A**t **A**ll **S**ports **E**vents

However, there is another problem in questioning that is frequently overlooked. The vast majority of questions asked in classrooms are by the teacher. Students ask few questions, other than for assistance or clarification. If we are to develop active minds, not just passive and reactive ones, we must encourage students to learn how to formulate effective questions, for it is through questions that productive thinking occurs. Pupils must learn to question so that they can be critical processors and consumers of information. This process should begin in elementary school and not be limited to the higher grades, for learning and thinking patterns begin at early ages and shape all learning thereafter.

Here are several techniques to involve students in questioning:

1. Classwork/Homework Questions—Have students make up questions for classwork and or homework. For example, tell your students, "Make up five questions that would test whether someone had really understood the assigned readings. Make sure the answers are not in any one sentence." This exercise promotes thinking, as well as learning how to write questions. As a bonus, you can choose a few of the best questions to duplicate and give to the class.

2. Journalist Style Questioning—Invite a guest to class, but instead of having a presentation followed by "Are there any questions?", have students prepare questions in advance. Help students write questions that go beyond facts and lower cognition levels.

For example, students might prepare questions such as these for a visit by the school principal:

"Why did you select education for your career?" "What's the toughest part of your job as principal?" "Imagine you had the resources and influence to do anything you wanted in this school. What would you do and why?"

3. Questioning Through Games, Simulation, Role-Playing—An excellent way for students to learn questioning is through games, simulation and role-playing. In each of these activities students are presented with a problem or situation in which they must ask questions to seek solutions.

For example, at a simple level, play games like "Changing Storybook History." Ask, "How could the gingerbread boy have outsmarted the fox?" "If you were Little Red Riding Hood, how would you have avoided the wolf?" For higher levels, simulations and role-playing offer opportunity for mini-investigations. For example, the teacher presents the following problem to science class: "Over the past five years, there has been a dramatic increase in lung disease and asthma-like conditions in a particular city in the United States. Desiring to find the reasons for the increase and to correct the situation, city officials have called in a group of scientists to solve the problem. You are the scientists."

The team, or teams, might begin by posing questions that gain general information, such as where and what are the characteristics of the city, whether the problem has occurred elsewhere, and what are the symptoms of the ailing residents. The students should lay a data foundation from which they can draw conclusions. Or the students might begin by listing possible reasons for the problem (pollution, a change in the people's diets) and then ask questions to gather data that might confirm or deny the hypothesis.

4. **Student Oriented Ouestions**—When a student is having difficulty making a point or is confused, ask that student to formulate a question. This technique helps the learner to identify the area of concern and obtain the help he or she needs.

5. **Wait Time**—What would your reaction be if someone started firing questions at you at the rate of two or three per minute? Such rapid questioning appears to be typical of teachers around the country. After asking a question, a teacher waits one second or less for a student to answer. Then the teacher typically repeats, rephrases or gives one second or less for a student to answer. Once the student has responded, the teacher typically waits less than one second before commenting on the answer or asking another question. We need to think about reducing the number of questions and getting more payoff per question.

In the pausing behavior of teachers, there are two important pause locations, called wait times. Wait time one is the pause following a teacher's question; whether students respond quickly or slowly, the teacher tries to wait. Wait time two is the pause after a student's response: the teacher tries to wait before commenting on the response or asking another question. When this second pause time is cut short, all the student's amplifying, qualifying, and speculation is chopped off by teacher intervention. Perhaps this is one reason that students in fast interactive systems speak in fragmented sentences. A child needs more time to verbalize.

Some Poor Types of Questions

1. Multiple —"What started the war with Iraq and why did we get involved?"

2. Chorus—"Were we right?"

3. Leading—"Aren't the terrorists bad? Don't you agree?"

4. Addressed to the teacher—"Give *me* the answer." "Tell *me*." (Use "us")

5. Yes–No—"Did the girl go to the store?"

6. Calling on student's name before question.

7. Not calling on nonvolunteers.

Procedure

1. List learning activities for the lesson

2. Include pivotal (main) questions

3. Include a brief sequential description of how the lesson will proceed

See lesson plans later in the chapter for sample "procedures" or "lesson development."

Review

1. Reviews prior lesson or knowledge at outset

2. Stops to review after difficult material is presented

3. Provides a medial review (in middle of lesson)

4. Provides a summative review (at end of lesson)

5. Allows students to explain what they know

6. Teacher checks for understanding

In some lessons you might provide for a brief definite review that will help to clinch the concepts, skills, and understandings that had been taught in the previous lesson. Reviews may be conducted in various ways. You can pose a few thought provoking and factual questions that ask for a summary of the previous lesson. You can pose a question that calls for a comparison or for an application. You can ask a student to present a summary of the previous lesson.

After such a presentation, the other members of the class should be asked to make corrections and additions.

Lesson in General

1. Well paced

2. Worthwhile

3. Individualized

4. Varied student activities

5. Transitions smooth

6. Medial and final summaries

7. Follow up

Tests

1. Appropriate to ability level

2. Clearly worded

3. Content valid

4. Clear directions

5. Sufficient time

6. Test format varies

See Chapter 9 for a more complete discussion of assessment that goes beyond testing.

Homework

1. Grew out of lesson

2. Specific and well-defined

3. Varied—option driven

4. Differentiated—allow for different abilities

5. Explained and understood

Homework can be an important part of the student's process of learning. It can be an extension of a day's lesson, preparation for a new lesson, or the culminating activity for a unit of study. Homework assignments should be well thought out and relevant to the subject matter being taught. Here are some suggestions on this particular aspect of teaching:

1. Place the homework assignment on the chalkboard indicating the date it is due. Students can then copy down this information and refer to it when needed.

2. Give the homework assignment during class when there is adequate time for explanation and student questions.

3. Vary the type of assignment.

4. When possible use the previous day's homework as the basis for a class discussion, for review purposes, or as a lead-in for the new lesson you are presenting.

5. Homework assignments should be realistic. Do students have enough knowledge to do the work assigned? Will they have the materials needed at home to successfully complete the work? How long should it take to do the assignment?

6. Always collect the students' work the day it is due.

7. Grade the homework papers and return them to the students as soon as possible.

8. Notify parents if a student continually fails to do the assigned homework. Parents have a right to know if their son or daughter is not doing the assigned work.

Good schools have a clear and consistent homework policy and teachers of different subjects in these schools coordinate homework assignments in terms of length and difficulty. Homework must be marked, reviewed, and graded. Know that research indicates that homework given and reviewed appropriately can raise student achievement (Walber, Paschal, & Weinstein, 1985).

Homework Guidelines

1. Develop classroom homework in line with school policy.

2. Coordinate amount and type of homework with other teachers.

3. Homework in early grades should not generally exceed 15 to 30 minutes, three times a week and in middle grades 45 to 90 minutes, four times a week. In high school, the time should be broken down by subject/class

because no teacher has a clue as to the amount of homework given in other classes.

4. Homework must be relevant, interesting, and appropriate to the ability level of the student.

5. Never use homework as a punishment.

6. Don't use homework to introduce new ideas or concepts below high school.

7. Homework should sometimes incorporate nontraditional sources such as television, newspapers, and the Internet.

8. Students should not be permitted to go home without fully understanding the homework (it's unfair to the students and it irritates parents).

9. Don't give homework unless you will grade, return, and review it with students.

10. Differentiate assignments.

11. Keep parents informed of homework policy and their expected role.

12. Develop procedures for collecting homework and for checking homework.

Evaluation

It is always wise to evaluate a lesson plan. It is especially important if the lesson plan fell short of your expectations the first time around. Effective evaluation can be accomplished by considering the following questions:

- Were my aims relevant and realistic?
- Was I well prepared?
- Was my presentation organized and clear?
- Was my presentation varied enough?
- Did my students understand what they were doing and why they were doing it?
- Were my questions well phrased in language the students could understand?
- Did the students respond properly to my questions?
- Did all the students listen to and take part in today's lesson?

Keep in mind these Strengths (S) and Weaknesses (W) of some aspects of your lesson:

MOTIVATION:

S: based on need or interests sustained

W: no real motivation, overlong, not related to aim or lesson

AIM:

S: definite, suitable, clear, achieved

W: lacking, not related to lesson, poorly worded, trivial

DEVELOPMENT OR PROCEDURE:

S: well paced, sequential, varied approaches

W: digressions, confusing, poor transitions, inadequate content, too abstract, summaries poor

QUESTIONS AND ANSWERS:

S: clear wording, good distribution, pivotal questions, stimulate critical thought

W: confused wording, talking after question, no wait time, reliance on volunteers, poor distribution, one-word answers, repeating answers, "Tell me"

OUTCOMES:

S: subject matter, skills, concepts, attitudes, lesson learned

W: not learned, no check for learning, skills not mastered, lack of remediation or enrichment

HOMEWORK:

S: clear, appropriate, motivated, explained, individualized

W: missing, inappropriate, vague or confusing, too brief or too long

---

Table 4.1   What's wrong or right with each scenario. Check the appropriate column.

	Good	Bad	Recommendations
1. Teacher to pupils who "chorus" out the answer: "Boys and girls, you shouldn't call out that way. Charles, why shouldn't we call out our answers?"			
2. A teacher in an 8th grade social studies class praises committee A for having just completed an excellent report on the Hindu religion in India. She was especially pleased to note that each member of the committee read the report in a loud, clear voice.			
3. Teacher: "John, can you point out the Erie Canal on the map?" John goes to the map in front of the chalkboard, but can't find the Erie Canal on the map. Teacher: "Can you help John, May?" May goes to the map and finds the Erie Canal. Teacher: "Class. Is May right?"			

(Continued)

Table 4.1   (Continued)

	Good	*Bad*	*Recommendations*

4. The reading teacher has organized four groups in her seventh-year corrective reading class. She starts instruction with the poorest group as they need her help the most.

5. In the industrial arts room, two boys are reading *Popular Machines* in the corner of the room while the other boys are at their respective stations working on projects.

6. The drill in the mathematics class (7th grade) consumes 10 minutes. All pupils work on the same example and answer the questions successfully.

7. The language arts teacher says to the class, "Before we start I'll tell you what to do. Read the story on page 8. Then answer the questions on pages 9 and 10. Write each word you don't know in your notebook. Now, get busy."

8. In a reading lesson, the teacher notes that some pupils are reading aloud. She comments: "I hear someone reading aloud. How should we be reading?" Pupil: "To ourselves. Only with our eyes." Teacher: "Why shouldn't we be reading aloud?"
Pupil: "It disturbs our neighbors." Teacher: "I'll read this paragraph. First I'll read it silently (10 seconds elapse). Now, I'll read it aloud (she reads slowly). Now which did I read more quickly?" Chorus: "The first time." Teacher: "Right. When you want to read to get information you read silently. In that way, you read faster. If you are reading to someone you would read aloud, but then you must read slowly or no one will understand you."

9. The class is reading a passage silently. The teacher circulates around the room. Teacher: "If you need help, raise your hand. I'll come to you." No hands were raised. The class continued to work. Many pupils finished their work, took out other books, and read silently.

10. In a social studies class: Teacher: "Howard, name the New England states." Student falters. Teacher: George, let's see if you can do a better job than that?

Some suggested sample answers (others may apply):

1. It's good to point out that choral responses do not allow teachers to assess who really understands the information.

2. Effective use of positive reinforcement is a good thing.

3. Several problems here. Don't call on student first and then ask a question. Other students will tune out. Avoid saying "Class, Is Mary right?" Call on a particular student. Allow for wait time.

4. Nothing particularly wrong unless she always groups her class that way.

5. Depends on teacher's objectives. Is the teacher aware of what is occurring?

6. Does the teacher check for understanding? Do pupils always work on the same problem at the same time? Does the teacher differentiate her examples?

7. Busy work. What is the educational purpose of this activity?

8. Teacher models desired behavior and stimulates student thinking.

9. Teacher circulates and students seem to know class routines and procedures.

10. No attempt to assist student and denigrates student.

RESPOND

Directions: Critique each of the following lesson plans using the criteria discussed and explained above. Indicate any strengths or weaknesses. See more detailed (much better) sample lessons at the end of this chapter.

LESSON #1: GRADE 5, INCLUSIVE, SCIENCE

Aim: To learn about fossils
Do Now: Read pages 123–187.
Motivation: Open books, and read aloud.
Procedure: Discuss fossils; read story about fossils; have students ask questions; show film about fossils, answer questions on board.
Questions: How were fossils made? And so on.
Homework: Answer questions on handout sheet after reading pages 187–199 in science book.

LESSON #2: GRADE 5, GIFTED CLASS, LANGUAGE ARTS

Aim: To define persuasive writing and write a persuasive composition.

Do Now: Should we have split session to ease school overcrowding?

Motivation: Refer to "Do Now" question and ask what a split session is. Would it solve overcrowding in our school? Why? Why not?

Procedure: How would you go about convincing someone that your opinion is the correct one? How would you write this in a composition?

Steps:

1. Read question carefully.

2. Plan out your opinion.

3. Make an outline.

4. Provide facts.

5. Choose a topic sentence.

6. Choose a summary sentence.

7. Write a first draft.

8. Proofread.

9. Write final draft.

Homework: Write 2nd draft of essay started in class. Include at least four reasons to support your opinion.

Evaluation: Check and review essays in class. Have children read to class.

LESSON #3: GRADE 8,
BELOW AVERAGE, SOCIAL STUDIES

Aim: To learn about the final battles of the American Revolution

Motivation: Direct students to page 65. Tell them that the picture shows George Cornwallis, the British commander, leading his army out of Yorktown after surrendering to George Washington. Explain that a band was playing a song called "The World Turned Upside Down." Ask, Why do you think the British surrendered? What do you think Cornwallis was thinking about? And so forth.

Development: Have students read pages 162–163. Ask, What did the Americans do when the British began to take the war to the southern states? Who was Swamp Fox? Have students describe the battles leading to the end of the war. Write what they say on board in list form. Ask further exploratory questions.

Summary: Have students list the reasons for the American victory as given on page 163.

Homework: Read pages 163–64.

LESSON #4: GRADE 3, AVERAGE, READING

Aim: Finding the main idea

Motivation: Show pictures of interesting historical events and have class determine the main ideas of each picture.

Vocabulary: List 10 new words on board and read aloud with the class.

Development:

1. Read out loud the first page of story to class.

2. Ask them to locate the main idea.

3. Ask another child to read next page and repeat procedure.

4. Have the answer main idea questions on a handout I will give them—they may refer to story.

5. Reading Sophistication Series pages 34–46.

6. Review homework.

Homework: Study handout on main idea.

Evaluation: Test on Monday on main idea.

LESSON #5: GRADE 1O, AVERAGE, ENGLISH

Aim: To appreciate Shakespeare

Motivation: Read a passage from *Hamlet* and discuss why Shakespeare may be boring to students. Discuss some exciting elements about Shakespeare that students can appreciate and even enjoy.

Procedure:

1. Hand out excerpts from *Hamlet.*

2. Read selected portions with class.

3. Point out relevant parts.

4. Ask questions.

5. Provide worksheet.

Homework: Read part I of Hamlet and answer questions.

Each of the previous lesson plans has deficiencies, primarily, no stated objectives, no attempt to differentiate instruction, and lack of detail. See much better plans in the sample lesson plans that follow.

SAMPLE LESSON PLANS

SAMPLE LESSON #1

Diagnosis:

Subject: Social Studies	*Topic:* Geography	*Grade Level: Third*
Ability: Heterogeneous. 2 Asian students, 4 Latino students, Average ability. A total of 18 students.		
Time: 30 minutes	*Sequence:* Introduction to world continents	

Goal:

Students will know the seven continents of the world by name and make a cultural/landmark association.

Objectives:

Students will be able to identify the continents by their shape and size. (Knowledge)

Students will be able to list and describe several different landmark or cultural habits to that continent. (Comprehension)

Students will be able to compare and contrast the land mass of the countries by categorizing them from smallest to largest. (Analysis)

Aim:

What is life like on another continent?

Prerequisite Knowledge:

Students are already familiar with their own community and the city they live in. They are also aware of some New Jersey history and U.S. history.

Rationale:

This lesson will emphasize the location and major attributes of the continents of the world. It will provide students with knowledge and understanding of the world and the place of North America within the world.

Standards:

Ties lesson to state, city, or local standards.

Motivation:

Who has ever traveled out of America?

Does anyone have any family members that are from another country? Ireland? Poland? South America?

Materials:

Globe, wall map of world

Do Now:

Name 3 places outside of the United States.

Instructional Strategies:

Table 4.2

_X_ whole group	_X_ direct instruction	_X_ small group
_X_ cooperative learning	___ review prior to test	___ guided reading
___ developmental lesson	___ shared reading	___ guided practice
___ reciprocal teaching	___ peer tutoring	___ test sophistication
_X_ skills development	_X_ individualized instruction	___ read aloud
___ paired reading	___ review after test	___ other

Procedure: Knowledge content, linguistic (based on Gardner's Multiple Intelligences)

1. Has anyone ever traveled outside of the United States? Is there anyone in the classroom who is from or has family from outside of the United States? Have map on board and globe available. First, we will look at the map and the globe and discuss how we already are familiar with these two maps and how they show the same areas.

2. Can anyone name for the class any of the continents? We will go over the definition of continent. I will then write the seven continents on the board and have them repeat the names.

3. Can anyone in the class think of a tune or a song where we can use the names? If not, I will sing them my song, (Music). We will use choral singing to remember the continents.

4. Okay, class, close your eyes. Imagine you are in a plane and we land in Asia. Before you open your eyes, think about what that part of the world might be like. Can you see the people? What kinds of foods might be eaten there? Okay, now open your eyes. Who can tell the class what they saw?

Comprehension/Knowledge: Linguistic

We will go over certain landmarks that the children might know. For example, kangaroos are a very familiar animal in Australia. Coffee is from parts of Africa and South America. Tea is plentiful from India and China.

Mathematical/Logical (based on Gardner's Multiple Intelligences)

By looking at this map, can anyone guess which continent is the largest? The smallest?

I will cut out several scaled shapes of the United States. I will ask the students to see how many United States can go into one continent (if time permits).

Class, which continent is the biggest in land mass? Which continent is the smallest?

Conclusion and Summary:

We will review the seven continents first by singing our song. Then students will write a one-minute paper saying what they learned today and what interested them.

Homework:

Write a paper on a day in the life of a child in a different continent. Use your imagination.

Evaluation:

Have class write a one minute paper saying what they learned and what has piqued their curiosity.

SAMPLE LESSON #2

Diagnosis:

Ninth of a ten lesson U.S. history unit on World War II. The students are of heterogeneous ability. This lesson will last approximately 40 minutes and be divided into three segments: 12 minutes for lecture-discussion, 13 minutes for group activity, and 15 minutes for class debate.

Goal:

This lesson will teach students the historical events leading up to Japan's surrender during World War II. It will also force them to criticize and assess their own opinions regarding the U.S. decision to use the atomic bomb.

Aim:

How did World War II end in the Pacific Theater?

Objectives:

Having listened to the brief lecture on the closing days of World War II in the Pacific Theater, and participating in the two group/class activities, students will be able to:

1. Understand the events that took place during this period. (Knowledge)

2. Discuss the event on a factual and interpretive basis. (Comprehension and application)

3. Decide for themselves whether or not the atomic bomb should have been used as a facilitator to end the war. (Evaluation)

Rationale:

Aside from the general knowledge of learned history, this lesson will emphasize the social responsibilities mankind must uphold in a technologically advanced world he creates.

Vocabulary:

Fatman—The short, egg-shaped bomb exploded over Nagasaki.

Little Boy—The more slender missile-shaped bomb used at Hiroshima.

Materials:

Video projector, VCR, picture handouts, quote handouts

Motivation:

Students will view a video of actual World War II footage concerning the events leading to the conclusion of the war.

Instructional Strategies:

Table 4.3

_X_ whole group	_X_ direct instruction	_X_ small group
___ cooperative learning	___ review prior to test	___ guided reading
___ developmental lesson	___ shared reading	___ guided practice
_X_ reciprocal teaching	___ peer tutoring	___ test sophistication
___ skills development	_X_ individualized instruction	___ read aloud
___ paired reading	___ review after test	___ other (e.g., debate)

Procedure:

1. Class will be adjusted to foment discussion in a U-shape.
2. Begin lecture on closing days of World War II:
   a. Germany has surrendered
   b. FDR has died, succeeded by Truman
   c. Potsdam Meeting
   d. Successful test of A-bomb
   e. Truman approves its use:
      i. Generals remind him of severe fighting/losses to date
      ii. Forecast of prospective losses if U.S. invades rather than bombs
      iii. Demonstration of bomb?
   f. Aug. 6 — Hiroshima 180,000 dead
   g. Aug. 8 — USSR declares war/Japan
   h. Aug. 9—Nagasaki 70,000 dead
   i. Aug. 15–22 — Formal surrender/ceremony

3. Show pictures of devastated cities.

4. Ask pivotal questions: Should the bomb have been used? Should the second bomb have been used? What were the alternatives? Why do you think they were not chosen?

5. Divide class into 3 groups:
   One group pro-bomb

   One group pro-invasion

   One group status quo

6. Explain roles:
   Recorder—writes ideas down

   Manager—keeps everyone focused and ensures their understanding

   Monitor—makes sure all participate

   Brainstormers—responsible for conveying ideas

7. Allow groups to work for 10 minutes or so to come up with arguments supporting their "belief' and anticipate adversarial critiques.

8. As a class, each group will propose its ideas and defend them against constructive criticisms from opposing groups. Each group will have the opportunity to state its case and defend at least one criticism from each group.

9. Conclusion: A brief summary verbally explained by each group relating what they have learned.

Homework:

Have students read last section on costs of war, human and monetary, in preparation for the next day's lesson.

Evaluation:

In addition to the discussions during the lesson, the unit exam will have numerous short-answer and essay questions to test their knowledge on this unit.

SAMPLE LESSON #3

Diagnosis:

Second of two seventh-grade science lessons on the tropical rain forest biome. The class is of heterogeneous ability (inclusive setting) with 19 of 25 students on grade level, three above, and three below. The lesson will last approximately 30 minutes.

Goals:

Students will learn about the tropical rain forest biome.

Objectives:

Having read the featured handout on the importance of tropical rain forests and participating in class activities, students will be able to:

1. Understand the importance of the world's rain forests. (Knowledge)

2. Identify and discuss issues concerning the rain forests. (Knowledge and Comprehension)

3. Role-play the different positions on rain forest usage. (Application)

4. Recognize and discuss contradictions. (Comprehension)

Aim:

Why are the rain forests important to all people?

Rationale:

This lesson will emphasize the importance of rain forests to the world's population. It will reinforce the idea of interdependence among all people and make students more thoughtful about the use of the environment.

Vocabulary:

Learned in previous lesson.

Materials:

Reading handouts, fact review sheet, homework sheet

Motivation:

Display of rain forest products (bananas, cloves, brazil nuts). Mayan proverb written on chalkboard: "Who cuts the trees as he pleases cuts short his own life."

Do Now:

Read handout "Why rain forests are important . . ." pages 142–143 and read Fact Review sheet:

More than 5,096 of all living things on earth live in tropical rain forests.

A form of leukemia common in children can be cured with a substance found in a rain forest plant called the rosy periwinkle.

Instructional Strategies:

Table 4.4

_X_ whole group	_X_ direct instruction	___ small group
_X_ cooperative learning	___ review prior to test	___ guided reading
___ developmental lesson	___ shared reading	___ guided practice
_X_ reciprocal teaching	_X_ peer tutoring	___ test sophistication
_X_ skills development	___ individualized instruction	___ read aloud
___ paired reading	___ review after test	___ other (e.g., debate)

Procedure:

1. Write "Tropical Rain Forest" on the chalkboard.
   Ask students what they think of when they see these words: trees, vines, orchids, hot, wet, monkeys.

2. Ask pivotal question: How would the disappearance of the rain forest directly affect you?
   Alter precipitation, add to expanding desert lands, alter temperature, and so on.

3. Divide class in half. One side argues for clearing the rain forest, the other against.

4. Explain roles to the students.
   a. If you wanted to clear the rain forest, who might you be? (farmer, rancher)
   b. If you wanted to protect? (environmentalist, scientist)

5. Ask students to think of arguments for their side.

6. Write answers in two columns on board.

7. Ask pivotal question: *Can all these opposing statements be true at the same time?*

8. Form students into groups of three or four and have them discuss ways to save the rain forests. Tell them to write down ways to use what they have learned for their homework assignment.

9. Review previous lesson.
   a. Located near the equator
   b. Climate warm and humid
   c. Seasons differ only in amount of rainfall
   d. Three levels: canopy, understory and forest floor
   e. Provides habitat for 5,096 plants and animals
   f. Scientists may discover new species—beneficial
   g. Helps regulate earth's climate.

Homework:

Write a science journal entry answering questions on homework sheet. Use rain forest product chart on sheet and group discussion to help you.

1. What rain forest products can people collect without harming its plants?

2. What will happen to earth if people continue to destroy rain forests?

3. How do you think we can save the rain forests?

Evaluation:

Check homework journal entries for concepts. Have children read ideas to class.

CONCLUSION

Writing lesson plans is vitally important. Whether you are a first-, fifth-, or fifteenth-year teacher, planning lessons is necessary. Even if you have previously learned much about lesson planning, there is always more to learn. I hope you learned at least a few useful ideas about lesson planning and delivery of a lesson in this chapter. As lifelong learners and professionals, good teachers continually strive to achieve excellence and professional growth.

*   *   *

FOLLOW-UP QUESTIONS/ACTIVITIES

1. What sections of this chapter will serve to help you write and deliver better lessons?

2. Write a lesson using the components explained in this chapter.

3. Read the Lesson Plan for Current Events that follows.

   What's wrong with this lesson? Identify one strength and one weakness, giving evidence for why it is a weakness and including a recommendation for improvement. Consider the aim of the lesson, the questioning techniques, the assignments, and teacher behavior in general. Can you write the lesson plan the teacher should have developed?

   Grade: 7
   Ability: Average
   Teacher: Mr. Jones
   Lesson: Current Events

   Mr. Jones, a well respected 7th grade teacher with 7 years of teaching experience, will be discussing violence in society for his weekly talk about current events.

Mr. Jones: "What can you tell me about violence in society?"

   [Calls on David, who has his hand raised.]

David: "It is a very serious subject."

Mr. Jones: "Yes, it is very serious, but what else can you tell me? What do you consider violent?"

[Calls on Alisa, who has her hand raised.]

Alisa: "Hitting someone would be violent."

Mr. Jones: "That's right, Alisa. What else can you tell me?"

Alisa: "How about rape?"

Mr. Jones: "Right."

[Calls on Billy Bob who has his hand raised.]

Billy Bob: "I guess most crimes are violent."

Mr. Jones: "No, Billy Bob, many crimes are not violent at all. What are some of the causes of violence?"

[Calls on Freddie, who has his hand raised.]

Freddie: "Violence on TV shows and in the movies."

Mr. Jones: "Right, TV shows and movies that contain violence. Who else can tell me something that may cause violence?"

[Calls on Skip, who has his hand raised.]

Mr. Jones: "Skip, what do you think?"

Skip: "Music."

Mr. Jones: "What do you mean, Skip?"

Skip: "Some music makes people violent."

Mr. Jones: "I guess you're right."

[Calls on Brian who has his hand raised.]

Brian: "Video games also contain violence."

Mr. Jones: "Right, Brian, and that is a hot topic right now. A rating system on video games is in the process of being created."

Mr. Jones: "What would you do, if you or someone you know was attacked?"

[Calls on Jimmy, who has his hand up.]

Jimmy: "I would get them."

Mr. Jones: "What do you mean, Jimmy? You mean you would call the police and let them get them, right?"

Jimmy: "No, I would do whatever they did to me and do it back, but worse."

Mr. Jones:	"That is why we have such a problem, because people want to get revenge instead of letting the police take care of things."
Jimmy:	"I don't care. I would do whatever it took to get them back."
Mr. Jones:	"Well Jimmy, that's wrong and you would just get yourself in trouble. It would also be dangerous and somebody could get severely injured."
Jimmy:	"Laws that say you have to get in trouble for doing something back to someone are stupid, and I don't care if I hurt the person that did something to me."
Eddie:	[Without being called on.] "He's right. I would get the person back, too. Why shouldn't I? And laws that do not let me are stupid."
Mr. Jones:	"Guys, you have the wrong idea. The best course of action would be to call the police and let them "get" the person for you."
Eddie:	[Without being called on again] "No way, cops are idiots, and they would never get them. I would make sure I got them."
	[At this point, the class is very noisy and Skip is yelling at Jimmy.]
Skip:	"I still never got you back for breaking my CD player."
Jimmy:	"Shut up, Skip. I told you it was an accident."
Skip:	"Don't tell me to shut up and it wasn't an accident." [Jimmy then punches Skip in the face.]
	[Mr. Jones separates the boys and sends them to the office. He instructs Eddie to escort them so they do not fight on the way. Skip can be heard yelling at Jimmy from down the hall.]
Mr. Jones:	"This is a perfect example of why there is so much violence today. People insist on getting even. This entire incident could have been avoided if Skip would have listened to Jimmy when he told him that it was an accident."
Eric:	"But it wasn't an accident. I saw him break it."

Mr. Jones: "We better just end this discussion right now, before another fight breaks out."

Mr. Jones then assigns the homework.

The homework assignment is to write an essay on what steps can be taken to protect people from violent crimes and make the neighborhood safe.

5

Can I Effectively Manage My Classroom?

Discipline problems are minimized when students are regularly engaged in meaningful activities geared to their interest and aptitudes.

—J. E. Brophy and T. Good

◆

FOCUS QUESTIONS

1. What is your greatest fear, if any, about dealing with student misbehavior?

2. Have you been adequately prepared to deal with serious misbehavior in the classroom?

3. Can you identify any classroom management theories or theorists that have helped you set up a discipline plan?

4. Do you have a well-thought-out discipline plan? Explain.

5. What do you want to know about classroom management?

Teaching is a challenging, complex art and science that demands not only knowledge and skill, but also empathy, caring, and commitment. Frequently frustrating and exhausting, good teaching encourages, inspires, and arouses that latent spark within each student. Still, teachers are confronted with difficult, seemingly insurmountable obstacles that can be puzzling and exasperating. Student misbehavior, for instance, may drive a teacher to the very limits of his or her endurance.

The principles and practices of effective discipline and classroom management are among the most important professional concerns that practicing educators confront daily. The public's attitude toward education, assessed by Gallup Polls sponsored by Phi Delta Kappan, indicate that discipline is one of the most intractable problems public schools must face. Further, teachers maintain that student misbehavior is perhaps the most troublesome and disconcerting problem they encounter in the classroom. The resultant frustration associated with student misbehavior not only increase levels of fatigue and stress, but also negatively impacts teacher performance.

Compounding the difficulties associated with classroom management and discipline is the fact that teachers are often ill prepared to deal with inappropriate student behavior. Ineffective suggestions such as "not to smile until Christmas" or that a well-planned lesson will always eliminate disruptive student behavior are out of step with current realities that confront classroom teachers.

Unfortunately, there aren't ready-made prescriptions to manage student behavior, nor are there specific techniques that apply to all classroom situations. Despite the assertions of some who attempt to promote their particular "discipline system," no "one best system" of classroom management exists. An effective teacher utilizes an array of sound strategies to meet specific problems in particular situations in the classroom.

My purpose in this chapter will be to:

1. Outline some practical strategies for dealing with classroom misbehavior.

2. Assist you in developing your own system of discipline based on your unique needs and circumstances (see sample at end of chapter entitled "My Personal System of Discipline").

Before introducing some key terms as a prerequisite for developing your own discipline plan, examine some of your preferences about student behavior. The following reflective activity might stimulate thought about some personal needs that will inevitably be manifested in your discipline plan.

REFLECT

What is your preferred teaching style? Do you prefer students to sit in rows and quietly pay attention to your lesson? Do you mind if students interrupt with questions? Do you structure lessons around group activities during wihch students work with each other on projects? Can you tolerate the inevitable noise that may result? Describe your preferred teaching style or styles. Also describe what you consider to be desirable student behavior. Finally, describe the relationship between your teaching style, student behavior, and how students learn best.

_____

_____

_____

_____

_____

_____

Share your responses with a colleague and see how your reflective comments above influence the discipline plan you develop later in this chapter.

Let's define some terms and review some key information (note that information here is gleaned from Charles, 2001, see Appendix A for this best resource on the topic):

Behavior—all the physical and mental acts people perform. For example, a hiccup, neither good nor bad, is a human act.

Misbehavior—is the label given to any behavior that is considered inappropriate in a given context or situation. That hiccup, for instance, when performed intentionally in midst of a reading lesson may be considered misbehavior.

Five Levels of Misbehavior—(in declining level of severity)

1. *Aggression*—the most severe form of misbehavior, including physical or verbal attacks by students

2. *Immorality*—acts such as cheating, lying, and stealing

3. *Defiance of Authority*—when students refuse to comply with regulations

4. *Class Disruptions*—perhaps the most common form of misbehavior—acts including calling out, getting out of seat without permission, and general fooling around

5. *Goofing Off*—included in this category are those students who, for example, don't participate, daydream, and don't complete assignments

Discipline—steps taken to cause students to behave acceptably

Classroom Management—the process by which discipline strategies are implemented

Rules—guidelines that inform students how to act in class (e.g., please walk in class)

Procedures—deal with a specific activity and how to do it (e.g., how you expect students to line up for lunch)

Three Stages of Discipline

1. *Preventive Discipline*—refers to those steps a teacher may take to preclude misbehavior from occurring in the first place

2. *Supportive Discipline*—refers to those steps a teacher may take to encourage student behavior during the first signs of misbehavior

3. *Corrective Discipline*—refers to those steps a teacher may take to restore order once misbehavior occurs

Six Elements to Consider About Classrooms

1. *Multidimensionality*—many events and acts occurring (i.e., the classroom is complex, not a simple, environment)

2. *Simultaneity*—many things happening at same time (i.e., teachers must remain cognizant and think quickly)

3. *Immediacy*—rapid pace at which events occur (i.e., events occur at an unbelievably fast pace)

4. *Unpredictability*—difficult to always know for sure what may occur (i.e., you are dealing with human beings, not inert raw materials, and therefore it's difficult to predict behavior)

5. *Publicness*—teach on stage (i.e., teachers are role models and must always remain aware of the affect they have on their students)

6. *History*—class develops a culture of experience and norms that provide the basis for future interactions (i.e., each class is different and assumes a "personality" of its own)

DEVELOPING YOUR PERSONAL SYSTEM OF DISCIPLINE

A plethora of effective strategies and techniques for maintaining classroom management are available to assist teachers in positively redirecting student misbehavior. Rather than developing a list of "do's and don'ts"—which have ephemeral benefits, to say the least, and more important, don't address your specific needs for maintaining classroom control—this chapter can assist you in developing your own system of discipline.

Student misbehavior, at some level, is inevitable. However, effective classroom managers are proactive, not reactive. They take effective steps to minimize occurrences of misbehavior. Preventive measures indicate a teacher's awareness that misbehavior might occur and establish guidelines for appropriate classroom behavior.

Still, misbehavior will occur in the best of classrooms. That's why supportive measures are necessary to quell disturbances at the outset. Corrective guidelines are necessary when preventive and supportive steps are inadequately implemented or ineffective with more severely disruptive students.

Developing a discipline system or plan that incorporates each of these three stages of discipline is essential to effective classroom management. Let's discuss some of the basic components of each stage and practical recommendations for their implementation.

Preventive Discipline

This is really the planning stage. It includes all the steps you'll take to establish a positive classroom environment conducive to student learning. Your effectiveness as a classroom manager depends on your ability to thoughtfully develop a plan that anticipates misbehavior and establishes guidelines for appropriate behavior.

1. Develop a Stimulating and Worthwhile Lesson—Although a well-planned lesson alone is not an assurance that misbehavior will never occur, it's certainly advantageous in motivating and encouraging student participation. Incorporate a wide array of teaching strategies such as discussion groups, oral reports, role playing, cooperative learning, and peer tutoring. Intentionally deliver instruction in a variety of ways to meet the diverse learning-style needs of your students. Here are some effective teaching strategies matched to each of three learning style preferences:

> *Visual Preference*—For those who learn best by seeing, use pictures, films, charts, flash cards, computers, and transparencies.

> *Auditory Preference*—For those who learn best through verbal instructions use lecture, oral directions, records, peer tutoring, mnemonic devices, and song.

> *Kinesthetic Preference*—For those who learn best by doing, use manipulatives, 3-D material, debate, projects, pantomime, interactive videos, physical movement, and plays.

2. Organize Your Physical Environment—Your seating plan can affect student interaction. Regardless of your physical setup (e.g., rows, groups, horseshoe, pairs, etc.), make sure all seats are positioned to ensure visibility and allow you to gain proximity to any student as quickly as possible. Ensure that your room is uncluttered and that learning centers, sinks, clothing areas, and entrance are accessible. Although I personally like a nicely decorated room, too many classrooms are overly decorated and some students may be easily distracted.

3. Develop five Rules and Procedures for Appropriate Behavior— Rules establish clear expectations for student behavior. Rules let the students know what performance and behaviors you deem acceptable. Develop five rules for acceptable classroom behavior that you'll review the very first day of class and reinforce throughout the year. You can have your students add a rule or two that they feel should be included. Guidelines for rules are:

> *State rules in a positive way* (e.g., "please walk in the classroom," not "don't run")

> *State rules clearly* (e.g., "listen in class" is too ambiguous—"look at the person who is speaking to you" is clearer and conveys the behavior expected)

> *Make certain rules are consistent with school rules*

Plan on common procedures you intend to review with your class (e.g., lineup procedures, what to do if students miss an assignment, and procedures for walking into the classroom after lunch).

Research indicates that effective managers spend time teaching rules and procedures. Don't worry that instructional time will be initially lost. Teaching and reinforcing rules and procedures are times well spent and may do much toward preventing inappropriate behavior.

4. Use Positive Reinforcement or "Catch 'Em Bein' Good"— Everyone wants encouragement and recognition. Effective teachers use varied and frequent reinforcement for acceptable behavior. As often as possible use some of these reinforcers:

Social Reinforcers—Use verbal acknowledgements such as "I appreciate your hard work," "Keep it up," "Wow, I'm impressed," "Excellent." As a classroom teacher for 16 years I always kept a list of 100 different expressions I could use. After a while, my students couldn't wait to hear which one they would receive! Use nonverbal reinforcers such as a smile, pat on the back, a handshake, etc. Reinforce every student at least once a day.

Graphic Reinforcers—Use marks, checks, stars, happy faces, etc.

Activities—Acknowledge students who comply with rules and regulations. Don't wait until they misbehave for them to receive your attention. Allow the student to: assume monitorial duties, sit near a friend, have free time, read a special book, have extra time at the learning center, care for the class pet, etc.

Tangible Reinforcers—Use a token reward system in which students can earn coupons, for instance, to obtain prizes. They can earn points to receive a special positive phone call from you to their parents!

5. Who's the Boss?—You are the authority in the classroom. Develop high standards for performance and expectations for behavior. Be fair and consistent when implementing your discipline plan.

Supportive Discipline

Any experienced teacher realizes that the best plan can't deter all misbehavior from occurring. Misbehavior is inevitable. Notice what happens in this scenario:

Jose throws a crumpled paper from his seat into the garbage pail. Teacher doesn't respond. A moment later Maria throws a paper. Teacher doesn't react. Then Ronald throws a paper.

Teacher: "Stop that, Ronald."

When a teacher ignores a breach of a class rule, others are likely to follow suit. In the case above, when the teacher finally did reprimand a student, it was too late. Ronald's complaint may be: "Why didn't you yell at Jose or Maria?" This may escalate into a verbal argument between teacher and student. In addition, Maria and Jose may be upset with Ronald for implicating them.

When you notice a student breaking a class rule don't ignore the behavior, but rather "nip it in the bud" by employing one of many types of supportive discipline techniques. Your personal discipline system should include numerous supportive strategies (see sample at end of chapter entitled "My Personal System of Discipline"). If you're a relatively new teacher, I suggest you keep these techniques written on small index cards for easy reference. These are some of the techniques that can be used to support discipline:

With-it-ness—Jacob Kounin (1977) maintained that teachers who were aware of what was happening in their classrooms were less likely to have problems escalate. For instance, you're working at the board with one student and notice Manuel throwing paper from his seat. You say, "Manuel, that's your first warning." You're "with-it." You've communicated to the entire class that you're aware of what's happening and have put Manuel on notice. Being "with-it" will nip problems in the bud when they first occur.

Send signals—When you see Ira misbehaving, communicate your dissatisfaction with a nonverbal signal such as a frown, stare, or wave of the hand.

Use physical proximity—When you either anticipate a problem or see one initially developing, walk over to Denise as nonchalantly as possible and stand near her.

Corrective Discipline

Despite your best efforts to prevent student misbehavior and support discipline, there will be times when more stern or corrective measures are necessary. Don't hesitate to use these corrective measures. They communicate that you care and are willing to insist on proper classroom behavior.

According to Charles (2001) "[Y]our corrective techniques should be neither intimidating nor harshly punitive, but instead only what is necessary to stop the misbehavior and redirect it positively." Consider the following corrective techniques:

Be Assertive—Lee Canter's (1989) model has gained popularity among some educators because it trains teachers to act more assertively. Canter's distinction between three different response styles is instructive:

1. *Nonassertive Style*—"For the fifth time, won't you please stop throwing that paper?"

2. *Hostile Style*—"If you throw that paper one more time I'll kick you out of here, stupid!"

3. *Assertive Style*—"I want you to stop throwing that paper and get back to solving those problems."

Assertive responses are effective corrective measures because they make your expectations known clearly and in a businesslike manner. Assertive teachers are ready to back up their response with action.

Invoke Consequences for Misbehavior—When you reviewed your class rules, students should have been apprised of the possible consequences for noncompliance. Therefore, when Ernest refuses to stop throwing paper you might say: "Ernest, you're refusing to work so you'll have to complete your assignment during recess." In developing your own system, you should note the nature and severity of each consequence tied to a specific type of misbehavior. These guidelines should be publicized and reviewed periodically.

Contracting—I have personally found this corrective measure very effective. Don't confront a student, if possible, in the midst of acting out in class. If the student must be removed (e.g., time-out), then do so. Try to meet with the student as soon after an incident as possible to develop a cooperative contract for appropriate behavior. This should involve an actual written document (usually effective in elementary or middle schools) in which an agreement between teacher and student is reached regarding rewards for good behavior and consequences for inappropriate behavior. Effective contracts should:

(a) Be mutually agreed upon, not teacher-imposed
(b) Be realistic and short-term
(c) Be specific (e.g., "Work on math problems for 30 minutes a day over the next week" is better than "study hard")
(d) Specify how long the contract will be in effect
(e) Specify rewards
(f) Be signed by student, teacher, principal, and parent

Time-Out—is a disciplinary strategy in which a student is removed from a situation and physically placed in a designated time-out area. Time-out is particularly effective when the student's misbehavior is precipitated by peer pressure. Although effective for younger children, time-out areas located outside your classroom are more effective with older students (plan time-out areas with your dean or assistant principal). Keep in mind these four steps when implementing time-out:

1. Designate a time-out area that is isolated to sight and sound as much as possible. The area should be undecorated and as disinteresting as possible.

2. Student must remain idle without work or amusement to occupy the time.

3. Establish a specific time for the punishment to last (e.g., 5 minutes)—I used to place a stopwatch at the desk so that the student could self-monitor.

4. Follow-up—When student returns to his or her seat make sure you say a few words about your expectations about future behavior. If you must briefly meet with the student after class then do so.

RECOLLECTION

As I reread the suggestions above for preventive, supportive, and corrective discipline, I was reminded of a former student for whom none of the above-mentioned strategies worked.

Shaheim was a student in my fourth-grade class in the South Bronx, New York, during my second year of teaching. Shaheim was a clever miscreant. My day was made, I am sorry to admit, when I took attendance and Shaheim did not respond because he was absent. Oh, what a day that was. Unfortunately, there were not many days that Shaheim was absent. He appeared to love school, or shall I say loved to make my day a horror. He would do anything and everything to get under my skin. His senseless tapping of the pencil on his desk, despite my protestations, and his throwing papers around the room annoyed me to no end. Hardly a day passed without Shaheim getting into a physical fight, harassing a fellow student, or arguing with a teacher or fellow student. I was at my wits end. I tried everything I learned in college. Positive reinforcement didn't work, nor did time-out. Private consultations with him were short-lived and his parents were no help. In fact, they looked to me to "solve" his problems. Visits to the assistant principal's office provided momentary respites, but before too long Shaheim was back in class. I referred him to guidance and even suggested he be tested for learning disabilities or something. Reports came back that he was fine and "normal." Never once, by the way, did they observe his behavior while in class. To make a long story a bit shorter, Shaheim made it through fourth grade but I barely did. One of the lessons I learned during that second year of teaching was that even one disruptive, unruly student can really disturb a class. "It only takes one" is a very true aphorism chanted and acknowledged by teachers. Still, I was glad the year was over and really hoped that Shaheim would mature enough in the following years so that his future teachers would have it easier than I did.

(Continued)

(Continued)

Six years passed and during my lunch period one day I had a visitor who wanted to meet with me. I looked up at this tall, lanky well dressed young man. Was this Shaheim?! Indeed, it was. He introduced himself and declared, "I came back, Mr. Glanz, just to see you because I am now half-way through high school and I'm doing really well thanks to you." "Thanks to me?!@#." I retorted. Shaheim made my day when he was absent. I yelled at him and threw him out of my class any chance I could. I did everything I could to no avail. In fact, I wish I could relive those early years of teaching. I made so many mistakes. Especially in the way I dealt with students like Shaheim. I now know better how to more positively work with students like Shaheim. In those days I'm sorry to admit, I resorted to anything to "get him to behave." I'm not particularly proud of the sarcastic, belittling remarks I would make in a vain attempt to pacify students like Shaheim. So when he declared that he wanted to thank me, I felt like apologizing to him! Also, I thought, "if he is praising me as his best teacher, could you imagine the other teachers he had?!" I listened.

"Mr. Glanz, yes, thanks to you. Sure you were rough with me, but I deserved it. Others threw me out and gave up. You never gave up. I remember the talks we had during lunchtime or after school. You never gave up on me. You cared." I was stunned. I was touched beyond words. A few moments passed in small talk and then he shook my hand. As I am now writing about this incident, I can feel his warm, generous, and firm handshake. I never saw Shaheim again. I hope he's reading this book. I want to thank him because he made my day that day. He affected me so deeply that I recall the incident in order to try to inspire you to realize that we, indeed, make a difference, even when we think we may not.

What are your recollections of any Shaheims you might have taught or tried to teach?

_____

_____

_____

_____

Seven Steps to Developing a Personalized Discipline System

1.   *What are your needs?*—The first step in developing a discipline system is to prioritize your needs for classroom management. Make a list of those conditions essential for your ideal classroom (e.g., students should have assigned seats, work quietly, respect fellow classmates and teacher, hand work in on time, etc.).

2.   *What are your rules and procedures?*—Develop a list of acceptable behaviors, culled from your needs list, that you want to teach and reinforce.

3.   *What are the consequences for compliance and noncompliance?*—Compose a list of positive and negative consequences tied to each rule and procedure.

4.   *What strategies will you employ?*—List specific strategies you feel comfortable implementing in each of the three stages of discipline: preventive, supportive, and corrective.

5.   *How will you implement your plan?*—Plan to teach your system through discussions, role-playing, and practice sessions. Review and reinforce your plan throughout the year.

6.   *How will you test your plan?* Start putting your system into action. Be fair and consistent, yet flexible. Modify your plan as needed.

7.   *If problems arise, as they most certainly will, should you give up?*—Never! All students can learn self-control. All students want acceptance and recognition. Your system can satisfy their needs for social acceptance. Always seek to expand the repertoire of strategies in your plan. Seek assistance and guidance from others. If you believe all children can learn, then believe that all children can become sincere, courteous, responsible, and disciplined.

CONCLUSION

Do experienced teachers need a plan? Regardless of experience, all teachers need to plan strategies for dealing with nonconformity to classroom rules and procedures. Your personalized plan should be reviewed periodically and matched to the unique needs of your current class. Not every technique will work with every student or class. There aren't quick-fix recipes to easily implement. Some students will definitely need special referrals. Nevertheless, develop your plan, share ideas with colleagues, and continue to find ways to help your students reach their full potential. See the sample discipline plan that follows. Hopefully it will guide you in developing your own. Then, assess your ability to effectively manage your classroom by completing the RESPOND beginning on page 123.

A SAMPE DISCIPLINE PLAN

My Personal System of Discipline by Rachel Schwab

I teach a first grade boys' mainstream class. My curriculum includes reading, writing, math, social studies, and science. My students are usually not used to the rules and behaviors that are expected in a first grade classroom. Rules, procedures, and reinforcers (especially negative ones), are a new experience for them.

Therefore, I must be careful to present and explain my rules, positive consequences and negative consequences in a clear, easy to understand, and precise manner.

Personal Belief Statement

One of my main goals as a teacher is *to make a difference in the life of a child*. I aim to accomplish this, first, by getting to know each child well, as the whole person that they are. I also aim to create a positive and warm atmosphere in my classroom, in which every child is encouraged to reach his full potential, knowing that I believe in him. I do my best to maintain a "fun" and interesting atmosphere as well, so that my students' early experience in learning will be one of fun and enjoyment. To this end, I show my students love and respect, yet at the same time set specific limits, so that my students' self-esteem grows while they learn responsible behavior.

These smaller goals are meant to fulfill my belief in making a difference in the life of a child, by helping their year in first grade be one of accomplishment and growth in a pleasant atmosphere. In this way, their first experience in "real" school is a positive one.

My Needs

One of my most basic needs is a well-managed classroom, where students know what is expected of them, the room is orderly, and routines are set with room for flexibility when necessary.

Another personal need is for each child to feel that he gets what he needs, academically and emotionally, so that he can grow in knowledge, self-esteem, and responsibility.

It bothers me when my students are mean to each other or laugh at one another; therefore I do not allow these behaviors in my classroom.

This includes teaching my students to act respectfully towards one another and to show caring for each other, both of which are important social skills.

Within the set routines, it is important for there to be a lively, warm and positive atmosphere in my classroom, so that my students can develop a lifelong love of learning.

My Rules

1. Follow directions.

2. Raise your hand before you speak.

3. Work quietly in your seat without disturbing others.

4. Be kind and polite to each other.

5. Speak with respect.

I selected these rules because they focus on two of my major concerns;

(a) maintaining order in the classroom, and (b) promoting a positive classroom atmosphere with warmth and respect. If these conditions are not met, the potential for learning cannot be fulfilled.

The first rule is important during independent work, group work, and during transition times, to promote good classroom management.

The second and third rules help maintain a calm, pleasant environment in a classroom. Of course there must be some flexibility within these rules, such as during discussions, and specific activities.

The third, fourth, and fifth rules are particularly helpful in maintaining an atmosphere of caring and respect and a positive environment. Caring, trust, and respect must be present between students as well as between the teacher and her students.

Rule four also encourages good social skills, which are important skills in a first-grade classroom.

I have separate rules for when the students work in cooperative groups. Since the nature of the setup is so different, my expectations when students work together differ from those when they are working independently or when I am teaching them.

Cooperative Group Rules

1. Take turns talking quietly.

2. Listen to each other's ideas.

3. Praise each other's ideas.

4. Help each other when asked.

5. Stay together until everyone is done.

6. Talk about how you worked well together and how you can improve.

So as not to overwhelm my students with so many rules, I do not present all the rules to my class the first week of school. Cooperative group rules are first presented and modeled when we begin working in groups.

Before posting the rules, I read them to my students and we discuss them and why they are so important in a classroom setting. We also role-play them to make sure that the students understand them.

I find that having rules for the various ways that we learn helps create an orderly classroom and a pleasant learning environment. Children like to know procedures and what is expected of them. The time spent teaching rules is always regained when a classroom can be managed well because of the rules and procedures that are in place.

Positive Consequences

1. Catch them being good—use verbal praise. Not only do children themselves respond to the praise they are given, it also causes a positive ripple effect. The other students also want to be recognized, so they imitate the behavior that was praised.

2. Students who behave well can get a positive note, a "happygram," sent home at the end of the day. I also make positive phone calls home, and I find that parents are thrilled to receive them.

3. My students love helping me, or being chosen to be my monitor. Students who follow the rules and behave are chosen to be monitors for various tasks.

4. Children earn the right to be first in line for library or recess, by behaving appropriately.

5. For extra special recognition, I have a child take a note to the principal, detailing his good behavior.

6. Depending on the class and the time of year, I have some type of reinforcement system set up, either individual or row charts, or classwide contests. In these ways, the children can accumulate a predetermined number of stickers to reach a larger reward. The rewards vary from tangible prizes to extra recess, planned trips, or miniparties. I also have small rewards that I give out randomly. In this way, the children get the incentives they need without constantly "working for a prize."

Negative Consequences

(In increasing order of severity)

1. Eye Contact—The student knows that I am aware of what he is doing, yet he has a chance to correct his behavior before it becomes an issue.

2. Warning—The child receives a verbal warning about the inappropriate behavior.

3. The child works away from the group for five minutes. I do not increase the amount of time spent working away from the group. I usually find that due to their age, it either works the first time or the child continues to act up, and a longer period of time only serves as a greater distraction to others.

4. Lose two minutes of recess. I do not take recess away completely, since children need that time to move around and be part of social interaction. I do find that losing two minutes of recess is very effective and still allows them some time to take part in recess activities.

5. Call parents.

6. Go to the principal.

Severe clause: Go to the principal.

My rules, positive consequences, and negative consequences are sent home to the parents as our classroom discipline plan. The parents discuss it with their children, sign it, and return it to me. This way, they know how I run my classroom and can better understand anything that might happen.

Preventive Discipline

1. My students and I discuss the rules at the beginning of the year. We review the rules and the necessity for them during the year. The class understands what is expected of them.

2. I plan the use of my classroom space to maximize visibility and proximity—and use these techniques.

3. "With-it-ness"—When students realize that you know what's going on, and that you won't put up with it, they don't try to test you as much. Also, if you exude self-confidence and an air of authority, students respond appropriately.

4. When my lessons are well planned, organized, interesting, and creative, students are less likely to misbehave since they are interested and actively participate.

5. Rewards from my list of Positive Consequences—They reinforce positive behavior and serve as an incentive for others as well.

Supportive Discipline

1. Establish eye contact with the student.

2. Use of nonverbal signals—shaking head, hand signals, and so on.

3. Proximity control/touch.

4. Verbal warning.

5. Discussion of relevant rules and firm demand for appropriate behavior (includes broken-record technique).

6. Use of rewards from my list of Positive Consequences.

Corrective Discipline

1. Firm demand for specific behavior.

2. Implement Negative Consequences (previously listed), based on the severity of the behavior.

Closing Statement

This plan will be the foundation of my personal system of discipline. The system gives me a way of addressing my classroom needs. It corresponds with my philosophy towards children and teaching. However, classes differ from year to year, so I need to be aware that not all methods will work every year. I also believe that it is important to remain flexible since students vary greatly from one another, since each child is an individual with specific needs. This is not in conflict with remaining consistent. Consistency is one of the most important details of any system of discipline. Students can understand what is expected of them and know the inherent consequences both positive and negative. However, there will always be students with special needs who demand greater understanding. Because of this, a certain amount of flexibility for rules and consequences must be anticipated. Sometimes students need individual behavior plans, charts, or systems. I have found that students understand and respect this concept, as long as they feel their needs are being addressed and they get what they need. They can accept that fair is not always equal since everyone has individual needs.

I feel that being aware of my needs in the classroom, as well as being aware of my beliefs in dealing with children, can help me become a reflective practitioner—a teacher who thinks about what I am doing in the classroom and what I hope to accomplish. This, together with knowledge and ideas of positive consequences and negative consequences and an understanding of my students, will hopefully assist me in reaching my goal of making a difference in the life of a child.

RESPOND

RUBRIC for Assessing Classroom Management

Directions: Assess how effective a classroom manager you are! Circle the Performance Dimension for each of the 8 categories

Performance Dimension	Unsatisfactory	Emerging	Proficient	Distinguished
Monitoring Seat Work	Teacher works extensively with one group while ignoring others; unaware of off-task students; fails to reinforce those on-task; employs ineffective supportive disciplinary techniques to off-task students; unaware of what students are doing; does not monitor students effectively	Teacher scans room occasionally; somewhat aware of what students are doing; misses some off-task behavior; stays near their desk or concentrates attention on one half of room; aware when arguments occur and separates students; tries to implement monitoring strategies, albeit inconsistently	Teacher aware of what is occurring in classroom; uses effective verbal and nonverbal communicative techniques to monitor student behavior; gives praise most of the time and reprimands those students who are not following class rules; spends a bit too much time with each child; help provided as needed; uses eye contact and scans the room every few minutes; attentive to monitoring seat work	Teacher very well aware of what is occurring in the classroom; appears to have "eyes in back of head"; able to do several tasks simultaneously; defines rules of what's expected from students during seat work; offers social praise to those who are working; able to immediately "nip in the bud" a child who may seem off-task; able to "overlap" and do two things at the same time; spends just the right amount of time with each child; monitors seat work very well
Transitions	No well-defined set of procedures for transitions; Students unsure how to proceed; remains in fixed position rather than circulates; long delays before start of activities; teacher unprepared for next activity and takes	Teacher may give instructions during transition; instructions vague; verbal praise may be given to students complying with the routine; teacher may put transitional times on the board; delays between	Teacher has a set schedule posted in a prominent place in classroom; students aware of when to expect changes; students can respond to instructions efficiently most of the time; procedures for transitions are reviewed weekly and practiced so that when	Actions of the students are seamless; students wholly responsible for their actions and teacher overlaps; teacher seldom behind desk during transitions; teacher walks among students and incorporates proximity control; visual and audio

(Continued)

123

Performance Dimension	Unsatisfactory	Emerging	Proficient	Distinguished
	time putting belongings away or taking out material for next subject; teacher has little idea of the importance of transition	activities are no more than five minutes; teacher prepares materials, but spends too much time setting up; teacher aware of the importance of transition but has difficulty in facilitation	actual transitions occur there is little loss of instructional time; students are reinforced for good transitions; teacher models desired behaviors to students; teacher aware of the importance of transition and implements strategies that facilitate smooth transitions	reminders are apparent; Little or no loss of instructional time; motivational devices displayed so students are encouraged to move and get ready quickly; teacher masterfully facilitates transitions
Classroom Setup	Furniture arranged in a way that is unsafe or impedes accessibility of both teachers and students; teacher has a hard time getting through desks and cubbies when trying to reach a student who needs help; materials stored in areas where both teachers and students cannot access them easily; not every student visible to the teacher and vice versa;	Classroom visibility impaired, but there is a constant rearrangement of desks and other furniture in an effort to ensure that all students can see teacher and board; classroom generally untidy; Students have a general area to keep their belongings; classroom generally safe except for clutter and occasional obstacles; seating arrangement not always followed	Teacher has access to every student; every student has a way of retrieving necessary materials; classroom neat and organized; classroom safe and aisles are clear; teacher aware of the importance of classroom setup	Furniture arranged for easy movement by both teacher and student; all students have access to each other and to necessary materials even during special activities; teacher can see all the students at all times; students can see teacher and board at all times; classroom neatly arranged; materials organized and labeled; materials in an appropriate location in close proximity to working area of students; each student has designated area for his or her

(Continued)

(Continued)

Performance Dimension	Unsatisfactory	Emerging	Proficient	Distinguished
	room poorly decorated; classroom untidy and disorganized; seating arrangement rigid			own personal belongings that is both organized and accessible; use of space in the classroom maximized
Classroom Atmosphere	Students hesitate to answer, and seem tense and anxious; teacher seems frustrated and tired; teacher barks instructions and uses lots of criticism and sarcasm; teacher often threatens to punish students; teacher inconsistent in discipline procedures; teacher appears disinterested and uncaring	Some students comfortable but others seem tense; students are not comfortable with offering their own opinions; teacher smiles less as the day progresses and is often moody; teacher compliments and criticizes; teacher gets frustrated with weaker students; teacher uses inconsistent discipline procedures; teacher shows warmth and care inconsistently; teacher tries to control her anger; classroom atmosphere not ideal for learning	Students generally participate and seem comfortable; teacher seems satisfied and pleased with the class and her teaching; teacher uses positive reinforcement most of the time; teacher generally consistent with discipline procedures; teacher cares about the students' well-being; atmosphere appears warm and open	Students supported by teacher; students motivated to participate and eager to achieve; students share information and risk giving their opinions voluntarily; teacher welcomes students enthusiastically in the morning; teacher gives lots of specific praise; teacher encourages constantly; students feel that class is safe and fun; students appear to trust the teacher; atmosphere open and students can share anything appropriate with teacher and class

(Continued)

Performance Dimension	Unsatisfactory	Emerging	Proficient	Distinguished
Response to Student's Misbehavior	Teacher unaware of what is transpiring most of the time; teacher often intervenes physically to misbehavior; teacher screams and sometimes threatens students with punishment; punishments are unreasonable or inappropriate; teacher uses humiliation or sarcasm to get the students to listen; teacher ineffective in dealing with misbehavior	Teacher generally aware of misconduct but unsure what to do; teacher responds verbally to a misbehavior but doesn't use other strategies; teacher takes misbehavior personally; teacher inconsistent in her discipline strategies; teacher eager to remove students who misbehave; teacher eager to learn positive strategies but has difficulty implementing them	Teacher alert and usually aware of misbehaviors; teacher responds to misbehaviors with verbal interventions that are private so as not to embarrass student; responses to misbehavior appropriate but inconsistent; teacher addresses the misbehavior, not the character of the student; teacher develops established rules and procedures; teacher uses logical consequences; teacher responds to early signs of misbehavior	Teacher consistent in dealing with misbehavior; develops a positive approach to classroom management; remains calm and does not overreact; clearly states academic and social expectations; elicits rules and procedures from students; reacts immediately and positively to misbehavior; Firm, fair, and caring; develops a systematic approach to classroom management
Reinforcement	Teacher infrequently uses positive reinforcement techniques; lacks a systematic approach to reinforcement; infrequent use of tangible or nontangible reinforcers;	Teacher occasionally uses reinforcement, although inconsistently; praises students superficially; reinforces only some students but ignores most others; lacks training	Teacher consistently incorporates reinforcement strategies; acknowledges most of the students in class every day; uses names of students most of the time; provides tangible rewards as soon as	Teacher provides constant and consistent reinforcement for positive behavior; all students are acknowledged and reinforced positively; students have developed, with teacher's assistance, intrinsic

(Continued)

126

(Continued)

Performance Dimension	Unsatisfactory	Emerging	Proficient	Distinguished
	seems uncomfortable or reluctant to use reinforcement	and experience in applying reinforcement	appropriate behavior observed; sends notes home about good behavior; realizes the importance of reinforcement	motivation; teacher develops systematic approach to reinforcement; reinforcement genuine, appropriate, and well distributed
Rules and Procedures	No set routine—different everyday; few set rules; no set consequences; too much freedom; children do not know what is expected of them; rules are stated negatively; no set procedures during transition time, etc.	Too many rules for students to remember; rules are not posted to remind students; unrealistic or unreasonable consequences; rules not elicited and reviewed; rules not vigorously enforced; procedures not well-defined; eager but lacks training and experience	Rules established and reviewed by teacher; students know what is expected of them; consequences established and evenly distributed; students obey rules, even though may not thoroughly understand them; rules stated positively; develops consistent rules and procedures	Rules and procedures are collaboratively established, posted, reviewed, practiced, monitored, and reinforced for all class matters
Lesson Presentation	Teacher unfamiliar with content/subject; lesson planning inadequate; lessons unsuitable for level of class; lecturing	Teacher somewhat familiar with content/subject; planning evident but has difficulty with delivery; objectives of lesson	Teacher plans lessons; goals and objectives stated; material organized; students encouraged to participate; teacher projects her voice and	Lessons well planned, interesting, and meaningful; teacher incorporates multifaceted approaches and methods to teaching; teacher

(Continued)

(Continued)

Performance Dimension	Unsatisfactory	Emerging	Proficient	Distinguished
	occurs most of the time; teacher speaks in monotone; teacher's explanations are vague; students appear uninterested and off-task; teacher relies heavily on textbook; needs training and experience with lesson plan development and presentation	are at times unclear; pacing and delivery problems evident; students not encouraged to participate; poor wait time; inability to project or use voice effectively; eager but needs additional training and experience	has good pacing; teacher uses visual aids; lesson has a clear beginning, middle, and end; incorporates medial summaries; teacher communicates lesson well	uses technology; projects voice and modulates at appropriate times; excellent pacing and wait time; sensitive to learning styles and multiple intelligences; lesson, although very structured with an introduction, body, conclusion, medial summaries, and reinforcing activities, is also innovative; students level of understanding monitored well; clearly, a master teacher

*   *   *

FOLLOW-UP QUESTIONS/ACTIVITIES

Based on the information in this chapter, develop your own system of discipline.

My Personal System of Discipline

1. Grade and instructional levels

2. Subject

3. Social realities

4. A personal belief statement

5. My Classroom Rules (list at least five rules and discuss briefly how you would implement them)

6. Positive Consequences (list)

7. Negative Consequences (list)

8. My Preventive Discipline Measures (list)

9. My Supportive Discipline Measures (list)

10. My Corrective Discipline Measures (list)

11. Closing statement

What useful information about managing your classroom did you learn in this chapter?

List ten suggestions you would offer to a beginning teacher about handling student misbehavior.

6

How Can I Help My Students Learn?

When I first began teaching, I visited with a former teacher who I respected greatly. I asked him for some advice. He responded without hesitation, "A good teacher must love his students." "Love?" I queried. "Yes, love. When you come to care about each student as your very own child, then you'll become a great teacher."

—Jeffrey Glanz

◆

FOCUS QUESTIONS

1. What factors affect student learning?

2. How *can* you help your students learn?

3. Do you really believe that what you do in the classroom makes a difference in student achievement? Explain.

4. What did your teachers do to help you learn?

131

5. How does cooperative learning promote student achievement?

6. Can you think of one very important element of good pedagogy often neglected by teachers and schools that directly impacts learning? Read on.

Many factors affect student learning. In the space provided below, list as many such factors as you can:

_____

_____

_____

_____

_____

_____

_____

_____

_____

_____

Did you include any of these?

- Organized, safe, and well-run school
- Strong, professional administrative leadership
- Active and positive parental involvement
- Sufficient federal, state, and local funding

These and other "external" factors, while important and, perhaps essential, do not have an immediate and direct impact on student achievement. If you've learned anything thus far in **Teaching 101** it's that *you*, the teacher, are the most critical element in the classroom. An experienced, credentialed teacher who possesses specialized content and pedagogical knowledge, instructional skills, and positive dispositions directly affects student learning more than any other factor (Darling-Hammond, 2003). Did your list above include any of these factors related specifically to what a teacher does in the classroom?

- Utilizes varied teaching strategies, including direct teaching, discussion, Socratic dialogue and cooperative learning (see discussion later in chapter)
- Sets high expectations
- Establishes a consistent classroom management and discipline plan
- Engages students in well-planned, meaningful lessons
- Stimulates critical thinking
- Communicates complex ideas simply
- Checks for understanding
- Employs strategies to keep students successfully on-task
- Responds well to individual learning differences
- Differentiates instruction so that low and high achievers' needs are met
- Uses culturally relevant pedagogy
- Offers appropriate, genuine praise and reinforcement
- Challenges students with thought-provoking activities
- Assesses student learning on a consistent basis
- Cares for the students

Although all of these factors, collectively are important to promote student achievement, I wonder how many of you listed *study skill instruction* as one important factor for promoting student learning. Teaching your students how to study, including listening, note-taking, and test-taking skills goes a long way towards helping them succeed in school. An often neglected aspect of learning is teaching students the essential skills for academic survival, such as how to study, memorize, take notes and tests, and generally succeed in school. This chapter is devoted, in large part, to introducing you to some of the key elements in an area of study officially known as "cognitive learning strategy instruction" (Pressley & Woloshyn, 1995). The strategies in this chapter, drawn from extensive research in the field, are relatively simple to learn and are very effective in promoting student learning. Cognitive learning strategy, or more simply known as study skill instruction, is premised on these key ideas:

- Our most important task as teachers is to ultimately promote student learning. Caring for students and even posing the right questions are important only to the degree to which students learn. Certainly, learning is more than scoring high marks on standardized reading tests. We need to broaden the way we assess student learning; more about that in Chapter 9.

- We, as teachers, have a powerful influence on student learning. Effective teachers do not lift their hands in defeat proclaiming "Well, what more can I do if Jerry doesn't get support from his parents and if I am continually harangued by administrators." Effective teachers have a high sense of self-efficacy; that is we feel and know that we make a difference, and we don't give up.
- We promote learning not only with rich, content-based instruction utilizing sound pedagogy, but we take an active role in fostering learning by teaching students how to think and process the information they learn.
- A student can learn almost anything as long as they have the necessary study skill strategies. Once students have practiced and developed these skills, they can apply them to any learning situation.

I have written this chapter to introduce you to this important area that impacts student learning and will provide several practical suggestions and strategies. The strategies included are based on sound theory and research in cognitive learning. While there are countless "how to study" books on the market, this chapter is unique in that I have translated cognitive learning theories into a simpler format. I have not included every possible skill that can assist in learning, nor have I treated these strategies comprehensively (that's for a separate book; actually, there are several good ones on the market, see Appendix A for a suggestion). I have only chosen, however, research-proven techniques that I have personally used with countless students in order to introduce you to these ideas. You may want to extend your understanding by consulting some of the reference works cited. Our goal as teachers is to make learning the skills easy and fun.

Very important: Spend time in class teaching your students the ideas below. Introduce the study skills as a unit of activity at the beginning and reinforce them throughout the year or semester. In fact, research indicates that when teachers actually refer to and teach these study skills as they teach lessons, student achievement rises dramatically (Mangrum II, Iannuzzi, & Strichart, 1998).

REFLECT

Although you may concur that study skills instruction is important, how, you might ask, can a teacher find the time to teach study skills in an already overcrowded curriculum? What are some ways you can

(Continued)

(Continued)

incorporate these study skills in your class? One hint or idea: Rather than think of cognitive strategy instruction as a separate curriculum area, how might you integrate such study in your teaching without really missing the proverbial "beat?" Jot some ideas down and then read the suggestion below. I'm sure you'll come up with other ways as well.

_____

_____

_____

_____

_____

Okay, here's one way to easily integrate study skill instruction in a lesson. For example, suppose you are teaching your students a science unit on erosion and you explain that weathering, a process that breaks down rocks, is aided by running water, ice, rain, plants, animals, and chemicals. You might assist student memory of the material by teaching them a quick and easy mnemonic strategy (refer to mnemonics later in this chapter) by asking, for instance: "Okay, these six forces help break down rocks, how might we remember them easily?" Perhaps, give them an opportunity to develop ways or say, "Why not use the first letters of the words such as in RIP RAC?!" "So, when I ask you on the test what are the six ways that weathering can break down rocks, you'll say RIP RAC and explain R = running water; I = ice; P = plants; R = rain; A = animals; and C = chemicals." Providing in-class time to develop these learning strategies may indeed take up some class time, but I assure the time will be well spent. Good teachers don't expect students to already have these skills. Good teachers actively teach the skills and incorporate them into their lessons. Although these study skills are particularly helpful for students with formally assessed learning disabilities, they are useful for all students, even for you and me.

Experience has taught me that all people can become successful learners. All that is needed is a plan, the right attitude, and study skill strategies.

The remainder of this chapter is divided into five sections:

1. Simple strategies for the early grades
   Study skill instruction should begin early on in a student's education.

The strategies listed below are simple yet powerful to get students to develop good study habits.

2. Strategies on how to improve note-taking skills

Success in school depends on how well your students can take notes. Since much instruction in schools is communicated in a traditional manner, that is, through lecture, note-taking skills are essential to success.

Many research studies demonstrate the importance of listening skills as a prerequisite to effective note taking. Listening is the foundation of all language skills as well. Success depends on how well students listen in class. The better listeners they are, the better notes they will take during class.

Students can indeed learn to become effective listeners and note takers. Guide them through the steps that follow. The more strategies they adopt, the better listeners and note takers they'll become.

3. Simple strategies on how to improve study skills

Obviously, success in school depends, to a large degree, on how well students study. Notice I didn't write "how hard they study." Too many students think that studying long and hard is the best way to study. Not true. Why study hard when they should study "smart"?

By learning and incorporating various study skill strategies, they will become more efficient and better learners. If they are "D" or "C" students, these skills will certainly help them do much, much better. Surprisingly, even if they are "B" or "A" students, they'll benefit with the use of these study techniques because they'll become more efficient learners. They may, in fact, reduce their study time by at least a third and still get those "A"s! I'm sure they'll appreciate that extra time, too.

Follow each strategy outlined below using the same format used above for listening and note taking. The more strategies your students adopt, the better at studying they'll become. With enhanced studying skills, they're on their way to that "A"!

4. Simple strategies on how to read material from a chapter or book

Students need guidance on gleaning material as they read. Often we tell students to read pages so and so without giving them strategies to cull relevant information. Research in study skills demonstrates that when teachers offer guidance to students as they learn and read, student comprehension and achievement increases.

As you introduce these aforementioned ideas to students, have them complete the following:

I use this strategy all the time. _____

I sometimes use this strategy. _____

I rarely use this strategy. _____

I will try this strategy. _____

This strategy works. _____

This strategy doesn't work. _____

This strategy works sometimes. _____

5. Cooperative Learning

Discussion of cooperative learning, although mentioned earlier in the book, is explained here in more detail because it has been proven to be one of the most valuable ways to promote student learning (Slavin, 1994). Research indicates that teachers who incorporate cooperative learning strategies promote student achievement. Cooperative learning is an especially useful strategy when employing cognitive strategy (study skills) instruction because many students learn best in cooperative groups. Cooperative grouping to promote study is particularly effective.

Some strategies in the sections, below require explanation, while others are self-explanatory.

SIMPLE SRATEGIES FOR THE EARLY GRADES

Strategy #1: Listen

Play listening games with students. Repeat a few words and have students repeat them. Award points, give out stars, and so on. Have students listen to songs on tape and have them repeat (sing) them.

Strategy #2: Thinking About Thinking and Learning

Ask students a simple question like "What do you want to do now?" As they answer, stop and encourage them to think about how they decided to answer the question. Encourage them to become aware of how they think, how they solve problems, and how they learn. Starting this metacognitive process early on will yield academic benefits years later.

Strategy #3: Taking Directions

Play games such as Simon Says. Select a student to play teacher. Have the child give directions to others. Discuss with class why following directions is important. Role-play how to follow directions.

Strategy #4: Breathe

Teach young students how to effectively deal with stress. Encourage them to talk about their concerns. Teach them simple breathing exercises.

SIMPLE STRATEGIES ON HOW TO IMPROVE NOTE-TAKING SKILLS

Strategy #1: Being Prepared

Ask students, "what does being prepared mean to you?" Elicit that being prepared means getting ready before they come to school. Being prepared includes having extra sharpened pencils, working pens, highlighters and/or markers, notebooks or loose-leafs with blank sheets for writing, textbooks, and any other materials needed. Have them make a list of what they need and have them check everything the evening before school.

Getting to school on time is also a form of preparation. Also, remind them to come to school with the right attitude—ready to learn! On an index card, have them write the following sentence and urge them to keep it handy: **"I'm Ready and Willing to Learn and I Will Learn!"** Repeating the sentence every morning for the next 10 school days and then once a week until the end of the school year is suggested. Obviously, depending on the age and grade level of your students you will have to modify this approach. But do tell your older students that "affirmations" are very powerful instruments of success for adults.

Therefore, being prepared means:

1. Bringing materials (Having the proper supplies will prepare them for note taking).

2. Arriving on time (Arriving on time is important because they'll likely hear the instructor review the lesson objective and overview).

3. Having a positive attitude (Self-affirmations, like "I'm ready and willing to learn and I will learn," are powerful and effective strategies because they affect one's subconscious in a positive way. With the proper attitude, they are more likely to succeed).

Strategy #2: Sit in the Front Row

Remind students to get to class early, especially the first day of class, to get a seat in the front row. Encourage them to sit in the middle of the row. Sitting near the entrance or a window will be distracting. If the teacher later requests them to move to the back, they should respectfully insist on sitting at the front. Simply say, "I learn best when I'm near the teacher!" Advantages of this approach include:

- Sitting in the front allows them to hear the teacher, even whispers or low intonations.
- Those who are seated at the front get the "goodies" first. For instance, handouts or special props are handed to those sitting nearest the instructor. If they are seated in the back, the handouts may run out.
- The teacher will naturally see those students seated in the front. He or she will interact with them, verbally and otherwise, far more than those students seated in the rear.
- There is also a psychological benefit to sitting up front. The teacher will consider them more involved and interested in class and that certainly can't hurt their chances of getting a better grade.
- They are more likely to pay attention and take better notes when they are seated near the instructor.

Strategy #3: Be an Active Listener: Look Attentive and Alert

Encourage students to look at the teacher and use good eye contact. Model behavior for students during your teaching. Give them examples by role-playing inactive listeners versus active ones.

Strategy #4: Don't Sit Next to "Talkers" and "Troublemakers"

Explain why doing so may keep them off-task.

Strategy #5: With the Teacher's Permission, Use a Tape Recorder for Difficult, Content-Laden Lessons

Would you allow a student to record a session? For some students this technique is a superb way to ensure that they at least get the information. That way they can play back the tape at home to record missing notes.

Strategy #6: Ask Questions and Ask Teacher to Repeat

Encourage students to ask questions. Inform class that you are willing to repeat and further explain any idea mentioned in class.

Strategy #7: Don't Write Down Every Word, Use Key or Main Words

Explain to students that they should not try to write everything down. They should record main ideas. Give them a mock lecture and have them record notes. Then, divide class into groups for them to compare notes. Discuss with class. Although this is a time-consuming activity, research again indicates that when teachers take the time to teach students how to study or in this case to take notes, student achievement increases.

Strategy #8: Listen, Then Put the Teacher's Ideas Into Your Own Words (Paraphrase)

Teach them to paraphrase. Model an activity for them and have them practice with your guidance and correction.

Strategy #9: Use Abbreviations/Symbols

Teach them to devise their own symbols for commonly used words. Let them use pictures to help as well. Give them examples.

Strategy #10: With the Permission of a Good Friend, Make Photocopies of Her or His Notes

Encourage students to exchange notes and to photocopy them as well.

Strategy #11: Know What Notes to Take and When

Explain to students to record the following:

- Key information written or highlighted on board
- Any questions the teacher asks and spends time getting class to answer
- Points stressed by teacher (teacher cues)—"Now, boys and girls, this is very important . . ."

Strategy #12: Write Legibly (Rewrite Notes)

Rewriting notes is time consuming, but one of the very best strategies for retention of information. Train students to do so right after class or at home that evening.

Strategy #13: Label or Date Notes

This simple suggestion helps organizes notes.

Strategy #14: Use Outlines

Model sample outlines such as:

    I. Main Idea
       A. Supporting Detail
       B. Supporting Detail
          1. sub-detail
          2. sub-detail

Strategy #15: Don't Miss the First and Last Minutes of Class!

Explain to class that that's when overviews and reviews occur—the most important parts of the lesson.

Strategy #16: Remember, FACT

F = focus
A = ask yourself questions
C = connect main ideas with each other
T = try to picture what the speaker is saying

Strategy #17: General Guidelines

Encourage students to:

- Focus on sentences, not words.
- Try to get general meaning.
- Don't jump to conclusions based on expectations rather than what's actually being said.
- While listening, ask questions about what the speaker is saying. Then try to answer questions.
- Try to "picture" what you are hearing in your mind's eye.
- Regularly summarize what the speaker has said.
- Listen first, judge later.
- Take notes to remember.

SIMPLE STRATEGIES ON HOW TO IMPROVE STUDY SKILLS

Strategy #1: Study Smart

Explain to students that there is no need to study hard and long. Tell them to "study smart—use the right tools." Much study time is wasted when students review what they already know. What they know they know. Spend time studying only areas of difficulty. Many of them use a yellow highlighter to identify important topics or ideas. After a while, they look back and everything in the chapter is highlighted! Encourage them to highlight *only* material they don't understand or know well. That way, they'll spend the time studying those areas that are difficult for them. This approach to studying can cut their study time in half.

Additionally, tell them to be prepared for study by:

- Bringing home their books/materials.
- Setting aside a specific location and time for study.
- Spending between 15–45 minutes studying at one time, then taking a break (5–15 minutes), then resuming.
- Having a positive attitude.

Strategy #2: Rewrite Notes Using 3 x 5 Index Cards for Easy, Quick Review

Rewriting notes aids review. Use of index cards allows students to carry them and study almost anywhere.

Strategy #3: Tape Record Your Notes and Chapter Content and Play It Back

Listening to a lesson on tape is a wonderful strategy for auditory learners.

Strategy #4: Study in Short Bursts

Tell students not to study for prolonged periods of time; say no more than 20 minutes at a time (varies with grade level). Four periods of study like that are much better than one prolonged study period.

Strategy #5: Study Five Minutes Each Night Reviewing Day's Lessons

The same concept applies.

Strategy #6: Avoid Cramming

Students will tell you, "It sure works for me." Well, if they are straight "A" students, fine. If not . . .

Strategy #7: Over-Study Areas of Difficulty

Research indicates that overstudying is good when one does so selectively.

Strategy #8: Meditate/Breath/Listen to Music (before and during study)

Strategy #9: Make Your Own Written Exam Questions

Students like to play teacher no matter what the grade level.

Strategy #10: When Studying a Book Chapter, Convert Headings and Sub-headings into Questions and Answer Them

Strategy #11: Form Study Groups (in person, over the phone, or via e-mail)

Strategy #12: Set Up a Special Study Space (Study in a comfortable setting, bright light, favorite chair, etc.)

Strategy #13: Study and Review Notes Soon After Class—Write an Outline

Strategy #14: Review Notes Out Loud and Ask Yourself Questions! (Use the mirror and role-play the teacher)

Strategy #15: Study in Morning/Night—Use Your Own Biological Clock

Strategy #16: Eat Before or After Study—Not During (Unless you ace your exams by studying during study periods)

Strategy #17: Ask for Help (teacher, friend, parent/adult, previous students)

Strategy #18: Use Mnemonics: Memory

Use Acronyms

- Use first letters for example, PGA for Professional Golf Association
- Make up your own
- Helpful for spelling (e.g., "embarrass" for Emily's Mom Broke A Red Rocker As She Sat)

Use Rhyming

- Established rhymes (e.g., "30 days have September, April, June, and November, all the rest have 31 except February")
- Make up your own rhymes

Use Linking

Linking can be used, for example, to remember parts of a flower: "Mr. Stigma shot a pink anther with a pistil while Miss Sepal fixed the stem of her bicycle petal." Or, for remembering parts of the eye: pupil, cornea, lens, iris, retina: "Iris watched a pupil through the lens of her Red Tin telescope eating corn-ea on the cob."

Use Keywords

Make up and memorize your own keywords (sometimes called "Pegs"). Use them to associate new information.

My key word	Words to memorize	How I associate
1. won	pin	I won a pin
2. pair	sunglasses	a pair of—
3. tree	monkey	__ up a tree
4. star	movie	movie star
5. foot	pencil	a 5-foot-long
6. 6-pack	squirrel	6-pack of
7. 7-up	hat	hat full of 7-up

8.	ate	cat	ate a
9.	9-iron	trumpet	__ shaped like a
10.	tent	pizza	tent made of __

Try the "body peg." Identify 10 spots on your body to place information: for example, on each foot (2), on each hand (2), on your lap (1), on your chest (1), on each shoulder (2), on your face (1), and on the top of your head (1). That should equal 10 spots (You can even use locations in your home and have up to 50 locations!). Now, place some information on each peg. Let's say I'm outside and have no pen to record information. Simply place the new information on each peg. You remember you have to call your mom and your best friend. Shrink their heads and place them mentally and visually on each foot. Hear them say, "Call me when you get home." Later, you remember that you have to take out the meat from the freezer. So, imagine a piece of meat on your lap. And so on . . . Now, when you arrive home and ask yourself, "What am I supposed to do?" Look, at your feet. What do you see? Of course, your mom and best friend. Now, what's on your lap? It's fun and it works.

Remember this mnemonic: **CAR**. Whatever you need and want to remember, make it **C**olorful, **A**ction-Oriented, and **R**idiculous. When you have to memorize anything, make it as colorful as possible, make it move, say up and down, and imagine it doing something ridiculous. For instance, I have difficulty sometimes remembering names of people I first meet. Let's say I am introduced to a woman named Jane. As I shake her hand and say hello, I imagine her hair in deep purple with globs of jam flowing on and down her long hair. Now, that is certainly colorful, action-oriented, and ridiculous. When I see her next, I envision that image and say, "Hi Jam, oh I mean Jane?!" Ha.

Try this one. Your parent or spouse tells you to pick up the following grocery items on the way home from work: Milk, loaf of bread, ketchup, and napkins. No need to write the info down. Simply mentally record the items using CAR in one of your pegs. Now, earlier I mentioned the body peg and the home peg. You can also have the "hood of the automobile peg." Place the items on the hood of your car so that when you get into it on the way home all you have to do is to look at your peg, the hood of the car. What do you see? Of course, white napkins all over sprinkled with red ketchup, and in the center is a container of milk with a loaf of bread balancing in see saw fashion. Now, that's certainly ridiculous, colorful, and action-oriented. You'll surely remember the groceries and, thus, avoid an argument with your spouse or parent!

Use Rote Memorization

As long as you rehearse, the good old-fashioned sometimes ain't bad.

SIMPLE STRATEGIES ON HOW TO READ MATERIAL FROM A CHAPTER OR BOOK

Strategy #1: SQ4R

Teach your students this popular technique: SQ4R (Survey, Question, Read, Reflect, Recite, and Review):

1. **S**urvey—get an idea of general organization and topics by skimming headings, subheadings, charts, and highlight words

2. **Q**uestion—turn headings into questions

3. **R**ead—the material, to answer the questions

4. **R**eflect—on the material and relate it to previous knowledge or information

5. **R**ecite—the information by asking or answering questions

6. **R**eview—the material then reread it; ask questions; complete practice exercises

Strategy #2: Don't Use a Highlighter

Students often highlight everything. When they are ready to study they are overwhelmed by the "sea of yellow." Instead, teach them to place check marks in margins next to information they feel they need to review. If they insist on highlighting, then teach them to highlight only parts they are unsure of; they should not highlight parts they know.

Strategy #3: Make Notes on 3 x 5 Index Cards

Strategy #4: Write Questions as You Read

Strategy #5: Write an Outline

After each major section or chapter, take a piece of paper and outline in your own words the main ideas.

Strategy #6: Read Aloud or Sing Portions

Just make sure students are alone.

COOPERATIVE LEARNING

In a chapter devoted to helping students learn, discussion of cooperative learning is imperative because it is such a powerful instrument to promote achievement as well as an invaluable means to reinforce study skill instruction. Students study more effectively, for instance, when placed in well-functioning cooperative learning groups.

What is Cooperative Learning?

Definition

According to Robert Slavin (1994), "cooperative learning refers to a set of instructional methods in which students work in small mixed ability learning groups. . . . The students in each group are responsible not only for learning the material being taught in class, but for helping their group mates learn" (p. 5).

What It Is Not

It's not enough just to place students in random groups, especially without specific guidelines or with minimal training.

Benefits

- Higher student achievement
- Increased self-esteem
- Greater enjoyment of school
- Decreased absenteeism
- Greater motivation to learn
- Respect for students with different backgrounds

Formation of Groups

Teachers can place students in appropriate groups based on academic and/or social considerations. Groups generally should be formed using the acronym SEA, that is evenly based on Sex (gender), Ethnicity, and Ability. A random placement technique often employed is the count off; for example, students count off 1, 2, 3, 1, 2, 3, and so forth. All one's for one group, two's another, and so on.

Elements of Learning

Use the acronym PIGS FACE.

Positive Interdependence—the success of the group depends on the success of each member. Therefore, it is vital that each member participates. How can you ensure that each member actively engages in the particular activity? Give, for instance, only one worksheet per group. This technique requires each member to look on with other group members. If you give out a sheet to each member, each would probably work alone, thus defeating your purpose.

Individual Accountability—each student is responsible for learning the material, completing assignments, and so on. Teachers hold each group member responsible for learning. In cooperative learning one person cannot sit back and let others do the work. Teachers can ensure accountability by giving each member a test, oral questions, and son on. Typically, each member is expected to sign the worksheet to indicate that he or she participated and learned the material.

Group Processing—group members reflect on how well they worked together or whether they have accomplished their task. Teachers have groups rate their work at the end of an activity. Teachers also provide feedback to each group.

Social Skills—the interpersonal and communication skills necessary for effective group instruction. One of the most critical elements is that students must be taught the social skills necessary to work in groups. Teachers spend significant time reviewing rules and procedures and incorporating role plays to ensure compliance.

FACE-to-face interaction—students interact with one another in close proximity. What can you do as a teacher to facilitate face-to-face interaction?

Roles

For students: Each group member must be assigned a specific and distinct role such as Reader, Recorder, Monitor, Captain, Encourager, Spell Checker, and so on. What impact does assigning each student a role have on group functioning and output?

For teacher: Determines group size; assigns students to groups; arranges classroom; determines academic and social tasks; makes expectations for group work clear; monitors, observes, and walks around; intervenes as needed; provides feedback; evaluates each member and group

Basic Types of Groups

Think-Pair-Share—just turn to your neighbor . . .

Focus Triads—working in small groups of three on specific short-term tasks

Reading groups

Jigsaw—each member assigned a different part to research and like a jigsaw puzzle comes together at the end.

Table 6.1   Comparing Cooperative Learning With Traditional (Competitive) Grouping

Cooperative Learning	Traditional Group
Group members depend on each other	Group members compete with one another
Mixed abilities	Homogeneous
Leadership roles are shared	One leader
Social skills taught	Social skills assumed or ignored
Teacher observes and interacts	Teacher not involved much
Group members assess their effectiveness	No group processing

Can you think of other differences?

Other Factors to Consider

Group size—varies depending on purpose

Physical arrangement of room

Duration of grouping

Selection of group members

Rotation of groups

What do you do when a group completes a task during a period and the rest of the class is still working? Plan activities from learning centers, silent reading, individualized instruction, and so on. Have brainteasers on the board, for example: What 7-letter word doesn't contain any of the 5 vowels? Or, what word contains 3 consecutive pairs of letters in it?

Answers: Rhythms, Bookkeeper

Sample Lesson Planning Format

Decisions:

Subject, Topic:
Group Size: __ 2 __3 __4 __5

Assignment to Groups: ___teacher assigned ___ heterogeneous by ability ___ randomly ___ self-selected ___other

Room Arrangement: ___ small cluster of groups ___ round tables with chairs ___ three desks together T-shaped ___other

Materials: ___ one set per group ___ one set per person __ other roles? ____ specify

Social Skills, Specify Social Objectives of Lesson:

Lesson:

Instructional Objectives

Positive Interdependence: ___ one paper per group ___ each member gets same reward ___ one set of material to share ___ each member has a special job ___ assign roles ___ team logo, name, song, etc. ___ each person has only part of information (jigsaw) ___ other

Individual Accountability: ___ signatures ___ individual quiz ___ test ___ random testing or quizzing ___ individual homework ___ other

Expected Behaviors: ___listening ___ encouraging others ___ moving quickly and orderly ___ staying in group ___ taking turns ___ listening ___ praising one another ___ checking for understanding ___sharing ideas ___ asking for assistance ___ paraphrasing ___ summarizing ___ challenging ___ other
Monitoring:
Feedback:
Group Processing:

See Table 6.2 for an overview of some cooperative learning models.

CONCLUSION

In an attempt to answer the question "How can I help my students learn?" this chapter introduced the importance of study skill instruction, including cooperative learning. Research indicates that teachers who actively teach study skills help students significantly, not only academically, but emotionally as well. Students equipped with study skills have the confidence to succeed in school and, most important, in life. I'd like to end this chapter by highlighting another answer to the chapter's question. Above all else, it seems to me, communicating to your students that they can succeed, indeed, that you expect them to, is imperative.

I think you need to remain aware of the extensive literature on the "self-fulfilling prophecy." The term as first coined by Robert Merton (1948). Later on Rosenthal and Jacobson (1968) in *Pygmalion in the Classroom* related Merton's

(Continued on page 152)

Table 6.2   Overview of Selected Cooperative Learning Methods

Method/Proponent	Brief Description/Comments
Learning Together	Emphasizing cooperative effort, Learning Together has five basic elements: • positive interdependence (students believe they are responsible for both their learning and the team's) • face-to-face interaction (students explain their learning and help others with assignments) • individual accountability (students demonstrate mastery of material) • social skills (students communicate effectively, build and maintain trust, and resolve conflicts) • group processing (groups periodically assess their progress and how to improve effectiveness)—uses four- or five-member heterogeneous teams
Student Teams-Achievement Divisions (STAD)	Four student learning teams (mixed in performance levels, sex, and ethnicity): teacher presents lesson, students work in teams, and help others master material. Students then take quizzes; cooperative efforts are not allowed on quizzes; team rewards are earned. Applicable to most grades and subjects.
Teams-Games-Tournament (TGT)	Using the same teacher presentation and teamwork as STAD, TGT replaces the quizzes with weekly tournaments in which students compete with members of other teams to contribute points to team scores. Competition occurs at "tournament tables" against others with similar academic records. The winner of each tournament brings six points to her or his team. Low achievers compete with low achievers (a similar arrangement exists for high achievers), which provides all students with equal opportunity for success. As with STAD, team rewards are earned. Applicable to most grades and subjects.
Jigsaw	Students are assigned to six-member teams to work on academic material that has been divided into sections. Each member reads a section; then members of different teams meet to become experts. Students return to groups and teach other members about their sections. Students must listen to their teammates to learn other sections.
Jigsaw 2	Students work in four- or five-member teams as in TGT or STAD. Rather than being assigned specific parts, students read a common narrative (e.g., a chapter). Students also receive a topic on which to become an expert. Learners with the same topics meet together as in Jigsaw, and then they

(Continued)

Table 6.2 (Continued)

Method/Proponent	Brief Description/Comments
	teach the material to their original group. Students take individual quizzes.
Team Assisted Individualization (TAI)	Uses four-member mixed-ability groups (as with STAD and TGT); differs from STAD and TGT in that it combines cooperative learning and individualized instruction and is applicable only to mathematics in grades three through six. Learners take a placement test, then proceed at their own pace. Team members check one another's work and help with problems. Without help, students take unit tests that are scored by student monitors. Each week the teacher evaluates and gives team rewards.
Cooperative Integrated Reading and Composition (CIRC)	Designed to teach reading and writing in upper elementary grades, CIRC assigns students to different reading teams. Teacher works with one team, while other teams engage in cognitive activities: reading, predicting story endings, summarizing stories, writing responses, practicing decoding, and learning vocabulary. Teams follow sequence of teacher instruction, team practice, team pre-assessments, and quizzes. Quizzes may not be taken until the team feels each student is ready. Team rewards are given.
Group Investigation	Groups are formed according to common interest in a topic. Students plan research, divide learning assignments among members, synthesize or summarize findings to the entire class.

SOURCE: *The Clearing House*, Vol. 63, No. 3, p. 211, Jan./Feb., 1991. Reprinted with permission of the Helen Dwight Reid Educational Foundation. Published by Heldfref Publications, 1319 Eighteenth St., NW, Washington, DC 20036-1802. Copyright © 1991.

theory to classrooms. Essentially, the principle goes something like this: If you expect someone to behave a certain way and treat them accordingly, then the person will likely fulfill your expectations; thus, your prophecy for them is fulfilled. The word "Pygmalion" comes from Greek mythology. Pygmalion was a sculptor who carved an ivory statue of the perfect woman. While doing so, he fell in love with his creation and longed for it to become real. Aphrodite, the goddess of love, feeling sorry for Pygmalion, allowed the statue to come to life. The sculptor's wish was fulfilled. The more modern version of the effect was the theme of George Bernard Shaw's play *Pygmalion* and the musical *My Fair Lady*. A crude, unrefined flower girl is transformed into a confident and charming lady. In the end, Eliza Doolittle proclaims, "The difference between a flower lady and a princess is not how she acts, but how she is treated." This is the essence of the self-fulfilling prophecy.

RECOLLECTION

I recall that a fellow teacher once told me the humorous story that follows to illustrate the essence and power of the self-fulfilling prophecy. It's probably not true, but you'll get the point:

There was an eighth-grade class that had five teachers quit within a 3-week period. The principal was at her wit's end. How can she find a suitable teacher for these seemingly incorrigible youngsters? Whenever she hired a teacher, he or she would invariably resign within a matter of days. The class was simply "dumb and uncontrollable."

She placed an advertisement in the local paper hoping to "sucker," I mean convince, some teacher to assume this position. Luckily, a young gentleman appeared at her office apparently interested in the job. The principal hurriedly interviewed him and offered him the position. (Of course, she conveniently neglected to inform him what he was in for!)

A week passed and no word from class 8–303. Two weeks. The principal was dumbfounded. Why had this young, inexperienced educator not resigned. Three weeks, yet no word.

One morning the freshman teacher was passing the principal's office. The principal could not resist. She reached out and yanked his sleeve asking him to step in her office. As he entered, she closed the door and asked him to have a seat. He complied.

"I must admit, I thought you'd have quit by now."

"Quit?!" wondered the new teacher. "Why should I have quit?"

"Well, you must know by now how difficult your class is?" replied the principal.

"The class is just fine," the teacher rejoined.

"Just fine? You have a group of undisciplined and dim-witted kids. You must know that."

"I know nothing of the sort. These kids are doing quite well. I don't know what you mean. You must have the class confused with some other class."

"I certainly have the right class. Did you know that five teachers quit before you assumed the job? They quit because they couldn't handle the class."

(Continued)

(Continued)

"Well, I find that hard to believe. The class I have is a group of hard-working, intelligent youngsters. Don't you remember you escorted me into the class that first day? You then handed me the class roster. On that roster was noted each child's I.Q. score beside each name: John-114; Mary-124; Jose-140; Louise-119; Trevor-139, and so on. These kids are smart!"

"Smart?" queried the dubious principal. That roster listed their locker numbers, not their I.Q.'s!!!"

How does the self-fulfilling prophecy actually work? The first step involves a teacher who forms a negative expectation about a student. Negative expectations may arise from a bias towards a student's ethnic group, gender, social class, and so on. Sometimes, the expectations stem from the student's behavior. For instance, if Alfredo has a history of being referred to the dean's office, the new teacher, having heard or read about Alfredo's indiscretions, may react by expecting the student to get into trouble. Once a teacher expects a certain behavior, the teacher acts in a differential manner. In Alfredo's case, the teacher, upon meeting the student for the first time, may state," I heard about you, now, you better not cause me any trouble. Alfredo may be unfairly targeted by the teacher for misbehavior. Even if another student acts in a similar way, the teacher may ignore the misbehavior but rather focus on Alfredo based on what she heard about his past.

One of the classic studies that addresses how teachers convey expectations was conducted by Ray Rist (1970) entitled "Student Social Class and Teacher Expectations: The Self-Fulfilling Prophecy in Ghetto Education." Teachers may convey low expectations in many ways, including direct verbal communications (e.g., "You'll never succeed"), indirect means (e.g., assigning menial tasks, providing low-grade curriculum materials, or giving these students little time to respond to teacher questions), among others. I encourage you to read Rist's study because his findings have been replicated and are just as relevant today as they were in 1970.

Tauber (1997) comprehensively and clearly reviews the research into "self-fulfilling prophecy." He provides the following testimonial:

A student who came to our school from another district was labeled as a discipline problem. His records were filled with discipline letters. The child's parent felt that her child's behavior deteriorated because he was living up to what the teacher expected of him. Right or wrong, I kept this young man's records from the teacher for his first 6 weeks in our district. He was assigned to a teacher with outstanding classroom organization and control. The teacher clearly related her academic and behavioral expectations for the boy. The boy apparently believed he was to behave in a certain manner, and he fulfilled these expectations. The teacher was surprised to find out that the child had a severe discipline problem in his prior school, and she disregarded the reports in the boy's file. (p. 124)

While the study of the self-fulfilling prophecy is intriguing and among the most interesting of educational topics, suffice it to say here that if you want your students to learn, perhaps the single greatest factor that may determine their success is understanding this self-fulfilling prophecy, how it works, and how it affects your behavior in the classroom. Maintain high expectations for all your students, regardless of their backgrounds or what others report about them. Avoid labeling students, for "labeling is disabling."

A quick story is in order. This first story I heard Lee Canter relate. One day, he said, I received a call from the district office that I was to expect a new admit to enter my school. I was warned to "watch out" because she apparently had a "rough and tough look." I got all worried. My grade levels had just achieved a degree of stability after three months of turmoil. Now it was early December, and to receive a new admit at this stage was, to put it plainly, a pain. My worst fears were confirmed when I saw her as she walked into the main office. She wore tattered clothing, her hair was strewn about, and she had this tattoo on her arm, partly concealed by her shirt. I could make out several words, however, "Born to . . ." "Oh no," I thought to myself. I know what that says, "Born to kill." I became abrupt with her and asked her for evidence that she in fact lived in our district. I wasn't very friendly towards her and I must have communicated my lack of enthusiasm for her presence because she responded in kind. To make a long story short, I placed her in a sixth-grade classroom. Although she had trouble adjusting at first, she turned out okay. In fact, she was a rather sweet girl once you got to know her. She had had a rather difficult life. She had no parents and was moved around from home to home. She craved to be loved and wanted. I felt very guilty after I discovered that her tattoo fully read, "Born to *be loved.*"

Teacher educators face an awesome challenge in preparing future educators to teach in a multicultural, multiethnic, and multiracial school environment. Extraordinary demands have been placed on teacher educators to prepare informed, dynamic professionals who have the requisite knowledge, skills, and dispositions to affect learning positively. Knowledge involves competence in content areas, and the ability to articulate philosophies, attitudes, and beliefs that guide instructional decision-making. Skillful teachers use a variety of instructional strategies, match curricular content with individual needs of students, and provide opportunities for active learning. These professionals also have dispositions or "mindsets" that radiate dedication, enthusiasm, empathy, resourcefulness, and imagination.

Expecting students to succeed is one such important disposition. Teachers who communicate high and affirming expectations to their students help them become self-confident, successful learners. Conversely, communicating negative expectations often produces disinterested and disaffected students. The literature is unequivocal; teachers' expectations of student performance is a major determinant for academic success and social adjustment to school/classroom life.

What we expect, all too often, is exactly what we get. Nowhere is this more true than in education, where teachers' expectations of students are crucial. As a teacher educator, I realize that teachers must be made aware of the self-fulfilling prophecy and how it functions within the classroom. The self-fulfilling prophecy functions whether or not we are aware of it. Becoming aware of how we tend to expect certain students to fail or not succeed more than others is crucial. Communicating positive expectations for all students regardless of gender, age, ethnicity, social class, and so on is a primary professional responsibility for all of us.

*   *   *

FOLLOW-UP QUESTIONS/ACTIVITIES

1. Describe how you would incorporate study skills instruction in your class.

2. What additional information do you need to know and how do you plan on obtaining the information?

3. Take one of the strategies previously mentioned and teach it to someone else not in your class, perhaps a family member. Did it work? Explain.

4. Share information in this chapter with a colleague.

5. How else can you help your students to learn?

7

How Can I Best Incorporate State and District Curriculum Standards?

A school's curriculum refers to the expectations for student learning embodied in the school's learning objectives, programs, and course offerings, and translates the state or district content standards into a sequenced series of statements about what students will learn through their school experiences

—Charlotte Danielson

◆

FOCUS QUESTIONS

1. What comes to mind when you think of the word "standards?"

2. When was the last time you referred to the Scope and Sequence in your curriculum area(s)?

3. Are you in favor of standards-based educational reform? Explain.

4. How do you, if at all, address your state or local standards? Is professional development provided to assist you?

5. What do you want or need to know about implementing or aligning standards in your lessons?

Continued dissatisfaction with the public schools has prompted still greater attention to the need for national, state, and local standards (O'Day, 2002). The debate about standards (see, e.g., Smith, Fuhrman, & O'Day, 1994), as far as classroom teachers are concerned, is moot. As a classroom teacher, under most circumstances, you are not in a position to determine the viability or suitability of a particular standard. This is not to say that teachers should not weigh in on the debate. In fact, teacher unions play a critical role in the politics of establishing standards. Moreover, teachers serving on school-based curriculum development teams may have an impact on the way standards are structured and presented. The fact remains, though, that the beginning classroom teacher is charged with the responsibility of ensuring that established national, state, or local standards are adhered to and addressed. Accepting various standards is part of your professional work, even though, for the most part, they have been imposed upon you by external bodies.

As a teacher you should become acquainted with the standards you are expected to implement. For purposes of describing the teacher's role, I will refer to the establishment of local district standards, although the discussion is equally relevant to state or national standards. Presumably your district via the principal or assistant principal has reviewed the curriculum standards you are expected to adopt. Hopefully, in-depth professional development to inform you of standards and expectations for implementing them has been provided. You have likely been informed of the various *benchmarks* established for your grade level. A benchmark is a more specific component of a standard, as in the following example:

English language standard: Analyzes Western and non-Western creative fiction

Benchmark, grades 9–12: Compares and contrasts the writing styles and plot development of William Shakespeare and Edgar Allan Poe with Homer and John Milton.

In this example, you may develop a unit on Western and non-Western creative fiction, but you will be expected to demonstrate that students are able to, among other benchmarks, compare and contrast the pieces of literature mentioned above. Lessons you design should indicate and demonstrate that you are attempting to assist students in accomplishing this objective.

REFLECT

State, local, or district standards are sometimes based on national standards. For this reflective activity, you'll first need to download the national standards in each of the disciplines noted below, in order to consider two questions: (a) How do these standards compare with standards established by your school or district? and (b) To what extent are you meeting or not meeting these national standards?

English: www.ncte.org/standards/index.shtml

Mathematics: www.standards.nctm.org

Science: www.nsta.org/onlineresources/nses.asp

Social Studies/History: www.socialstudies.org/standards/toc.html

_____

_____

_____

_____

_____

_____

_____

_____

In this chapter, I will provide a concise overview of curriculum development as you plan for instruction. Implementing standards is meaningful only within a sound and firmly grounded curricular program. You should, therefore, have some understanding of curriculum. As a teacher, you are expected to design curricula and plan instruction based on knowledge of the subject matter, student needs, community and curriculum goals (including state and local performance standards). I will then briefly give you some historical perspective of the current standards-based movement that has driven instruction in the classroom and profoundly affects classroom teachers. The chapter will conclude with suggestions for implementing and teaching to the numerous statewide and local standards-based reforms while at the same time developing creative, interdisciplinary lessons.

WHAT IS CURRICULUM DEVELOPMENT?

Discussion of standards in isolation of an analysis of curriculum development, albeit brief, is not fruitful. Curriculum development is a dynamic, interactive, and complex process that serves as the foundation for good teaching practice. Teachers, as instructional leaders in their own right, must be actively involved in curriculum development. Such involvement is even more critical today because of national, state, and local attention to standards. Teachers, as mentioned earlier, are pressured to respond to the national movement towards standards-based education, including high-stakes testing, by raising student academic achievement.

What is curriculum? Before we can address this question, three more fundamental questions must be framed. What is education? Why is obtaining one so important? What are the purposes of an education? Curriculum cannot be studied in isolation of these fundamental questions. Ask a few people "Why do we need to be educated?" You might get some of these responses: to learn practical skills, for intellectual fulfillment, to make money, to appreciate democracy, and to respect other cultures. An educated person seeks the following four notions, which form four basic purposes of education:

1. *Self-Realization*—included in this broad category are ideas such as striving for intellectual growth, pursuing aesthetic interests, personal development, character building, and enhancing self-worth.

2. *Human Relationships*—included in this broad category are ideas such as developing friendships, respecting others, fostering cooperation, developing ethical and moral reasoning, and promoting democracy.

3. *Economic Efficiency*—included in this broad category are ideas such as work, career, money, and becoming an educated consumer.

4. *Civic Responsibility*—included in this broad category are ideas such as seeking social justice, avocating tolerance for others, promoting world peace, respecting law and order, and fulfilling obligations to government.

Education is conceived as the deliberate, systematic and sustained effort to transmit the knowledge, skills, and values that a society deems worthy. Schooling represents a small part in one's overall education. Life indeed educates. You may walk down the street one morning and meet a friend who "educates" you about a specific matter. Museums, televison, family, religious institutions, theater, library, salespeople, and prisons educate. Schools certainly play a vital role in education. Three purposes can be identified:

1. Helping children acquire knowledge and skills

2. Transmitting ideas and values of society

3. Preparing children to live creative, humane, and sensitive lives

These purposes of education and schooling are meant to stimulate your own ideas. Other educators may select different definitions and aspects to accentuate when speaking about education and schooling. The point, however, is that when we as educators attempt to translate these broad purposes in schools into a program that offers intellectual and educational substance we enter the purview of curriculum. The curriculum field is devoted to the study and examination of the decisions that go into determining what gets taught. Hence, curriculum theorists deal with the following issues and concerns: epistemological ("what knowledge is most worthwhile?"); political ("who controls this knowledge?"); economic ("how is this knowledge linked to power and goods and services?"); technical ("how should this knowledge be made accessible to all students?"); and ethical ("is this knowledge morally sound?"). As a teacher, you may address these theoretical concerns from an academic perspective, but, when you work on a daily basis, you and your supervisors are most concerned with translating the broad or specific curriculum goals (standards) into practical lessons and units of instruction.

Of Definitions

Schubert (1993) notes that "the term curriculum is shrouded in definitional controversy" (p. 8). A discussion of this controversy, its history, and implications goes beyond the purposes of this chapter. Suffice it to say, that curriculum has been variously defined. Some common definitions include (see Beach & Reinhartz, 2000):

- All planned and unplanned learning experiences in a school.
- All that is planned and directed by teachers to achieve educational goals.
- Planned and guided learning experiences and intended learning outcomes, formulated through the systematic reconstruction of knowledge and experience, under the auspices of the school, for the learner's continuous and willful growth in personal—social competence.
- Plans for guiding teaching and learning.
- A work plan that includes both the content and the strategies for teaching and learning.
- Includes careful planning, with the ultimate goal of increasing student achievement and is not only the written plan or construct but also the content, learning experiences, and results.

What does curriculum mean to you? Many educators take curriculum for granted. It is sometimes and regrettably synonymous with the textbook. For many teachers curriculum is prescribed by district, city, or state agencies and presented as prepackaged mandates. Over the past several years, with great emphasis on high-stakes testing and standards-based education, educators at the school level have felt that they have had little control over what gets taught. Your principal and assistant principal can play important leadership roles here in conveying to you that mandated curricula do not necessarily stifle creativity and curriculum innovation. You can be guided by a particular standard or benchmark but still be free to create meaningful learning experiences for your students that promote achievement.

One of the most helpful curriculum development models for teachers to easily implement is the one developed by Ralph Tyler (1949). His model is practical in the sense that teachers must establish curriculum goals that can then be translated into instructional objectives. Through curriculum development, teachers identify learning activities to provide students with meaningful learning experiences.

Widely known as the Tyler Rationale, this useful model identifies four steps in curriculum development:

1. What educational purposes should the school seek to attain?

2. What educational experiences can be provided that are likely to attain these purposes?

3. How can these educational experiences be effectively organized?

4. How can we determine whether these purposes are being attained?

According to Tyler, general goals must be stated in behavioral terms or objectives so that teachers can assess the extent of student learning.

REFLECT

How might the Tyler Rationale help you develop curriculum? Be specific, giving examples.

_____

_____

_____

_____

_____

_____

_____

_____

_____

_____

Three criticisms have been leveled at Tyler's model. First, learning that is merely identified with observed changes in behavior is limited in the sense that while some kinds of learning are likely to be manifested in observable behavior, many other kinds are not. Sometimes change may not occur immediately but may blossom months after a particular unit is taught. Long-term development of intellectual patterns of thought are not considered in the Tyler model.

A second problem arises when teachers precisely identify learning objectives in advance of instruction. Progressives like John Dewey, for instance, saw objectives as arising out of activity, giving that activity a richer, deeper meaning. Objectives, according to this criticism, do and should not always precede activity.

A third criticism of the Tyler Rationale arises from a simplistic view of evaluation or assessment. A unit of instruction, according to the Tyler model, is successful when measured outcomes match prespecified objectives.

Sometimes the most important outcomes may not have been anticipated. Therefore, simply measuring outcomes aligned with prespecified objectives may miss significant student learning outcomes.

Notwithstanding these criticisms, teachers can use the Tyler model, keeping in mind its limitations, to help them identify learning outcomes, develop learning strategies, and establish criteria for assessment. Note that alternate models exist. Consult, for instance, Pinar, Reynolds, Slattery, and Taubman's 1995 work.

Of the Curriculum Development Process

Three key curriculum development steps for teachers can be identified:

1. Planning for teaching and learning

2. Implementing the plan

3. Assessing teaching and learning

According to Beach and Reinhartz (2000), "These three steps provide a framework for . . . teachers . . . as they develop a blueprint for teaching and learning in classrooms and schools" (p. 199). Figure 7.1 illustrates the three steps of the curriculum development process. The steps are cyclical as the process begins and ends with planning. Units or lessons are modified and improved through this process.

Developing curriculum at the planning stage involves determining prior knowledge and skills of learners, establishing instructional outcomes, and reviewing appropriate resources and materials. As teachers and their supervisors plan together at this stage, they reflect on the teaching and learning process. During a grade conference, for example, teachers and the assistant principal can examine mandated curricula (local standards) but still be free to develop and match instructional objectives with learner needs and abilities. Curricular modifications at this stage are possible and indeed recommended to plan for the most meaningful unit of instruction as possible. Instructional practices, for instance, in an inclusive classroom will differ dramatically from a more homogenous grouping of students. During this stage, teachers can review availability of appropriate resources and materials that support instruction. During this stage, teachers address possible teaching strategies and activities, goals and objectives, assessment procedures (always keeping the end in mind), content or subject matter, and standards that must be met. Teachers must always keep in mind:

- Content matched to the developmental level of students
- Prerequisite knowledge and skills before undertaking a new unit of instruction

Figure 7.1

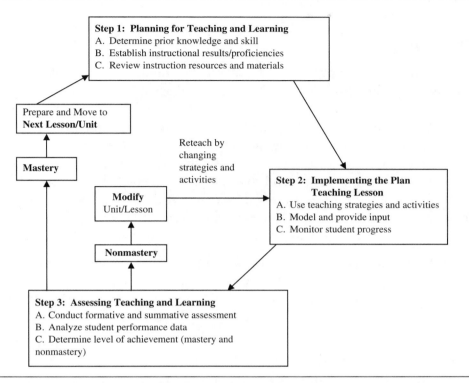

SOURCE: From Don M. Beach & Judy Reinhartz, *Supervisory Leadership:* Focus on *Instruction.* Published by Allyn and Bacon, Boston, MA. Copyright © 2000 by Pearson Education. Reprinted by permission of the publisher.

- Inductive and deductive teaching approaches
- Selection and appropriateness of learning experiences
- Sequencing of learning experiences
- Selection and appropriateness of assessment instruments

Beach and Reinhartz (2000) remind us that "the success of the curriculum depends on the quality of planning and the decisions that teachers make as they prepare for instruction" (p. 201).

During the second step of the curriculum development process plans are implemented. Teaching is the process of implementing curricular plans. Curriculum and teaching are conceived as very much interrelated. During this step, teachers present their lessons using appropriate and varied strategies and activities. Teachers also model skills and monitor student progress (see Figure 7.1).

The third step of assessing teaching and learning is critically important. If students are not learning, the curriculum development process requires modifications. Perhaps instructional objectives need reconsideration, teaching strategies may need revision, or reteaching and review may be necessary.

Of Quality

Glatthorn (2000, pp. 11-12) highlights several guidelines for developing quality curriculum, some of which are reviewed below:

- Structure the curriculum to allow for greater depth and less superficial coverage. Teachers should engage students in meaningful and detailed lessons that involve problem-solving projects and activities and critical thinking teaching strategies. Such activities and strategies form the basis for any topic to be covered during the course of the school year. Rather than rushing to "cover" topics or "teaching for the test," teachers should give students the problem solving and critical thinking skills that they, on their own, can apply to any topic.

- Structure and deliver the curriculum so that it facilitates the mastery of essential skills and knowledge of the subjects. Providing students a rich and deep knowledge base is primary but should be incorporated with problem solving strategies that are realistic and meaningful to students.

- Structure the curriculum so that it is closely coordinated. Coordinating content within lessons and among units over the course of the school year is imperative so that curriculum is sequential and well organized.

Emphasize both the academic and the practical. Relating content to the lived experiences of students is important to increase student learning. Hands-on activities, when feasible, are very much warranted.

According to Danielson (2002, p. 83), a "curriculum in a school organized for high-level learning by all students must first of all be rigorous and should demand high levels of cognitive engagement from students." The curriculum, Danielson continues, is the "school's description of what it will teach its students; it gives meaning to the school's academic goals." Curriculum must be connected to state or district content standards and the school's goals for student learning. A poor curriculum bears no relation to state or district standards or to the schools' goals for student learning.

RECENT HISTORY OF THE HIGH STAKES TESTING AND STANDARDS MOVEMENT

Many school systems around the country are pressured to raise student achievement levels as measured on standardized tests. These school systems are implementing a rigorously enforced standards-based curriculum that sometimes means a common curriculum for all students. The motivation for mandating a common school curriculum came from an analysis of declining standardized scores in reading and mathematics. In New York City, the largest school system of its kind in the country, for instance, most schools have been mandated to follow various curriculum programs: "Month by Month Phonics" for grades K–3, published by Carson-Dellosa Publishing Company; "Everyday Mathematics" for grades K–5, published by Everyday Learning and developed by the University of Chicago Mathematics Program; "Impact Mathematics" for grades 6–8, created by the authors of "Everyday Mathematics"; and "New York Math A: An Integrated Approach" published by Prentice Hall for high school students.

The national movement towards standards-based education, including high-stakes testing, has served to support raising local standards and promoting uniformity of curricular offerings to raise academic achievement. Standards has been a long-established reform proposal (Seguel, 1966) in this country. Present efforts at establishing national or state standards should be viewed within a historical context. The first significant attempt to improve and "modernize" the American curriculum occurred in the 1890s. The Committee of Ten, issued its report in 1892 under the leadership of Charles W. Eliot, the president of Harvard University. The committee sought to establish new curriculum standards for high school students. Standards were established to enable all students to receive a high-quality academic curriculum (Kliebard, 1987).

Notwithstanding the lofty aims of this committee, it wasn't until the establishment of the Commission on the Reorganization of Secondary Education that the school curriculum actually changed. The commission issued its report in 1918 and advocated a diversified curriculum that made allowances for a variety of curriculum "tracks" for the varied abilities of students. Known as the "Cardinal Principles of Education," the findings of this commission endorsed a differentiated curriculum that emphasized, in part, the importance of vocational training for a large segment of students (Krug, 1964).

During the first half of the twentieth century, the College Entrance Examination Board (formed in the 1890s), the Scholastic Aptitude Test (the first SAT was administered in 1926), and the American College Testing Program (established in 1959) were the guardians of standards, as applied to the academic curriculum. As a result of the Russian launch of the first artificial satellite (Sputnik) in 1957, American education was attacked vociferously. Only months after the Sputnik launching, Congress passed the National Defense Education Act (NDEA) which poured millions of dollars into mathematics, sciences, and engineering. For several years following Sputnik, enrollments in high schools increased dramatically as did achievement scores in many academic areas. Academic standards, up until this time, continued to be driven by levels of student achievement and assessed by national standardized tests (Ravitch, 1995).

By the mid-sixties, however, the American school curriculum shifted from an academic orientation to a nonacademic one. Prompted by political and social reforms, educational reformers reconsidered their longstanding emphasis on academic curriculum standards. The easing of high school graduation and college entrance requirements were just two of many effects of educational reforms during this tumultuous era. Yet, by the late 1970s, criticism of nonacademic curricula focused on declining SAT scores and what was perceived as a general lowering of standards. With the election of Ronald Reagan in 1980, an era of unprecedented educational reform, focusing on a conservative political and educational agenda, was about to begin.

With the publication of "A Nation at Risk: The Imperative for Educational Reform," a report by the National Commission on Excellence in Education (1983), attention was drawn to the assertion that schools had lowered their standards too much and that American students were not competitive with their international counterparts. The authors of this 1983 report were perturbed by the fact that American schoolchildren lagged behind students in other industrialized nations. The National Commission on Excellence in Education reported that, among students from various industrialized nations, U.S. students scored lowest on 7 of 19 academic tests and failed to score first or second on any test. Similar results were reported by the Educational Testing Service (1992). Moreover, the study found that nearly 40 percent of U.S. 17-year-olds couldn't perform higher-order thinking skills.

Pressure to improve the quality of American education by articulating concrete standards for performance increased. Consequently, a spate of national and state reports continued through the 1980s, each advocating fundamental educational change. Commitment to democratic ideals and the influence of public education were reinforced once again in 1986 with the publication of the report, sponsored by the Carnegie Foundation, "A Nation Prepared: Teachers for the 21st Century" (Carnegie Forum on Education and the Economy, 1986) and the Holmes (1986) report. The national curriculum reform movement was catapulted into prominence and action with the Education Summit held in 1989 by then President George Bush and state governors. A year later, in his State of the Union Address, President Bush affirmed his commitment to excellence in education by establishing six national education goals to be achieved by the year 2000. Signed into law by Congress during the Clinton administration on March 31, 1994, "Goals 2000" proclaimed, in part, that by the year 2000 "U.S. students will be first in the world in science and mathematics achievement" and "Every school will be free of drugs and violence and will offer a disciplined environment conducive to learning."

The adoption of national goals has been a major impetus for the increased attention to standards at the state level. In 1991, the U.S. Congress established the National Council on Educational Standards and Testing (NCEST), which encouraged educators and politicians to translate somewhat vague national goals into content curriculum standards. NCEST recommended that educators establish specific standards in specific subject areas. The National Council of Teachers of Mathematics (NCTM) led the way by publishing standards that quickly influenced textbook companies and testing agencies. These national curriculum reforms inevitably affected state educational reforms. More than 40 states have revised their curricula to reflect the standards that NCEST established.

Continuing in the tradition of standards-based education, President George W. Bush signed into law the No Child Left Behind Act of 2001, a reauthorization of the Elementary and Secondary Education Act of 1965. The purpose of the new legislation was to redefine the federal role in K–12 education and to help raise student achievement, especially for disadvantaged and minority students. Four basic principles were evident: stronger accountability for results, increased flexibility and local control, expanded options for parents, and an emphasis on teaching methods that presumably have been proven to work.

What does this history of standards-based education teach us about the current interest in revising curriculum and raising standards? Striking is the persistence of reform efforts and the influence of political and ideological agenda on national and state educational policies. Since the emergence of public education, attempts to improve curricular standards have abounded. Over the last hundred years or so, the American school curriculum has been influenced by different philosophies and ideological frameworks (Pinar et al., 1995). Yet, since the election of President Reagan in 1980, an essentialist and perennialist orientation has held sway in education, one that was not thwarted by the election and reelection of President Bill Clinton. This ideological commitment, spurred on by conservative political alliances, explains why so much emphasis has been placed on a call for the return to traditional academic content, usually in the form of core curriculum standards.

With the exploding knowledge and information ages and the rapid changes in technology, a growing demand for internationally competitive workers placed inordinate pressures on schools. Schools have been continually pressured to confront society's economic and social crises. Consequently, an advocacy for standards has been promulgated.

Although standards-based reforms have been criticized (Hostetler, 2003), many agree that they can help educators raise expectations for all students to achieve academically. Standards should, of course, be rigorous and world class. Standards, to be useful, must develop what is needed for citizenship, employment, and lifelong learning. Good standards represent by discipline the most important knowledge and skills so that high standards are kept for writing, mathematics, sciences, and the arts, as examples. Standards, to be useful, must allow for flexibility in implementation, allowing for differing individual interests. Assessments of standards must be deliberately aligned to determine whether or not students are meeting academic expectations. Aligning, for instance, English language standards with the standardized state examination for English language competence is imperative. Does the examination test students in areas covered by the curriculum? Does the curriculum reflect state and other assessment instruments?

SUGGESTIONS FOR IMPLEMENTING STANDARDS

Below are some practical suggestions for implementing state and local curriculum standards:

1. Seek Assistance—You are probably unfamiliar with your local curriculum standards. Seek advice from the assistant principal. Assistant principals and principals play a key role in curriculum standards implementation as they challenge and lead teachers to consider:

- Content matched to the developmental level of students
- Prerequisite knowledge and skills before undertaking a new unit of instruction
- Inductive and deductive teaching approaches
- Selection and appropriateness of learning experiences
- Sequencing of learning experiences
- Selection and appropriateness of assessment instruments

Teachers should be provided with standards-based Scope and Sequence charts and the performance standards for the particular grade and/or subject. Simply distributing these booklets is insufficient. Teachers should be provided with professional development workshops on how the school wishes teachers to use the standards.

2. Refer to the District Curriculum Guides—Schools and districts design and select curriculum materials across grades in order to make the course of study consistent from year to year. Scope and Sequence charts serve as valuable reference tools for teachers in planning appropriate individual, small-group, and whole-class instruction.

As you refer to a district curriculum guide that outlines the scope and sequence of various curriculum units, make certain that the curriculum guide meets the following criteria, among others (Glatthorn, 2000, p. 42):

- Guide is organized for easy use, is up-to-date, and is "teacher-friendly."
- Guide reflects current thinking about the subject.
- Guide focuses on key objectives.
- Objectives are developmentally appropriate.
- Objectives are developed and coordinated from grade to grade without repetition.

In addition, review the Scope and Sequence of expected knowledge and skills to obtain a sense of the overall curriculum in each content area in which you teach. Think about which formal and/or informal assessment instruments you will apply to determine student achievement.

Example: You are a fourth-grade teacher and you discover the following objectives stated in the Scope and Sequence document as follows:

Science: Examine, describe, investigate, and measure the effects of erosion and other natural events on Earth materials, such as on land, water, and air.

Social Studies: Locate information by investigating different types of primary and secondary sources, such as maps, globes, graphs, charts, newspapers, magazines, cartoons, media, and brochures.

Mathematics: Use knowledge of place value to read and write numbers up to the hundred millions.

English/Language Arts: Keep a record of what has been read, reflecting goals and accomplishments.

As an elementary schoolteacher, you are responsible to teach each of these content areas. Referring to the Scope and Sequence chart, you know in advance what knowledge and skills are expected of students at the end of the year. In each of the four cases above you will, for example, develop lesson plans that address the particular outcome. You will also identify assessment instruments that will measure student success in meeting these objectives.

3. Review Curriculum Goals—Review the types of curriculum goals established by your district. According to Danielson (2002) they may include:

- Knowledge—What should students know and understand after the unit? Students should know facts, for instance, but also be able to apply their knowledge to different situations or settings.
- Thinking and Reasoning Skills—Although conceptual knowledge is important, students must be able to reason, draw conclusions, compare and contrast, interpret information, and think deeply about a topic.

- Communication Skills—Although reading and writing are paramount, students must also become conversant in other means of communication (e.g., visual representation and the performing arts).
- Social Skills—Getting along with others and interacting effectively.
- Physical Skills—Skills developed as part of a physical education program are important as are physical skills developed in other curriculum areas, such as handwriting and the playing of musical instruments.

4. Familiarize Yourself and Utilize Content Area Performance Outcomes (Standards)—Thoroughly review performance standard guides in each content area you teach. Use the guides every day you plan lessons. Specify how your lesson plan addresses a particular standard. The performance standard curriculum guide gives you the details while the Scope and Sequence charts give you the overview of what is expected by the end of the year in a given subject.

5. Integrate Curriculum Through Use of Thematic Units and Interdisciplinary Study—Integrating curriculum has a number of substantial educational advantages including teaching students to become independent problem solvers and understanding the interrelationships among varied disciplines or subjects (Roberts & Kellough, 1996). Teachers may plan subject-specific material in a scope and sequence outline on tropical rain forests, for instance. Teachers can then develop thematic units that address the topic from various disciplines such as language arts, social studies, mathematics, and science. Identify, specify, and implement standards that cut across these various disciplines.

CONCLUSION

Implementing and teaching to the numerous statewide and local standards-based reforms while at the same time developing creative, interdisciplinary lessons is a challenge, but one that is not insurmountable. The standards, you will find, are useful to guide and reinforce instruction. Following them is a way to make sure that as a classroom teacher you are on the right track to ensure your students are meeting rigorous standards. Certainly, I am not advocating simply "teaching to the standards" without developing relevant and worthwhile lessons. Although you are required to adhere to the standards, you can still create interesting lessons and units of instruction. Try to maintain your positive attitude, despite those around you who might decry the imposition of standards. Use them wisely to enrich the educational experiences of your students.

*   *   *

FOLLOW-UP QUESTIONS/ACTIVITIES

1. Interview an experienced teacher and ask how he or she has integrated standards-based reforms.

2. Develop an interdisciplinary curriculum unit that incorporates district standards.

3. What is the connection between assessment and standards?

4. Give advice to a teacher newer than yourself on how best to incorporate district standards.

5. What more do you need to know about standards? Ask your assistant principal, curriculum coordinator, or principal.

8

How Can I Begin to Incorporate Technology into My Teaching?

The World Wide Web can be a source of unlimited resources that can bring exciting learning opportunities to students anywhere at anytime. In order to effectively and meaningfully integrate an online resource, teachers must first thoroughly plan a place for it in the comprehensive curricular sequence.

—Gary Bitter and Melissa Pierson

◆

FOCUS QUESTIONS

1. Were you adequately prepared to integrate technology into teaching in your teacher preparation program? If so, describe.

2. What are some major advantages of incorporating technologies in teaching?

3. How might you use the Internet as a teaching tool?

4. How might you use email as a teaching tool?

5. Do you know how to incorporate a PowerPoint presentation in your teaching?

Over the last twenty years computer technology has played an increasingly important role in schools and classrooms. Preparing students for the global workplace by teaching them to use computer technologies has been imperative. Teachers who incorporate technologies in their teaching model for students the practicality and usefulness of technology. Teachers have found that technology is a powerful means to promote teaching and learning. Although technology can never replace a competent teacher, it can aid the instructional process. Today's teachers must feel comfortable using technology to promote learning when and wherever feasible. Knowing how and when to employ technology in your teaching is the essence of good teaching with technology.

RESPOND

How technologically competent are you?

Check off below the technologies and/or instructional strategies you feel most proficient in using in your teaching:

_____ Word processing

_____ Faxes

_____ E-mail

_____ DVD player

_____ Attaching files to e-mail

_____ Scanners

_____ Video cameras

_____ Digital cameras

_____ Information retrieval on WWW

_____ Computer assisted instruction (CAI)

_____ Web page design

_____ PowerPoint presentations

_____ Desktop publishing

_____ Electronic grade book

_____ Other

Did you check off "word processing?" Typing, using grammar and spell checks, merging documents, using the Thesaurus, cutting and pasting . . . all familiar to you? Do you accept and encourage student work that has been word processed? What about using a spreadsheet to record student grades? Have you placed all your students in a database file for easy access to information on each student? Do you at times allow students to use handheld spell-checkers, dictionaries, electronic calendars, and the like? Have you supported your teaching with CAI—computer assisted instruction? If so, in what curriculum areas? Did CAI improve student learning of the material? Although you may regularly use cassette players/recorders and televisions (VCR and/or DVD), have you ever used encyclopedia, atlas, or dictionary CD-ROMS? Have you set up a Listerv with your students? If not, what about use of e-mail as a form of communication and discussion?

If you are not comfortable with using technology as a personal means of communication or learning, you are unlikely to want to incorporate it into your teaching. All new teachers, it sees to me, must understand the importance of technology in society, why it's imperative for students to become technologically literate, and how to use some aspect of technology as a teaching tool. Research demonstrates that when teachers model technology use in their classrooms, students are more likely to incorporate it as a meaningful learning tool (Bitter & Pierson, 2002).

Although not using technology to assist and augment instruction simply doesn't make sense, don't think technology, alone, makes for effective teaching. Teaching is an art form that certainly can be enhanced by presenting information in innovative and creative ways. Become familiar with how technology can help you present information in different, more efficient ways. Incorporate use of technology into your lessons. Using PowerPoint to present content, for instance, is a very effective use of technology (see PowerPoint lesson plan later in this chapter). PowerPoint is a simple graphics program that can be used to create slides to display information in creative ways. Attend a seminar or take a class on how to develop a PowerPoint presentation (for a PowerPoint tutorial, visit http://homepage.cs.uri.edu/tutorials/csc101/powerpoint/ppt.html). It's not difficult at all (visit http://www.microsoft.com/office/PowerPoint/default.asp). A great Web site to help students learn to use PowerPoint, including a teacher's guide, can be found at http://www.actden.com/pp/. Become familiar with the use of a laptop along with the LCD projector. What other ways have you seen technology used in the classroom?

The purpose of this chapter is not to teach you how to use a word processor or to design a Web page. Rather, the purpose here is to highlight a few practical strategies or ideas to improve student learning. Discussion will center on using the Internet as a teaching tool (Leu & Leu, 2000). Readers interested in a comprehensive treatment of many technologies in a relatively easy to understand format consult, Bitter and Pierson's (2002) *Using Technology in the Classroom*.

In light of our discussion of standards in Chapter 7, I have extracted below (with permission) important technology standards published by the International Society for Technology in Education (ISTE), the major association promoting good teaching and learning in technology (subscribe to their outstanding journal, *Learning & Leading with Technology*). Peruse these standards to get a sense of what students are expected to know and do throughout the various grade levels. Then, see the reflection activity that follows.

K–12 TECHNOLOGY STANDARDS

NT.K–12.1 Basic Operations and Concepts

- Students demonstrate a sound understanding of the nature and operation of technology systems.
- Students are proficient in the use of technology.

NT.K–12.2 Social, Ethical, and Human Issues

- Students understand the ethical, cultural, and societal issues related to technology.
- Students practice responsible use of technology systems, information, and software.
- Students develop positive attitudes toward technology uses that support lifelong learning, collaboration, personal pursuits, and productivity.

NT.K–12.3 Technology Productivity Tools

- Students use technology tools to enhance learning, increase productivity, and promote creativity.
- Students use productivity tools to collaborate in constructing technology-enhanced models, prepare publications, and produce other creative works.

NT.K–12.4 Technology Communication Tools

- Students use telecommunications to collaborate, publish, and interact with peers, experts, and other audiences.
- Students use a variety of media and formats to communicate information and ideas effectively to multiple audiences.

NT.K–12.5 Technology Research Tools

- Students use technology to locate, evaluate, and collect information from a variety of sources.
- Students use technology tools to process data and report results.
- Students evaluate and select new information resources and technological innovations based on the appropriateness for specific tasks.

NT.K–12.6 Technology Problem-Solving and Decision-Making Tools

- Students use technology resources for solving problems and making informed decisions.
- Students employ technology in the development of strategies for solving problems in the real world.

SOURCE: Reprinted with permission from *National Education Technology Standards for Students Connecting Curriculum and Technology*, copyright © 2000, ISTE (International Society for Technology in Education), iste@iste.org. All rights reserved. Permission does not constitute an endorsement by ISTE.

PROFILES FOR TECHNOLOGY-LITERATE STUDENTS

Performance Indicators for Technology-Literate Students—Grades PreK–2

Prior to completion of Grade 2, students will:

1. Use input devices (e.g., mouse, keyboard, remote control) and output devices (e.g., monitor, printer) to successfully operate computers, VCRs, audiotapes, and other technologies. (1)

2. Use a variety of media and technology resources for directed and independent learning activities. (1, 3)

3. Communicate about technology using developmentally appropriate and accurate terminology. (1)

4. Use developmentally appropriate multimedia resources (e.g., interactive books, educational software, elementary multimedia encyclopedias) to support learning. (1)

5. Work cooperatively and collaboratively with peers, family members, and others when using technology in the classroom. (2)

6. Demonstrate positive social and ethical behaviors when using technology. (2)

7. Practice responsible use of technology systems and software. (2)

8. Create developmentally appropriate multimedia products with support from teachers, family members, or student partners. (3)

9. Use technology resources (e.g., puzzles, logical thinking programs, writing tools, digital cameras, drawing tools) for problem solving, communication, and illustration of thoughts, ideas, and stories. (3, 4, 5, 6)

10. Gather information and communicate with others using telecommunications, with support from teachers, family members, or student partners. (4)

Grades 3–5

Prior to completion of Grade 5, students will:

1. Use keyboards and other common input and output devices (including adaptive devices when necessary) efficiently and effectively. (1)

2. Discuss common uses of technology in daily life and the advantages and disadvantages those uses provide. (1, 2)

3. Discuss basic issues related to responsible use of technology and information and describe personal consequences of inappropriate use. (2)

4. Use general purpose productivity tools and peripherals to support personal productivity, remediate skill deficits, and facilitate learning throughout the curriculum. (3)

5. Use technology tools (e.g., multimedia authoring, presentation, Web tools, digital cameras, scanners) for individual and collaborative writing, communication, and publishing activities to create knowledge products for audiences inside and outside the classroom. (3, 4)

6. Use telecommunications efficiently to access remote information, communicate with others in support of direct and independent learning, and pursue personal interests. (4)

7. Use telecommunications and online resources (e.g., e-mail, online discussions, Web environments) to participate in collaborative problem-solving activities for the purpose of developing solutions or products for audiences inside and outside the classroom. (4, 5)

8. Use technology resources (e.g., calculators, data collection probes, videos, educational software) for problem solving, self-directed learning, and extended learning activities. (5, 6)

9. Determine which technology is useful and select the appropriate tool(s) and technology resources to address a variety of tasks and problems. (5, 6)

10. Evaluate the accuracy, relevance, appropriateness, comprehensiveness, and bias of electronic information sources. (6)

Grades 6–8

Prior to completion of Grade 8, students will:

1. Apply strategies for identifying and solving routine hardware and software problems that occur during everyday use. (1)

2. Demonstrate knowledge of current changes in information technologies and the effect those changes have on the workplace and society. (2)

3. Exhibit legal and ethical behaviors when using information and technology, and discuss consequences of misuse. (2)

4. Use content-specific tools, software, and simulations (e.g., environmental probes, graphing calculators, exploratory environments, Web tools) to support learning and research. (3, 5)

5. Apply productivity/multimedia tools and peripherals to support personal productivity, group collaboration, and learning throughout the curriculum. (3, 6)

6. Design, develop, publish, and present products (e.g., Web pages, videotapes) using technology resources that demonstrate and communicate curriculum concepts to audiences inside and outside the classroom. (4, 5, 6)

7. Collaborate with peers, experts, and others using telecommunications and collaborative tools to investigate curriculum-related problems, issues, and information, and to develop solutions or products for audiences inside and outside the classroom. (4, 5)

8. Select and use appropriate tools and technology resources to accomplish a variety of tasks and solve problems. (5, 6)

9. Demonstrate an understanding of concepts underlying hardware, software, and connectivity, and of practical applications to learning and problem solving. (1, 6)

10. Research and evaluate the accuracy, relevance, appropriateness, comprehensiveness, and bias of electronic information sources concerning real-world problems. (2, 5, 6)

Grades 9–12

Prior to completion of Grade 12, students will:

1. Identify capabilities and limitations of contemporary and emerging technology resources and assess the potential of these systems and services to address personal, lifelong learning, and workplace needs. (2)

2. Make informed choices among technology systems, resources, and services. (1, 2)

3. Analyze advantages and disadvantages of widespread use and reliance on technology in the workplace and in society as a whole. (2)

4. Demonstrate and advocate legal and ethical behaviors among peers, family, and community regarding the use of technology and information. (2)

5. Use technology tools and resources for managing and communicating personal/professional information (e.g., finances, schedules, addresses, purchases, correspondence). (3, 4)

6. Evaluate technology-based options, including distance and distributed education, for lifelong learning. (5)

7. Routinely and efficiently use online information resources to meet needs for collaboration, research, publications, communications, and productivity. (4, 5, 6)

8. Select and apply technology tools for research, information analysis, problem-solving, and decision-making in content learning. (4, 5)

9. Investigate and apply expert systems, intelligent agents, and simulations in real-world situations. (3, 5, 6)

10. Collaborate with peers, experts, and others to contribute to a content-related knowledge base by using technology to compile, synthesize, produce, and disseminate information, models, and other creative works. (4, 5, 6)

REFLECT

How might you address these aforementioned standards in your teaching?

_____

_____

_____

_____

_____

_____

_____

_____

_____

THE INTERNET AS A TEACHING TOOL

The Internet has changed the way we view the world and the way we access information. The Internet is an exciting teaching tool when used appropriately. This section will highlight some ways you can use the Internet in the classroom to promote student learning.

First, what is the Internet? Simply, the Internet is a set of computers that are connected to one another by virtue of a shared language. The Internet includes e-mail and the World Wide Web (WWW or simply, the Web). Although the U.S. Department of Defense in the 1960s first developed the Internet, the first Web pages didn't appear until the early 1990s. Today there are millions of Web pages. The Internet is ideal for communication and the exchange of information. E-mail is used to send messages. The Web of the Internet is an invaluable source of information for teachers and students. But how can the Web be used as a teaching tool? Here are some suggestions:

- **Researching topics or reinforcing learning**—Why not encourage Internet use by guiding students to various Web sites with relevant information on a given topic. Why not encourage your students, in Boston, to visit the Australian rain forests? (Send them to http://www.latrobe.edu.au/botany/rainforests/.) Say you just completed that topic and wish students to compare and contrast rain forests around the world. Guide them to the Internet. Acquainting them with various search engines is critical. Although many search engines exist (e.g., www.yahoo.com, www.infoseek.com, or www.dogpile.com), why not lead them to my favorite, www.google.com? Students can simply type in the information they are seeking. Using quotation marks around their key words will help focus the search, as in, "tropical rain forests." Similarly, if the class has read a novel, the teacher may gather information for herself from the Internet (see below) as well as lead students to follow-up information on the Web. For instance, if fifth or sixth grade students have read *The Devil's Arithmetic* they may be guided to various relevant Web sites as a follow-up activity. Students are generally enthused about learning more about a topic on the Web that was first discussed in class.

The Devil's Arithmetic, Jane Yolen, 1990, Puffin (Reprint edition), ISBN: 0140345353

Summary: This popular novel among ages 9 to 12, tells the story of Hannah, a young girl living in New Rochelle, New York who goes with her family to her grandparents' house for the Passover Seder. She wonders why she always has to celebrate holidays with her relatives, and why she is always told, "remember." Finally, she finds out. That night when Hannah opens the front door as part of the Passover ceremony, she is somehow transported to a strange place. She finds herself in a Jewish shtetl (village) in the 1940s. Everyone she meets seems to know who she is and keeps calling her Chaya. As her past life in New Rochelle quickly fades, the Nazis suddenly take her, along with her family, to a concentration/annihilation camp. While in the camp, she learns why she must "remember." Chaya [Hannah] gradually forgets her old identity and begins to live just to survive another day. When three of her friends are selected to be sent to the gas chambers, Chaya heroically changes places with Rivka, thereby saving Rivka's life. Chaya is sent to the gas chambers where she is killed. The final chapter of the book transports Chaya [Hannah] back to modern day to the exact moment she left, during Passover dinner. Hannah returns to the table to complete the celebration where she talks with her aunt and discovers that in her aunt's Polish village she was known as Rivka. The story is well written, poignant, and has wide appeal not only for younger audiences, but also for young adults.

Authenticity: Though the time travel may seem contrived, the author's powerful writing style captivates readers. The book is well researched and full of accurate historical facts about the Holocaust experience, especially in the annihilation camps.

Cautions: This book deals primarily with the realities of life in concentration and annihilation camps. The teacher should be sensitive to how some students may react to the horrors that befell people there. Only the barest facts about the camps should be related to this age group. Also, some reviewers have difficulty with the book's use of fantasy. I personally do not find its use offensive.

Teaching ideas: While I do not recommend that concentration and annihilation camps be discussed in any great length to this age group, this book, more than any other, is a sensitively written account. Students should be able to recognize the value of family traditions, friendship, and courage as well as to be able to analyze the factors that contributed to survival in the camps. The following guiding and follow-up statements/questions are suggested:

- Have you ever imagined yourself at another time and another place? Describe.
- What do you think it would feel like to live during the 1940s in Europe as a Jew?
- Describe, through Chaya's experiences, what life was like in the camp?
- What qualities did Chaya possess?
- How did the author make you believe that Hannah was actually "there"? Could the author have done a better job? Explain.
- Pretend you are Hannah and tell your mom what happened in all its detail and how it felt.
- What lessons did Hannah learn from her unique experience?
- Describe how this story moved you to better understand what the Holocaust means.
- Why is it important to remember those that were victims of the Holocaust?
- Create a piece of art (watercolors, oil painting, pen and pencil drawing, charcoal drawing, sculpture, mobile, etc.) depicting life in a concentration camp.

After the book is analyzed in class, the teacher could show the well made movie (video) by the same title. To gain further information about concentration and annihilation camps, the teacher is urged to consult: *Hitler's Death Camps*, Konnilyn G. Feig.

Try this Internet search: www.google.com. Type in *The Devil's Arithmetic*. At least ten different Web sites can be explored for more ideas on using this novel with students. Some sites include interactive lesson plans and online discussion groups for students who have read the book. See, for example, wwwjaneyolen.com/tchrsideas.html. This site is composed of shared ideas and experiences in relation to this novel. It includes child-created artwork, thoughts, and e-mails reacting to the novel.

As we use sources on the web for ourselves or to enhance student learning, we must remain cognizant of the fact that not all Web sites contain accurate information or are useful. Teachers should *always* preview a Web site prior to use in the classroom. Below are some guidelines to assist you in determining the authenticity and usefulness of a site.

CRITERIA FOR EVALUATING WORLD WIDE WEB SITES

Authoritativeness

Poor   Fair   Excellent

The authors are respected authorities in the field.

The authors are knowledgeable.

The authors provide a list of credentials and/or educational background.

The authors represent respected, credible institutions or organizations.

Complete information on references (or sources) is provided.

Information for contacting the authors and webmaster is provided.

Comprehensiveness

All facets of the subject are covered.

Sufficient detail is provided at this site.

Information provided is accurate.

Political, ideological, and other biases are not evident.

Presentation

Poor   Fair   Excellent

Graphics serve an educational, rather than decorative, purpose.

Links are provided to related sites.

What icons stand for is clear and unambiguous.

The Web site loads quickly.

The Web site is stable and seldom, if ever, nonfunctional.

Timeliness

The original Web site was produced recently.

The Web site is updated and/or revised regularly.

Links given at the Web site are up-to-date and reliable.

SOURCE: From F. W. Parkay & B. H. Stanford, *Becoming a Teacher*, 5/e. © 2001. Published by Allyn and Bacon, Boston, MA. Copyright © 2000 by Pearson Education. Reprinted by permission of the publisher.

- **Communicating via e-mail, Listserv, or Newsgroup**—Most students know very well how to communicate via e-mail. Unfortunately, they develop poor habits of writing when they use what my daughter calls short-cuts as in:

> hey sup? . . . nm hows skewl? . . . lol me 2 ill brb . . . back so wats doin? . . . o kool wat u doin in the summer? . . . o well idk yet prob work btw wanna go 2 the park tom? . . . ur so mean!! jk go 4 me ok? ok w/e well neways . . . omg ppl are annoying me!! wats ur # again? . . . kk well srry i gtg gn ttyl mb ill c u tom i dunno kk bb oh b4 i go happy b-day!!! lol!!

Got it? If not, see below:

> Hey what's up? . . . nothing much how's school? . . . lol (that's laughing out loud) me too, I'll be right back . . . back. . . . So what's doing? . . . Oh cool, what are you doing in the summer? . . . Oh, well, I don't know yet, will probably work. By the way, want to go to the park tomorrow? . . . You're so mean!!! Just kidding. Go for me ok? Okay, what-ever well anyways. . . . Oh my gosh, people are annoying me!! What's your number again? . . . Okay, well sorry, I have to go. Good night. Talk to you later. Maybe I'll see you tomorrow. I don't know. Okay, bye-bye. Oh, before I go, "Happy Birthday!!!" lol (laughing out loud)!!!

You can give them better opportunities for writing by using e-mail as a teaching tool. Why not communicate with them, for instance, via e-mail, say, distributing homework assignments. Teach them various skills you want to reinforce, such as writing in complete sentences. In fact, use e-mail to improve writing in general (e.g., punctuation, sentence structure, etc.). Although e-mail is generally used without attention to writing standards, it can be an ideal way to motivate yours students. Also, teach them other skills, such as attaching files. You can require students, for instance, to submit their assignments and papers via e-mail as attachments.

Facilitating use of an appropriate Listerv is a good teaching tool to enhance communication about a particular topic in the curriculum. A Listerv is a network of individuals who communicate with each other on a common topic of interest. With a Listerv you type a message and the entire group will receive it. In essence, it is an automatic e-mail system that receives incoming messages to the subject-specific list and sends out copies to all subscribers. You can establish your own classroom or school Listerv or have students subscribe to ones that you have previewed and approved.

Newsgroups are also very useful ways to exchange information. A newsgroup is a discussion group devoted to a single topic. Users can post messages to the group, read the discussion, and reply to the author individually or post replies that can be read by the whole group. Although similar to a Listserv, a newsgroup is devoted to only one topic at a time and allows individuals to converse with each other on an ongoing basis.

• **Planning instruction**—The Internet can be an invaluable resource for planning instructional activities and units for your students. Many sites exist. In fact, the best book on the topic is *The Internet and the World Wide Web for Teachers* by Eugene Provenzo, Jr. (2002). It is the best resource for accessing excellent Web sites for planning and for student use. Below is a list of some valuable sites:

Musée du Louvre—http://www.paris.org:80/Musees/Louvre/

The Library of Congress—http://lcweb.loc.gov/homepage/lchp.html

The Victoria and Albert Museum—http://www.vam.ac.uk/

Mars Pathfinder—http://mars.jpl.nasa.gov/MPE/index1.html

National Aeronautics & Space Administration—http://www.nasa.gov

Nine Planets Tour—http://www.seds.org/nineplanets/nineplanets/nineplanets.html

Friends and Partners—http://solar.rtd.utk.edu/friends/home.html

Index of Slave Narratives, University of Virginia Hypertext Library—http:// xroads.virginia.edu/~HYPER/wpa/wpahome.html

Ellis Island—http://www.ellisisland.org/

Paris Virtual Tour—http://www.paris.org/AfterHours/

Perseus Project—http://www.perseus.tufts.edu/

Project Libellus—http://www.hhhh.org/perseant/libellus/

Aquarium Museum—http://aqua.ucsd.edu

Monterey Bay Aquarium—http://www.mbayaq.org/

Bartlett's Familiar Quotations—http://www.columbia.edu/acis/bartleby/bartlett

Roget's Thesaurus—http://humanities.uchicago.edu/forms_unrest/ROGET.html

Virtual Reference Desk—http.//thorplus.lib.purdue.edu/reference/index.html

Webster's Dictionary—http://www.m-w.com/netdict.htm

World Atlas on the Web—http://pubweb.parc.xerox.com/map/

Kathy Schrock's Guide for Educators—http://www.capecod.net/schrock-guide/index.htm

Web66—http://web66.coled.umn.edu

Web66 and Web66NT Mailing Lists—http://web66.coled.umn.edu/List/Default.html

Teacher Talk—http://www.mightymedia.com/talk/working.htm

Teachers Helping Teachers—http://www.pacificnet.net/~mandel/

National Education Association—http://www.nea.org/

American Federation of Teachers—http://www.aft.org/index.htm

American Educational Research Association—http://aera.net/

Florida Department of Education—http://www.firn.edu

Diversity—http://www.execpc.com/~dboals/diversit.html

Inclusion Resources—
http://www.hood.edu/seri/serihome.htm#inclusion_resources

Walk a Mile in My Shoes—http://www.wmht.org/trail/explor02.html

Multicultural Pavilion—
http://curry.edschool.Virginia.EDU/go/multicultural

Getty Information Institute—http://www.gii.getty.edu/giibroch/index.html

Exploring content resources on the web—*Using Technology in Classroom* (The following excellent and most up-to-date information is reprinted with permission from Bitter & Pierson, 2002, pp. 166–172. Published by Allyn and Bacon, Boston, MA. Copyright © 1999 by Pearson Education. Reprinted by permission of the publisher.)

The largest category of educational resources on the World Wide Web, and those that are most easily incorporated into instructional plans, are those sites providing some type of content information. National organizations, research institutions, or even individual Internet users with a great interest in a particular topic might maintain these sites. The quality and extent of information will vary greatly between sites, necessitating thorough preview by teachers before students are asked to use them. These types of content sites can be used as minimally as a supplemental or enrichment resource or can supply the backbone of a series of lessons.

Language Arts

Children's Literature Web Guide http://www.ucalgary.ca/~dkbrown/

This is a complete resource locator for those who teach literature to children. The site compiles an annual guide to newly published literature and points the user to annual award lists, such as Newbery and Caldecott. There are discussion areas, links to other children's literature online resources, a multitude of teaching ideas, and lists of current children's best-sellers. Still more links guide users to information on recommended books, authors, and movies based on books, as well as further resources for teachers, parents, and students.

Teaching Tip: Have book clubs in your class select their readings from a list you approve and join a discussion list about the author.

Edsitement <http://edsitement.neh.gov/>

This partnership of the National Endowment for the Humanities and MarcoPolo is the center for humanities resources, lesson plans, and activities on the Web. Separate sections on literature, foreign language, arts, and history create a complete selection of information organized by grade level.

Teaching Tip: High school foreign-language teachers can begin with the provided resources and then branch out to related sites to bring to life the unique cultures students are learning about.

Shakespeare Web <http://www.shakespeare.com/>

Whether used to enrich an established curriculum or to spur an individual interest, many gems of information can be found on Shakespeare Web. Itineraries on a traveling Shakespearean theater company and tidbits on Shakespeare history are highlights.

Teaching Tip: Use this site at the beginning of a middle school Shakespeare unit to research background history.

Mathematics

The Geometry Center <http://www.geom.umn.edu/>

Funded by the National Science Foundation, the Geometry Center develops methods in which technology can be used to visualize and communicate mathematics and related sciences. Serving both academic and industrial fields, this site provides links to geometry references, software, course materials, and distance learning resources. Current projects include such areas as spacecraft design, solar system visualization, and satellite constellation visualization.

Teaching Tip: Have intermediate math students work together to design a space station using geometrical principles. Encourage them to check back with this site frequently to verify calculations and confirm hunches.

Illuminations <http://illuminations.netm.org>

Presented by the National Council of Teachers of Mathematics (NCTM) in partnership with MarcoPolo, Illuminations is a wealth of interactive multimedia lessons, video teaching vignettes, and innovative lesson plans centered on the NCTM standards.

Teaching Tip: Use the math interactive figure for investigating triangles with the whole primary class. Then have students find triangles in your school.

Mega-Mathematics <http://www.c3.lanl.gov/mega-math/>

Mega-Mathematics, a product of Los Alamos National Laboratory, brings very complex mathematical concepts to students in understandable, original ways. Lessons on such topics as colors, graphs, infinity, and algorithms are outlined completely so that teachers are prepared to facilitate the lessons. Lesson components include activities, vocabulary, background information, key concepts, evaluation ideas, relation to NCTM standards, preparation and materials, and indications for further study.

Teaching Tip: Have small groups of students work independently through the "A Usual Day at Unusual School" play. Encourage each group to record their thinking processes on paper. Have groups prepare charts to share their strategies with the rest of the class at the end of the activity. How do the strategies compare?

Science

The Franklin Institute Online <http://sin.fi.edu/tri/welcome.html>
The Franklin Science Museum's online presence is a must-see resource that not only allows a glimpse into the real museum but also gives teachers and students rich learning activities. Content units, problem-solving opportunities, resource "hot lists," and multimedia enhancement are among the many learning resources.

Teaching Tip: Use "The Heart: An Online Exploration," in the Learning Resources section, with younger students studying basic circulatory properties or with older students studying advanced human anatomy and physiology. Students can read the text of the units independently or with a partner. Consider projecting the photo slide shows in front of the whole class as discussion prompts.

Ology <http://ology.amnh.org/>
The American Museum of Natural History presents Ology to demonstrate its belief that "everybody wants to know something." The Ology Web site tells children that if they are curious about something, they are "ologists." The highly interactive and informative resource links students with expert scientists in engaging content-based investigations.

Teaching Tip: Have students collect, sort, and compare "ology cards" to explore more about the specific content, such as the dinosaur varieties in the paleontology exhibit.

SeaWorld and Busch Gardens Animal Information Database <http://www.seaworld.org/>
SeaWorld and Busch Gardens maintain this vast Web site in order to provide an enthusiastic, imaginative, and intellectually stimulating atmosphere for students. Within the site, learners will encounter a list of topics on animal information that spans animal rescue to zoological park careers, including sea turtles, penguins, and even Clydesdales along the way. Teachers can depend on numerous lesson resources and activities designed by the SeaWorld Education Department. Current animal-related news and "Ask Shamu," a frequently asked questions area on animals, round out the resource.

Teaching Tip: Have PreK students choose an animal and work with older "buddy" classes to research their animals. Prereaders can illustrate using photos from the Web site as guides. Older students can synthesize factual information into a format their younger buddies can understand.

Volcanoworld <http://voicano.und.nodak.edu/>

Learn about volcanoes from the experts! This NASA-supported site is loaded with everything you ever wanted to know about volcanoes (see Figure 9.4). You can find the latest information on currently erupting volcanoes, observatories, and monuments, and research on the topic. Learners can access pictures, videos, stories, games, and activities, and they can even send a message to a real volcanologist. Teachers have available extensive lesson plans, and anyone can arrange to be alerted through e-mail of any new eruptions.

Teaching Tip: Use the email alert system to have your students embark on a year-long project to track volcano eruptions. Locate eruptions on a map, use the Web to research the countries in which the eruptions happen, and construct detailed scenarios predicting how the eruptions will impact the affected communities.

Social Studies

The American Civil War Home Page <http://sunsite.utk.edu/civil-war/warweb.html>

The American Civil War Home Page gathers together in one place hypertext links to the most useful electronic files about the American Civil War. The lengthy list of links points to resources on timelines, photographs, specific battles, original documents such as letters and diaries, information on state participation, reenactment groups, and other Civil War organizations.

Teaching Tip: Students can use the vast resources available from this site to plan the sequence of a Civil War unit. After a couple of hours exploring the information available, have students develop concept maps about what they know about the Civil War. Then encourage them to plan how best to "fill in" the gaps in their understanding.

Congress.org <http://congress.org>

This federal site links learners with information on activity in the legislative branch of the government. There is a directory of members, a calendar of events, and a list of legislative committees.

Teaching Tip: Secondary government students can compare information on this site with online news sources and state government sources to interpret different versions of the same events.

EconEdLink <http://www.econedlink.org/>

EconEdLink, produced by the National Council on Economics Education, highlights the economics standards through real-world scenarios. The site provides lessons on authentic, up-to-date economics topics, real financial data, and economics-related news. This is a MarcoPolo partner site.

Teaching Tip: Use the lessons in EconomicsMinute to enrich weekly current events studies by encouraging students to think beyond the news to consider the economic implications of events.

National Geographic Xpeditions <http://www.nationalgeographic. conVxpeditions/main.html>

Xpeditions brings the national geography standards to life in innovative ways that make the most of emerging Web technologies. Students can use the atlas to search for global locations and print detailed maps of any location in the world. They also can locate relevant Web sites to be used to meet the geography standards and explore at home with their families through readings, games, and virtual field trips. By visiting the stunning virtual world of the Expedition Hall, the geography standards come to life in compelling and intriguing ways. Xpeditions is a MarcoPolo partner site.

Teaching Tip: As part of a unit on international relations, use the Culture Goggles feature with the whole class. Have students make predictions about how each of the cultures will respond.

Arts

Artsedge: The National Arts And Education Information Network
<http://artsedge.kennedy-centerorg/artsedge.htmi>

Operating under an agreement between the Kennedy Center for the Performing Arts and the National Endowment for the Arts, and supported by the U.S. Department of Education and MarcoPolo, this massive site is designed to help artists, teachers, and students communicate to support the arts in the K–12 curriculum. The listed projects, performances, and study guides are given to further the stated mission: to connect people to people, to connect people to information and resources, and to build a new base of knowledge in arts and education.

Teaching Tip: Rather than having art students create projects and simply hang them up in the hallway, have students communicate with other classes around the country who are working on similar projects. Comparisons among techniques of artists at different locations can be valuable in the development of artistic skills.

Metropolitan Museum of Art <http://www.metmuseum.org>

The Metropolitan Museum of Art, one of the largest and best-known art museums in the world, presents on this Web site collections of several hundred thousand exhibits at any given time. Exhibits cover world culture from prehistory to the present. The site features a calendar that details special exhibits, concerts, lectures, films, and other museum activities.

- **Using Computer Assisted Instruction (CAI)**—CAI relies on computer programs that provide students with structured drill-and-practice tutorials. Advantages include: enhanced opportunities for individualizing instruction; students can monitor their own work; students can work at their own pace; multisensory experiences (e.g., voice, sound, text, graphics, animation); motivating for students; proven excellent for students at-risk, low functioning students, and students who are English language learners. (For more information see, e.g., http://www.nwrel.org/scpd/sirs/5/cu10.html.) One of the leading companies that sells excellent CAI programs can be found at www.sunburst.com.

Although a list of programs is not provided (because their suitability is ultimately dependent on your needs and given the fact that there are a plethora of programs), see the criteria below to help you evaluate a program that provides for CAI.

CRITERIA FOR EVALUATING SOFTWARE PROGRAMS

User Friendliness

Poor Fair Excellent

How easy is it to start the program?
Is there an overview or site map for the program?
Can students easily control the pace of the program?
Can students exit the program easily?
Can students create their own paths through the
program and develop their own links among elements?
After first-time use, can student bypass
introductory or orientation material?
Does the program include useful hotlinks to
Internet sites?

Inclusiveness

Can students with hearing or visual impairments
make full use of the program?
Can students navigate the program by making
simple key strokes with one hand?
Does the material avoid stereotypes and reflect
sensitivity to racial, cultural, and gender differences?

Textual Material
Poor Fair Excellent

How accurate and thorough is the content?
Is the content well organized and clearly
presented?
Is the textual content searchable?
Can the content be integrated into the curriculum?

Images

Is the image resolution high quality?
Is the layout attractive, "user friendly," and
uncluttered?
Do the graphics and colors enhance instruction?
How true are the colors of the images?
Are the images large enough?
Does the program have a zoom feature
that indicates the power of magnification?
Does the program make effective use of video
and animation?

Audio

Are the audio clips high quality?
Does the audio enhance instruction?

Technical

Is installation of the program easy and trouble-free?
Are instructions clear and easy to follow?
Is user-friendly online help available?
Are technical support people easy to reach, helpful,
and courteous?

Motivational

Does the program capture and hold students' interest?
Are students eager to use the program again?
Does the program give appropriate, motivational
feedback?
Does the program provide prompts or cues to
promote students' learning?

SOURCE: From F. W. Parkay & B. H. Stanford, *Becoming a Teacher*, 5/e © 2001. Published by Allyn and Bacon, Boston, MA. Copyright © 2000 by Pearson Education. Reprinted by permission of the publisher.

• **Creating PowerPoint presentations with Internet links—** Learning to develop your own PowerPoint presentations is exciting for you and will most importantly serve to enthuse your students. Learning PowerPoint is really easy since the program is menu driven. Besides, an excellent tutorial guides you through the program (see tutorial link cited earlier in the chapter). Below is part of a PowerPoint presentation developed by Anthony Vavallo, a master's degree candidate at my institution. His presentation actually teaches his students how to use PowerPoint.

USE OF POWERPOINT IN THE CLASSROOM

Anthony Vavallo

ABSTRACT AND RATIONALE

This unit plan takes students through a five-step process to teach them how to compile a PowerPoint project. It will be implemented to do the following:

1. Enhance writing skills.

2. Enhance computer skills.

3. Promote social interaction in the classroom.

4. Introduce what a PowerPoint project is.

5. Promote the use of technology in the classroom.

Lesson 1

Goals and Objectives:

• Students will be given an opportunity to compile a PowerPoint project.
• Students will prepare the materials to use for their slide project.

Activities:

Students are shown what a PowerPoint project looks like.

Students are given the opportunity to compile an 8-slide template out of folded card stock paper.

Lesson 2

Goals and Objectives:

- Students will have a final draft of their 8-slide template.
- Students will critique each other's work.

Activities:

Students are required to finish the final draft of their 8-slide template.

Students are shown how to "bullet" an idea instead of typing long sentences.

Students are also given the opportunity to critique each other's work.

Lesson 3

Goals and Objectives:

- Students are given an introduction in how to type a PowerPoint project.
- Students will be able to transfer their templates to the actual PowerPoint slides.

Activities:

Students are assigned their own computers to use for the project.

Students are given a tutorial on how to begin a basic PowerPoint project.

Lesson 4

Goals and Objectives:

- Students will be given an introduction to improving their PowerPoint projects.
- Students will be able to change the font, font style, font size, and color.

Activities:

Students are shown how they can change the font, font style, font size, and color in their slide show.

Students are also given an opportunity to add a picture of themselves in the project.

Lesson 5

Goals and Objectives:

- Students will be able to change the format of the slides in their project.
- Students will be given the opportunity to refine their projects for submission to be graded as a final project.

Activities:

Students are given the knowledge and the opportunity to reformat their slide show.

Students will have ample time to complete their projects.

Below is the text file (without the actual PowerPoint slides) of a student who followed Mr. Vavallo's lessons above. You can probably figure out the types of slides the student developed based on the text. Counting the title, the student created 8 slides:

MY YEAR OF THE ROOSTER

By Jacky Yan

Contents

Celebrating Chinese New Year

Chinese Zodiac

Dance of the Dragon and Lion

Food

Clothing

About the Author

Celebrating Chinese New Year

People celebrate Chinese New Year, well, to celebrate the New Year.

Money is given to their family members.

The money represents good luck.

In the New Year festival, the color red appears everywhere.

That's why red is a lucky color.

Chinese Zodiac

People are born in different years.

There is an order of each animal. It goes like this: rat, rabbit, horse, rooster, ox, dragon, goat, dog, tiger, snake, monkey, and pig.

February 1, 2003 is the year of the Goat.

The Goat is artistic and shy.

Dance of the Dragon and Lion

People believe that the dance of the dragon and the lion scare away evil spirits.

Some people believe that firecrackers scare away evil spirits.

People that work in stores put lettuce at the top of the store for the lion.

Sometimes, the lettuce has a red envelope inside.

The money is to help the environment.

Food

People have a big feast with lots of food.

People eat the food to celebrate Chinese New Year.

These are some examples of the food of Chinese New Year: fish, noodles, duck, chicken, pig, rice, and seafood.

Clothing

People wear red to represent the color of China.

They also wear red to celebrate the Chinese New Year.

The idea of wearing red is taken from the red money envelopes.

About the Author

Hi, my name is Jacky Yan.

My favorite year is the year of the Rooster.

I was born in the year of the rooster.

I am 10 years old.

I am in fourth grade.

I was born in 1993.

I think Chinese New Year is cool.

I live in New York.

CONCLUSION

We can't ignore technology. Technology is a tool we can use as educators to enhance the educational experiences of our students. As a professional educator, you are obligated to become technology proficient to the extent to which you can model best practice with students and use it as a viable teaching tool. Although I advocate technological integration in your teaching, you are still the most critical element in the classroom. Technology cannot, by itself, transform lives. Only you can do so. As bell hooks reminds us, "To teach in a manner that respects and cares for the souls of our students is essential if we are to provide the necessary conditions where learning can most deeply and intimately begin."

* * *

FOLLOW-UP QUESTIONS/ACTIVITIES

1. Interview a more experienced teacher and ask how he or she integrates technology in teaching or visit another school that is known for technology integration (if you are really interested in technology, ask your principal to release you for a morning to go visit that school). Find out what technologies are used and how they promote student learning.

2. Create a PowerPoint presentation in a specific content area. Be sure to include Internet links.

3. Which ideas presented in this chapter were of most value? Explain.

4. What further professional development technology activities would you find most useful?

9

How Should I Assess and Grade My Students?

If you want to determine if students can write, have them write something. If you want to determine if students can operate a machine, have them operate a machine. If you want to determine if students can conduct an experiment, have them conduct an experiment. In short, if you want to determine if they can perform a task, have them perform the task.

—Norman E. Gronlund

◆

FOCUS QUESTIONS

1. How will you determine whether or not students in your classroom have learned the material?

2. What is the relationship among measurement, evaluation, and assessment?

3. What is the relationship among performance assessment, alternative assessment, and authentic assessment?

4. What is portfolio assessment?

5. What do you want to learn about assessment?

6. Do you know how to obtain an electronic grade book?

When I began teaching, the only methods I used to determine student achievement were teacher-made tests, primarily, and results from standardized achievement tests. Traditional assessment and evaluations consisted of multiple choice questions, true or false, matching, fill-ins, and so on. Recently, these test formats have received severe criticism (Popham, 2002). It is true that such narrow views of assessment do not really capture all facets of student learning. Relying on these traditional forms of assessment does not consider the full range of student work and achievement. Professional educators today view student achievement in a much more comprehensive way that accurately reflects the varied learning styles and achievements of students.

REFLECT

What forms of assessment were you exposed to as a student in college during teacher preparation? How do teachers in your school currently assess students? How do you plan on doing so?

_____

_____

_____

_____

_____

_____

_____

What's wrong with traditional assessment? The problem is not the traditional testing format itself, but the misuse of the format. We have taken a perfectly good tool and used it for the wrong purpose. A hammer is great for driving nails; it's poor for cutting wood. Multiple-choice tests are very good for comparing to norms and standards; but they are not very good for measuring integration of skills, for providing continuous feedback during the school year, and for evaluating particular are as such as creativity and performing arts ability.

In addition to misusing this format, the scores of traditional assessment affect major decisions such as class placements, promotion, and funding. Moreover, the results do not show well enough how instruction can be improved. It is as if curriculum, evaluation, and teaching methods are three separate areas with very little connection. To overcome these deficiencies, teachers must find the right tools for the right jobs. Certainly, no single test method is the cure for all evaluation needs. Multiple-choice and true-false tests serve their purposes and so do essays, group projects, and the like. By using each effectively, you can take advantage of their strengths.

How should you assess and grade your students? The same way you would want to be assessed and graded. You would want someone to consider the varied ways you learn and not to rely on one or two assessment instruments or tests to determine your grade or readiness for learning. Remember taking a standardized test and how a teacher, administrator, or admission's office might have come to an erroneous conclusion about your readiness for learning based on a single assessment? If you're like me, you would resent such a generalization and categorization of your abilities. My guess is that if you're like me, you'd want to be assessed based on a variety of criteria or assessment instruments that draw a clearer picture of your abilities. That's what holistic assessment is all about; relying on data from a variety of sources in order to inform some sort of decision.

RECOLLECTION

I recall that as a high school student I was a hard worker. I was not brilliant; subject knowledge did not come easy for me, but I always did well in school (an A-student). To achieve high grades I worked and studied very hard and long. I attended class regularly, did the assigned homework, participated eagerly in class, and studied for all exams. Teachers thought highly of me and my potential to succeed.

All that changed rather abruptly, as I recall, after my English teacher saw my score on what was then called the Iowa Achievement Test. I don't know if the test even still exists, but in those days, the 1960s, they were

(Continued)

(Continued)

very popular and were used a great deal. The principal explained to my parents the purpose of the test was to determine the "potential for academic success" of students. "Jeffrey," exclaimed my English teacher in private to me, "I would have thought you'd score much higher." Her look of extreme disappointment and surprise shocked me. "Maybe," I thought to myself, "I am dumb . . . I will not succeed." I can tell you with certainty that my English teacher and several others treated me much differently after reviewing my Iowa score. No longer was I their favorite. I was called upon in class with less frequency. It took me years later to realize how caught up they were with the presumed predictive value of that Iowa test and probably standardized tests in general. We now realize, at least many of us, that to stigmatize students unfairly based on a single score from a standardized test is misdirected. Had teachers at my high school understood the holistic way we should assess student performance they would have utilized and valued alternate forms of assessment to realize that I might have had a bit more potential than my score on that Iowa test indicated.

Have you ever been stigmatized by a standardized test? Explain.

_____

_____

_____

The theme of this chapter is that classroom assessment and grading should rely on a variety of sources in order to make an informed decision about student achievement or even potential for learning. The best way, in my view, for a teacher to make a decision about student learning is to collect data from a variety of sources and to encourage students to develop portfolios that demonstrate their achievement. This chapter introduces you to assessment via the use of portfolio assessment as an ideal, holistic way to accurately assess student learning. First, let me define several terms:

- **Assessment** refers to the process by which a teacher gathers data to determine student achievement in order to provide constructive feedback to improve learning success.
- **Measurement** relies on quantitative data from traditional tests to specify student success in a particular subject (e.g., an 80% on a spelling test)

- **Assessment instrument** refers to any device used to collect data about student achievement, such as a teacher-made test, essay exam, oral presentation, standardized test, and so on.
- **Evaluation** refers to the decision made about student achievement or potential for learning.
- **Grade** refers to the numerical designation given to summarize a student's achievement in a given test or subject.
- **Traditional assessment** refers to the common ways teachers gather information to measure learning that rely exclusively on paper-and-pencil tests, including teacher-made tests and standardized achievement tests.
- **Performance assessments** require students to demonstrate their achievement by actually performing a task (e.g., writing a composition or essay).
- **Alternative assessments** include data from a variety of sources that go beyond traditional paper-and-pencil testing (e.g., oral presentations).
- **Authentic assessments** require students to demonstrate understanding by performing an activity that resembles a real-life situation (e.g., if you wanted to assess the extent to which a student can dribble a basketball you would have the student actually demonstrate dribbling as opposed to asking her to write an essay on dribbling).
- **Holistic assessment** considers traditional forms of assessment along with alternative means to obtain a complete or accurate picture of student learning.
- **Rubric** is a set of scoring guidelines (criteria) for evaluating student work. A rubric specifies standards of performance from minimal to outstanding. See sample rubric for assessing classroom management in Chapter 5.
- **Portfolio assessment** is a vehicle or framework by which a teacher and/or a student collects and presents evidence of student achievement. A student's portfolio, then, will include evidence of learning in a variety of ways. Assessment, therefore, does not rely solely, for example, on paper-and-pencil traditional testing to determine student learning. Alternate forms of assessment (including authentic and performance-based assessments) are encouraged (e.g., essays, oral presentations, artwork, musical performances, videos, etc).

This chapter highlights portfolio assessment as an ideal way to collect evidence of student learning. Portfolio assessment is a form of holistic assessment that includes traditional and alternative forms of assessment. A portfolio would include performance and authentic assessments, where relevant. The portfolio is a vehicle to evaluate student learning so that a teacher might more accurately arrive at a final grade. Suggestions for setting up a system of portfolio assessment are the main foci of the chapter. I also will highlight suggestions for constructing teacher-made tests (true-false, completion, multiple-choice, matching, and essay questions), developing rubrics, and grading students.

In order to reflect upon your own knowledge of assessment and related areas take the self-test instrument that follows in From 9.1, and read the accompanying explanations highlighting some fundamental assessment principles that form a foundation for the remainder of the chapter.

Form 9.1

RESPOND				
SA = Strongly Agree ("For the most part, yes") *A = Agree ("Yes, but . . .")* *D = Disagree ("No, but . . .")* *SD = Strongly Disagree ("For the most part, no")*	*SA*	*A*	*D*	*SD*
1. Teachers need to know about assessment because they need to monitor students' progress.				
2. Effective instruction requires that we expand our concern to a teaching-learning-assessment process, with assessment as a basic part of the instructional program.				
3. Paper-and-pencil testing must be replaced with more realistic and meaningful performance assessments.				
4. Teachers should be skilled in choosing assessment methods appropriate for instructional decisions.				
5. Teachers need to know how valid and reliable a test is.				

SOME FUNDAMENTAL PRINCIPLES OF ASSESSMENT: AN ANALYSIS OF YOUR RESPONSES ABOVE

Teachers indeed need to know about assessment because they need to monitor students' progress. Assessment as a process whereby a teacher gathers data from a variety of sources to help determine the extent of student learning is critical. Without it, a teacher would not know that after a lesson a particular student was experiencing learning difficulty. Teachers, however, need to know about assessment for other reasons. Teachers need to be able to diagnose a student's strengths and weaknesses. If Edward is not comprehending while reading, then you'll have to make some instructional adjustments. Conversely, if Edward already knows how to multiply fractions then preassessing his knowledge would save instructional time. A third reason why teachers need to know about assessment is to assign grades properly. Popham (2002) concisely explains, "The best way to assign grades properly is to collect evidence of a student's accomplishments so that the teacher will have access to ample information before deciding whether to dish out an A, B, C, D, or F to a student" (p. 9). A fourth reason teachers need to assess student progress is to determine the effectiveness of their own instructional program. In other words, how will you know whether or not you are successfully promoting learning unless you pretest students prior to teaching a unit and then posttest them to determine student learning? Results from this pretest/posttest design will indicate whether or not you need to make some instructional alterations. Finally, current pressures reflected in high-stakes testing makes it imperative that teachers become knowledgeable in assessment. High-stakes testing refers to the use of tests to make decisions that strongly impact students, teachers, and schools. Various states, for example, have employed state-delivered tests to determine which students will be granted high school diplomas. High stakes test results also are used by several states to make promotional decisions. High-stakes tests are also used to make judgments about teacher and school performance. Many schools around the nation, for instance, have been labeled as "failing" based on results of standardized tests (Kubiszyn & Borich, 2003). Consequently, teachers are expected more than ever to be conversant in educational testing procedures. As Kubiszyn and Borish (2003) state, "With increasing public pressure for accountability, it does not appear likely that the average teacher will be able to get ahead or even get by without a good working knowledge of test and assessment practice" (p. 16).

The relationship between instruction and assessment is vital. Instructional planning must include assessment planning. As the teacher begins instruction, student readiness for learning must be assessed in order to provide an instructional program relevant to the learner's needs. Pretests of basic skills, arithmetic, or biology will contribute to a rich instructional program by providing the teacher with information to help remedy deficiencies, place students in appropriate learning groups, or use the results as a baseline for future assessments. Although the role of assessment in preplanning is crucial, equally important is its role during instruction. As students are progressing through the curriculum unit, good teachers use tests, to monitor student progress. These formative assessments are "typically designed to measure the extent to which students have mastered the learning outcomes of a rather limited segment of instruction, such as a unit or a textbook chapter" (Gronlund, 2003, p. 6). Diagnosing and remedying student learning problems along the way is key to any successful instructional program. Finally, at the end of instruction, summative assessments are undertaken to determine the extent to which students have mastered the learning outcomes and to determine what grade the teacher should assign.

Paper-and-pencil testing should not be replaced with more realistic and meaningful performance assessments. Rather, teachers should consider *all* forms of assessment to determine student achievement. Teachers should determine which assessment instrument is most appropriate for a particular instructional situation. At times, paper-and-pencil testing is a more practical and accurate measure than an oral presentation. As in the case of portfolio assessment (see below), teachers use a variety of assessment instruments to determine student achievement.

Teachers should indeed be skilled in choosing assessment methods appropriate for instructional decisions, as was mentioned above. How should teachers do so? They should match the specific objective with the assessment instrument or procedure as in, for instance, "Objective: Student will be able to interpret pictographs; Assessment Procedure: Student writes explanation at end of lesson (Minute Paper) and student answers worksheet questions related to pictograph interpretation with at least 2 out of 3 correct. If the teacher stated that she would wait to see results of a teacher-made test given, perhaps, two weeks later or a score on a standardized test, then she would have selected two inappropriate assessment methods in order to make an immediate instructional decision about a student's ability to interpret a pictograph. Obviously, this example is simple. Teachers have to match objectives with assessment procedures on an ongoing basis in all units of instruction. But teachers need other standards for teacher competence in student assessment (*Standards for Teacher Competence in Educational Assessment of Students*, 1990; as cited in Gronlund, 2003). Below you will find the standard, a brief explanation, and a practical suggestion for implementation:

Teachers should be skilled in developing assessment methods appropriate for instructional decisions. When teachers use external assessment instruments (e.g., city standardized reading test), they should utilize the results as part of their overall assessment approach in order to come to some sort of decision about student learning. One practical suggestion for implementing this standard would be for the teacher to identify the subject or specific skill being assessed (e.g., reading comprehension). Then, the teacher should list the various data he will use to arrive at a final report card grade in reading comprehension. He may indicate that he will choose the following list of assessment methods in determining the grade: (a) average of grades on teacher-made tests; (b) responses to questions in in-class reading assignments and activities; (c) average of grades on homework assignments related to reading comprehension; (d) grade given on student-developed portfolio demonstrating reading comprehension; and (e) score obtained on reading comprehension on the citywide standardized test in reading. The teacher would actually organize this list in a form (see Form 9.2) and record a desired weight for each assessment method.

Form 9.2   Using Prespecified Standards to Interpret Data for Student X on "Reading Comprehension"

Assessment Method	Standard Desired	Weight	Final Grade
Teacher-made tests	A = 90% B = 80%+, etc.	30%	
In-class reading	Satisfactory rating on rubric	25%	
Homework	A = 90% B = 80%+, etc.	5%	
Portfolio section	Satisfactory rating on rubric	25%	
Citywide test	Grade-equivalent score (on-grade level, etc.)	15%	

Teachers should be skilled in administering, scoring, and interpreting the results of both externally produced and teacher-produced assessment methods. Teachers must not only be able to select appropriate assessment methods, they must also be able to apply them properly. One practical suggestion for implementing this standard would be for the teacher to become familiar with, for instance, standardized achievement tests. Widely used in schools, these tests are primarily norm-referenced tests in that they compare student performance to the performance of a representative sample of students in a norm group (e.g., a group of seventh graders at the national, regional, or state level). Administration of these tests follows a prescribed simple format. Scoring of these tests is beyond the purview of teachers. Interpreting the scores, however, is within a teacher's purview, although greatly influenced by the interpretations of school administrators and school board members who are, in turn, influenced by public perception. Nevertheless, the teacher should become familiar with two of the most common ways scores are compared: percentile ranks (e.g., a student who scores at the 70th percentile scores higher than 70% of students who took the exam) and grade equivalent scores (e.g., a third-grade student who scores a 3.5 in reading, according to the test results, is in the fifth month on the third grade level. If another student scores a 6.4, it doesn't mean that the student is reading at the sixth grade and four month level; it does indicate that the student is reading very well for his grade level). Although books on assessment explain in detail the meaning of standard scores, standard deviations, z scores, T-scores, and so on, these scores are infrequently used in comparison to the two previously mentioned ones and are, in my estimation, not essential knowledge for classroom teachers.

Teachers should be skilled in using assessment results when making decisions about individual students, planning teaching, developing curriculum, and school improvement. Teachers must play a vital role when participating in decision making at each of these levels. Administrators must include teachers in such decision-making activities. One practical suggestion for implementing this standard is for schools (i.e., principals) to develop ongoing and meaningful professional development for teachers in these areas and to involve teachers in decision-making processes (e.g., school-based decision teams handling curriculum development and school improvement). Teachers should advocate for such participation.

Teachers should be skilled in developing valid pupil grading procedures that use pupil assessments. For example, teachers must understand and appreciate the significance of grading as an essential part of professional practice. Grading procedures should be made known to students in advance of learning. After all, don't you want to know in your graduate course how you will be graded? Grades should be assigned based on the extent to which instructional objectives have been achieved. In determining a grade, will attendance and participation count? If so, how much? One practical suggestion for implementing this standard is for teachers to discuss with students during the first day of instruction how he or she will grade student performance. The class requirements that follow describe the grading procedure I use with my college students.

CLASS REQUIREMENTS

The course requirements are as follows:

1. Book Review (20%)

Student will select a book on a topic that has been approved by the professor. A brief book review is to be written (2 to 5 pages). Review must include a title page, summary, implications, and recommendation. Review should be divided into three labeled sections: summary, implications, and recommendation. Evaluation criteria are:

Content: Is reviewer knowledgeable of content and related critical issues?

Citation: Is book cited in APA form?

Coherence: Is paper well organized and are ideas developed clearly? Are implications reflectively developed?

Conciseness: Are summary, implications, and recommendation relevant, yet concise?

Control: Does writing style reflect "good" technical control?

2. Critical Issues Paper (20%)

Student will select an issue or perspective and write a well-reasoned essay in 3 to 5 pages. Evaluation criteria are:

Content: Knowledge base, relevance, and significance

Coherence: Organization

Clarity: Readability

Control: Writing style

Analysis: Reflective insights

3. Research Paper (20%)

Student will collect three articles on a preselected, approved topic. The research paper will include summary and implications sections. Evaluation criteria are:

Content

Format

Citation

Control

4. Discussion Groups (20%)

Students will select a theme to report on to class. Class discussions will ensue. Evaluation criteria are:

Content

Presentation style

Poise

Sufficient discussion time

Response to audience questions

5. Final Examination (20%)

Student will be administered an examination based on class lectures and relevant readings. Course grade will be computed by averaging scores on the above mentioned assignments. Numerical equivalents for grades are:

    90+   average = A
    88–89 average = A–
    85–87 average = B+
    80–84 average = B
    70–79 average = C

Incompletes are offered at 1/2 reduction of grade. Extra credit assignments (with the prior approval of professor) can raise a grade by a half, as long as assignment is handed in by last class session.

6. Attendance and Participation in Class Are Important

Up to 3 points can be added to the student's average for attendance and participation, as follows:

Attendance points (0–3)

    (0–1 absence) = 3 points

    (2 absences) = 2 points

    (3 absences) = 1 point

    (4 absences) = 0

    (5 or more) = failure

    (Note: two tardies = 1 absence)

Participation points (0–3)

    Very active and coherent participation = 3 points

    Active and coherent participation = 2 points

    Occasional, yet coherent participation = 1 point

    Little, if any, participation = 0 points

You can ask professor at the end of the course how many points you earned. Attendance and participation points will be totaled and divided by 2, resulting in the points added to your average to determine your final course grade.

Teachers should be skilled in communicating assessment results to students, parents, other lay audiences, and other educators. Teachers should publicize their assessment plan not only to their students but also to parents and school officials. Publicizing the plan will avert misunderstandings and possible misuses of results. One practical suggestion for implementing this standard is for teachers to first share their assessment plan with the building supervisors to solicit their input and approval. Teachers should then write a detailed letter to parents explaining the assessment plan. Teachers should use conferences with parents as additional opportunities to open lines of communication and parent involvement. Such practices will, at the very least, minimize parent complaints (e.g., "Why and how did my child receive *that* grade?").

Teachers should be skilled in recognizing unethical, illegal, and otherwise inappropriate assessment methods and uses of assessment information. Teachers should justly administer their assessment plan so that all students are treated and evaluated fairly. Teachers should behave ethically by avoiding cheating or illegally providing students, for instance, with answers or information that would give them advantages on a particular test. Teachers should not teach-to-the-test nor be caught up in the pressures, usually placed on them by administrators, to ensure student achievement at all costs. We've all heard horror stories of teachers providing students with actual test questions in advance or actually changing answers on exams. One practical suggestion for implementing this standard is for teachers to assign grades that accurately reflect student achievement. The following six guidelines for effective and fair grading (drawn, in part, from Gronlund, 2003) are important:

1. Inform students, parents, and administrators at the beginning of instruction what grading procedures will be used, as explained above.

2. Base grades on student achievement, and achievement only. Extraneous factors such as misbehavior and tardiness should be dealt with separately from grading. If you, for instance, detract points from a student's exam because she misbehaved in class, then you lessen the impact of the achievement test. No longer does the score indicate achievement in science, for example.

3. Base grades on a wide variety of valid assessment data. As intimated earlier, sole reliance on paper-and-pencil tests is unfair because they assess only a narrow range of abilities. Alternative forms of assessments should be employed (e.g., evaluations of oral presentations, projects, laboratory work, recitals, etc.).

4. Ensure that students do not cheat. Many studies demonstrate that most students have cheated at one time or another. My guess is that most teachers would claim that no cheating ever goes on in their class because they are vigilant about student cheating. My guess is also that many of these teachers are unaware of the prevalence of cheating in their classrooms. Teachers can discourage cheating by changing the exam format and questions asked during each administration. Students may have copies of previous examinations and if the teacher does not change the items, some students (those who have the previous exams) have an unfair advantage. I know of one teacher who claims she collects the exam booklets, therefore "none of my students could possibly have the exam." Consequently, she rarely, if ever, altered the exam format or questions. We later discovered that copies of her exam were distributed on a Web site. Teachers cannot effectively grade if cheating is not kept in check.

5. For essay-type exams have students write their names on the back of the exam booklet to avoid the dangers of negative or positive teacher

expectations. If Mario is a stellar student and you know that you are reading Mario's paper you will naturally tend to expect Mario to do well on the essay. Conversely, if Donald is a low-achieving student, you might tend to grade it accordingly. Grading exams without knowing whose paper you're grading might avert the influence of teacher expectations that might affect grading.

6. Don't give undue added weight to standardized achievement tests, especially when they radically contradict in-class or school-wide assessments. Some students simply don't perform well on high-stakes tests. Although these tests should not be ignored, consider student performance over time on these tests rather than relying on a single score in a given year. Try to diagnose a student's weakness area on these exams and provide proper instructional support to improve achievement. Moreover, consider the range of assessment instruments holistically in determining a final grade in a particular subject.

Teachers indeed need to know the validity and reliability of a test. According to Gronlund (2003, p. 201), "The two most important questions to ask about a test or other assessment procedure are: (a) To what extent will the interpretation of the results be appropriate, meaningful, and useful? (that's validity), and (b) To what extent will the results be free from errors? (that's reliability)."

Validity

Validity refers to the extent to which a test, survey, or some other instrument measures what it is intended to measure. If I wanted to assess your knowledge of some aspect of educational research, I could administer a test. If the pretest was comprised of mathematical questions only, then the test would *not* be valid, as it did not measure your knowledge of research but rather your ability to compute and solve mathematical problems. For a test to be valid, it must, in simple language, test what it's supposed to test.

There are four general types of validity: *concurrent, construct, content,* and *predictive.* Descriptions of each type of validity are not necessary since most classroom teachers are unlikely to ever need to use all four types of validity.

Perhaps the only exception would be use of *content* validity. When administering a test to assess your knowledge of research, I would undertake a content analysis of the curriculum or knowledge base of educational research, as I intend to teach it. The test items would be compared to the *content* base to ascertain that the questions on the test reflect the content.

Have you ever taken a test in which you said, "We never covered this stuff!"? If you were to administer, for example, a test to a group of 12th graders

based on Chapter 10 in their social studies textbook, you would check for
content validity after writing the test to see whether or not answers to each
question can be found in the chapter. If each question is, in fact, derived from
the content of Chapter 10, then your test may be said to have *content* validity.
By the way, determining content validity for standardized tests involves more
sophisticated procedures.

Two other types of validity, although not thought of highly by many experts
in the field, are useful for classroom teachers: *consensual* and *face* validity.

Consensual validity would be ascertained by asking people who will not be
administered the test or survey (e.g., a colleague or a student in another
class) whether or not the questions selected for inclusion are appropriate
given the purpose of the assessment. Reviewers of these test or survey
items may indicate ambiguously worded items, for instance, thus causing
you to revise the item. Once an instrument is shown to several individuals
and corrections made, the survey or test is said to have achieved consensual
validity.

Face validity would be ascertained by asking participants or subjects to
share their views about how valid a test or survey appears. Ever take an examination that was fair because it accurately reflected the content of the course?
Such an exam might have high face validity. The converse could, of course, also
be true if the content of the course didn't match the questions asked on the
exam.

Reliability

Reliability refers to the degree to which an instrument yields consistent
results under repeated administrations. When you hear the term "reliability,"
you should immediately think of "consistency." Usually, if you wanted to know
whether a particular instrument was reliable, you would consult the test
maker's manual. Reliability, whether reported by a manual or computed on
one's own, is reported in terms of a correlation coefficient. The closer the coefficient of correlation, which is expressed in hundredths, comes to + 1.00, the
higher the reliability factor. Thus, for instance, a reliability coefficient of .80
would indicate that the instrument (e.g., a test) is reliable. Remember that no
test is ever 100% reliable.

Common reliability tests include:

1. *Test-retest method,* in which the same test is repeated over a period of
   time. Two test administrations are required. Correlations are taken
   between the two sets of test results. The resultant correlation coefficient
   is the index of reliability. Note that correlations can be inflated if the time
   interval between tests is short. Why do you think this is so?

2. *Parallel (or equivalent) forms method is* similar to the previous method, in which you retest the same group with an equivalent form of the test. This method requires two administrations (Form A of the test administered, for instance, in September, and then Form B administered to the same group in March). The two sets of scores are correlated as they were in the test-retest method.

3. *Split-half method,* in which the test is split into two parts (or halves), such as odd-numbered items and even-numbered items. The test is administered to the same group. Two sets of scores are obtained for each person: a score based on the odd-numbered items and a score based on the even-numbered items. These two sets of scores are correlated to obtain a reliability coefficient. Note that the longer the test, the more reliable the test will be. Why do you think this is so?

4. *KR-21* (Kuder-Richardson Formula), used to measure the consistency of an instrument in which all items have the same characteristic or degree of difficulty. Tests that include diverse items or varied levels of difficulty should be subjected to split-half reliability assessments.

5. *Interrater reliability* (also known as *internal reliability)* involves comparing ratings or rankings given by independent observers. The more similar the rankings, the higher the reliability. Interrater reliability, therefore, refers to the percentage of agreement among independent observers. Teachers use this form of reliability in grading standardized writing tests. Three teachers rate a given essay separately and an average score is then computed. In this way, no single rating is given preference. This is sometimes referred to as holistic scoring.

Reliability is enhanced by use of multiple data sources. In other words, the more assessment instruments you use, the more reliable your grade for a student will be in a given subject. Why do you think this is so?

Discussion of validity and reliability leads us to consider the construction of classroom tests, which are the traditional and main ways teachers assess student learning. The information that follows outlines guidelines for general test construction and preparing objective test items including true-false, completion, multiple-choice, matching, and essay questions. The bulleted items are meant to serve as general guidelines rather than detailed prescriptions for use in test construction. It is likely you were introduced to these ideas in a graduate course on measurement and evaluation or will receive some professional development or coaching as a new teacher in your school. If your experience is like mine, then you'll have to fill in the gaps on your own. Hopefully, these guidelines, drawn from the work of MacDonald and Healy (1999), are useful.

CONSTRUCTING CLASSROOM TESTS

General Guidelines for Test Construction

The following are some general guidelines to keep in mind as you approach the work of test construction:

1. Have some questions that are easy enough for every student in the class to answer correctly. Begin with the least difficult question so all students will get a good start and will be encouraged to go on to the questions that follow.

2. Make test items reflect instructional aims and the content taught. Test teaching objectives in proportion to their importance. If the test overemphasizes, under emphasizes, or omits representative portions of learned content, it will lose validity.

3. Watch the vocabulary level of test items. To be valid, your test should measure the content students have learned, not reading ability (unless previously stated).

4. Make it easy for students to demonstrate what they have learned. Do not allow writing ability, or speed in test taking to be a factor in student success. Everyone should have a chance to do well on the test.

5. Make sure test directions are entirely clear to students. Ensure that students don't miss an item because they misunderstood the details for answering it.

6. Place all items of the same type together so students are not confused.

7. Include several test items for each objective. This will give students ample opportunity to demonstrate competence, thus avoiding the possibility that a chance error could give a false assessment of ability.

8. Include all the information and material students need to complete each item. When you have to provide missing information or when students find it necessary to stop working to seek clarifications, the reliability of the test is affected.

9. When one of your purposes is to determine differences in students' achievement, do not allow choices in the questions to be answered.

You must use exactly the same measuring instrument for everyone, otherwise you jeopardize validity.

10. Make more items than you will use. Select only the best items, then rework them as necessary to make the test reflect your best professional effort. The final product off the duplicating or copy machine should be neat, grammatically perfect, and clear.

Choosing and Preparing Objective Test Items

The preceding guidelines for constructing tests in general apply specifically to the development of objective tests. Among the most common varieties of objective test items are true-false, completion, multiple-choice, and matching questions.

True-False Questions

In this familiar type of objective test item, students are given statements they are to judge for accuracy. This kind of test can be useful for finding out if students can discriminate fact from opinion and valid from invalid generalizations. To rule out guessing (which would affect the reliability of the test item), students need to be called on to justify their answers with a sentence telling why they answered one way rather than another. On the surface, a true-false test seems simple to construct, but to produce true-false items that are free from ambiguity or false leads is usually a challenge. By taking the following precautions, however, you can avoid some of the main snags in making good true-false tests:

1. Avoid broad generalizations. Words like *always* and *never* can serve as clues that statements are false.

2. Attempt to keep a balance between true (T) and false (F) statements.

3. Avoid using negative statements as items when possible. If you do use a negative construction, be sure the key word is underlined or capitalized to call attention to it (e.g., not, NEVER).

4. Use clear language for questions. Textbook wording is likely to test memory rather than understanding.

True-false tests have the following major advantages:

1. Items can be scored easily.

2. Directions for true-false items are easy for students to understand.

3. A good number of items can be answered in a short time.

4. They are good for initiating discussions and for pretesting.

5. They are a quick way to test for simple factual knowledge.

These are their main weaknesses:

1. It is difficult to avoid ambiguous items because a statement is seldom entirely true or entirely false.

2. Unless students are required to give reasons for their answers, student performance is subject to guessing and chance effects, thus affecting test validity.

3. True-false tests tend to encourage memorization and guessing.

Completion Questions ("Gap-Fillers")

These are statements with important words or phrases left out that are to be written in by the test taker. These items are useful in testing whether students actually know anything because they require the student to supply information that is not visible in the test. The following ideas should be helpful to you in developing completion questions:

1. Be sure students know what is expected in terms of length and detail in their answers.

2. Word the item so only one correct answer is possible. "Michelangelo was a famous_____" would be a poor question of this type because there are a number of answers that would be equally correct (among them "Italian," "male," "painter").

3. Supply enough context in the statement to give the item meaning. The following is an example of an item with an inadequate ratio of words provided to words omitted: "The_____protects_____, liberty, and _____.

4. Avoid grammatical clues such as a blank following the letter a, which indicates that the missing word(s) would begin with a consonant.

5. Design questions so only significant words are omitted. A poor example would be, "Washington _____the Delaware to defeat the Hessians."

6. Use a direct question if possible, and avoid textbook language.

The main advantages of completion items:

1. They are easy to construct and relatively easy to mark.

2. They allow a rapid survey of information over a large area of content.

3. Students find it difficult to guess right answers.

4. They are useful when recall is all that is required.

Their central weaknesses are:

1. It is difficult to construct items for which there is only one correct answer.

2. When used exclusively, or excessively, completion items tend to encourage memorized learning of isolated facts rather than understanding.

Multiple-Choice Questions

These are the most commonly used form of objective test items, and they can be used in all subject areas. A multiple-choice item contains two major components, its stem and its alternative answers. The stem may be phrased as a question or a simple statement: "Most automobiles are propelled by." Of the alternative responses, one is the correct answer and the others are the distractors, so-called because they are intended to mislead students who are not certain of the correct answer. In this case, the alternative responses might be:

a. A steam engine
b. An electric storage battery
c. An internal combustion engine
d. A solar cell

Multiple-choice questions are relatively versatile types of test items because, depending on the complexity of the item, they can assess recognition of information that has been memorized as well as some kinds of higher-level thinking. To produce good items requires considerable skill and attention to detail. The following guidelines apply to the development of multiple-choice tests:

1. The stem of the question should be clear and contained separately from the possible answers. If the stem is in the form of an incomplete

statement, it should provide enough meaning so students will not have to read the answers to understand the question.

2. At least four responses should be provided. This will decrease the likelihood of guessing correctly and increase the validity of the item by requiring students to be more discriminating.

3. Questions that call for "best answers" are more useful for measuring higher thought processes than those that call for correct answers.

4. Make all the responses plausible, and when testing at higher levels, increase the similarity in the choices under each item in order to better test the powers of discrimination.

5. If you can, avoid the use of negatively stated items. These tend to be somewhat more ambiguous than positively stated items.

6. Distribute the order of correct answers randomly and equally, avoiding any discernible pattern, such as favoring first or last choices.

7. Each item should test isolated information that gives no clues to other items in the test.

8. Make the wording simple and clear. The language should be clear enough for even the poorest readers.

These are the primary virtues of multiple-choice items:

1. A wide range of subject matter can be tested in a short time.

2. They can be administered and scored quite rapidly.

3. Items can be written to test for relatively fine discriminations in students' knowledge in a number of subject areas.

4. They can be used to test both simple memory and higher mental processes.

The most significant disadvantages of multiple-choice tests are:

1. Good items are difficult and time-consuming to write.

2. Like all structured response items, they do not require students to provide information in their own words.

3. They normally require a level of concentration and discrimination on the part of the test taker that may make them inappropriate for use with younger learners.

4. Mechanical scoring of items requiring complex thinking provides no basis for checking the thought processes of students.

5. It is never possible to be sure that the student identified the "right" answer for the right reason, that is, knows the right answer (as opposed to getting it by guesswork, or for the wrong reason).

6. They encourage a view of learning that plays down thinking and rewards recognizing or guessing.

7. They encourage a process of learning in which students read by "biting," concentrating on identifying discrete pieces of information of the kind that turn up in tests, rather than on "texting," reading for meaning.

8. The use of "distractors" to mislead students puts the teacher in the position of being seen by his or her students as trying to trick them into making a mistake.

Matching Questions

Matching items are a convenient means of testing for correct associations between related classes of information, such as names and dates, people and events, authors and books, terms and definitions, laws and illustrations, and the like. They are well suited to testing who, what, where, and when but not to measuring understanding as distinct from mere memory.

In constructing these items, two lists are drawn up and the test taker must match an item in the first list with the one in the second list to which the relationship is closest. The following are suggestions for constructing good matching items:

1. Include no more than 10 to 12 items to be identified or matched.

2. There should be more items in the "answers" column than in the "questions" column. If the numbers are equal, students will be helped to make correct choices at the end through a process of elimination.

3. All items in each column should be in the same general category. For example, events and their dates should not be mixed with events and the names of historical characters.

4. Directions should clearly state what the basis for matching is. The directions should specify if choices may be used more than once.

The main advantages of matching questions are:

1. Their compactness allows you to test a good deal of factual information in a short period of time.

2. They are particularly appropriate for surveying knowledge of definitions, events, personalities, and so forth.

3. They are easy to score.

The most prominent weaknesses of matching items are:

1. They cannot check the understanding of concepts or the ability to organize and apply knowledge.

2. It is difficult to avoid giving clues that tend to reduce validity.

3. The format requires the use of single words or very brief phrases.

Essay Questions

Essay tests require the learner to supply an unprompted, extended written response to a stated question or problem. They are appropriate for measuring ability to select and organize ideas, writing abilities, and problem-solving skills requiring originality. The student must create an answer from memory or imagination, so these items are capable of testing a higher level of knowledge than most objective tests. Essay tests are widely used, particularly by high school teachers, although they are often criticized for their subjective nature. The following are guidelines to be used in writing essay questions:

1. Make the wording of the question as clear and explicit as possible. It should precisely define the direction and limits of the desired response. It is important that all students interpret each question in the same way.

2. Include some items that expressly call for a paragraph response, requiring shorter answers, rather than a very few questions requiring long answers. This allows a better sampling of subject-matter knowledge and encourages more precise responses.

3. Decide whether or not to include grammar and sentence structure in your evaluation of answers. You may wish to give two marks, one for the substance of the answers and the other, less crucial grade, for form and writing style. Be sure to announce to the class the basis on

which you will be grading their answers before they begin the exam, and leave time to answer their questions.

4. Provide students with guidance on how to use their time in answering the items. Suggest approximate time limits and answer lengths for each question, so students will distribute their time appropriately.

5. Write the question while planning the unit of instruction rather than near the conclusion of the unit. This will help you to focus more clearly on the objectives of the unit as you are constructing the test.

6. In general, do not allow students a choice on essay items unless there are different objectives for different students in the course. All students must take the same test if you are to have a sound basis for comparing scores.

7. In general, do not ask questions that only sample a student's opinion or attitude without having the student justify the answer in terms of the cognitive content of the course.

8. Have a colleague critique the test as a means of eliminating ambiguity and possible misinterpretations.

Essay questions have the following main strengths as evaluative instruments:

1. They can measure more than the ability to remember information.

2. They encourage students to learn how to organize their own ideas and express them effectively.

3. Students tend to use better study habits when preparing for essay tests.

4. They permit teachers to comment directly on the reasoning processes of individual students.

5. A teacher need only write a few items for a test.

6. Guesswork is largely ruled out.

Essay tests are subject to these drawbacks:

1. Answers may be scored differently by different teachers or by the same teacher at different times.

2. They are usually very time-consuming to grade.

3. Only a relatively few questions on limited areas of knowledge can be responded to in a given period of time.

4. Students who write slowly may not be able to complete the test even though they may possess adequate knowledge.

SOURCE: From MacDonald & Healy, *A Handbook for Beginning Teachers*, 2e. Published by Allyn and Bacon, Boston, MA. Copyright © 1999 by Pearson Education. Reprinted by permission of the publisher.

WHAT IS PORTFOLIO ASSESSMENT?

Portfolios are used with increasing frequency by classroom teachers as a means of assessment. According to Gronlund (2003, p. 157), a portfolio "is a collection of student work that has been selected and organized to show student learning progress (developmental portfolio) or to show samples of student's best work (showcase portfolio). Portfolios are arranged by the student, with the guidance of the teacher, to demonstrate learning over time in each content area. Although students should be allowed to demonstrate their achievement in any reasonable way in the portfolio, the portfolio should also include assessment instruments that the teacher deems appropriate and important. For example, students may want to include writing samples, computer reports, and diary entries to demonstrate effective use of English grammar. The teacher would also want the student to include scores in English grammar as measured by teacher-made tests and standardized achievement tests. A portfolio would include student self-assessment, peer-assessment, and teacher-assessment data.

Grading occurs as a result of examining the contents of a portfolio. Students must document achievement of each curriculum goal and/or learning objective specified by the teacher. Portfolios are advocated in this chapter as an ideal way to assess student's learning because they encourage holistic assessment and thus provide sufficient and varied information to demonstrate student achievement. Portfolio use mitigates the use of one form of assessment over another or to the exclusion of another. Portfolios have a number of other advantages, including encouragement of student reflection about learning and meeting learning outcomes, engagement of student in instruction and assessment, and increasing collaboration between student and teacher in the teaching-learning process.

You should be aware that portfolio assessment is more time-consuming than traditional assessment and much harder to standardize. Portfolios can focus on specific subjects or on activities that integrate several areas. A few examples include:

- Self-evaluation through an "All About Me" portfolio in which students choose items through which they can express themselves, as to their likes, dislikes, hobbies, personality, and family.

- Written literacy portfolios, with such works as timed writing samples, best notes, log and journal entries, essays, critiques, and short stories
- Creative expression, such as art, music, dance, and photography
- Math portfolios with such items as diagrams of problem-solving and steps, written description of math investigations and responses to open-ended questions and problems
- Projects, such as science and social studies investigations
- Videotapes and written analysis of progress for physical skills such as gym, swimming, and dance

Portfolio Assessment Guidelines

The following suggestions for setting up, maintaining, and evaluating a portfolio are recommended:

- Introduce portfolio assessment on the first day of class. Explain in detail the purposes and uses of the portfolio. Try to show students a sample portfolio (it'll be easier to do this after your first year of teaching). Review all aspects of the portfolio (see below).

- Organize the portfolio by including a table of contents, an introduction, a list of learning outcomes addressed by subject or topic, a notation referring to district standards addressed, and a short reflection on each artifact included to indicate why the artifact was chosen and how it demonstrates learning.

- Include only artifacts and evidence related specifically to each learning outcome or objective. You cannot include every piece of evidence in a portfolio. The portfolio would become too cumbersome. Selection of artifacts are determined by both the teacher and student. For each entry (e.g., work samples, test scores, drawings, projects, multimedia, etc.), the student should explain why the entry was selected and what it demonstrates.

- Make certain students assume responsibility for portfolio maintenance. Reinforce notion that grades will be determined solely on the evaluation of the portfolio (see evaluative criteria later). Obviously, in the early grades, teachers will maintain each portfolio with student participation to every extent possible.

- Schedule portfolio conferences with each student at least once a month. Ultimately, you are responsible for overseeing the portfolio process. A period or portion of the day can be devoted to portfolio inspections or whatever else you'd like to call it.

- Involve parents, where appropriate and feasible, in the portfolio process. Reviewing portfolios, for instance, during parent-teacher conferences is suggested.

• Evaluate each portfolio. Preparing and evaluating a portfolio should be the joint responsibility of teacher and student. Teachers should, to every extent possible, involve the student in the evaluative process. Portfolio evaluation should consider these factors:

1. Standards must be established ahead of time.

2. Standards should be very clear and specific.

3. Criteria should be related to learning goals.

4. Decide if the score should be based on performance against a standard, on a student's growth over time or both.

5. Use a checklist rather than writing in portfolio for feedback.

6. Develop a rubric.

I am a strong advocate of scoring rubrics. Form 9.3 is a sample rubric to assess a portfolio.

Form 9.3   Portfolio Rubric

Directions to Evaluators: Place an X on the continuum that reflects your evaluation of each of the following portfolio aspects. Use the comments section to provide feedback regarding your assessment

1. Introduction to portfolio

1	2	3	4	5
Little information about purpose and organization of portfolio			Significant information about purpose and organization of portfolio	

Comments:

2. Evidence cited

1	2	3	4	5
Little evidence provided and not varied enough			Significant evidence and from varied sources	

Comments:

(Continued)

Form 9.3   (Continued)

3. Documentation/Choice of Artifacts

1	2	3	4	5
Limited artifacts that do not provide substantial evidence in support of performance standards or categories			Variety of artifacts that provide irrefutable evidence in support of performance standards or categories	

Comments:

4. Reflective Entries/Explanations

1	2	3	4	5
Unclear narratives; lacking insight, critical thinking, and problem-solving; little evidence of commitment			Clear narratives revealing significant insight, critical thinking, problem-solving, and commitment to growth and learning	

Comments:

5. Writing Mechanics

1	2	3	4	5
Poorly written narratives, containing errors in grammar, spelling, and punctuation			Clearly written narratives with complete and correct grammar, spelling, and punctuation	

Comments:

6. Organization and Appearance of Portfolio

1	2	3	4	5
Unprofessional appearance; poorly organized			Neat, professional appearance; logically organized	

Comments:

(Continued)

You can quantify evaluative results for the rubric. There are six items, each with a 5-point scale. Therefore, a score of 30 would be the highest score. Although you would develop a specific grade for each content area highlighted in the portfolio (e.g., math, science, reading, etc.), you could assign a grade to the portfolio itself as in:

PORTFOLIO TOTAL SCORE

25–30 = Outstanding = A
20–25 = Good = B
15–20 = Satisfactory = C
10–15 = Needs revision = D
< 10 = Unsatisfactory = F

Score: _____

Rubrics are very important tools to evaluate student progress. The best Web site on rubrics is www.odyssey.on.ca/~elaine.coxon/rubrics.htm. Other good links, such as www.rubrics.com, can be accessed from this Web site as well.

Grading

A grade is awarded as a result of the evaluative process. You have accumulated data on student performance from a variety of perspectives. You've used a portfolio to document student progress. You can use a traditional gradebook to record your grades or an electronic grade book, which is increasingly being used across the country. Schools or districts may have a grade book they prefer. If you are free to select one on your own, I'd recommend one of these: http://www.classmategrading.com/, http://www.jacksoncorp.com/, or http://www.teacherease.com/home.asp.

The more essential question is "How will you now determine a student's grade?" Earlier in the chapter, in Form 9.2, I explained that you should list each assessment method, specify a success standard, weight each assessment method, and then determine the grade. As I also mentioned earlier, students should be apprised in advance of the criteria used in determining grades.

Here are some very good and general common sense tips on grading extracted from http://teaching.berkeley.edu/bgd/grading.html:

• *Grade on the basis of students' mastery of knowledge and skills.* Restrict your evaluations to academic performance. Eliminate other considerations, such as classroom behavior, effort, classroom participation, attendance, punctuality, attitude, personality traits, or student interest in the course material, as the basis of course grades. If you count these nonacademic factors, you obscure the primary meaning of the grade, as an indicator of what students have learned.

- *Avoid grading systems that put students in competition with their classmates and limit the number of high grades.* These normative systems, such as grading on the curve, work against collaborative learning strategies that have been shown to be effective in promoting student learning. Normative grading produces undesirable consequences for many students, such as reduced motivation to learn, debilitating evaluation anxiety, decreased ability to use feedback to improve learning, and poor social relationships.

- *Try not to overemphasize grades.* Explain to your class the meaning of and basis for grades and the procedures you use in grading. At the beginning of the term, inform students, in writing how much tests, papers, homework, and so forth. Will count toward their final grade. Once you have explained your policies, avoid stressing grades or excessive talk about grades, which only increases students' anxieties and decreases their motivation to do something for its own sake rather than to obtain an external reward such as a grade.

- *Keep students informed of their progress.* For each paper, assignment, midterm, or project that you grade, give students a sense of what their score means. Try to give a point total rather than a letter grade. Letter grades tend to have emotional associations that point totals lack. Do show the range and distribution of point scores, and indicate what level of performance is satisfactory. Such information can motivate students to improve if they are doing poorly or to maintain their performance if they are doing well. By keeping students informed, you also prevent unpleasant surprises at the end.

CONCLUSION

Teaching 101 would not be complete without attention to the important relationship between instruction and assessment. Someone once advised me to "always keep the end in mind." Although that's good advice in general, it certainly makes sense in teaching as it relates to assessment. How can anyone become an effective teacher without attending to the way we view assessment of student progress and to the way we intend to grade our students? Our important responsibility is to ensure that our students develop the requisite knowledge, skills, and dispositions that will serve them well in school and in life. Holistic assessment, as advocated in this chapter, is the fairest way I know to determine the extent to which we meet this responsibility.

*   *   *

FOLLOW-UP QUESTIONS/ACTIVITIES

1. Interview an experienced teacher and ask why he or she awards grades.

2. How will or do you use portfolio assessment in your class?

3. Which ideas about assessment in this chapter were new to you and which do you think are most useful?

4. Construct a short-answer test based on the criteria cited in this chapter.

5. Develop a portfolio assessment system along with grading criteria and share it with your principal for her/his reaction.

10

How Can I Build a Professional Portfolio?

Teaching is difficult, demanding, draining work.

—William Ayers

◆

FOCUS QUESTIONS

1. Thus far in *Teaching 101,* I have presented much information that I deem essential for new teachers. Have I given you "everything" you "ever" need to know? Of course not. Teaching is a lifelong endeavor of self-discovery and continuous learning. What other areas of competency do you still need or want to know or learn about?

2. Make a list of knowledge, skills, and dispositions that you have gleaned from this book. Recall the K-W-L activity presented in Chapter 2. We are now up to the "What You Have Learned" part. Complete that column.

3. What is your essential mission as a teacher?

4. Why is developing and maintaining your own portfolio important?

5. If teaching is so difficult, demanding, and draining as the quote at the outset of this chapter indicates, why would anyone want to become and remain a teacher?

We have covered a lot of ground in *Teaching 101*. With experience in teaching, you will inevitably hone your skills and learn about many others necessary to become an expert educator. It takes between 5 and 7 years to truly master various aspects of teaching and become more comfortable in the classroom. Even then, you realize there is so much more to learn. But committed to lifelong learning and loving your chosen profession, you will succeed and know that you have made a difference in the lives of others.

RECOLLECTION

Thinking about succeeding, I recall a great story told by Dr. Charles Garfield, author of *Peak Performance*, as related by the "The Executive Speechwriter Newsletter." The story and its interpretation address our professional commitment as educators.

A very wealthy man bought a huge ranch in Arizona and he invited some of his closest associates in to see it. After touring some of the 1,500 acres of mountains and rivers and grasslands, he took everybody into the house. The house was as spectacular as the scenery, and out back was the largest swimming pool you have ever seen. However, this gigantic swimming pool was filled with alligators. The rich owner explained it this way: "I value courage more than anything else. Courage is what made me a billionaire. In fact, I think that courage is such a powerful virtue that if anybody is courageous enough to jump in that pool, swim through those alligators, and make it to the other side, "I'll give him anything he wants, anything—my house, my land, my money." Of course, everybody laughed at the absurd challenge and proceeded to follow the owner into the house for lunch . . . when suddenly they heard a splash. Turning

(Continued)

(Continued)

around, they saw this guy swimming for his life across the pool, thrashing at the water, as the alligators swarmed after him. After several death-defying seconds, the man made it, unharmed to the other side. The rich host was absolutely amazed, but he stuck to his promise. He said, "You are indeed a man of courage and I will stick to my word. What do you want? You can have anything—my house, my land, my money—just tell me what and it's yours." The swimmer, breathing heavily, looked up at his host and said, "I just want to know one thing—who the hell pushed me into that pool?"

Well, no one is going to, nor can, "push" you to do anything you don't want to do. But, each of us has enormous resilience, tenacity, grit, guts, and determination to accomplish anything despite difficult circumstances. Not unlike the swimmer, you may need that extra "push" or encouragement, but once you get going you can achieve success at anything you put your mind to! Teaching is fraught with challenges that may lead to feelings of despair and a sense of failure. But such feelings are short-lived because teaching has so many positives to offer. The excitement of seeing a young mind become aware of something new is incredible. The thrill of working with young people and making a real difference in their lives is unparalleled. As lifelong learners and professionals, good teachers continually strive to achieve excellence and professional growth.

In this final chapter, in order to affirm your professional commitments, I encourage you to frame a Mission Statement to guide your continued practice as a teacher, and to develop and maintain a portfolio demonstrating your competencies and aspirations as a teacher. The chapter closes with an appropriate poem for first-year teachers and a few words of advice.

DEVELOPING A MISSION STATEMENT

Throughout *Teaching 101*, you were encouraged to reflect on your beliefs about students, education, learning, and teaching. A number of exercises or activities challenged you to reflect or respond to certain critical ideas. As a new teacher, framing a philosophy or belief system is important. Certainly, your experiences in teaching will help you refine your beliefs. Still, every good teacher, in my view, has a well-defined, articulated mission. Framing such a mission in the form of a statement helps to guide one's practice and serves as a moral compass as one inevitably confronts the travails of teaching. Successful teachers have such a well-defined mission that reflects their beliefs at the moment. Although a mission may develop and change over time, good teachers can at once articulate succinctly what they are trying to accomplish and why they have chosen teaching as a career. I am encouraging you to articulate such a Mission Statement in this final chapter. You'll find the activity empowering; and it will keep you in good stead through difficult times.

I really believe that all teachers should actually compose a written Mission Statement and keep it handy. I keep mine in my wallet everywhere I go. When I am having that proverbial tough day, I read my statement to remind myself that all will be okay. It serves as my anchor, affirming why I have chosen this great profession.

A Mission Statement is concisely worded, usually no more than a sentence or two. In order to frame, one think about why you went into teaching in the first place. Think about what you hope to accomplish and what you want for your students, given an ideal situation. Try not to be too general, as in, "To change the world for the better." Or, too Pollyannaish, "I will ensure that all students become geniuses." Think about what drives and motivates you. Think about why you wake up in the morning. Let this statement serve to inspire you and remind you what teaching for you is all about. Pause now and re-read all the exercises I have encouraged you to take throughout this book (including Appendix C). After doing so, jot down some ideas, thoughts, and beliefs about what you hope to accomplish below:

_____

_____

_____

_____

RESPOND

Recall your first interview for a teaching position? Below you will find some questions commonly asked during an interview. Jot some responses down. Your responses will further assist in developing a Mission Statement.

1. Can you tell me what you want your students to learn?

_____

_____

2. What essential knowledge do effective teachers need?

_____

_____

3. What essential skills do effective teachers need?

_____

_____

4. What essential dispositions (values) do effective teachers need?

_____

_____

5. In your estimation, what are the qualities of an effective teacher?

_____

_____

Here are some sample Mission Statements that some of my colleagues have framed:

- To treat students as special, unique individuals with boundless potential and to encourage them, every step of the way, to fulfill their potential.
- To value and cherish the process of education by teaching my students the knowledge and skills necessary to become contributing members of society.
- To love my students so much that I will never give up in helping them to succeed academically and socially.
- To teach my students the value of democratic living and to teach them the importance of justice and opportunity for all.

Try framing your statement now based on these samples and the ideas you jotted down in the exercise above.

_____

_____

_____

Refine your statement over the next week and write it down on an index card. Place it in a convenient location and read it at least once a day. Feel free to refine the statement. Share it with a close colleague, if you like. Now, keep the statement over the next month and see if reading it daily or every other day helps you focus your teaching energies.

Research indicates that teachers who have a well framed mission (whether formally articulated or not) are more likely to persevere and maintain their enthusiasm about teaching. Your statement is likely to change as you continue to grow as a teacher and that is expected. As you continually refine your Mission Statement, keep in mind some of these guiding questions:

- What is it about teaching that inspires me?
- What do I want for my students?
- How has my philosophies or beliefs about teaching changed?
- What do I want to accomplish as a teacher?
- Am I satisfied with my work as a teacher?

DEVELOPING A PROFESSIONAL PORTFOLIO

Teaching ultimately requires judgment, improvisation, and conversation about means and ends. Human qualities, expert knowledge and skill, and professional commitment together compose excellence in this craft.

—National Board for Professional Teaching Standards

Why a Portfolio?

You probably began a portfolio as part of your undergraduate or graduate training, and may have even used one to secure a position. A portfolio is a document that is produced by reflective professional educators to demonstrate their ever-growing competencies in knowledge, skills, and dispositions. A portfolio is developmental in the sense that it reflects professional growth and accumulated competencies. In my view, the portfolio should not end with securing a job, as is currently commonplace. Portfolios are important vehicles to indicate continued professional growth that should end with retirement. Imagine the accumulated information at that point. You can be proud of your portfolio as it reflects your uniqueness as a professional educator. For those of you who have not started developing one, who are in the midst of doing so, or who have used one extensively in preservice settings, I am urging you to develop and maintain a portfolio of accomplishments to inspire and empower you as a professional educator.

A professional portfolio can also come in handy as you work towards National Board certification, as I hope many of you do. The National Board for Professional Teaching Standards (NBPTS), established in 1987, offers nationally accredited certification to teachers who meet rigorous standards of excellence. Although specific certifications exist in more than 30 certification areas, here are some general areas in which you must demonstrate excellence:

- A commitment to students and their learning
- Knowledge of subject taught and how to teach the subject to students
- Responsibility for managing and monitoring learning
- Thinking systematically about practice

Currently, there are about 23,000 Board-certified teachers nationally. The goal of the NBPTS is to have 100,000 Board-certified teachers by 2006.

As part of Board certification, candidates must develop and maintain a professional portfolio to demonstrate teaching competence. For more information on Board certification, visit http://www.nbpts.org/. The following information is excerpted from the Web site:

The National Board for Professional Teaching Standards is rooted in the belief that the single most important action this country can take to improve schools and student learning is to strengthen teaching.

The National Board for Professional Teaching Standards is leading the way in making teaching a profession dedicated to student learning and to upholding high standards for professional performance. We have raised the standards for teachers, strengthened their educational preparation through the standards, and created performance-based assessments that demonstrate accomplished application of the standards.

The mission is to advance the quality of teaching and learning by:

- Maintaining high and rigorous standards for what accomplished teachers should know and be able to do
- Providing a national voluntary system certifying teachers who meet these standards
- Advocating related education reforms to integrate National Board Certification in American education and to capitalize on the expertise of National Board Certified Teachers

The success of the National Board came from the power of a good idea: Quality teachers are necessary for student learning.

And it has been teachers who have led the formation and implementation of the work of the National Board. Together, we tackled the difficult job of identifying what it means to be an excellent teacher. Our first policy statement, "What Teachers Should Know and Be Able to Do," ignited widespread discussion between teachers and other educators. It also led to broad accord and real enthusiasm for the idea that teachers are the unifying substantive framework for guiding the teaching profession. This statement describes a vision of teaching based on the Five Core Propositions that outline what the National Board values and believes should be honored in teaching.

Using the core propositions as a foundation, the NBPTS further details what constitutes accomplished teaching in every subject and for students at all stages of their development. For individual teachers, National Board standards provide a careerlong learning curriculum for accomplished teaching. For the nation, these standards are the keystones in efforts to improve teaching and thereby improve student learning.

National Board Certification measures a teacher's practice against these high and rigorous standards. The process is an extensive series of performance-based assessments that include teaching portfolios, student work samples, videotapes, and thorough analyses of the candidate's classroom teaching and student learning. Teachers also complete a series of written exercises that probe the depth of their subject-matter knowledge, as well as their understanding of how to teach those subjects to their students.

Teachers who have participated in National Board Certification have over-whelmingly stated it is the most powerful professional development experience of their careers. They say the experience changes them as professionals and that through the process they deepen their content knowledge and develop, master, and reflect on new approaches to working with their students.

National Board Certification is voluntary and open to all people who have a baccalaureate degree and three years of classroom experience in either a public or private school. It is valid for 10 years, after which a teacher must seek renewal. The fee for National Board Certification is $2,300.

Write for the latest Guide to National Board Certification by calling 1-800-22TEACH or visit the Web site noted above. See Appendix A for the best resource on National Board Certification.

What Is a Portfolio?

An educational portfolio is a collection of artifacts, evidence, and reflections documenting your achievements over the course of time. It might include, but is not limited to, writing samples, performance evaluations, teacher facilitated student projects, evidence of student learning, photographs, observation reports, lesson/unit plans, and audio/video files. The format of the portfolio may be traditional print or as an electronic, multimedia file.

How Should I Compile My Portfolio?

Although your portfolio can be developed in any unique way you'd like, here are some key components (note that you are advised to check with the NBPTS for specific format preferred if you intend to eventually apply for Board certification):

1. A Table of Contents of the artifacts in the portfolio organized into a framework of your choosing. One way is to divide the contents into the following sections: Introduction, Knowledge, Skills, Dispositions/Values, and Conclusion.

2. A Philosophy Statement that addresses your view of the essence of education. The focus should be on the student and how the classroom can help develop the student into an effective citizen based on what you have learned.

Keep the statement to a readable length of no more than two to three pages double-spaced. Share your statement with a colleague or supervisor.

3. A short Reflection on each artifact and what it demonstrates. In other words, what did you choose and why? A reflection should include perceptions, analyses, reactions, evaluations, and integration of knowledge, skills, and dispositions.

What is an artifact? (Adapted from *Student Teacher's Portfolio Handbook*, Phi Delta Kappa, 2000.)

An *artifact* is any piece of evidence used for demonstration purposes. Most items will come from the everyday materials, plans, and student work completed in the classroom. Additional items will come from other materials (e.g., observation notes, evaluations, notes to/from parents).

Listed below are many types of artifacts. This list is not intended to be all-inclusive but to serve as a guide for you.

Caution: When including student work, photos, and reflections in your portfolio, use first names only when referring to students. Confidentiality must be maintained in both written and oral presentation of samples.

What Artifacts Should I Include?

General
- Resume
- Letters of reference from university supervisors, fellow teachers, parents, or administrators of school where you have worked
- Journal entries; anecdotal notes
- Videos or audiotapes of instruction along with reflective narratives
- Informal and formal evaluations from others
- Photographs that provide evidence of your work or skills, including captions and supporting evidence

Knowledge
- Academic transcripts (if outstanding)
- Standardized certification scores
- Honors, certificates, awards
- Evidence of proficiency in a second language
- Evidence of knowledge of cooperative teaching methods, technology, and current curriculum content and trends
- Original lesson plans: plans or directions highlighted with captions showing evidence such as tapping prior knowledge, use of technology, cooperative learning, critical thinking, and community activities

- Demonstration of writing competence: professional writing, anything published, philosophy statement, essays, research papers
- Case studies
- Critique of a test/essay, and so on
- Evidence of knowledge of databases, distance learning equipment, and the Internet; use of technology to research and communicate with educators worldwide. Print out examples of online news groups and LISTSERV memberships
- Bibliographies of sources and materials used

Skills

- Assessments of teaching performance
- Student work samples: student samples before/after significant instruction; pre/post student scores demonstrating improvement (These are very strong pieces of evidence.); children's writing, webbing, or projects; students' work demonstrating a high degree of understanding based on challenges you presented; evidence of comprehensive integration of instruction over time
- Copies of teaching materials you developed: learning packets, learning centers, and so on.
- Demonstration of media/technology skills: samples of discs, photos, plans, and so forth, including electronic grade book, templates for lesson plans or activities, lists of Web sites used for teacher and students; lessons showing use of computers/Internet to enhance instruction; PowerPoint presentations; use of distance learning labs; use of camcorder/VCR, interactive video, laser discs, and cable and educational television
- Self-assessments: video evaluations, journal entries, and narratives that analyze your teaching along with your problem-solving strategies
- Record-keeping: rubrics, checklists, grade book excerpts, contracts; anything that demonstrates your ability to organize, manage, and assess student progress
- Photos: pictures of environmental print and bulletin boards with explanations; seating arrangements; photo essays of student-teacher interactions (with parental permission)
- Assessments: tests created; authentic performance-based assessments with scoring rubrics; informal assessment strategies; evidence of student progress over time
- Additional diagnostic tools: instruments used to get to know students; critiques of standardized tests; samples of checklists or organizational systems used for informal assessment

Dispositions/Values

- Evidence of meeting students' individual needs: evidence of understanding multiple intelligences; individualized plans or IEP adaptations; behavior modification plans; modifications of lessons with student samples; challenge material presented to individual students or small groups; evidence of student's change in attitudes toward learning over time
- Evidence of professional development/lifelong learning: lists of workshops/conferences attended; follow-up on how you incorporated new knowledge; handouts or notes from workshops attended; reflections describing how you used this information in your teaching
- Evidence of professional involvement: memberships in professional organizations; self-initiated volunteerism; evidence of teaming—team-teaching, participation in faculty planning
- Evidence of community involvement: invitations to speak, study trips, community resource materials organized by you
- Demonstration of communication with parents: samples of newsletters, notes, progress reports; responses to parent concerns, notices, letters written to parents, records of phone contacts, and so on
- Demonstration of family involvement: parent volunteer activities initiated; involvement of families in curriculum or assignments; letters of appreciation from parents, children

Note: You should begin collecting potential artifacts early and consistently. As you write journal entries and lesson plans, create assessments, design management strategies, and so forth, consider which items might serve as good evidence of your growth and competence. You will, of course, gather more artifacts as you gain more teaching experience. Remember that the intent of the portfolio is not to create extra work for you, but rather to have you consistently collect evidence of your good teaching, and to document your growth as a professional.

CLOSING WORDS

Top 10 Reasons You Still Want to Be a Teacher

#10   Walking into school and being called "hey, teach . . ."

 #9   Sitting in the teachers' lounge, listening to gossip

 #8   Having your own chalk holder

 #7   Having students call you by your full last name, instead of by the first initial as when you were student teaching

#6   Talking to other teachers behind a piece of paper

#5   Laughing when people tell you that you have it easy because your day ends at 3 o'clock

#4   Using a grade book

#3   The "<u>HUGE</u>" paycheck

#2   Knowing that a student has "<u>Gotten it</u>"
And the #1 reason you still want to be a teacher is . . .

#1   **MAKING A DIFFERENCE**

SOURCE: Printed by permission of Erika O'Rourke

   With your mission in hand and a portfolio in development, you are on the path to success as a teacher. The first years of teaching are certainly challenging. You understand, though, that teaching is a growth process. Keep the words of this poem in mind:

First Year Blues
By Charles Smith, Jr.

I
Got me those rookie teaching blues,
Feel lonely and low, got to pay my dues.
At workshops told to be mean and nasty,
Control and power is the game.
But discipline is hard after 17 years of studentship.
Evaluation time comes, and the tears start,
Pushing your limits, but progress like a snail,
Facing the morning, sentenced to jail.

II
Frustrations: No one understands the pressure.
Taking everything home—problems, papers,
Pressures, livin' from day to day on lesson plans hectic,
Other teachers help, but the pain of constant stress remains.
Experience is a relentless taskmaster.

III
Lesson plans fizzle and sputter, like my temper,
"Can I go to the restroom?" a familiar litany.
(Why is it always in the middle of . . .)
A respect grows, between the kids and me

As our purposes become clear to us—
Each dependent on, and learning from, each other.
After six months, the jail sentence is bearable.

IV
Spring break, relief (No School!!!), tension
(Got to get all this work done).
Vacations, like the year, are bittersweet.
Extra-curriculars crop up, taking their toll,
The principal doesn't like "No's" from first-yearers.

V
The last month drifts by in a fog,
Hey!, I think I'm going to survive!!
With relief comes realization—
I've learned and done well.
I am a teacher.

SOURCE: Permission to reprint the poem by *Kappa Delta Pi Record*, 22(4): 104. Published by Kappa Delti Pi, International Honor Society in Education.

Those of you who strive for professional excellence will inevitably realize, as you gain more teaching experience, that teaching as a field of study and practice is a complex enterprise. Although it may be true that "anyone can teach," those who "teach well" are in the minority. Teaching is both an art and a science. Those of you who conceive it as such realize there is much to learn. Michael Fullan (1995) makes the point even stronger, "Quality learning for all students depends on quality learning for all educators" (p. 5). As you gain experience, you will inevitably learn more about critical pedagogy, content area strategies, advanced cooperative learning groupings, reflective practice, peer coaching, action research, transformative teaching practice, literacy development, . . . oh, there is so much more to learn and do. But that is what makes this field so exciting and growth oriented. Each day is different and new, and those who envision teaching as a lifelong growth process will hone their skills and continually learn. The best teachers are the best learners.

In **Teaching 101** I have highlighted the importance of taking your study and practice of teaching seriously by viewing yourself as an esteemed professional. Learning as much as you can about your chosen field is as necessary as it is empowering professionally. Understanding the essential knowledge, skills, and dispositions to good teaching is imperative. Knowing the learning needs of your students, understanding how children learn, and appreciating and accommodating the diverse abilities of your students are all critical. Writing effective lessons and developing the ability to communicate well is foundational to good teaching practice. Assisting your students through study skills instruction is significant. No matter how knowledgeable and skillful you are, you can't succeed in the classroom without a systematic approach to classroom management and the skills to work effectively with students. Developing a comprehensive student assessment plan, incorporating technology as a teaching tool, and working to meet local or state standards are further challenges. But above all else, remain proud of your profession. Feel empowered and grow as a professional. Continued success . . .

Appendix A: Annotated Bibliography

The literature on teaching is extensive. The list below is not meant to serve as a comprehensive resource by any means. The titles I have selected to annotate are few but, in my opinion, are among the most useful references on the subject. I may have missed, of course, many other important works. Nevertheless, the list below is a good start. Don't forget that life is a long journey of continuous learning. Continue to hone your skills by reading good books and articles on the topic. No one is ever perfect and everyone can learn something new by keeping current with the literature in the field. Share your readings and reactions with a colleague.

Assessment

Gronlund, N. E. (2003). *Assessment of student achievement* (7th ed.). Boston: Allyn & Bacon.

Clearest, most concise work on the subject.

Becoming a Teacher

Abbey, O. F., Jr., (2003). *A practical guide for new teachers: Getting started, surviving, and succeeding.* Norwood, MA: Christopher-Gordon Publishers.

A short, practical guide for new teachers that includes advice on how to obtain a teaching position an introduction to what life in school is like, and tips on how to survive in the classroom.

Armstrong, T. (1998). *How to awaken genius in the classroom*. Alexandria, VA: Association for Supervision and Curriculum Development.

> Some may consider this book "far-out," but I think its thesis is true and it is a must-read—a really short book.

Ayers, W. (1993). *To teach: The journey of a teacher*. New York: Teachers College Press.

> Inspiring introduction to teaching.

Feeney Jonson, K. (1997). *The new elementary teacher's handbook.* Thousand Oaks, CA: Corwin Press.

> Nice, brief, and easy-to-use handbook to guide a teacher.

Kane, P. R. (Ed.). (1991). *My first year as a teacher*. New York: Signet.

> Short, practical stories from new teachers.

Kohl, H. (1984). *Growing minds: On becoming a teacher*. New York: Harper & Row.

> Classic book that greatly affected my own teaching practice.

Kottler, J. A., & Zehm, S. J. (2000). *On being a teacher: The human dimension* (2nd ed.). Thousand Oaks, CA: Corwin Press.

> Inspirational, practical, and current—reminds you why you went into teaching in the first place.

Palmer, P. J. (1998). *The courage to teach: Exploring the inner landscape of a teacher's life.* San Francisco: Jossey-Bass.

> Clear, refreshing work to get you going when you don't feel particularly inspired.

Brain-Based Education

Sousa, D. A. (2001). *How the brain learns* (2nd ed.). Thousand Oaks, CA: Corwin Press.

> Practical and easy-to-understand volume devoted to synthesizing brain research to assist educators in maximizing student learning—packed with teaching ideas.

Wolfe, P. (2001). *Brain matters: Translating research into classroom practice.* Alexandria, VA: Association for Supervision and Curriculum Development.

> Practical classroom applications and brain-compatible teaching strategies.

Classics

Anyon, J. (1981). Social class and school knowledge. *Curriculum Inquiry, 11*(1), 3-41.

> Required reading for every education student—insights into prejudice, discrimination, and differential treatment.

Banks, J. A. (1997). *Teaching strategies for ethnic studies* (6th ed.). Boston: Allyn & Bacon.

    Important and popular work by a noted educator.

Bloom, B. S. (Ed.). (1956). Taxonomy of educational objectives: The classification of educational goals. *Handbook I: Cognitive domain.* New York: David McKay.

    One of the most familiar educational books of all time—Bloom identified six levels of intellectual behavior within the cognitive domain.

Cremin, L. (1964). *The transformation of the school.* New York: Vantage.

    One of the 20th century's noted educational historians.

Dewey, J. (1929). *The sources of a science of education.* New York: Liveright.

    How can one not include a work by the foremost educator in the previous century? This work is short and clear, unlike many of his other works.

Giroux, H. A. (1983). *Theory and resistance in education: A pedagogy for the oppression.* Hadley, MA: Bergin & Garvey.

    Although not an easy read, his views are avant-garde and insightful.

Goodlad, J. I. (1984). *A place called school.* New York: McGraw-Hill.

    Prolific and noted educator.

Greene, M. (1988). *The dialectic of freedom.* New York: Teachers College Press.

    One of the greatest educational philosophers of our time—her other work, *Teacher as Stranger,* shaped my beliefs about teaching.

hooks, b. (1994). *Teaching to transgress: Education as the practice of freedom.* New York: Routledge.

    A wonderful read.

Howard, J. (1991, March 27). *Getting smart: The social construction of intelligence.* The Efficacy Institute, Inc.

    Groundbreaking work on the social construction of intelligence—every teacher must read this piece.

Hunter, M. (1982). *Mastery teaching.* Thousand Oaks, CA: Corwin Press.

    How can one not read a book by Madeline Hunter, who influenced teaching practice almost more than anyone else?

James, W. (1902). *Talks to teachers on psychology: and to students on some of life's ideals.* New York: Henry Holt.

    One of the most influential works on teaching.

Katz, M. B. (1971). *Class, bureaucracy, and schools: The illusion of educational change in America.* New York: Praeger.
> A classical treatise on bureaucracy in American education.

Kozol, J. (1991). *Savage inequalities: Children in America's schools.* New York: Crown.
> Classic work on school inequities.

Lortie, D. (1975). *Schoolteacher: A sociological study.* Chicago: University of Chicago Press.
> The classic study on becoming a teacher.

Noddings, N. (1992). *The challenge to care in schools: An alternative approach to education.* New York: Teachers College Press.
> Noted educational philosopher—her "ethic of caring" has become axiomatic.

Oakes, J. (1995). *Keeping track: How schools structure inequality.* New Haven, CT: Yale University Press.
> A belief-changing work—greatly influenced me.

Pyne, S. L. (1951). *The art of asking questions.* Princeton, NJ: Princeton University Press.
> The essence of good teaching—practical.

Rist, R. C. (1970). Student social class and teacher expectations: The self-fulfilling prophecy in ghetto education. *Harvard Educational Review, 40*(3), 411-451.
> Classic article on the influence of teacher expectations.

Sadker, D., & Sadker, M. (1999). *Failing at fairness: How our schools cheat girls.* New York: Simon & Schuster.
> An eye-opener to gender inequities—also affected me deeply.

Sarason, S. B. (1971). *The culture of the school and the problem of change.* Boston: Allyn & Bacon.
> The classic on educational change.

Schlechty, P. C. (1990). *Schools for the 21st century.* San Francisco: Jossey-Bass.
> Futurists must read this one.

Vygotsky, L. (1978). *Thought and language.* Cambridge: MIT Press.
> Vygotsky, along with Dewey, are among the elder statesmen of education.

Wong, H. K., & Wong, R. T. (1998). *How to be an effective teacher: The first days of school.* Mountain View, CA: Harry K. Wong Publications.

> National best-seller, Wong is an inspirational speaker and his book is a must read not only for every beginning teacher but even for experienced teachers to remind them of the basics and to inspire them.

Classroom Management

Arnold, H. (2000). *Succeeding in the secondary classroom: Strategies for middle and high school teachers.* Thousand Oaks, CA: Corwin Press.

> One of the better resources for the upper grades—as a teacher in the upper grades, I could have used this practical book. Hands-on strategies and practical techniques, especially for prospective and beginning teachers, make this book a must read.

Belvel, P. S., & Jordan, M. M. (2002). *Rethinking classroom management: Strategies for prevention, intervention, and problem solving.* Thousand Oaks, CA: Corwin Press.

> Few resources deal effectively with preventive, supportive, and corrective stages of discipline—this work does the trick. Encouraging reflective thinking, this useful resource reviews excellent intervention techniques and problem-solving strategies.

Burden, P. R. (2000). *Powerful classroom management strategies: Motivating students to learn.* Thousand Oaks, CA: Corwin Press.

> Nice combination of theory and practical strategies for effective classroom management. I especially like its easy reading style. Emphasizing the importance of motivation theory, this compact work is very user-friendly.

Canter, L. (1992). *Assertive discipline.* Santa Monica, CA: Lee Canter and Associates.

> The very best book on corrective discipline out there! One of three books I require my students to read. Learn and practice the three response styles. Although controversial (some hate the system, others swear by it), I'm in the latter camp. Use it! A lifesaver!!

Charles, C. M. (2001). *Building classroom discipline.* New York: Longman.

> Best textbook on the subject.

Curwin, R. L., & Mendler, A. N. (1999). *Discipline with dignity.* Alexandria, VA: Association for Supervision and Curriculum Development.

Classic—most useful. It's one of three books I require my students to read in a course I teach on classroom management. Their creative ideas have caught on nationally and their work is used extensively at all levels. A must read.

Gill, V. (2001). *The eleven commandments of good teaching: Creating classrooms where teachers can teach and students can learn* (2nd ed.). Thousand Oaks, CA: Corwin Press.

Really concise and useful. Don't let the catchy, perhaps simplistic, title fool you—this book is excellent. Full of tactics and strategies, this resource is written by a veteran teacher who has practical and wise advice.

Ginott, H. G. (1972). *Between teacher and child.* New York: Macmillan.

If I could recommend only one book, this is it! Sensitive, insightful, and practical, this work is a classic in the field. An "oldie but goodie."

Gootman, M. E. (2000). *The caring teacher's guide to discipline: Helping young students learn self-control, responsibility, and respect* (2nd ed.). Thousand Oaks, CA: Corwin Press.

Another Corwin favorite of mine—I believe a good classroom manager is above all else a "caring" human being. Thoughtful, practical, and extremely sensitive.

Rosenblum-Lowden, R. (2000). *You have to go to school . . . you're the teacher: 200 tips to make your job easier and more fun* (2nd ed.). Thousand Oaks, CA: Corwin Press.

One of my favorites—I read a tip a day. Filled with pearls of wit and wisdom, this very brief resource will help you develop rapport with students and manage everyday school problems.

Cognitive Strategy Instruction (Study Skills)

Mangrum C. T., II, Iannuzzi, P., & Strichart, S. S. (1998). *Teaching study skills and strategies in grades 4–8.* Needham, MA: Allyn & Bacon.

Easy and ready-to-use strategies to effectively teach students study skills.

Pressley, M., & Woloshyn, V. (1995). *Cognitive strategy instruction that really improves children's academic performance.* Brookline, MA: Brookline Books.

Classic book that reviews many study skill strategies in various content areas. Offers specific suggestions for teaching cognitive learning strategies.

Scheid, K. (1993). *Helping students become strategic learners: Guidelines for teaching.* Brookline, MA: Brookline Books.

> A most practical guide that helps beginning or experienced teachers adopt practical teaching tools for learning in the basic skill areas.

Critical Pedagogy

Freire, P. (1994). *Pedagogy of the oppressed.* New York: Seabury Press.

> Also a classic on innovative teaching practices.

Freire, P. (1994). *The pedagogy of hope: Reliving pedagogy of the oppressed.* New York: Continuum Publishing Group.

> Classic follow-up to previous work.

Kohl, H. (1998). *The discipline of hope: Learning from a lifetime of teaching.* New York: Simon & Schuster.

> How can a "best book" list not include a work by Kohl?

McLaren, P. (1998). *Life in schools: An introduction to critical pedagogy in the foundations of education* (3rd ed.). New York: Longman.

> A guru of critical pedagogy.

Wink, J. (2000). *Critical pedagogy: Notes from the real world* (2nd ed.). New York: Addison Wesley Longman.

> Powerful and accessible, opens doors on a broad and deep perspective of teaching and learning.

Diversity

Banks, J. A. (1999). *An introduction to multicultural education* (2nd ed.). Needham Heights, MA: Allyn & Bacon.

> Classic overview of the subject.

Delpit, L. (1988). *Other people's children: Cultural conflict in the classroom.* New York: The New Press.

> One of most widely read books on the subject.

Jelloun, T. B. (1999). *Racism explained to my daughter.* New York: The New Press.

> Small book—contributors are William Ayers, Lisa Delpit, and Bill Cosby, among others.

Nieto, S. (1996). *Affirming diversity: The sociopolitical context of multicultural education.* New York: Longman.
>   Also a classic on diversity.

Nieto, S. (1999). *The light in their eyes: Creating multicultural learning communities.* New York: Teachers College Press.
>   Her superb follow-up to the previous work—just as good.

Paley, V. (2000). *White teacher.* Cambridge, MA: Harvard University Press.
>   Moving personal account of her experiences as a kindergarten teacher in an integrated school in a predominantly white middle-class area.

Shapiro, A. (1999). *Everybody belongs: Changing negative attitudes toward classmates with disabilities.* New York: Routledge Falmer.
>   A colleague of mine, a great detailed book with practical suggestions.

Sleeter, C. E. (1996). *Multicultural education as social activism.* New York: Albany State University of New York Press.
>   Clear and useful.

Stalvey, L. M. (1989). *The education of a wasp.* Madison: University of Wisconsin Press.
>   Honest and passionate, a white woman's chronicle of discovering racism—disturbing.

Tatum, D. B. (1997). *Why are all the black kids sitting together in the cafeteria?* New York: Basic Books.
>   Phenomenal, life-changing, and practical.

West, C. (1993). *Race matters.* New York: Vintage.
>   Classic treatise on the topic—one of the most brilliant and controversial thinkers of our time.

General Education

Berliner, D., & Biddle, B. (1995). *The manufactured crisis: Myths, fraud, and the attack on America's public schools.* New York: Addison Wesley Longman.
>   Defend yourself as an educator—read this one.

General Teaching

Brause, R. S., Donohue, C. P., & Ryan, A. W. (2002). *Succeeding at your interview: A practical guide for teachers.* Mahwah, NJ: Erlbaum.
>   One of the most practical and detailed books on the topic.

Jackson, P. (1968). *Life in classrooms.* New York; Holt, Reinhart & Winston.
　　Classic on classroom life—insightful.

Joyce, B., & Weil, M. (1996). *Models of teaching.* Boston: Allyn & Bacon.
　　Classic on teaching strategies.

Morrison, G. S. (2003). *Teaching in America* (3rd ed.). Boston: Allyn & Bacon.
　　Comprehensive textbook—one of best.

Nagel, G. (1994). *The Tao of teaching.* New York: Primus.
　　Esoteric yet practical—pithy advice such as "obey your instincts," "have
compassion, practice frugality, be willing to follow."

Parkay, F. W., & Hardcastle Stanford, B. (2001). *Becoming a teacher* (5th ed.).
Boston: Allyn & Bacon.
　　Appendixes are great and include a list of many professional teacher
organizations you should become familiar with, if not join.

Warner, J., & Bryan, C. (1995). *The unauthorized teacher's survival guide.*
Indianapolis, IN: Park Avenue Publications.
　　Handy, easy-to-read, and really practical.

Warner, J., & Bryan, C. (1997). *Inside secrets of finding a teacher's job: The unauthorized teacher's survival guide.* Indianapolis, IN: Park Avenue Publications.
　　Among the best on the topic.

Inclusion

Peterson, J. M., & Hittie, M. M. (2003). *Inclusive teaching: Creating effective schools
for all learners.* Boston: Allyn & Bacon.
　　Comprehensive, up-to-date and practical.

Winebrenner, S. (1996). *Teaching kids with learning difficulties in the regular classroom: Strategies and techniques every teacher can use to challenge and motivate
struggling students.* Minneapolis, MN: Free Spirit Publishing.
　　Packed with practical tips, this book is a must read for all teachers.

Inspirational

Bluestein, J. (Compiler). (1995). *Mentors, masters and Mrs. Macgregor: Stories
of teachers making a difference.* Deerfield Beach, FL: Health Communications, Inc.
　　Delightful book that reminds me why I became a teacher—to deeply
and profoundly affect the lives of others—inspirational.

Whitaker, T., & Whitaker, B. (2002). *Teaching matters: Motivating and inspiring yourself.* Larchmont, NY: Eye on Education.

> Inspirational—taking care of yourself.

Journals and Newspapers

The Clearing House

Educational Leadership

The Educational Forum

Educational Studies

Education Week

The Elementary School Journal

Equity & Excellence in Education

Harvard Educational Review

Journal of Curriculum & Supervision

Kappan

Multicultural Education

Phi Delta Kappa Fastbacks

Teachers College Record

Legal Issues

Imber, M., & van Geel, T. (2001). *A teacher's guide to education law* (2nd ed.). Mahwah, NJ: Erlbaum.

> Primer including sections on student's rights, discipline, discrimination, special education, negligence, hiring, due process, and tenure.

Literacy

Beaty, J. J., & Pratt, L. (2003). *Early literacy and preschool and kindergarten.* Columbus, OH: Upper Saddle River, NJ: Merrill/Prentice Hall.

> An invaluable textbook for early childhood educators focusing on preschool learning. Superb treatments of the foundations of literacy specific strategies for reading.

National Board Certification

Berg, J. H. (2003). *Improving the quality of teaching through national board certification: Theory and practice.* Norwood, MA: Christopher-Gordon Publishers.

> Nuts and bolts approach for prospective National Board candidates.

Personal Growth

Glanz, J. (2000). *Relax for success: An educator's guide to stress management.* Norwood, MA: Christopher-Gordon Publishers.

My suggestions for a successful life and career.

Whitaker, T., & Winkle, J. (2001). *Feeling great: The educator's guide for eating better, exercising smarter, and feeling your best.* Larchmont, NY: Eye on Education.

Wonderful reference work.

Practical Strategies

Chuska, K. R. (1995). *Improving classroom questions: A teacher's guide to increasing student motivation, participation, and higher-level thinking.* Bloomington, IN: Phi Delta Kappa Educational Foundation.

The key to effective teaching is posing "good" questions—this is a short practical guide.

Gregory, G. H., & Chapman, C. (2002). *Differentiated instructional strategies: One size doesn't fit all.* Thousand Oaks, CA, Corwin Press.

Practical strategies and techniques.

Harmin, M. (1994). *Inspiring active learning: A handbook for teachers.* Alexandria, VA: Association for Supervision and Curriculum Development.

If I could only recommend one book for you to read on practical strategies to promote learning, then this book would be the one! Don't miss it. See http:// www.inspiringonline.com/History.html.

Raffini, J. P. (1996). *150 ways to increase intrinsic motivation in the classroom.* Boston: Allyn & Bacon.

Action-packed with great ideas.

Scruggs, T. E., & Mastropieri, M. A. (1992). *Teaching test-taking skills: Helping students show what they know.* Brookline, MA: Brookline Books.

One of the clearest and most useful brief books packed with practical ways of helping students Develop skills necessary to do well on tests, including essay, short answer, multiple choice, and so on.

Silver, H. F., Strong, R. W., & Perini, M. J. (2000). *So each may learn: Integrating learning styles and multiple intelligences.* Alexandria, VA; Association for Supervision and Curriculum Development.

Fascinating and useful.

Spreyer, L. (2000). *Teaching is an art: An A-Z handbook for successful teaching in middle and high schools.* Thousand Oaks, CA: Corwin Press.

   Geared for the upper grades—this is a practical book loaded with practical teaching strategies and resources.

Tauber, R. T. (1997). *Self-fulfilling prophecy: A practical guide to its use in education.* Westport, CT: Praeger.

   Invaluable tool for introducing and summarizing the vast literature into the impact of the self-fulfilling prophecy.

Tomlinson, C. A. (2001). *How to differentiate instruction in mixed-ability classrooms* (2nd ed.). Alexandria, VA: Association for Supervision and Curriculum Development.

   Provides easy-to-read and useful practical strategies for how teachers can navigate a diverse classroom. If you want to learn how to teach students of different abilities at the same time, read this book—great case studies of classrooms at all levels in which instruction is differentiated successfully.

Whitaker, T., & Fiore, D. J. (2001). *Dealing with difficult parents: And with parents in difficult situations.* Larchmont, NY: Eye on Education.

   Great resource—practical.

Professional Development

Glickman, C. D. (2002). *Leadership for learning: How to help teachers succeed.* Alexandria, VA: Association for Supervision and Curriculum Development.

   Practical guidance to help teachers improve classroom teaching and learning.

Reflective Thinking

Schon, D. A. (1983). *The reflective practitioner: How professionals think in action.* New York: Basic.

   Advocates reflection on the practice of teaching.

Special Education

Shelton, C. F., & Pollingue, A. B. (2000). *The exceptional teacher's handbook: The first-year special education guide for success.* Thousand Oaks, CA: Corwin Press.

Practical guide for the new special education teacher—includes checklists, forms, and so on.

Teaching Characteristics

McEwan, E. K. (2002). *10 traits of highly effective teachers.* Thousand Oaks, CA: Corwin Press.

Outstanding work that identifies 10 traits of effective teachers: passionate, positive, leader, with-it, style, motivational expert, instructional effective, learned, street smart, and reflective.

Rosenshine, B. (1971). *Teaching behaviors and student achievement.* London: National Foundation for Education Research in England and Wales.

Classic book in the field.

Teaching Effectiveness

Danielson, C. (1996). *Enhancing professional practice: A framework for teaching.* Alexandria, VA: Association for Supervision and Curriculum Development.

Author has developed a framework or model for understanding teaching based on current research in the field.

Marzano, R. J., Pickering, D. J., & Pollock, J. E. (2001). *Classroom instruction that works: Research-based strategies for increasing student achievement.* Alexandria, VA: Association for Supervision and Curriculum Development.

Authors examine decades of research in education to come up with nine teaching strategies that have positive effects on student learning—one of the books that is a must read.

Stronge, J. H. (2002). *Qualities of effective teachers.* Alexandria, VA: Association for Supervision and Curriculum Development.

Most recent and one of the best summaries of current research on teacher effectiveness.

Technology in Teaching

Bitter, G., & Pierson, M. (2002). *Using technology in the classroom* (5th ed.). Boston: Allyn & Bacon.

Very helpful, comprehensive, and packed with practical ways to help teachers incorporate technology into teaching.

Jukes, I., Dosaj, A., & Macdonald, B. (2000). *NetSavvy: Building information literacy in the classroom.* Thousand Oaks, CA: Corwin Press.

    Easy-to-follow guide for assisting students to use the Internet.

Leu D. J., Jr., & Leu, D. D. (2000). *Teaching with the Internet: Lessons from the classroom* (2nd ed.). Norwood, MA: Christopher-Gordon Publishers.

    Easy-to-use guide to teaching with the Internet. Packed with great Web sites in content areas.

Appendix B: Some of the Best Web Sites for Teachers

Below are some of the best resources on the Web. I offer them as suggestions because the voluminous material that exists on the Web can actually turn you off. Begin with the sites below. You will find them enormously helpful and they'll lead you to others.

The best book for resources for the Internet and the World Wide Web is Eugene F. Provenzo's *The Internet and the World Wide Web for Teachers*, published in 2002 by Allyn & Bacon—you won't believe how many great resources are listed.

http://isis.csuhayward.edu/alss/engl/TESOL/CALL_01_1998/TEACHING_TI
   PS.html#b7
   Brief, practical Web site filled with good "teaching tips." It'll take 15 minutes to go through so it's really convenient.

www.google.com
   Great advice: search Google by typing in "classroom management"—now, spend the day exploring. (Also, try typing in "discipline." Because many non-school discipline sites are included, you'll have to pick and choose. It's worth exploring though.) Google is the most accessible, easy-to-use, and current search engine.

www.masterteacher.com

This for-profit Web site is a phenomenal storehouse of educational resources (some for free) that includes videos, books on a host of relevant topics (e.g., leadership, inclusion, mentoring, etc.)—a must to browse with loads of teaching ideas. Subscribe for free materials at list@masterteacher.com—great free catalog 1-800-669-9633.

http://soupserver.com
Daily inspirational sayings—uplifts the soul.

www.newteachercenter.org
Promotes excellence and diversity in schools—very teacher friendly.

www.alfiekohn.org
Useful site packed with the ideas and writings of a noted critic of public education.

www.effectiveteachers.com
Harry Wong's site (see Appendix A)– packed with information

www.inspiringteachers.com
Great action-packed site that includes tips for new teachers, resources, opportunity to interact with colleagues.

www.proteacher.com and www.innovativeclassroom.com
Both sites contain many useful ideas and tools (including lesson plans in content areas) on a variety of educational topics—easy to navigate.

http://www.ed.gov/
The home page of the U.S. Department of Education provides timely news regarding the state of education in our country, answers to frequently asked questions, links to related governmental officials, updates on legislation, application information for federal grants, and links to federally funded publications.

http://teachersnetwork.org
Teachers Network Web site connects innovative teachers with one another. Loads of useful information. Click on the site's *For New Teachers* link for access to a Helpline, which allows you to ask a question of veteran teachers, and you receive a response within 72 hours.

http://www.splcenter.org/
Tolerance and diversity issues.

http://www.ascd.org
Consult *Educational Leadership*, ASCD journal (see Appendix A)—"Web Wonders"—great resources on a plethora of topics.

Web-questing is hot. Do a Google search for WebQuest.
WebQuest Portal. Find links for "Top," "Middling," and "New." http://webquest.org

http://www.corwinpress.com
Refer to the veritable storehouse of wisdom contained in other Corwin publications. Send for a catalog at 800-818-7243.

Appendix C: Self-Assessment Instrument

$\mathbf{C}$harlotte Danielson, in a 1996 work titled *Enhancing Professional Practice: A Framework for Teaching* published by the Association for Supervision and Curriculum Development (see Appendix A), developed a framework or model for understanding teaching based on current research in the field. She identified "components" clustered into four domains of teaching responsibility: *planning and preparation, classroom environment, instruction,* and *professional responsibilities.* I developed the questionnaire below based on her framework. Please take the questionnaire because it will serve as an important reflective tool. A short activity to assess your responses can be found at the end of the questionnaire.

Analyzing Your Responses

Note that the items draw on research that highlights good educational practice. Review your responses and circle responses that concern you. For instance, if you checked *Strongly Agree* for "I ask multiple questions that sometimes confuse students," ask yourself, "Why is this is a problem?" "How can I remedy the situation?" and "What additional resources or assistance might I need?" If you agree, share, and compare responses with another educator, the dialogue that will ensue will serve as a helpful vehicle to move towards more effective teaching practice.

Self-Assessment Instrument

Directions: Using the key below, check the appropriate box for each item.

SA = Strongly Agree ("For the most part, yes")
A = Agree ("Yes, but . . .")
D = Disagree ("No, but . . .")
SD = Strongly Disagree ("For the most part, no")

Planning and Preparation	SA	A	D	SD
1. I make many errors when I teach in my content area.				
2. I display solid content knowledge and can make connections with the parts of my discipline or with other disciplines.				
3. I rarely consider the importance of prerequisite knowledge when introducing new topics				
4. I actively build on students' prior knowledge and seek causes for students' misunderstanding.				
5. Although I am content knowledgeable, I need additional assistance with pedagogical strategies and techniques.				
6. I am familiar with pedagogical strategies and continually search for best practices to emulate in my teaching.				
7. I don't know too much about the developmental needs of my students.				
8. I know the typical developmental characteristics of the age groups I teach.				
9. I am unfamiliar with learning styles and multiple intelligences theories.				
10. I have a solid understanding of learning styles and multiple intelligences theories and can apply them to instructional practice.				
11. I do not fully recognize the value of understanding students' skills and knowledge as a basis for my teaching.				
12. I understand the importance of students' skills and knowledge, even those students with exceptional needs.				

(Continued)

Planning and Preparation	*SA*	*A*	*D*	*SD*
13. I don't believe that setting goals for my class is ever helpful because they may influence my expectations for them in a potentially negative way.				
14. Goal setting is critical to my success in planning and preparing for my class.				
15. I am unfamiliar with teaching resources to assist me in the classroom.				
16. I am very aware of teaching resources and seek to use them in preparing for lessons.				
17. I don't develop appropriate learning activities suitable for my students.				
18. I plan for a variety of meaningful learning activities matched to my instructional goals.				
19. I teach the whole class most of the time without utilizing instructional groups.				
20. I use varied instructional grouping.				
21. My lessons, generally, have no clearly defined structure.				
22. My lessons are well planned, organized, and matched to my instructional goals, most of the time.				
23. I usually don't have a systematic plan for assessment of student learning.				
24. I have a well-defined understanding of how I will assess my students after a unit of instruction.				

Classroom Environment	*SA*	*A*	*D*	*SD*
1. I realize I sometimes use poor interaction skills with my students, such as use of sarcastic or disparaging remarks.				
2. My interactions with students are generally friendly and demonstrate warmth and caring.				
3. Students in my class, generally, don't get along with each other and conflicts are not uncommon.				
4. Student interactions are generally polite and friendly.				
5. I convey a negative attitude towards the content suggesting that the content is mandated by others.				

(Continued)

Classroom Environment	SA	A	D	SD
6. I convey a genuine enthusiasm for the subject.				
7. Students in my class demonstrate little or no pride in their work and don't perform to the best of their ability.				
8. Students meet or exceed my expectations for high-quality work.				
9. I don't always communicate high expectations for all my students.				
10. I communicate high expectations for all my students.				
11. Students in my class are sometimes on-task, but often off-task behavior is observed.				
12. Students in my class are highly engaged and on-task.				
13. I have difficulty managing my class during transitions, e.g., change of subjects or at dismissals.				
14. Transitions in my class occur smoothly, with little loss of instructional time.				
15. Routines for handling materials and supplies in my class are not well organized causing loss of instructional time.				
16. Routines for handling materials and supplies in my class are well organized, with little, if any, loss of instructional time.				
17. I have not established a well-defined system of rules and procedures.				
18. I pride myself on the well-established system of rules and procedures in my class.				
19. I have difficulty enforcing standards for acceptable conduct in my class.				
20. Standards for conduct are clear to all students.				
21. I monitor student behavior and I am aware of what students are doing.				
22. I am alert to student behavior at all times.				
23. I have difficulty responding effectively to student misbehavior and consequently students are disruptive.				
24. My response to misbehavior is appropriate and successful most of the time.				

(Continued)

Classroom Environment	SA	A	D	SD
25. I don't consider safety issues in my classroom in terms of room arrangement.				
26. My classroom is safe and the furniture arrangements are a resource for learning.				

Instruction	SA	A	D	SD
1. My directions are not clear to students often causing confusion.				
2. My directions are clear and appropriate.				
3. My spoken language is often inaudible and crude.				
4. I speak clearly and appropriately, according to the grade level of my students.				
5. My use of questions needs improvement.				
6. My questions are uniformly of high quality.				
7. I mostly lecture (talk) to my students without enough student participation.				
8. I encourage students to participate and prefer for students to take an active role in learning.				
9. Only a few students participate in class discussions.				
10. I engage all students in class discussions.				
11. My ability to communicate content is poor.				
12. My ability to communicate content is sound and appropriate.				
13. Activities and assignments are inappropriate to students, and don't engage students mentally.				
14. Activities and assignments are appropriate to students, and encourage student understanding.				
15. I don't know how to group students appropriately for instruction.				
16. I am very familiar with grouping strategies to promote instruction.				
17. I select inappropriate and ineffective instructional materials and resources.				

(Continued)

Instruction	SA	A	D	SD
18. Instructional materials and resources are suitable and engage students mentally.				
19. My lessons have little, or no structure and my pacing of the lesson is too slow, rushed, or both.				
20. My lessons are highly coherent and my pacing is consistent and appropriate.				
21. I rarely provide appropriate feedback to my students.				
22. Feedback to my students is consistent, appropriate, and of high quality.				
23. When I do provide feedback, it's inconsistent and not timely.				
24. Feedback is consistently provided in a timely manner.				
25. I rely heavily on the teacher's manual for instruction.				
26. I rarely, if ever, rely on the teacher's manual because I can adjust a lesson to make it appropriate to the needs and level of my students.				
27. I often ignore students' questions or interests.				
28. I consistently encourage student questions.				
29. I often blame my students for their inability to learn by attributing their lack of success to their background or lack of interest or motivation.				
30. I don't give up with slow learners and try to encourage them all the time.				
31. I tend to go off on tangents.				
32. I ask multiple questions that sometimes confuse students.				
33. I use wait time effectively.				

Professional Responsibilities	SA	A	D	SD
1. I have difficulty assessing my effectiveness as a teacher.				
2. I can accurately assess how well I am doing in my classroom.				

(Continued)

Professional Responsibilities	SA	A	D	SD
4. I am aware of what I need to do in order to become an effective teacher.				
5. I don't have a system for maintaining information on student completion of assignments.				
6. My system for maintaining information on student completion of assignments is effective.				
7. I don't have a system for maintaining information on student progress in learning.				
8. My system for maintaining information on student progress is sound.				
9. I rarely encourage parental involvement in my class.				
10. I actively and consistently engage parents in my classroom.				
11. I rarely reach out to parents.				
12. I reach out to parents consistently.				
13. I have difficulty relating to my colleagues in a cordial and professional manner.				
14. I collaborate with my colleagues in a cordial and professional manner.				
15. I rarely participate in school events.				
16. I often volunteer to participate in school events.				
17. I avoid becoming involved in school and district projects.				
18. I volunteer to participate in school and district projects.				
19. I rarely seek to engage in professional development activities.				
20. I seek out opportunities for professional development to enhance my pedagogical skills.				
21. I am rarely alert to students' needs.				
22. I am active in serving students.				
23. I am not an advocate for student's rights.				
24. I am an advocate for student's rights.				
25. I rarely desire to serve on a school-based committee.				
26. I volunteer to serve on departmental or schoolwide committees.				

In summary, review your responses for each of the four domains and circle your summary response (SA, A, D, or SD) for each of the domains below.

RESPOND

Domain 1: Planning and Preparation. This domain demonstrates your content and pedagogical knowledge, knowledge of students and resources, ability to select instructional goals, and the degree to which you assess student learning.

SA   A   D   SD   I am satisfied that my planning and preparation knowledge and skills are satisfactory.

Domain 2: The Classroom Environment. This domain assesses the degree to which you create an environment of respect and caring, establish a culture for learning, manage classroom procedures, manage student behavior, and organize physical space.

SA   A   D   SD   I am satisfied that my knowledge and skills of classroom environment are satisfactory.

Domain 3: Instruction. This domain assesses the ability to communicate with clarity, use questioning and discussion techniques, engage students in learning, provide feedback to students, demonstrate flexibility and responsiveness to student's instructional needs.

SA   A   D   SD   I am satisfied that my knowledge and skills of instruction are satisfactory.

Domain 4: Professional Responsibilities. This domain assesses the degree to which you reflect on teaching, maintain accurate records, communicate with parents, contribute to the school/district, grow and develop professionally, and show professionalism.

SA   A   D   SD   I am satisfied. I am professionally responsible.

References

Allan, J. (1999). *Actively seeking inclusion.* London: Falmer Press.

Barton, L. (1998). *The politics of special educational needs.* Lewes: Falmer Press.

Beach, D. M., & Reinhartz, J. (2000). *Supervisory leadership: Focus on instruction.* Boston: Allyn and Bacon.

Bitter, G., & Pierson, M. (2002). *Using technology in the classroom* (5th ed.). Boston: Allyn and Bacon.

Bolotin J. P., & Burnaford, G. E. (2001). *Images of schoolteachers in America* (2nd ed.). Mahwah, NJ: Lawrence Erlbaum.

Bolt, R. (1962). *A man for all seasons.* New York: Basic Books.

Brezak, D. (2002). *Education in turbulent times: Practical strategies for parents and educators.* Brooklyn, NY: Mesorah Publications.

Canter, L. (1989). *Assertive discipline for secondary school teachers: Inservice video package and leader's manual.* Santa Monica, CA: Lee Canter and Associates.

Capper, C. A., Frattura, E., & Keyes, M. (2000). *Meeting the needs of students of all abilities: How leaders go beyond inclusion.* Thousand Oaks, CA: Corwin Press.

Carnegie Forum on Education and the Economy. (1986). *A nation prepared: Teachers for the twenty-first century.* New York: Carnegie Corporation.

Charles, C. M. (2001). *Building classroom discipline* (7th ed.). New York: Longman.

Clough, P., & Corbet, J. (2000). *Theories of inclusive education.* Thousand Oaks, CA: Sage.

Cochran-Smith, M. (2002). Reporting on teacher quality: The politics of politics. *Journal of Teacher Education, 53*(5), 379-382.

Danielson, C. (2002). *Enhancing student achievement: A framework for school improvement.* Alexandria, VA: Association for Supervision and Curriculum Development.

Darling-Hammond, L. (2000). *Studies of excellence in teacher education.* Washington, DC: American Association of Colleges for Teacher Education and National Commission on Teaching and America's Future.

Darling-Hammond, L. (2003). Keeping good teachers: Why it matters what leaders do. *Educational Leadership, 60,* 6-13.

Darling-Hammond, L., Chung, R., & Frelow, F. (2002). Variation in teacher preparation: How well do different pathways prepare teachers to teach? *Journal of Teacher Education, 53*(4), 286-302.

Davis, O. L., Jr. (1998). Beyond beginnings: From "hands-on" to "minds-on." *Journal of Curriculum and Supervision, 13,* 119-122.

Dewey, J. (1899). *The school and society.* Chicago, IL: The University of Chicago Press.

Educational Testing Service. (1992). *The second international assessment of educational progress.* Princeton, NJ: Educational Testing Service.

Elliott, D., & McKenney, M. (1998). Four inclusion models that work. *Teaching Exceptional Children,* 54-58.

Fisher, D., Frey, N., & Williams, D. (2002). Seven literacy strategies that work. *Educational Leadership, 60,* 70-73.

Freire, P. (1974). *Pedagogy of the oppressed.* New York: Seabury Press.

Freire, P. (1994). *The pedagogy of hope: Reliving pedagogy of the oppressed.* New York: Continuum Publishing Group.

Fullan, M. (1995). In M. J. O'Hair, & S. J. Odell (Eds.). *Educating teachers for leadership and change* (pp. 1-10). Thousand Oaks, CA: Corwin Press.

Gardner, H. (2000). *Intelligence reframed: Multiple intelligences for the 21st century.* New York: Basic Books.

Ginott, H. (1993). *Teacher and child: A book for parents and teachers.* New York: Macmillan.

Glanz, J. (2002). *Finding your leadership style: A guide for educators.* Alexandria, VA: Association for Supervision and Curriculum Development.

Glasser, W. A. (1975). *Reality therapy.* New York: HarperCollins.

Glatthorn, A. A. (2000). *The principal as curriculum leader: Shaping what is taught and tested* (2nd ed.). Thousand Oaks, CA: Corwin Press.

Good, T. L., & Brophy, J. E. (1997). *Looking in classrooms* (7th ed.). New York: Addison-Wesley.

Goodlad, J. (1970). *Behind the classroom door.* Belmont, CA: Wadsworth.

Gronlund, N. E. (2003). *Assessment of student achievement* (7th ed.). Boston: Allyn & Bacon.

Herrell, A., & Jordan, M. C. (2004). *Fifty strategies for teaching English language learners* (2nd ed.). Upper Saddle River, NJ: Pearson/Prentice Hall.

Holmes Group. (1986). *Tomorrow's teachers: A report of the Holmes Group.* East Lansing, MI: Holmes Group, Inc.

Hostetler, K. D. (2003). Responding to the technicist challenge to practical wisdom in teaching: The case of INTASC standards. *Educational Foundations, 16,* 45-64.

Huber, T. (2002). *Quality learning experiences for ALL students.* San Francisco, CA: Caddo Gap Press.

Jordan Irvine, J. J., & Armento, B. J. (2003). *Culturally responsive teaching.* Boston: McGraw-Hill.

Kessler, R. (2000). *The soul of education: Helping students find connection, compassion, and character at school.* Alexandria, VA: Association for Supervision and Curriculum Development.

Kliebard, H. M. (1987). *The struggle for the American curriculum: 1893–1958.* New York: Routledge & Kegan Paul.

Kochhar, C. A., West, L. L., & Taymans, J. M. (2000). *Successful inclusion: Practical strategies for a shared responsibility.* Upper Saddle River: NJ: Merrill.

Kohl, H. (1998). *The discipline of hope: Learning from a lifetime of teaching.* New York: Simon & Schuster.

Kottler, E., & Kottler, J. A. (2002). *Children with limited English: Teaching strategies for the regular classroom* (2nd ed.). Thousand Oaks, CA: Corwin Press.

Kounin, J. (1977). *Discipline and group management in classrooms.* New York: Holt, Rinehart & Winston.

Krug, E. A. (1964). *The shaping of the American high school, 1890–1920.* New York: Harper & Row.

Kubiszyn, T., & Borich, G. (2003). *Educational testing and measurement: Classroom application and practice* (7th ed.). New York: John Wiley and Sons.

Ladson-Billings, G. (1994). *The dreamkeepers.* San Francisco: Jossey-Bass.

Leu, D. J., Jr. & Leu, D. D. (2000). *Teaching with the Internet: Lessons from the classroom* (2nd ed.). Norwood, MA: Christopher-Gordon Publishers.

Lieberman, A., & Miller, L. (1984). *Teachers, their world and their work.* Alexandria, VA: Association for Supervision and Curriculum Development.

Lortie, D. (1977). *Schoolteacher: A sociological study.* Chicago: University of Chicago Press.

MacDonald, R. E., & Healy, S. D. (1999). *A handbook for beginning teachers* (2nd ed.). New York: Longman.

Macedo, D. (Ed.). (1994). *Literacies of power.* Boulder, CO: Westview Press.

Mangrum II, C. T., Iannuzzi, P., & Strichart, S. S. (1998). *Teaching study skills and strategies in grades 4–8.* Needham, MA: Allyn & Bacon.

McLaren, P. (1994). Critical pedagogy: Constructing an arch of social dreaming and a doorway to hope. In L. Erwin, & D. MacLennan (Eds.), *Sociology of education in Canada: Critical perspectives on theory, research, and practice* (pp. 137-160). Toronto: Copp Clark Longman.

McLeskey, J., & Waldron, N. (2001). *Inclusive schools in action: Making differences ordinary.* Alexandria, VA: Association for Supervision and Curriculum Development.

Merton, R. K. (1948). The self-fulfilling prophecy. *Antioch Review, 8,* 193-210.

Morse, T. E. (2002). Designing appropriate curriculum for special education students in urban schools. *Education and Urban Schools,* 4-17.

National Commission on Excellence in Education. (1983). *A nation at risk: The imperative for educational reform.* Washington, DC: U.S. Department of Education.

Oakes, J., & Lipton, M. (1999). *Teaching to change the world.* New York: McGraw-Hill.

O'Day, J. A. (2002). Complexity, accountability, and school improvement. *Harvard Educational Review, 72*(3), 293-329.

Ogle, D. (1986). The K-W-L: A teaching model that develops active reading of expository text. *The Reading Teacher, 39,* 564-570.

Ornstein, A. C. (1990). *Institutionalized learning in America.* New Brunswick, NJ: Transaction Publishers.

Osterman, K. F., & Kottkamp, R. B. (1993). *Reflective practice for educators: Improving schooling through professional development.* Newbury Park, CA: Corwin.

Parkay, F. W., & Stanford Hardcastle, B. (2001). *Becoming a teacher* (5th ed.). Boston: Allyn & Bacon.

Pinar, W. F., Reynolds, W. M., Slattery, P., & Taubman, P. M. (1995). *Understanding curriculum: An introduction to the study of historical and contemporary curriculum discourses.* New York: Peter Lang Publishers.

Popham, W. J. (2002). *Classroom assessment: What teachers need to know* (3rd ed.). Boston: Allyn & Bacon.

Pressley, M., & Woloshyn, V. (1995). *Cognitive strategy instruction that really improves children's academic performance.* Brookline, MA: Brookline Books.

Provenzo, E., Jr. (2002). *The Internet and the World Wide Web for teachers.* Boston: Allyn & Bacon.

Ravitch, D. (1995). *National standards in American education: A citizen's guide.* Washington, DC: The Brookings Institution.

Rist, R. C. (1970). Student social class and teacher expectations: The self-fulfilling prophecy in ghetto education. *Harvard Educational Review, 40,* 411-451.

Roberts, P. L., & Kellough, R. D. (1996). *A guide for developing an interdisciplinary thematic unit.* Englewood Cliffs, NJ: Merrill.

Rosenthal, R., & Jacobson, L. (1968). *Pygmalion in the classroom.* New York: Holt, Rinehart, & Winston.

Schubert, W. H. (1993). Curriculum reform. In *Challenges and achievements of American education: The 1993 ASCD yearbook.* Washington, DC: Association for Supervision and Curriculum Development.

Seguel, M. L. (1966). *The curriculum field: Its formative years.* New York: Teachers College Press.

Slattery, P. (1995). *Curriculum development in the postmodern era.* New York: Garland Publishing.

Slavin, R. (1994). *Cooperative learning: Theory, research, and practice.* Boston: Allyn & Bacon.

Smith, C., Jr. (1986). First year blues. *Kappa Delta Phi Record,* p. 104.

Smith, M. S., Fuhrman, S. H., & O'Day, J. (1994). National curriculum standards: Are they desirable and feasible? In R. F. Elmore & S. H. Fuhrman (Eds.), *The governance of curriculum* (pp. 12-29). Alexandria, VA: Association for Supervision and Curriculum Development.

Stronge, J. H. (2002). *Qualities of effective teaching.* Alexandria, VA: Association for Supervision and Curriculum Development.

Tauber, R. T. (1997). *Self-fulfilling prophecy: A practical guide to its use in education.* Westport, CT: Praeger.

Tyler, R. W. (1949). *Basic principles of curriculum and instruction.* Chicago: The University of Chicago Press.

Walber, H. J., Paschal, R. A., & Weinstein, T. (1985). Homework's powerful effects on learning. *Educational Leadership,* 76-79.

Wolfendale, S. (2000). *Special needs in the early years: Snapshots of practice.* London: Routledge.

Zukav, G. (2000). *Soul stories.* New York: Simon & Schuster.

Index

CORWIN PRESS

The Corwin Press logo—a raven striding across an open book—represents the union of courage and learning. Corwin Press is committed to improving education for all learners by publishing books and other professional development resources for those serving the field of K–12 education. By providing practical, hands-on materials, Corwin Press continues to carry out the promise of its motto: "**Helping Educators Do Their Work Better**."

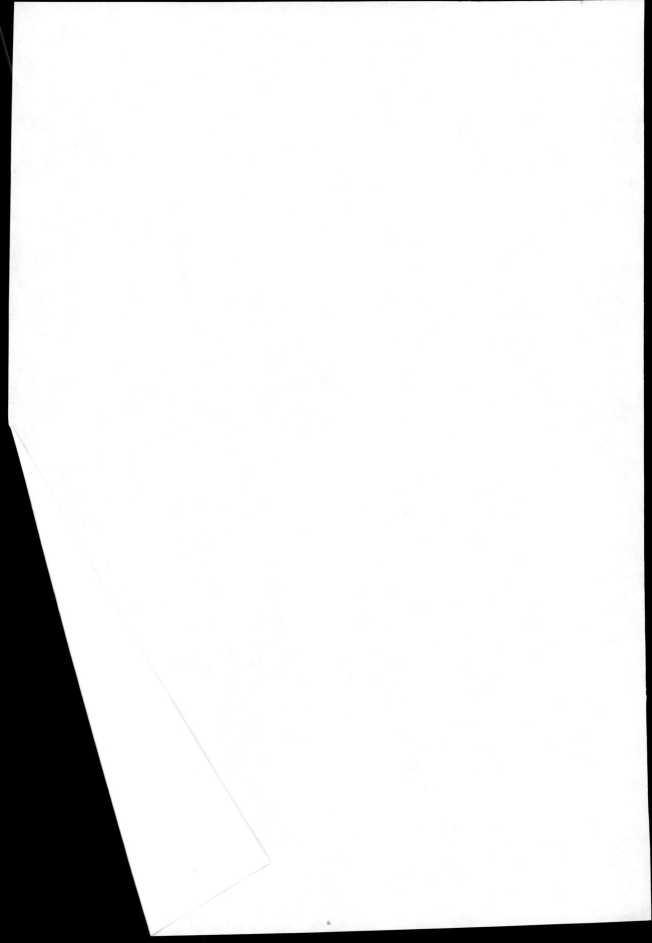

National Council for the So

Teaching About
Canada
and
México

Edited by
William W. Joyce
John F. Bratzel
Michigan State University

Published in association with
The Michigan State University
Canadian Studies Centre *and*
Center for Latin American and
Caribbean Studies

 **NCSS**
Bulletin 104

National Council for the Social Studies

8555 Sixteenth Street • Suite 500 • Silver Spring, Maryland 20910

www.**socialstudies**.org

Editorial staff on this publication: Michael Simpson, Chi Yang
Design/Production: Cowan Creative, San Jose, California | www.cowancreative.com

Library of Congress Control Number: 2006927480
ISBN: 978-0-87986-098-1

Printed in the United States of America

5   4   3   2   1

ACKNOWLEDGEMENTS

We are grateful to Alane Enyart, office assistant, MSU Canadian Studies Centre, for processing the manuscript for this publication. Her diligent, tireless efforts were invaluable. Cartographic materials were created under the competent direction of Sarah Acmoody, Center for Remote Sensing and Geographic Information Science, Michigan State University.

Also, we would like to thank John Hudzik, Former Dean of International Programs at Michigan State University, for his support of our international outreach efforts; and the Canadian Studies Centre and Center for Latin American and Caribbean Studies for encouraging and supporting this publication.

Finally, we are indebted to Dan Abele, Academic Relations Officer, Canadian Embassy, for supporting this publication; to the Canadian government for providing much-needed financial assistance; and to Michael Simpson, NCSS Director of Publications, and Chi Yang, NCSS Publications Assistant, for their competence in translating this publication into reality.

Table of Contents

NORTH AMERICA

Introduction

OVER THE YEARS, Canada and México have received minimal attention in U.S. social studies classes. Admittedly, these countries are taught in some schools at the sixth grade level, but this is by no means a national reality. It can be argued that this neglect is attributable to our nation's tendency to take these nations for granted. Canada and México are our major trading partners, we share a common history and geography, and many of our friends and family members are of Mexican and Canadian origin. Our nations share many views on world affairs. Indeed, we have much in common.

Canadians and Mexicans believe that it is in their best interests to keep abreast of U.S. affairs. U.S. television and radio provide them with a continuous flow of information on the U.S., including its policies on North American and global issues. In contrast, most Americans cannot receive Canadian and Mexican T.V. and radio broadcasts, and thus are deprived of Canadian and Mexican perspectives and vital aspects of their cultures.[1] That Canadian and Mexican newspapers can be purchased only in major U.S. urban areas and border towns further limits Americans' opportunities to keep abreast of events to the north and south of our borders. The net result: John and Mary Average American know very little about Canada and México.

Social, cultural, economic, and political events in both Canada and México have a greater impact on Americans than we would expect. Perhaps the most convincing evidence of the growing importance of this close, tripartite relationship occurred on September 11, 2001, when the people of our nation quickly learned that our ability to protect ourselves against further terrorism will be predicated on our efforts to build a North American-wide anti-terrorist capability, without jeopardizing our trade with Canada and México, and impairing the movement of people across our common boundaries.

We Americans desperately need to expand our knowledge of Canada and México, their historical antecedents, achievements, and the persistent problems of each country, as all three nations work toward harmonious continental integration. The essays in this publication are an important first step in this process, as they expose the reader to what is best and unique about these nations, and how we can craft a viable North American community. Further, we hope that the essays will provide a sound, reliable basis for further study and research by teachers and their students, and that the suggested activities at the end of the chapters will offer challenging, worthwhile learning experiences for students.

The Canada section opens with a chapter by Terry McDonald on the history of Canada, beginning with an account of the first Europeans who settled and colonized this nation. The chapter then analyzes major political and social developments in Canada from 1763 to the present, against the ever-changing US-Canada background.

"How We're Governed: People, Politics, and Law in Canada," by Desmond Morton, probes the historical foundations and contemporary policies and practices of Canada's parliamentary system of government, and this nation's relations with the United States.

Martin N. Marger's chapter, "Canadian Society: The North American Other," analyzes Canada's people, their primary values, and Canada's national identity through the perspectives of Canadians, Americans, and people of other nations. Also explored in this chapter is the growing gap in political ideology separating conservative Americans from liberal Canadians.

What is Canadian? David McKnight grapples with this question as he describes the processes by which Canadians have created rich cultural works, which express their unique identity as a nation, and are now attempting to preserve this culture. Distinctive features of Canadian literature, art, music, and other art forms are emphasized.

The 2003 Québec election is the focal point of Philip J. Handrick's chapter, which examines Québec's separatism in light of social and cultural perspectives that transcend traditional party affiliation models. It concludes with an analysis of the implications of Jean Charet's 2003 election as premier of Québec.

The México section begins with Amy J. Hirshman's chapter on this nation's rich history, which is discussed in terms of the rise and fall of various civilizations in México. To Hirshman, these societies are made up of real people with real lives, and as such, she allows the reader to relate to a time past.

Dina M. Berger and John F. Bratzel discuss the Spanish arrival in México, the conquest, and the resulting society. Following independence from Spain, the failure of México to achieve a stable government led to chaos and a loss of a third of its territory, as well as French meddling. Ultimately, out of this chaos came a strong government under Porfirio Diaz. While Diaz brought stability, he also generated pent up resentment of his people, and ultimately a terrible revolution.

Paloma Bauer de la Isla discusses Mexican politics from the revolution of 1910 to today, with the emphasis on the last few years. She discusses the structure of the official party and system of control that ruled México for seventy years. She also describes what recently brought that structure to an end, and speculates on the future.

Mexican culture is found at many levels from high-quality novels and poetry, to television soap operas and comic books. In his chapter, Daniel J. Nappo reviews Mexican literature, television, and movies, with an emphasis on the last seventy years.

"United States Images in México," by Manuel Chavez, examines what Mexicans think about the United States. Chavez does not deal with México as a single entity, but differentiates based on region and other factors. Where a person lives in México and the amount of contact an individual has had with Americans affects one's views. The result is a fascinating pattern of views that many will find surprising.

The final chapter on México was written by a well-known political commentator and author, Dr. Leonardo Curzio of El Centro Investigaciones sobre América del Norte (CIESAN) at the Universidad Nacional Autónoma de México (UNAM). He examines the last twenty years in México's history, and the considerable changes that have taken place. He provides his thoughts about what México has achieved, and what challenges the country will face in the future.

The final section by Dimitry Anastakis demonstrates why the North American Free Trade Agreement remains a constant central theme in U.S.-Canada-México relations. The author explores the impact of NAFTA and related agreements on the continuing economic integration of the three nations, and speculates on what the future portends as continental trade, employment, the environment, and sovereignty dominate the behavior of North Americans.

At the end of each chapter is a list of suggested activities designed by Dean V. June and Ruth Writer (Canada and NAFTA sections) and by Kristen Janka Millar (México section). Intended to assist teachers in using the major ideas in these chapters in their teaching, the classroom activities are organized according to the NCSS standards.

Notes

1. For an intensive discussion of the profound lack of reciprocity between U.S. citizens' access to Canadian media and their Canadian counterparts' access to U.S. media, see Avner Segal, "What do Prospective Social Studies' Teachers in the U.S. Know About Canada?," *Michigan Social Studies Journal* 14 (spring 2003): 7-10.

Canada

Arctic
Ocean

Yukon

Northwest
Territories

Nunavut

★ Whitehorse

★ Yellowknife

Hudso
Bay

British
Columbia

Alberta

Saskatchewan

Pacific
Ocean

Manitoba

Ontario

Edmonton
★

● Calgary

Vancouver
Victoria

Regina
★

Winnipeg
★

Canadian Capital

Capital City

Major City

United States of America

Miles
0   125   250   500

0   200   400   800
Kilometers

Canadian Provinces and Major Cities

Iceland

Greenland

Iqaluit

Newfoundland and Labrador

St. John's

Quebec

PEI Charlottetown

Nova Scotia

Quebec Fredericton

Halifax

Ottawa Montreal

New Brunswick

Toronto

Atlantic Ocean

A History of Canada: From the First Europeans to the Twenty-first Century

By Terry McDonald
Centre for the Study of Britain and its Empire
University of Southampton

European visitors to North America often find it difficult to tell the difference between the United States and Canada. In a number of ways, the United States and Canada look alike and to the untutored ear, they sound alike. The two countries are in one respect, intertwined for the Canadian province of British Columbia separates the American state of Alaska from its partners in the "lower 48." Indeed, it can be argued there should not be two countries occupying much of North America because the natural geography of the continent rules against it. The rivers and the mountain ranges, features that frequently create borders in other parts of the world, all run (more or less) north to south. The boundary between the United States and Canada, which mostly runs along the 49th parallel, is obviously an artificial construct. If the continent had to be split into the political entities that today we call "nation states" they ought, logically and practically, to have borders that run from north to south, rather than the east to west as they exist today.

Yet there are two countries and they have an east-west border. They are so large in area that both are federal countries although the smaller, the United States, has around ten times the population of Canada and is by far the more powerful economically and militarily. So, why haven't the ten Canadian provinces and three territories simply merged with the United States and allowed it to finally fulfill its manifest destiny? Why should there be a country called Canada? And, given that there is, why should it be a monarchy and have a parliamentary system, rather than a republic with a presidential system of government? Why should it have a social system more in common with the countries of Western Europe than with the United States?

The answer to all of these questions lies in the history of North America, and the long and fierce rivalry between two European powers which invariably resulted in war.

Britain and France, so close geographically but so different in many ways, created two of the great global empires and Canada was literally a battleground for their ambitions and antagonisms. Thus the history of modern Canada is, from the outset, a history of two European peoples, the French and the English, their impact on the land, on those already living there and on those who came later. It is also the history of a country that was always determined to be different to the United States.

The First Europeans

Although the first Europeans arrived in the Americas around the year 1000, they only touched upon the edge of the continent and their stay lasted only about three years. These were the Norse, traces of whose occupation can still be seen at Anse aux Meadow, on the northern tip of Newfoundland. This, though, had little or no impact on the continent. It was to be almost five hundred years before Europeans returned, but when they did, it was (eventually) to result in permanent settlement.

They came to a land already populated by nomadic aboriginal peoples but, given its sheer size, it was an empty country. To the Europeans it was theirs for the taking. The majority came in search of fish and furs, which were available in unprecedented quantities and also in hopes of finding vast quantities of precious metals, as the Spanish and Portuguese had in South America. Even if precious metals were not to be found in North America, there was still the tantalizing prospect of a sea route to Asia, where many of the luxuries that the European elite craved could certainly be found. The search for the North West Passage was to occupy the minds of European explorers for over three hundred years and the French were among the earliest people to attempt it. In so doing they began to penetrate the Canadian hinterland.

Jacques Cartier was the first of these, making three visits to North America between 1534 and 1541. On his first voyage he claimed the lands around the Gulf of St Lawrence for France and, on his second he traveled as far as present day Montréal. From the indigenous peoples he learned of a river that led to a great body of water which he assumed would be the Pacific. In fact, he was the first European to become aware of the existence of the Great Lakes although he never reached them.

New France

Jacques Cartier, on his third visit to North America in 1541, attempted to establish a colony. This failed and it was to be another Frenchman, Samuel de Champlain, who successfully established a permanent French presence in Canada. He traveled as cartographer in 1604, with 125 settlers who arrived in a region that they named Acadia but is today called Nova Scotia. The French settlers eventually founded Port Royal, present day Annapolis Royal, but in 1608 Champlain sought a new site for colonization and chose a strategically significant location on a bend in the St Lawrence River which he called "Québec." Here, high above the river, he built a fort, thus laying the foundations for what was to become the most solidly French city in North America. Thirty four years later, another settlement was established on an island in the river which was named Ville Marie de Montréal. The future city of Montréal was another step towards cementing the French presence in the New World.

France was not alone in attempting to colonize the newly discovered lands. England, too, made tentative attempts to plant people in the Americas in places as diverse as Virginia and Newfoundland. These first colonies were usually unsuccessful but later ones succeeded. France and England, however, had different approaches to the management of their overseas possessions. In 1663 "New France" had been designated as a Royal Province whose settlers were there because of the French government's strategic policy of hand-picking them and subsidizing their existence in order to secure the territory. English policy was commercial and individualistic, as the creation of the Hudson's Bay Company reveals. It was founded in 1670, and was to be instrumental in ensuring Britain's eventual ownership of the vast territories of what is now the Canadian north.

However, it was the French who pressed ahead with the colonization of Canada, with emigration increasing the population of New France from around 3,000 in the 1660s to around 75,000 by the mid eighteenth century. At its peak, French settlement was centred upon the northern bank of the St Lawrence River as far as the Saguenay River and the southern bank as far as the Gaspé Peninsula. There were also colonies in Île Royale (now Cape Breton) where the mighty fortress of Louisbourg had been built, and Île St. Jean (now Prince Edward Island), Acadia and Newfoundland. The French also owned Louisiana (a much larger area than the modern state of that name) and dominated vast territories around the Great Lakes.

The French, though, were never to emigrate in huge numbers, unlike the inhabitants of the British Isles. In the seventeenth century it is estimated that 400,000 English, Scots and Irish emigrated to the Americas but, overwhelmingly, they settled in those areas that were to become the United States. This exodus continued in the eighteenth century and by 1763 Britain possessed eighteen colonies in North America, from Florida to Newfoundland as well as others in the Caribbean. In continental North American the population of the thirteen most prosperous colonies had reached two and a half million. Thus when war broke out again between Britain and France, the latter country's population in North America was miniscule compared with that of Britain.

The Conquest

On the other side of the Atlantic, the balance of power in Europe was changing. Spain was in decline and there was a long and bitter struggle between England and France for economic and political supremacy. Between 1688 and 1763 the two countries fought each other on four occasions, not only in Europe but also in North America. The most important of these was to be the Seven Years War,[1] which began in 1756 and was to bring about the end of French power in North America.

At first the War did not go well for the British but in 1759 they were to win one of most unexpected military victories in modern history. This occurred after the French army, under the Marquis de Montcalm, had concentrated its forces in the city of Québec, high above the St Lawrence River which was now controlled by British forces. In September the British, under the command of General James Wolfe, were able to land their army below the cliffs and the soldiers "clambered up one of the steepest precipices that can be conceived being almost perpendicular and of an incredible height."[2]

When the French awoke on the morning of September 13, they found a British army just a mile from the city gates and ready for battle. In a twenty minute engagement, fought in a traditional European manner and which saw the deaths of both Wolfe and Montcalm, the French were defeated. On that morning, French power in North America effectively came to an end and the British were masters of almost the whole of the eastern side of the continent. The war dragged on until 1760, when the city of Montréal surrendered and in the subsequent Treaty of Paris, in 1763, France lost all its territories except for the two islands of St Pierre and Miquelon which lie a few miles off the south coast of Newfoundland. Louisiana was awarded to Spain.

In the aftermath of the war, Britain had to govern these vast territories with their French settlers and a hostile native population. Indeed, under their Chief, Pontiac, the Ottawa Indians led a rebellion against the British that was to last for five years and force them to develop a new strategy for dealing with the native peoples. Britain was, however, surprisingly tolerant towards the French who remained in North America. Some, such as government officials, military officers and a few merchants, returned to Europe but for the majority of the population, life continued much as before. By the Royal Proclamation of 1763 a Legislative Assembly was to be established (although this did not come into being for another thirty years), the Roman Catholic religion tolerated[3] and all citizens were protected under the laws of England. In 1774 the British Parliament passed the Québec Act which greatly increased the territory designated as "Canada," the Catholic church's position was strengthened, the semi-feudal seigneurial system of land ownership was allowed to continue and the Civil Law remained French. Plans to Anglicize the colony by immigration never came to fruition and it remained predominantly French in language and tradition.

The American Revolution and its Aftermath

British rule over the whole of eastern North America was, of course, short-lived. Just sixteen years after the fall of New France, the original thirteen colonies of the U.S. began their fight against what they saw as a repressive and greedy British government. By 1783 Britain had lost a war and the United States of America had been born. Yet not all of the inhabitants of the rebellious colonies were against Britain and, once the war was over, a movement of peoples

occurred that was to help in the creation of Canada as an English speaking, parliamentary democracy. Those who remained loyal to Britain and refused to lived in the new republic had two basic choices—to go home (although "home" was for the majority somewhere they had never seen) or to go to those parts of North America that were still British. The vast majority took the latter course.

The most obvious places to move to were the British colonies to the north of the United States, especially the area called Nova Scotia, and in 1783, the year that the war ended, it is estimated that 32,000 people arrived there. Several thousand more moved to the newly conquered Canada, settling in its western fringes, thus laying the grounds for the territory's division, in 1791, into French speaking Lower Canada and English speaking Upper Canada. Nova Scotia had already been divided into smaller units, including (for a short time) Cape Breton as a separate colony, and, more permanently, the creation of New Brunswick in 1784. The people who left the United States were helped by the British government and given land, tools, and livestock. With between 80,000 and 100,000 Loyalists having moved to British North America, the Anglicization of Canada had begun.

Over the next half century the British North American colonies continued to expand, despite the huge strains placed upon Britain by the Napoleonic wars. Fortunately for Britain its French-Canadian population opposed the ideas from revolutionary France and this helped consolidate its North American character. The English speakers, too, were strengthened by the "war within a war",[4] known today as the War of 1812. As France and Britain fought each other the United States found an excuse to attack British possessions in North America. For three years Americans fought the British and Canadians, on land and on the Lakes, and although the outcome was inconclusive, the War of 1812 was to be another of the factors that helped produce a Canadian identity. When peace returned, the United States had failed to gain any territory from Canada.

In 1815, after 22 years of war, peace also returned to Europe. This was followed in Britain and Ireland by a steep rise in unemployment brought about by the demobilization of thousands of soldiers and sailors, and the introduction of new machinery to industry and agriculture. One obvious solution to the "problem of the poor" was emigration and British North America was to receive its first major influx of English speaking peoples. In the quarter of a century between 1815 and 1840, thousands of people settled in Upper Canada, modern day Ontario. All along the shores of Lake Ontario and Lake Erie new settlements were established, largely populated by English, Scots and Irish immigrants and by 1834 Toronto had a population of almost 10,000. This wave of emigration from the British Isles was at its peak in the early 1830s, when around 50,000 settlers a year arrived in Québec. They then traveled by river to Montréal, but very few stayed in French Canada. One English immigrant, a single woman named Sylvia Lawrence, initially stayed in Montréal but told her father in a letter home:

> I went to work at the millinery, at a French family, my mistress taught me a great many French words. She said by next summer I should speak French well enough to sell bonnets for her, as she wanted one that could speak both languages; but its being a Catholic family, we could not agree upon our religion, so I left them. ...everyone says it is better going on farther.[5]

And go on farther they did. Upper Canada saw its population rise to almost 400,000 in 1838 compared with 125,000 in 1824, whilst in Nova Scotia it reached 200,000. For all of British North America it rose from 750,000 in 1820 to almost two and a half million by 1851. Not all of these new people were fleeing poverty in the British Isles. Many were comfortably off, drawn by the opportunities offered in a country where land seemed to be theirs for the asking.

The West

Thus far this history has concentrated on eastern Canada but Britain also possessed, through the Hudson's Bay Company, huge tracts of the north known as Prince Rupert's Land. There was also the question of the western side of the continent where, at the beginning of the nineteenth century, Spain, Britain and Russia all claimed part-ownership. Gradually the Spanish lost ground as California and Texas passed into the hands of the United States. Russia's claim over Alaska, which had begun in 1741, saw the establishment of its first settlement there, on Kodiak Island, in 1784. Britain, too, had become interested in the Pacific coast of North America and in the late eighteenth century had explored, charted and claimed much of the region. The west was also becoming more accessible by land as explorers from the North West Company, a Montréal

based grouping of Scots and French fur-traders founded in 1787, ventured beyond the prairies. In effect there was a two pronged attack upon the West by overland explorers such as Mackenzie, Fraser, and Thompson (whose names are remembered by the great rivers that they discovered), and by sailors such as Cook and Vancouver.

Even the prairie regions were receiving British settlers, beginning with a scheme promoted by a Scots aristocrat, the Earl of Selkirk, in the early years of the century. Despite clashes with the Métis people, of mixed French and Native origins, and the rivalry between the Hudson Bay and North West Companies, the region gradually developed and eventually formed the basis of the province of Manitoba. Thus, aided by economic and social developments in the east, British North America was, by the 1850s and 60s, clearly evolving into the country that is now Canada. The question, therefore, was what should be done with it?

Confederation

If there was ever a case of the British learning from the lessons of history, it was in the creation of the Dominion of Canada. The American Revolution was a defeat for Britain and, as the population of British North America continued its rapid growth, there was clearly a fear in London that history might repeat itself. Demands for reform had already manifested themselves in both English speaking Upper Canada and (largely) French speaking Lower Canada and in what have become known as the 1837 rebellions, both parts of Canada challenged the existing political establishment.

In Upper Canada the rebellion was led by the Scots journalist William Lyon Mackenzie and in the Lower province it was Louis Joseph Papineau. Both were opposed to the conservatism of the ruling class and the churches and sought the introduction of democratic institutions in the American manner. They wanted the ending of appointed government and greater control over commerce and industry and, in Lower Canada, more power to French speakers. When their demands were rejected, Papineau issued a call to arms and for around three weeks his supporters were in open rebellion. There was a similar rising in Upper Canada, albeit on a smaller scale, and with virtually no bloodshed. In Lower Canada, though, there were some deaths. Both Mackenzie and Papineau fled to the United States but were eventually able to return to Canada.

Britain's response to the rebellions was, with hindsight,

a prudent one in that it sent Lord Durham to investigate the situation in British North America and his subsequent Report, published in early 1839, was to form the basis for self government. In the short term, Upper Canada and Lower Canada were united under the Act of Union in 1841, but sub-divided into Canada West and Canada East. Each sent 42 members to a new Legislature although the Government was still mainly appointed and controlled by the Colonial Office in London. This was, to both English and French speakers, an unsatisfactory arrangement and the demands for responsible government continued. London gradually accepted these, and in 1848, it was granted to Nova Scotia. Self government in all domestic matters for Canada East and Canada West followed a few months later. It was granted to New Brunswick in 1854, Newfoundland in 1855 and Prince Edward Island in 1862.

Once again, it was events in the United States that were to help shape the future Canada. In the west new states were emerging and there was a serious dispute over the Oregon territory. The Americans regarded gaining the western half of the continent as a further step towards their "manifest destiny," something that the Russians who owned Alaska recognized in the years before they sold that land to the United States. As one Russian wrote in 1853, "...the United States are bound to spread over the whole of North America... Sooner or later we shall have to surrender our North American possessions."[6] London disagreed, but was concerned about American intentions. The Oregon dispute was settled when the 49th parallel became the agreed border in 1846, although Britain retained control of the crown colony of Vancouver Island whose southern tip, including the city of Victoria, is below that line. Britain also replaced the Hudson's Bay Company as the authority in the west and created the crown colony of British Columbia in 1858.

The 1860s were a crucial decade for both Canada and the United States. Trade links had improved and the British colonies were enjoying unprecedented prosperity. The most important event of the period was undoubtedly the American Civil War of 1861-65 and there was a feeling on the Union side that Britain supported the Confederacy. There were some sympathizers within the British government but the public generally supported the North, as did the population of British North America. There was, however, a fear that once the northern armies were victorious, they might turn their attentions towards the British pos-

sessions. Given that the United States now had a population of 31 million as against just over three million in the British territories, there would be little that Britain could do to defend the Canadas and the Maritimes. This forced the British authorities and those living in the colonies to contemplate bringing them together under one government, to finally create an alternative North American country, as implied in the Durham Report.

The formal debate on confederation began at Charlotte-town, on Prince Edward Island, in September 1864 and was attended by delegates from all three maritime colonies, whose idea it was. They were joined by self-invited delegates from both Canadas, but the remaining colony, Newfoundland, failed to send anyone. It did, however, send two observers to the follow-up conference in Québec City, which began on October 9, 1864, and they became involved in the negotiations. Once home, they were unable to convince their electorate of the benefits of confederation and Newfoundland was to remain a separate country for another 85 years.

Confederation was clearly an attainable goal to the other delegates and luminaries as Sir John A. Macdonald from Canada West, and George-Etienne Cartier from the Eastern half led the discussions. They had been instrumental in creating a new political party, the Liberal-Conservatives who, as their name suggests, wanted moderate reform of Canada and its institutions. Another "Father of Confederation" was Alexander Galt, a Montréal businessman, who recognized that the only way to truly unite the colonies was by making travel and communication between them much quicker. He therefore argued for the building of a railway that would, initially, link the Atlantic coast to Québec and would eventually be extended westward. After two weeks of discussion, with Macdonald arguing persuasively for a federal union, the delegates produced a package now called the "Seventy Two Resolutions." These included assurances that the peoples who made up British North America would retain their identity and traditions, something of great importance not only to the French-Canadians but also the Maritimers. Each of the new "provinces," one of which would be predominantly French speaking, would retain considerable power over its own affairs. The federal government in the newly designated capital city of Ottawa would have overall control in areas such as economic planning and decision making, including the proposed railway line from the Atlantic westwards.

With the success of the Québec conference, the next

stage was to talk to the British government in London, and in 1865 Canada's leading politicians held talks with the Colonial Office in England. No representatives from the Maritimes were present, not least because there was still considerable resistance to a federal union in those colonies. Newfoundland and Prince Edward Island had already rejected the Québec Resolutions and New Brunswick was wavering. In Nova Scotia, too, there were problems but, under pressure from London, the two colonies eventually accepted the concept and their representatives joined their colleagues from the Canadas in a second visit to London. There, under the watchful eye of the Colonial Office, proposals for uniting the willing North American colonies were discussed.

London was, once again, gently coercing the colonials towards the form of union that it wanted. In effect, the new country was to have a British system in a federal context. The regional tensions that had always existed within the colonies meant that a way had to be found to ensure that each province would feel it was an equal partner in the new federation and that its identity would be preserved. Thus it was agreed that a new country would be created, called the "Dominion of Canada" rather than "Kingdom" because of American sensibilities. It would have four provinces, Nova Scotia, New Brunswick, and the two Canadas, these being re-named Ontario and Québec. The central government in Ottawa would have responsibility for matters of national interest, whilst the provinces controlled matters of local interest. Canada was to have a monarch and a bi-cameral parliament, just as in Britain, and the monarch was, of course, the British queen, Victoria. She would be represented in Canada by a "Governor-General" who was, until after the Second World War, always British. The parliament was made up of an elected House of Commons, with Québec having 65 of its 181 members, and a Senate whose members were appointed by the Prime Minister, with each province having an agreed quota.

It was also agreed that an "inter-continental" railway should be built, the concept of a "trans-continental" one coming later. All of these measures were passed by the British parliament and the British North America Act became law on March 29, 1867. It was to be the Constitution of Canada until 1982.

The New Dominion

The Dominion of Canada came into being on July 1, 1867, and was the first British possession to become, on the face of it, an independent state. However, its people remained British citizens and the parliament in London could veto bills passed by its counterpart in Ottawa. Britain also retained control over immigration, and Canada's relationship with other states was to be through Britain.

Nevertheless the new state existed and its first government was led by Sir John A. Macdonald. He wisely involved men from all four provinces, deftly alleviating the possibility of any regional, linguistic or religious group feeling left out. Over the next few years, more provinces joined the new confederation, and its territory increased. In 1870 Prince Rupert's Land and the North West Territories were passed to Canada by Britain, after an Act of Parliament of 1868 ended the Hudson's Bay Company charter. In that same year, two more provinces were admitted into the confederation, Manitoba and British Columbia.

Manitoba's accession was troublesome in that the government failed to take into account the feelings of the 7,000 French speaking people living around the Red River, the Métis. They had a distinct sense of identity and their reaction to Ottawa's plans resulted in violence. Fearing a threat to their Catholicism and their traditional territories being taken over by English speaking Protestants, they seized Fort Garry (modern day Winnipeg) and set up their own provisional government. Their leader, Louis Riel, executed a Protestant settler charged with "antagonism towards his government," thus creating enormous tension between Ontario and Québec. To the former, Riel was a murderer, to the latter a defender of French Catholic rights from attack by Protestants. Ottawa managed to restore order and Riel went into exile in the United States. Manitoba became a Canadian province on July 15, 1870 with, under the Manitoba Act, English and French as official languages and of equal status. The two linguistic groups had separate schools and the Métis were granted lands of their own.

Like Manitoba, where there had been fears in both Ottawa and London of annexation by the United States through American settlers seeking new lands, in the far west, the Crown Colony of British Columbia was also subject to American pressures. These were caused by people crossing the border seeking gold in the late 1850s and early 1860s, mainly in the Cariboo region, and from others simply seeking new land. More American expansion occurred in 1867 when Alaska was bought from Russia, thus threatening to encircle the British territories. The two crown colonies of Vancouver Island and British Columbia had been re-united in 1866 and there was growing support for joining Canada within them. In 1870 negotiations began between the colony and the federal government with the latter offering to connect the west coast to eastern Canada by railway. British Columbia became part of Canada on July 20, 1871. Manitoba and British Columbia's entry into confederation reveal the two strands that have bedevilled Canada since its creation. These were the relationship between the English and French speaking sections of its population, and the one between a Canada based largely on "British" institutions and the United States. These tensions still exist today, of course, although those between Canada and the United States are largely economic.

By 1871 there were now six Canadian provinces and there remained two more candidate colonies waiting in the wings. One of these, Prince Edward Island, finally became part of the Dominion in 1873, but Newfoundland continued to stay aloof and did not become a Canadian province until 1949. During the first few years of the new Dominion's existence, the priority was clearly the consolidation of its territories and peoples, but the men in Ottawa who had been responsible for the birth of the new country had several other problems facing them.

Sir John A. Macdonald served as prime minister for six years, until 1873. He was a Tory, the informal British name for Conservatives, and a term that is still used today in both countries. His successor was from the "Liberal" party, the new name for the Reformers. This replicated the two party system of Conservatives and Liberals that had recently emerged in Britain. The new Prime Minister, Alexander Mackenzie, was faced with a number of problems, particularly economic ones. There was also the promised railway to the far west which was proving to be both expensive and time-consuming and, for a while, there seemed a possibility that British Columbia's membership of the Canadian confederation would be short lived. Mackenzie's government also had to cope with the regional tensions that were seemingly endemic in the new state and with organizations such as "Canada First" that promoted a vision of a more independent and overwhelmingly "Anglo Saxon" country. Eventually, in 1878, the Liberals were heavily defeated in the election of that year and were replaced by Macdonald's Conservatives.

One of Macdonald's first tasks was to honor his promise to British Columbia and the building of the railway be-

came a priority. It was completed as the Canadian Pacific Railway in 1885. Another problem from his first period in office returned as Louis Riel continued to involve himself in Canadian politics. Convinced that his role was to resist the westward expansion of Canada by English speaking settlers and to establish a Roman Catholic state in the west, he led the Métis and the native population in rebellion. This "North West Rebellion" cost 200 lives and was suppressed by the federal government, who were able to use the new railway to move troops from the east to Winnipeg. Riel, despite obvious mental health problems, was tried for treason and hanged in 1885. He immediately became a martyr to the Francophone and Catholic section of Canadian society and remains a controversial figure today.

Throughout Macdonald's second term in office his government was dogged with problems that may seem eerily familiar to modern Canadians. The relationship between the federal government and its provincial counterparts was never easy, particularly where money was concerned. There were also the always potent linguistic skirmishes and the even more divisive issue of religion. By the time of the next election, in 1891, Macdonald was an old man; indeed he made a virtue of it with the party's rallying cry of "The Old Flag, the Old Man, the Old Policy." He and the Conservatives won the election of 1891 but he died in 1894. At the next election, in 1896, the Liberals returned to power and gave Canada its first Prime Minister from Québec.

Wilfrid Laurier was to dominate Canadian politics for the next fifteen years, and pursued policies similar to those of his predecessor. He was able to resolve a problem with Manitoba's schools by suggesting a compromise acceptable to all religious denominations and gave strong support to Canadian industry and commerce. He also took Canada to war for the first time since confederation when he supported Britain's attempt to defeat Boer aspirations in South Africa between 1899 and 1902. French Canada reacted strongly, for there was some empathy among French Canadians for the Boers, who they saw as a minority linguistic group under attack from English speakers. In a typical compromise, Laurier personally authorized the raising, equipping and transporting of a volunteer Canadian regiment of 1,000 men to South Africa where they fought under British command. Eventually almost 8,000 Canadians served in South Africa.

The Laurier years also saw the beginning of an important change to Canadian society with an increase in immigration from Europe. Although much of it came from

Britain, there were also substantial numbers from Germany, the Ukraine and Scandinavia. During the fifteen years of Laurier's Liberal administration, around two million immigrants settled in Canada, with the wheat fields of the West experiencing dramatic growth. Such was the increase in population that, in 1905, two new provinces were created from the prairies, Saskatchewan and Alberta, bringing the total to nine.

The West was also the source of another dispute with the United States, this time over the boundary between British Columbia and Alaska. The gold rush that began in earnest in 1898 made it necessary to clarify just where the boundary between the United States' territory of Alaska and the Canadian territory of the Yukon lay. This was an important question because access to the Pacific for miners, merchants and traders would be through ports in either American or Canadian territory, to the benefit of either Seattle or Vancouver. The dispute was sent to arbitration by a panel consisting of six judges, three American, two Canadian and one British. To intense Canadian annoyance, the British judge sided with the Americans and the Yukon found itself cut off from the ocean by the Alaska 'pan handle.' Once again Canada found itself caught between Anglo-American interests.

Canada and the Two World Wars

In August 1914, a war in Europe began that was to traumatize the western world. Designated as the "Great War" when it ended in November 1918, it caused death on a scale never before experienced. Among the millions of men who died in the battlefields of France and Belgium were thousands of Canadians and Newfoundlanders.

At the general election of 1911, Laurier's Liberals had been replaced by the Conservatives and the new Prime Minister was a Nova Scotian lawyer named Robert Borden. Although at odds with Britain over Canada's right to be involved in decision making that affected it, Borden fully accepted that the moment Britain declared war on Germany, Canada was also at war. Within six months the first Canadian division had arrived in France, and three more would eventually arrive. On total, over 600,000 Canadian soldiers fought in the War, along with 8,000 who served in the Navy and 24,000 who joined the new "Flying Corps" of the British Army. Although not yet Canadian, 500 Newfoundlanders left for England in October 1914, and were the nucleus of a regiment that came, more than

any other, to exemplify the horrors of the First World War. On July 1, 1916, 810 men of the Royal Newfoundland Regiment left their trenches near the French village of Beaumont Hamel to attack the Germans. Within minutes over 100 were dead, 210 were missing and 374 wounded. Three months later, at Gueudecourt, the Regiment now consisting of around 500 men suffered losses on a similar scale to those at Beaumont Hamel. The Canadians, too, suffered terrible losses with over 60,000 men killed. This was 10,000 more than the United States which, from 1917, sent two million men to Europe. In some of the most difficult battles of the war, at Ypres and Passchendaele, for example, Canadian soldiers were heavily involved, gaining themselves a reputation for bravery and discipline. From this experience came the beginnings of a new Canadian nationalism.

At home, the Borden government had to cope with another conflict between the country's Anglophone and Francophone populations. Whereas the English speakers still retained strong links with Britain, the French speakers had little or no interest in France. Thus when the government began planning to introduce conscription there was a hostile reaction in Québec. There were, of course, French Canadians fighting alongside their English speaking compatriots in France, and the 22nd Royal Regiment of Québec had as distinguished a war record as any Anglophone Canadian regiment. But the war had proved to be another divisive factor in Canada's troubled Anglo-French history.

The war ended on November 11, 1918 and Canadians could breathe a sigh of relief. Their troops had fought gallantly and had given Canada a new status within the Empire and in the wider world. Yet, despite the benefits to the economy that the war had brought, the next twenty years were to be ones of frustration and depression.

The general election of 1917 had been a flawed one and had created new divisions in Canadian politics that persist to the present day. Borden had won the election as head of a coalition of Conservatives and Liberals who supported conscription. The remaining Liberals had support only in Québec, and the resulting government became the first one in Canadian history that did not include a major figure from that province. Borden retired in 1920 and the election of December 1921 saw the coming to power of a man who was to set new records for prime ministerial tenure, William Lyon Mackenzie King. He was, as his name reveals, the grandson of the leader of the Upper Canada rebellion in 1837.

In Canada the 1920s was a time of rising prosperity but it also saw the beginnings of a particularly Canadian phenomenon, new political parties with a strong regional base. Thus, in 1921, the Progressives, a new party drawing most of its support from western Canada, won 64 seats. This was fourteen more than the Conservatives, who were the traditional opposition to the Liberals. The most significant feature of the Progressive party was its left-of-centre platform and this is, again, an aspect of Canadian life that is more British than American. The Progressives' influence was not to last long and their parliamentary presence had declined by the end of the decade.

However, other parties from the west and from Québec emerged from the 1940s onwards as part of a trend away from a strict two-party system. The Albertan based Social Credit Party, the Co-Operative Commonwealth Federation (also from Western Canada) and the Union Nationale all had an impact. This last example was to take control of Québec and can be seen as the forerunner of the Parti Québécois, a powerful force in provincial politics in the late twentieth century, even affecting the national scene.

A major factor in producing these new parties was the "Great Depression" that began in 1929 and which had a devastating effect on Canadian industry and agriculture, especially industries such as timber, mining, fishing, and wheat growing. The prairies in particular suffered from the world-wide fall in wheat prices and the suffering in this region contributed towards the new political dissent and the creation of new parties. Ontario and Québec, with their manufacturing base, fared better. Eventually the economy began to recover although the government's efforts at emulating the American concept of a "New Deal" contributed little towards this. Two government innovations, however, were to prove of lasting benefit to Canada. One was the creation of the Bank of Canada, which took the control of monetary policy from the Government, whilst the other was the Canadian Broadcasting Corporation. This radio service, modeled on Britain's BBC, was to prove a stable and unifying force in Canadian society.

The inter-war years finally resolved the difficult constitutional position of countries such as Canada and their relationship with Britain. In 1931 the British Parliament passed the Statute of Westminster which made the dominions of the Empire independent countries, whose only relationship with Britain was loyalty to the Crown and membership in the British Commonwealth of Nations. Canada was now free to pursue its own foreign policies and to negotiate treaties without reference to Britain. However, Canada's neighboring dominion, Newfoundland, was to enjoy its new freedom for just three years. In 1934 its serious economic problems led to its government asking Britain to resume its colonial role and it was run by three British and three Newfoundland civil servants for the next fifteen years.

It had been believed that the allied victory of 1918 heralded the end to war but this optimism was short lived. The rise of new dictatorships in Europe and their expansionist policies had made yet another war on that continent inevitable. Mackenzie King believed, like Britain's Neville Chamberlain, that war could be avoided and even visited Germany to discuss the international situation with Hitler. He warned him that Canada would stand by Britain if war should occur. On September 3, 1939 Britain declared war on Germany. On this occasion, Canada did not automatically declare itself at war alongside Britain but, seven days later, the Canadian parliament voted on the matter. With only three of the 245 M.P.s dissenting, a state of war was declared between Canada and Germany.

The Second World War was a very different conflict than the First World War. For Canada it was its first venture onto the international stage as a full-fledged military power, although this did not seem likely at the outset. Its forces were miniscule compared with those of Britain, but when the war ended six years later, it had a navy of 100,000 men, 365 warships, and dozens of lesser vessels. The Royal Canadian Air Force also grew rapidly, peaking at almost 250,000 personnel, and 94,000 of them served overseas. Many Canadians served in the British air force but there were 48 RCAF squadrons based in Britain and other overseas theatres of war. The largest of the three services was the Army, with 730,000 men and women. For a country whose total population was still only twelve million, this was an astonishing achievement.

Although all three services played a full part in the fighting, it was the army that bore the brunt of Canadian losses. In 1942, when an attack was made on the French port of Dieppe in order to test the German defenses and the viability of an eventual invasion, the force was largely made up of Canadian troops. The Dieppe raid was to prove a disaster and of the 6,000 men who took part, 1,000 were killed and 2,000 were taken prisoner. The great majority of the losses were among the Canadian forces. When the

Allies invaded France in force, three countries were involved, the United States, Great Britain and Canada. On June 6, 1944, the great invasion took place, and of the 130,000 men who landed on the beaches of Normandy, 14,000 were Canadian. The "D-Day" invasion cemented Canada's role as a true partner to the United States and Britain.

At home, domestic politics continued and many of the disputes that arose were familiar ones including federal-provincial relations. Québec, which looked likely to re-elect a strongly nationalist government, reacted strongly to the possibility that conscription would be introduced, despite King's government having promised that there would be no calling up of men to serve overseas. With Canada's total commitment to the war effort, the Prime Minister needed to devise a way out of this pledge. He chose a plebiscite and sought the consent of the people to conscription being introduced if the government deemed it necessary. The outcome was that 80% of English speakers supported the government but 72% of French speakers opposed it, regarding the war as a European matter that was nothing to do with them.

For the Canadian economy the war had been beneficial. Whereas at the start of the war, much of the economy was still based upon primary resources, by the end Canada had become a genuinely industrialized country. Its agricultural sector was still important, of course, and it had been a major supplier of food to Britain both during and after the war. But its role as a major arms manufacturer was to lead to a permanent industrial base and Canada became the Americas' second largest industrialized country and (for a while) the world's fourth largest economy. This advance, though, was at a heavy price. 45,000 Canadians died during the war, fewer than in the First World War but still a large number for a country of twelve million people.

Coming of Age

The war ended on May 8, 1945 and it was, in many ways, a new Canada that faced the peace-time future. Within three years of the war's end, Mackenzie King retired after serving more than 22 years as Prime Minister and his successor was the second French speaker to hold the country's highest office, Louis St Laurent. Following policies similar to those of Mackenzie King, St Laurent presided over an increasingly confident and affluent country. In 1949 Canada, with the United States, became a founding member of the North Atlantic Treaty Organization (NATO), along with Brit-

ain and other west European countries as a defensive pact against the growing threat from the Soviet Union.

This new confidence was largely the result of events at the federal level. In 1949, eighty years late, Newfoundland became Canada's tenth province. It had prospered during the war, thanks mainly to the presence of American and Canadian troops, who were there because of its strategic location. Britain held two referendums in 1948 on its future, with the first offering three choices, a return to responsible government, union with Canada, or continuation of government by Commission. This last was decisively rejected by the people of Newfoundland and so, once again, was union with Canada. This was not the result that London and Ottawa wanted, so a second referendum was held, this time offering only "confederation" or "responsible government." By a majority of just 7,000 votes, the people finally chose to become Canadian and on April 1, 1949 Canada was, at last, deemed to be complete.

A further sign of Canada's growing maturity was the appointment, in February 1952, of its first Canadian born Governor-General. This office, which performed the duties of the (usually) absent Monarch, had always been held by a member of the British aristocracy, but after the appointment of Vincent Massey, the Governor-General has always been a Canadian. Other obviously British links were quietly dropped, including the term "Dominion" although it should be noted that many Canadian institutions retain the prefix "Royal", most notably the federal police force, the "Mounties."[7]

Domestic politics was also changing, most significantly in Québec where the Union Nationale regained power and held on for thirteen years, presiding over a growing sense of self-identification among the French speaking majority. The "Québec question" has come to bedevil Canadian politics since that time. At the federal level the Liberal Party continued its seemingly permanent hold over Parliament and government. Their stranglehold was finally broken in 1957 when the Progressive Conservatives, under John Diefenbaker, won the first of two successive election victories. A charismatic man with considerable skill as an orator, Diefenbaker was from Saskatchewan, and pursued policies promoting Canadian interests at home and overseas. In 1963 the Liberals returned to power under the leadership of Lester Pearson.

Pearson's Liberal government was fortunate in that the 1960s saw growth in the economy, rising prosperity and an increasing role for Canada on the world stage, through organizations such as the United Nations. His enduring legacy, though, was a small but vital addition to Canada's identity and image around the world. This was the adoption of the maple leaf flag in place of the former British red ensign with the Canadian coat of arms in its bottom right hand quarter that had been the national flag since 1867. The new red and white tricolor, with its distinctive red maple leaf in the center section, gave Canada one of the world's instantly recognizable flags.

Both Diefenbaker and Pearson helped improve Canadian society and the Canadian economy, especially in continuing the development of what Europeans term a "welfare state." Like Europeans, Canadians enjoy family allowances, state pensions and a health service, a fundamental difference between them and their American neighbors. What neither Prime Minister realized, though, was that Québec was also changing and that the 1960s would be seen in that province as the years of the "Quiet Revolution." Québec nationalism, always a latent force in Canadian politics, took on a new dimension and a new optimism. Ironically, the Quiet Revolution took place at a time when Canada was to get its third French speaking Prime Minister and a man who came to epitomize the new Canada and the new Québec, Pierre Elliott Trudeau.

Trudeau was even more charismatic than Diefenbaker; indeed the term "flamboyant" is probably a better descriptor. A bilingual lawyer from a wealthy Montréal family, he was superbly educated, well traveled and with a French-speaking father and an English speaking mother, he could be described as the archetypical Canadian. As a young man he had been active in promoting radical change in Québec, helping in the overthrow of the old guard that had run the province since the eighteenth century. The far reaching powers of the Catholic Church were greatly reduced and the education system was radically overhauled. Industries such as hydroelectric power were taken into provincial ownership and the French language was given new life as an everyday means of communication in government and business. Trudeau, who had been an active promoter of these changes, had entered parliament in 1965 and became Minister of Justice in Pearson's government in 1967. The following year he became Liberal Party leader and prime minister of Canada.

Trudeau's premiership is remembered for three reasons. The first is his personality and his life style, which gave rise to the term "Trudeaumania." A bachelor when he became prime minister, he was frequently seen at social events with leading figures from the world of entertainment, and when he married, it was to a woman 33 years his junior. The second was his reaction to the crisis that arose when a militant group from Québec who sought complete separation of that province from Canada embarked on a campaign of violence to help achieve their aims. In 1970 they kidnapped a British diplomat and, five days later, a minister in the Québec government. The latter was killed by the group. Trudeau invoked the War Measures Act, putting troops on the streets of Montréal and Ottawa, and his whole attitude towards the terrorists can be summed up in his famous response to a journalist who asked him how far he would go. "Just watch me," he said.

Québec separatism had been growing as a political movement since the Quiet Revolution and had been encouraged by the fiercely nationalistic President of France, Charles de Gaulle, during his visit to Montréal in 1967. His cry of 'Vive le Québec Libre' (Long Live Free Québec) infuriated Canadian politicians but struck a chord with many people in Québec. In 1980 the province's government, the separatist Parti Québécois which had come into being in 1968 and formed its first administration in 1973, held a referendum on whether Québec should remain a full member of the Canadian confederation. The separatists were defeated by 60% to 40% but it served as a warning to the rest of Canada that the Québec problem was not going to go away.

The third reason why Trudeau is remembered is his constitutional changes, which were largely a response to the "Québec problem." In 1969 he brought in the Official Languages Act which made Canada a bi-lingual country, with English and French having equal status. All government offices and institutions work in both languages. More significantly, Trudeau succeeded in "patriating" the Canadian constitution, a goal of many earlier prime ministers. The British parliament was asked to repeal the British North America Act that had formed the basis of Canada's constitution since 1867. This it did willingly, embarrassed that such a relic of Empire was still on the statute books. Ironically, when the Canada Act was passed into law in 1982, it was signed in Ottawa by the British Queen, Elizabeth II, in her capacity as Queen of Canada. In addition to the new constitution, Trudeau had added a Canadian Charter of Human Rights, which was to have far reaching consequences for the many minority groups within Canadian society.

Trudeau was Prime Minister for fifteen years, from 1968 until 1979 and from 1980 to 1984. It is not an exaggeration to say that he changed Canada, both internally and externally. He sought to make Canada independent, not just from the remnants of British imperialism, but also as a full player in international affairs. He was not popular with American administrations and famously defined the relationship between the two countries as "sleeping with an elephant—no matter how friendly and even tempered is the beast... one is affected by every twitch and grunt." Trudeau died in 1999 at the age of 80.

In the last quarter of the twentieth century Canada continued to grow and change. It had experienced large scale immigration since the war, initially from Britain but increasingly from the 1960s onwards, from other European countries and from Asia. It also formed closer economic ties with the United States in a number of areas and remained a major industrial power. Its oil industry, especially in Alberta, flourished and there was enormous American investment in the country. However, it continued to be plagued by its regional divisions, its tendency for new political parties to emerge, and a volatile electorate.

In 1984 the Progressive Conservatives returned to power under the leadership of a Quebecker whose mother tongue was English, Brian Mulroney. His victory was a spectacular one, the Tories winning 211 of the 282 seats in the House of Commons, and a new economic era began for Canada. Under Mulroney's leadership Canada adopted the economic policies advocated by Ronald Reagan and Margaret Thatcher, and became more active in world affairs. It joined bodies such as the Organization of American States, the "Group of Seven" (the world's most industrialized countries) and the Francophonie, France's version of the Commonwealth.

Mulroney won again in 1988 in an election that focused upon the projected North American Free Trade Agreement, albeit with a reduced majority of 43 over the Liberals and the New Democrats. By 1993, with the economy in recession, and the untried Kim Campbell as Mulroney's successor, the Progressive Conservatives faced the country. The result was astonishing. At the dissolution the Tories held 169 seats but when the results were declared, they had just two. The Liberals had returned but they were just the largest of five parties in the new House of Commons. The most significant feature of the new parliament was the presence of two parties that had not fought the previous election, the Bloc Québécois and Reform. Canada was about to enter a new period of volatility and intense self scrutiny.

The Reform Party was a product of the Canadian West. Formed in 1986, its policies were populist and right of centre. It was vehemently opposed to any more concessions being granted to Québec, which it regarded as something of a spoilt child within the Canadian family. Its slogan for the election reflected the growing sense of alienation in its homeland, "The West wants in", it claimed. In the event it won 52 seats, all but one of them in the four western provinces, and had similar results in subsequent elections. It became the official opposition in 1997. It has yet to make the hoped for breakthrough in eastern Canada but has pursued a strategy of merging with the Progressive Conservatives in order to present a united right of center challenge to the Liberals. In 2003 a merger was agreed, and the two parties formed the Conservative Party of Canada.

The Bloc Québécois was created in 1990 as the federal version of the Parti Québécois. Its candidates only fought for Québec seats but in 1993 it won 54 seats, making it (ironically) Her Majesty's Loyal Opposition. Since then its parliamentary representation has fallen by about a third. Its presence in Canadian federal politics was a direct result of the failures of the Mulroney government to settle once and for all the question of Québec's relationship with the rest of Canada. The 1982 Constitution had never been signed by Québec and Mulroney, after exhaustive discussions in 1987 with the ten provincial premiers at Meech Lake, a resort in Québec, agreed on an Accord which recognized that the province was different from the rest and that it would be seen as being a "Distinct Society." The Accord had to be ratified by all ten provinces within three years. However, because of opposition from Newfoundland and from an aboriginal leader from Manitoba, it ran out of time and was never ratified. A second attempt at resolving Québec's grievances, the Charlottetown Accord, was put to the public in a referendum in 1992 but, on a 72% turn out, was rejected by 54.3% to 45.7%. To Québec and the Parti Québécois, Meech Lake and Charlottetown were proof that they were not welcome in the Canadian federation. In October 1995 the Québec Government held a second referendum on separation and on this occasion the result was breathtakingly close. By 50.58% to 49.42% the people of Québec voted to remain Canadian. After more than 200 years of living together, the English and French speaking portions of the Canadian population were as far apart as ever. The pursuit of national unity thus continued to be the supreme goal of Canadian governments.

A New Century

The century began with Canada being led by the ever present Jean Chrétien, who was first elected to Parliament in 1963 and became prime minister in 1993. As leader of the only party to win seats in all thirteen provinces and territories, he has faced few conventional political challenges but many that have come from within Canadian society. His party's hold on power was heavily dependent on the province of Ontario where, in the 2000 election, it won 101 seats. With another 36 of its 172 seats in the 301 seat House of Commons coming from Québec, the Liberals are still an over-whelmingly eastern Canadian party. Of the 88 seats from the prairies and the west, they won only fourteen. They fared better in the Atlantic Provinces but the first parliament of the new century suggests that Canada is still troubled by its traditional regional differences. It was also elected on a turn-out of only 61%, the lowest in Canadian history, and this implies a new and worrying indifference to the nation's most important institution. In December 2003 Chrétien resigned and was replaced by Paul Martin, whose scandal-plagued administration was succeeded after the January 2006 election by a government headed by Stephen Harper, leader of the Conservative Party of Canada.

The Québec question remains a thorny one although a judgment by Canada's Supreme Court in 1998 clarified the situation by ruling that a province could leave the federation but only if its people voted by a clear majority to a clear question. Further respite came when the Parti Québécois was defeated by the Liberals in the provincial election of 2003, the latter winning 76 of the 125 seats in the National Assembly.

An optimistic development was the creation, in 1999, of a third territory. The North West Territories were divided into two and the eastern half was named Nunavut, or "Our Land," in the Inuit language. It gave a homeland to 40,000 Inuit people, the inhabitants of Canada's vast Arctic territories, and was seen as a welcome and inclusive move by Ottawa towards the indigenous peoples.

Canada has entered the new century as a major industrial power and a country which "punches above its weight." It is, by population, easily the smallest of the G8 group of countries. It is the second largest financial contributor towards the Francophonie and plays a senior role in the 52 nation Commonwealth.[8] It remains a distinct country from the United States, something that is clearly visible by its adoption of the metric system and its bi-lingualism. Yet it still has something of an identity crisis. Its many successful entertainers and actors are usually thought of as being Americans, on both sides of the Atlantic.

Traditionally Canada has been described consisting of "two solitudes," the English speakers and the French speakers who live separate lives, and cannot talk to each other. Arguably this is changing. Pessimists see Canada as now having no less than five solitudes, based upon the regional political differences. Optimists see these differences as making a major contribution to the Canadian whole and believe that it is a dynamic whole. Because of its post war immigration policy, Canada has become a multi-cultural society where differences are encouraged in the belief that they make for a richer society. As the world's second largest country enters a new century, its liberal traditions and its willingness to contribute towards making the world a safer and a better place for all suggest that it will, despite its divisions, survive and prosper.

Notes

1. The "Seven Years War" is also known as the "French and Indian War" in North America.
2. Captain John Knox, *The Siege of Québec and the Campaigns in North America, 1757-1760* (London: 1976 edition of the 1769 original), 196
3. England was (and still is) an overwhelmingly Protestant country.
4. It has been said that both Canada and the United States think they won the war, but the British have no memory of fighting in it!
5. Thomas Bunn (attrib.), *Letters from Poor People who Emigrated from the parish of Frome in the County of Somerset* (Frome, 1834).
6. Nikolai Muraviev, cited in Hector Chevigny, *Russian America—the Great Alaskan Venture, 1741-1867* (Portland, OR: 1965), 223.
7. The Royal Canadian Mounted Police. Other examples include the armed forces, and the Canadian navy's ships are prefixed H.M.C.S., or 'Her Majesty's Canadian Ship.'
8. With one exception—Mozambique—the Commonwealth is made up of countries that were once part of the British Empire.

A History of Canada

By Dean V. June and Ruth Writer

❶ CULTURE

▶ Discuss why it has been so difficult for the Canadians to answer the question: "What is a Canadian?"

▶ Discuss the dilemmas posed by the language issue in Canada from 1760 to the most recent referendum in Québec.

❷ TIME, CONTINUITY, AND CHANGE

▶ Create a time line of major historical events discussed in the article.

▶ Discuss why the creation of the territory of Nunavut is being closely monitored by aboriginal peoples around the globe.

❸ PEOPLE, PLACES, AND ENVIRONMENTS

▶ Using a Venn diagram, plot early French and English attempts to establish North American colonies. Be sure to include the effects of location and environment.

❹ INDIVIDUAL DEVELOPMENT AND IDENTITY

▶ Debate what the results of the French and Indian War might have been, if "The Conquest" hadn't occurred and the French were victorious.

▶ Compare and contrast George Washington's political career with that of Canada's first Prime Minister—John A. Macdonald.

❺ INDIVIDUALS, GROUPS AND INSTITUTIONS

▶ Evaluate the impact of the Loyalists on the settlement of Upper Canada and the Maritimes.

▶ Compare the history of Louis Riel's rebellions with that of any U.S. human rights movement.

❻ POWER, AUTHORITY, AND GOVERNANCE

▶ Compare and contrast a parliamentary system of government with a republican system of government.

❼ PRODUCTION, DISTRIBUTION, AND CONSUMPTION

▶ Use the internet to research if the U.S. Civil War had an economic impact on Canada. If so what was it? Speculate about what you think the economic impact on Canada would have been if the North had lost the Civil War.

❾ GLOBAL CONNECTIONS

▶ Create a political cartoon or a short news bulletin on the Alaskan/Canadian boundary dispute.

❿ CIVIC IDEALS AND PRACTICES

▶ Write a letter to the editor or your elected representative concerning conscription during World War II from an English-Canadian or French-Canadian point of view.

▶ Compare and contrast the personalities of Diefenbaker, Pearson, and Trudeau.

CHAPTER TWO

How We're Governed: People, Politics and Law in Canada

By Desmond Morton
McGill University

Because Canadians have come from many other countries, because their prosperity depends on trading with the world, and because Canada has never been allowed to have illusions of super-power status, Canadians are also affected by the decisions of other nations. Canada owes its existence to a refusal by most of its people to join the revolution that created the United States. Since then it has learned to live in close harmony with its closest neighbor, biggest trading partner and its major source and destination for immigrants. However, an unbroken history of seeking and depending on alliances has persuaded Canadians to depend on international organizations like the United Nations (UN) or the North Atlantic Treaty Organization (NATO), sometimes to gain leverage with its powerful southern neighbor. International organizations and their agencies adopt policies that sometimes have the force of law for Canadians.

Bureaucrats

People everywhere are governed by individuals we call "officials" and sometimes, combining a French and a Greek word, "bureaucrats." The word is not an insult since it underlines that the women and men who face us in a government office must treat us equally and according to law. No official can favor her cousin or be mean to someone with a different accent. Sometimes people who condemn "bureaucracy" are really complaining that they don't get more generous treatment than the law allows.

Confederation

Canada is a huge country—second largest in the world—at the northern end of North America. Between 1775 and 1784, the forebears of Canadians in the present-day provinces of Nova Scotia and Québec said no to the American Revolution. From 1812 to 1814, they fought American invaders and, with British help, survived the War of 1812 to become a self-governing pillar of Britain's 19th century empire. In 1867, three of Britain's North American colonies formed a Confederation of four provinces, Ontario, Québec, Nova Scotia and New Brunswick.

There were several reasons for Confederation. The American Civil War (1861-1865) told the British they could no longer save Canada in another War of 1812. It seemed a good idea to reorganize their colonies before they pulled out. In Canada West—the future Ontario—local leaders wanted to create a government strong enough to keep Americans out of the North West Territories, then managed by the fur-trading Hudson's Bay Company. Montréal, Canada's biggest commercial city, strongly agreed. Other Quebeckers, mostly French-speaking and Catholic, were reluctant to become a minority in an English-speaking, Protestant Canada. They demanded special safeguards in the British North America Act, as Canada's new constitution was called. Britain's Atlantic colonies resisted Confederation but the two mainland colonies, Nova Scotia and New Brunswick, were pushed into the Union by shrewd politics, pressure from Britain, and threats by Irish-American terrorists called Fenians.

Over the next eighty years, Canada took shape. In 1870, the Hudson's Bay Company's Red River colony became a new province of Manitoba. British Columbia joined in 1871 on the promise of a trans-continental railway. A financial crisis forced tiny Prince Edward Island into Confederation in 1873. The southern part of the Northwest Territories became Alberta and Saskatchewan in 1905. Britain's oldest colony, Newfoundland, had been a self-governing country but in 1949, Newfoundlanders narrowly chose to become Canada's tenth province. North of the 60th parallel are three territories: Yukon to the West, the Inuit-dominated Nunavut in the east and the North West Territories in the middle. Territories have elected governments but federal taxes pay most of the costs of government.

Federal and Parliamentary

The British North America Act made Canada a federal, parliamentary, self-governing colony of Britain. Some "Fathers of Confederation," who believed that too many "States Rights" had led to the U.S. Civil War, wanted a strong central government. Federalism was a concession to Québec and the Maritime provinces. As in the United States, the powers of government were divided between provinces and the central government.

The centralizers believed that Canada controlled powers that really mattered, such as defense, criminal law, and railways and canals. In the new capital of Ottawa, Parliament controlled banking and finance and it could levy "indirect taxes"—the ones people don't notice, like tariffs on imported goods. Ottawa was responsible for "Indian Affairs." Provinces looked after education, municipal government, the sick and the poor, law enforcement, and "property and civil rights". Provinces could levy only "direct taxes"—the ones ordinary people know about, like income tax or license fees. Immigration and agriculture are shared by both levels of government.

Times change. No one in 1867 had heard of radio or television. That year, Canada's first automobile was built and then crashed for lack of brakes. Cars and highways would not worry governments for another forty years. No one knew whether Ottawa or the provinces would cope with them.

Federally or provincially, Canadians adopted a "parliamentary" style of government, based on the British model. Ministers were "responsible" to an elected assembly. If most members of the assembly defeated a serious government proposal, the government had "lost the confidence" of the assembly and had to resign. If another party could form a government that won votes in the assembly, it could govern. Or the defeated government could call a general election and let the voters decide. In theory, Canadians could change the government by persuading elected representatives to defeat the current regime. More often, they wait as long as five years for a government to call an election. Any government that waits that long usually is defeated.

Kingdom or Dominion

The Fathers of Confederation called Canada a kingdom, but the British warned that the Americans might be annoyed by the word. Instead, New Brunswick's Leonard Tilley checked his Bible and found the phrase "He shall have Dominion from Sea unto Sea." The words gave Canada a title, "Dominion", and a motto, *A mari usque ad mare*. These days, Canadians have dropped the word "Dominion" because it never translated easily into the other official language, French. Since Canada extends to the Arctic as well as the Atlantic and Pacific oceans, Canadians express their motto as: "From sea to sea to sea."

The British also warned Canada to prepare for war with the U.S., and promised to help out. After 1867, few took the threat seriously. As long as Americans had nothing to fear on their northern frontier, Canada would be safe. A weak militia controlled disorders and the red-coated Mounted Police, sent to western Canada in 1874, ended any need for the U.S. Cavalry to cross the border. The "longest undefended border in the world" dates from 1871, when the British brought their last troops home from central Canada.

Canada's sovereign is Queen Elizabeth II of England and her heirs and successors. She is represented by a Governor General, currently a former journalist and broadcaster of Haitian ancestry, Michaëlle Jean. Canada's Constitution seems to give the Governor General awesome powers but, as befits a democracy, they are exercised solely through the will of a Parliament which consists of a 104-member Senate, appointed until age 75 by the prime minister, and an elected 307-member House of Commons, based on the principle that small provinces and rural voters should have more influence than people in big provinces and major cities. Each province has a lieutenant-governor, guided by a premier responsible to an elected legislature.

Parliamentary Power

Unlike the United States with its separation of legislative, executive and judicial power, governments in Canada are formed by the leader of the party which has "the confidence" of the elected House of Commons or legislature. From 1993 to 2003, that person was Jean Chrétien of the Liberal Party of Canada, a veteran politician first elected to represent his home-town of Shawinigan, Québec, in 1963. On December 12, 2004, Paul Martin, his former finance minister, replaced him after a power struggle. A prime minister chooses or dismisses the ministers in his or her government and most other key government officials, including senators and senior judges. More important, a prime minister can call an election when he or she chooses within a five-year term. Since timing is everything in politics, this is a big advantage.

However, prime ministers or provincial premiers lose their power the minute they lose their parliamentary majority in an election, or if supporters in the House of Commons or provincial Assembly switch their allegiance. When Canadians vote in a federal or provincial election, they choose only the "member" or representative for their electoral district, normally from candidates selected by national or provincial parties. The winner is "the first past the post," or the person who wins the most votes, even if she or he gets less than half the votes cast. The party that wins the most "ridings" or districts gets first chance to form the government, though sometimes a close contest results in a coalition or partnership of parties. Since Canada has had several federal parties since 1918, only four times since 1917 has a majority of Canadians actually backed the winning party in a federal election.

Political Parties

Canada's Liberal Party held power for seventy years and the Conservatives for only thirty. Moderation and lots of luck associated the Liberals with good times while the Conservatives usually held power during wrenching crises. Western Canada has sometimes formed protest movements to make its concerns heard, most recently the Reform Party in 1993, which amalgamated with Conservatives in 2003. Once devoted to the British connection, modern Canadian Conservatives sound a lot like U.S. Republicans. Members of a Bloc Québécois (BQ) support a sovereign Québec. A labour-backed New Democratic Party (NDP) has won acceptance for policies like universal health insurance without ever forming a government.

Canada's federal system split government responsibilities more clearly in 1867 than now. Ottawa controls Canada's foreign and defense policy. By controlling banking and interest rates, it tries to manage the economy. It collects the bulk of taxes, a thankless chore, but it also hands much of the money back to the provinces to spend on health, education and social welfare. It is never enough: both provinces and city governments want more revenue sources to pay for what voters want, from improved public schools and affordable day-care to the soaring costs of modern health care.

While premiers exercise the same enormous influence in their provinces as a federal prime minister, they also exercise a national role. When the prime minister meets provincial and territorial premiers, federal-provincial issues and constitutional change are discussed by politicians with real power. That power makes compromise difficult, particularly in open sessions, with the media listening and television recording each crowd-pleasing phrase.

Provincial Politics

Canada's provinces favor very different political styles. Ontario pioneered "progressive" Conservatism when a Conservative government forced private electricity companies into a huge publicly-owned corporation later called Ontario Hydro. The result was cheap energy and rapid industrial growth. Since 1935, Alberta voters have elected one conservative government after another, leaving few seats for the opposition. Saskatchewan, the farming province next door, has mostly elected social democrats since 1944, while Manitoba, the third prairie province, has switched between moderate Conservatives and moderate New Democrats. In Canada's four Atlantic provinces, Liberals and Conservatives change places often.

In 1867, provinces had minor roles. Roads were muddy tracks; schools offered a few years of education, and people got sick and died at home. Today, provinces spend sixty per cent of Canada's public revenue to provide highways and hospitals, and to subsidize public transit. They regulate municipalities and protect the environment from the grosser forms of pollution. They manage and finance school systems that provide twelve years of primary and secondary education. In some provinces, schools serve the separate interests of French and English, Catholics and Protestants. With federal help, provinces fund universities, though students and private donors now pay more of the cost.

Quebeckers boast that their province "n'est pas une province comme les autres" ("Is not a province like the others".) For one thing, French is the only official language, and rules restrict the use of English (the language of 18 per cent of Quebeckers) on signs and in public places. Until the 1960s, Québec seemed the most Catholic and conservative region in Canada. A "quiet revolution," silently building among people whose minds were opened by education and television in the affluent post-1945 years, burst in the 1960s. French-speaking Quebeckers turned to the government, not the Church, to exercise power. The logical next step, for many, was a sovereign country, independent of Canada but associated for many common interests. From 1970 to 2003, Québec voters switched every two elections between the federalist pro-business Liberals and a more left-wing, pro-sovereignty Parti Québécois (PQ) In 2003, after the usual two terms in opposition, Québec Liberals regained power.

Tangled Responsibilities

From the outset, federalism in Canada was tangled in the arguments of premiers and their lawyers, seeking a bigger role than the first Canadian prime minister, Sir John A. Macdonald, intended them to have. Until 1950, the judges were often members of the Empire's highest court, the Judicial Committee of the Privy Council. They believed in a federalism that made provinces as sovereign over its jurisdiction as the central government was over its responsibilities. In 1950, Canada decided that its Supreme Court would have final jurisdiction. Still, many precedents had been set. As in the United States, the division of powers inherent in federalism, complicated by changes un-imagined in 1867, invites judges to interpret the constitution. Canadian judges have used their powers with relish.

When BSE ("mad cow disease") was found in an Alberta cow in 2003, and beef exports were halted at the U.S. border, was Ottawa or Alberta responsible? Agriculture is a joint responsibility. Both governments inspect slaughterhouses, but Alberta (and the Cattlemen's Association) insisted on a minimum of government meddling. Still, Canada's entire beef industry was hard hit by the U.S. ban, and few resisted the urge to blame Ottawa and demand federal funds.

Peace, Order and Good Government

If Americans declared their independence for the sake of "Life, Liberty and the Pursuit of Happiness", Canada's constitution promised "Peace, Order and Good Government." Happy the government that can administer from day to peaceful day. Unhappily, if human nature produces sin, politics generates demands. Canadians wrestle with an environment made sick by over-consumption of its resources and the illusion that nature was too vast and forgiving ever to be irreversibly damaged. Intermittent seven-year drought cycles have helped devastate the prairie wheat economy while over-fishing, domestic and foreign, wiped out cod stocks on the Atlantic coast and salmon on the Pacific.

As heirs of a resource-based economy with a single major customer, the United States, Canadians are as vulnerable as third-world nations to world commodity prices. In addition to drought, prairie wheat farmers were victims in the 1990s of a subsidy war between the European Union and the United States. Canada, on its own, could afford to compete. Trade

disputes fostered by U.S. competitors closed down Canada's softwood lumber and cattle industries. Canadians dominate some key niches in high technology, notably robotics and telecommunications, but foreign ownership means that management and research decisions are made somewhere else. As elsewhere, existing but declining industries can outshout newcomers in their demands for government aid.

For two decades, 1974 to 1995, a gap between revenue and spending forced Ottawa to borrow at a huge cost. Business persuaded sympathetic governments to switch from taxes on wealth to consumption taxes like the European-style Goods and Services tax of 1991.

Rights and Freedoms

Canadian feminists denounce patriarchalism, demand effective enforcement of paternal support and won suspension of laws restricting abortion. Canadian women are not yet equal partners in the workforce. They still earn less, on average, than men, and single mothers and their children are a major component of the four million Canadians who are poor. This troubles many Canadians, but probably not most of them. Canadians are closer to U.S.-style individualism than they used to be.

From 1968 to 1979, Canada's prime minister was Pierre Elliott Trudeau. A charismatic, public figure, he alternately charmed and enraged Canadians but when he was defeated by the Conservatives in 1979, he left little as a memorial. In 1980, voters gave him a second chance. Trudeau decided to replace the British North America Act with a Made-in-Canada constitution which Canadians could amend. Trudeau's centerpiece was a Charter of Rights and Freedoms to protect all residents of Canada from oppression and injustice. In a titanic political struggle with the provinces and the Conservative opposition, Trudeau prevailed. On some issues, especially the amending formula, he yielded to the provinces, but never on his Charter. By the spring of 1983, Trudeau could invite Queen Elizabeth II to Ottawa to sign a Constitution Act that reduced her role in Canada but which enormously enhanced the power of Canada's courts as defenders of human rights and freedoms, and especially those of women, visible minorities, Native Peoples, and the disabled.

Though judges had always helped define Canadian federalism, they rarely imitated the interventionist role of American judges in reviewing state and federal laws, partly because they had no counterpart to the Bill of Rights. The

Charter filled that role and, with two additional centuries of experience, went beyond it. When they want to change a law they consider unjust or an unfair government policy, Canadians now consult lawyers, not their member of parliament or provincial legislature. Thanks to the Charter and judges who interpret it, Canada's armed forces must recruit and train women for combat, homosexual couples won the legal right to marry and Native fishermen have greater access to shrinking fish stocks. As judges have grown in political significance, critics have argued that their appointments must involve provincial as well as federal approval, and should no longer be the sole prerogative of the current prime minister.

Baby Boomers and a Baby Bust

In the 1950s, Canada had one of the highest birth-rates in any developed country; now it has one of the lowest. Since 1964, the birth-rate has been too low to replace the elderly. In Québec, large families used to help *Canadiens* keep pace with surges of immigration. Modern Quebeckers refuse to have large families. Nationalists fear the vanishing of French Canadians and passed laws to allow Québec to attract French-speaking immigrants and to educate newcomers *en français*. One exception to the baby-bust has been Canada's First Nations or Native population, half of whom are under twenty.

An aging population adds to Canadian worries about the cost of maintaining the universal health insurance system in effect since 1967. Healthcare costs are lower in Canada than in the United States where medicine-for-profit still reigns, but people resent the waiting lists that are an alternative to price rationing, while taxpayers resent the cost unless they are old or sick. Immigration is an obvious answer to demographic decline, but it brings the challenge of cultural diversity since the Third World, not Europe, provides most of Canada's inflow.

Culture, Race and Poverty

In 1973, the Liberal government of Pierre Elliott Trudeau proclaimed that Canada had two official languages—English and French—and many cultures. However multiculturalism starts to look like a smug evasion when major cities feel the resentment of Asian and West Indian newcomers whose beliefs, lifestyle and skills finds little acceptance. If Islam is as good as any other religion, will Canada's legal system incorporate *shari'a* law and, if so, which of its many versions?

Another inequality, shared by other countries, divides provinces and regions into "haves" and "have-nots," measured by whether they are now recipients or donors in a constitutionally-mandated system of equalization payments. Three provinces, Ontario, Alberta and British Columbia, usually contribute, six provinces take the money, and Québec is close to the borderline. All three northern territories depend heavily on Ottawa. Have-not Canada is a resource hinterland, where spikes in world prices produce brief interludes of prosperity amid bleak poverty. Encouraged by their leaders to live a traditional lifestyle, many of Canada's native people live on the lowest rung of the resource economy, heavily dependent on government payments, sometimes victims of corrupt band oligarchies.

The southern, urban, industrialized regions of Canada are as prosperous as anywhere in the world, but northern regions and hinterland provinces complain that little durable wealth reaches them. A seventy-year old cartoon depicted a cow being fed by hard-working prairie farmers and milked by eastern bankers while its back end is planted firmly over the Maritimes. Occasionally it reappears. Inequality in Canada's cities also grew since the 1970s when income disparities between rich and poor stopped shrinking and started to grow again. Prime Minister Trudeau's vision of a "Just Society" began fading long before he left office in 1984.

Trade Opportunities and Dependency

Free trade was always a hinterland solution for regional ills. Tariffs forced farmers to buy tractors from foreign-owned factories in Ontario but their exported wheat faced world competition. Canada's Conservatives created and defended tariffs to create industry in Canada, and they claimed working-class votes because they created jobs. Times had changed when Brian Mulroney led Progressive Conservatives to power in 1984. In 1980, Ronald Reagan had made a North American free trade area part of his Republican platform. The stage was set for a Canada-U.S. Free Trade Agreement signed by Mulroney and President Reagan in 1989, after Canadians re-elected the Conservatives in 1988 after a bitterly-fought campaign.

Liberals promised to scuttle the deal but after Jean Chrétien annihilated Mulroney's party in 1993, the Liberals agreed to expand the agreement and México, the United States and Canada signed a North American Free Trade

Agreement (NAFTA) in 1994. Serious trade irritants continue, but by 2001, a billion dollars worth of Canadian products moved across the American border daily, representing more than eighty per cent of Canada's foreign trade and millions of jobs. Canada had long since replaced Saudi Arabia as the main source of U.S. oil and natural gas. Critics worry about dependence on a single, sometimes capricious customer, but where else would Canadian producers find as close or as wealthy a market?

Québec and Canada

Some Fathers of Confederation hoped that French and English Canadians would share Canada. That has not happened. When Louis Riel, a Métis leader, was deposed at the Red River in 1870 and executed after a violent rebellion in Saskatchewan in 1885, Quebeckers decided not to move to the North West but to continue moving to jobs in the New England states, losing their French and keeping their Catholicism. Many western Canadians resent an Official Languages Act that entitles Canadians to receive federally-regulated services in French or English. Youngsters who fail to learn both languages have a hard time getting ahead in government, the armed forces or federal politics. With brief exceptions, every Canadian prime minister since 1968 has come from Québec.

In 1976, the Parti Québécois (PQ) was elected in Québec. Its language law made French Québec's only official language. Immigrants to Québec had to send their children to French schools. Everywhere signs in French replaced signs in English. Thousands of English-speaking Quebeckers abandoned the province where they were born. However, when the PQ held a referendum on sovereignty for Québec in 1980, claims that French was in danger made no sense when the language flourished on billboards and on the street. Opponents of sovereignty won sixty per cent of the vote.

The referendum had pitted an elfin, chain-smoking René Lévesque against Pierre Elliott Trudeau, who despised nationalism as reactionary tribalism. Trudeau fought Lévesque with the promise of a constitution that would guarantee Quebeckers an acceptable place in a federal Canada. Of course, what was acceptable to Trudeau could not be tolerated by Lévesque or his followers. The new Constitution Act of 1982 offered a special status for women, multicultural interests, language minorities and even Native peoples but not for the province of Québec.

Trudeau's province was a province like any other. Most Quebeckers felt differently. As a minority in Confederation, Quebeckers needed the right to veto future constitutional amendments that might affect it.

Québec's claim to a veto grew out of a theory devised by a Québec judge in the 1880s and taken up by many Quebeckers with enthusiasm. Judge Thomas Loranger argued that Confederation was a pact between two peoples, the French and the English, now represented by Québec and Canada. Like any pact, it could only be altered by the agreement of the original parties. Loranger's theory was more ingenious than historical but it became an article of faith to many Quebeckers. One reason Canada waited so long after other Dominions to take control of its own constitution was that the bitterly divisive issue of a Québec veto would have to be settled. Though Trudeau boasted that he had ended a colonial relationship, it was not the British but Canadian politicians who had refused to grasp a very hot potato. Trudeau and Canadians soon learned how hot it still was.

As a Quebecker, Brian Mulroney did his best to win a special status for Québec. He failed. Other Canadians saw no need to conciliate a province that had rejected sovereignty or a Conservative prime minister who had become unpopular. In 1992, a nation-wide constitutional referendum on a complicated compromise failed. Indignant Quebeckers turned back to the Parti Québécois in 1994. A year later, on October 28th, Quebeckers went to the polls in a second referendum. Pollsters warned that the results were too close to call. They were right. The Yes vote won 49.4%, the No vote, 50.6%.

Afterwards, Ottawa spent millions to raise the profile of Canada in Québec. The Supreme Court ruled that people in a Canadian province could secede but only if the issue was made clear. Parliament passed a Clarity Act, setting out conditions for a vote that were more demanding than Québec's rules for the 1980 and 1995 referenda. The wording of the question had to be clear and the winner needed more than a single-vote margin. Sovereignty support declined in Québec after 1995 and most Quebeckers had always confessed that Canada was a good place to live. Still, most believed that someday, Québec would be independent, and that day would come sooner if they felt that their fellow Canadians had treated them unfairly.

Canada's First Nations

When one of Mulroney's constitutional compromises seemed close to passing in 1990, Elijah Harper, a lone Native legislator in Manitoba, cast the key negative vote. This was theatre, of course. Most Manitobans opposed the Accord. Harper's protest was not against Québec. Instead, he complained that all attempts to define the rights of his people had been shelved until Québec's concerns were addressed. First Nations, after all, had been here first!

It took a Native blockade and violence between police, troops and a Mohawk community at Oka, near Montréal, in 1990 to push Ottawa to appoint a Royal Commission to investigate the claims of First Nations on Canada. The Commission's seven-volume report forthrightly gave a Native view of how Canada's first peoples had fared in everything from formal treaties to their depiction in school textbooks. The result was massive unfinished business for Ottawa and for provincial governments, caught between the demands of resource industries, native negotiators made intransigent by their own deep and legitimate resentments and millions of non-Native voters with other priorities. The challenge is made more complex by a million natives who have left reserves to find success, or sometimes renewed poverty, in Canadian cities and towns, by the related claims of millions of Métis or people of mixed ancestry, and by the distinctive Inuit of northern Canada.

A Holiday from Politics?

Despite the excitements of Meech Lake and Oka, the 1995 Québec referendum and spill-over effects of the terrorist attacks of September 11, 2001 in the United States, many Canadians willingly took a holiday from politics after the Liberals were elected in 1993. The two next largest parties, the Bloc Québécois and Reform (later renamed the Canadian Alliance), were regional protest movements from Québec and the West, with nothing in common and no chance of winning on their own. In 1993, Brian Mulroney's government was so unpopular that under Canada's first woman prime minister, Kim Campbell, the Conservatives saved only two parliamentary seats. The New Democrats also lost their official party status for four years. The Liberals seemed to be safely in power until defeated in 2006 by Stephen Harper's Conservative Party of Canada.

Despite Jean Chrétien's election promises, his government did not renegotiate Free Trade or scrap Mulroney's Goods and Services Tax. Instead, they did what the Conservatives had promised and failed to do: by cutting services and payments to the provinces, Chrétien and his finance minister, Paul Martin ended the federal deficit by 1996 and began reducing the national debt. They left the Canadian dollar at 65 U.S. cents, to make Canada's exports cheaper.

Relations with the U.S.

In 1984, Brian Mulroney told *The Wall Street Journal* that "good relations, excellent relations" with the United States were his priority. With Ronald Reagan as president, he achieved them. The Chrétien government was equally close to Bill Clinton. The Prime Minister and President shared many ideas about the world and politics. For that reason, good relations were hard to renew with President George W. Bush. It was hardly a secret that Jean Chrétien hoped Al Gore would win in 2000. Opinion polls suggested that most Canadians, even in conservative Alberta, agreed.

Of course, good relations with Washington are vital to Canada, whoever forms the government. After all, the two countries are the other's best customer. Efforts by Prime Minister Trudeau to pressure Canadian business to diversify trade links never had a chance. Nor did Prime Minister Chrétien's annual trade missions to Asia or Europe make much difference. Trudeau tried to force foreign investors—almost always Americans—to respect Canada's interests. The Mulroney government scrapped the rules and welcomed any and all investment.

War on Terrorism

After September 11, Canada spent billions to improve border security, less out of fear of terrorists than in fear that Washington would slow or stop cross-border trade. Security concerns made as good a cover for protectionist lobbies in Washington as it did for authoritarians on both sides of the border. Canadian lives are influenced increasingly by decisions taken in Washington on defense, trade, security, and all the other concerns of the world's only super power. However, Canadians have no votes in U.S. elections, and Washington knows it. Giving honest advice from the sidelines may be a good friend's best service but it is seldom, if ever, appreciated, least of all when it might be right.

When Washington moved unilaterally against Saddam Hussein in Iraq, Canadians were split. Who could defend a cruel tyrant, especially in a Canada where many of Saddam's victims had found refuge? Yet Canadians were deeply skeptical about the claim of links between Saddam's secular regime and Islamic terrorists, and about Saddam's holdings of weapons of mass destruction. Above all, Canadians wondered about the aftermath of a military victory by a U.S.-led coalition. How would the United States handle a deeply-divided, bitterly impoverished country in a region seething with resentment against the West? Instead, Ottawa decided to help complete the unfinished business the United States seemed about to forget in post-Taliban Afghanistan.

Neither a Superpower Nor a Colony

As a huge country with a small population, Canada has always needed allies—France from 1608 to 1760 and Great Britain from 1760 to 1940, when Canada and the United States created the Permanent Joint Board of Defense on the eve of the U.S. entering the Second World War. In 1948, Canada's armed forces set out at the start of the Cold War to abandon their British training and to model themselves on their American counterparts. Canadians are proud of their peacekeeping record since they helped organize the United Nations Emergency Force in 1956, but they forget that almost all Canadian peacekeeping served allied, and often American interests.

In 1914, when Canada was still a colony, without any consultation, Canadians suddenly found themselves at war with Germany. By 1919, 630,000 Canadians out of a population of eight million had enlisted. More than 60,000 had died and even more had been permanently disabled in mind or body. Canada emerged from the war in 1919 close to bankruptcy. Canada also emerged with a conviction that it would be a colony no longer. In 1939, Canadians took over a week to decide to fight Hitler. In 1950, Canada contributed, proportionally, more than any other United States ally to the Korean War and a year later, it did even more to answer General Dwight D. Eisenhower's urgent appeal to back the North Atlantic Treaty Organization (NATO).

Canada is neither a superpower nor a colony. It was a founding member of the United Nations and a keen sponsor of most of its agencies. Canadians have roots in so many parts of the world that their government would find it impossible to be isolationist or unilateralist. Like Prime Minister Mulroney, they want "good relations, excellent relations" with the United States. It is no coincidence that one of Washington's biggest embassies, on a prime site on Pennsylvania Avenue, bears Canada's flag. Canadians would have to look very hard in the world to find a better neighbor. They also believe that most Americans would probably say the same.

Canada has survived wrenching economic changes and an accelerating technological revolution but, to its people, it remains the "peaceable kingdom." When the fireworks go off around Canada's Parliament Buildings on the night of July 1st, the neighbors might suspect a catastrophe but Canadians know that it's just an old-fashioned way to celebrate another year of their history.

How We're Governed: People, Politics and Law in Canada

By Dean V. June and Ruth Writer

❶ CULTURE

▶ Create a bulletin board that shows the British and American influence on Canadian culture and politics.

❷ TIME, CONTINUITY AND CHANGE

▶ Create an illustrated time line depicting the major political developments in Canada since the last referendum on Québec secession.

❸ PEOPLE, PLACES AND ENVIRONMENTS

▶ Summarize the dilemmas Canadian politicians face due to the size of the nation and the diversity of its people.

❹ INDIVIDUAL DEVELOPMENT AND IDENTITY

▶ Debate the merits of Québec's distinct society goals.

❺ INDIVIDUALS, GROUPS AND INSTITUTIONS

▶ Using a graph of the Canadian birth rate, in all ten provinces, from 1964 to the present, predict what it will be in the next 35 years if all birth rates remain the same.

❻ POWER, AUTHORITY AND GOVERNANCE

▶ Debate this question: "The American Civil War was a primary cause of Canadian Confederation."

▶ Write an editorial arguing for Québec's separation from the rest of Canada and another arguing against separation.

❼ PRODUCTION, DISTRIBUTION AND CONSUMPTION

▶ Conduct an internet search to determine the type and percentage of Canadian industries which are foreign owned.

❽ SCIENCE, TECHNOLOGY AND SOCIETY

▶ Explain how Canada and the U.S. are interconnected in terms of technology, i.e. power grids, internet, media, etc.

❾ GLOBAL CONNECTIONS

▶ Using the internet, locate an issue of current concern between the U.S. and Canada such as the soft wood dispute; then analyze the issue, taking a U.S. and a Canadian position. Defend the positions.

❿ CIVIC IDEALS AND PRACTICES

▶ Using a copy of the U.S. Bill of Rights and the Canadian Charter of Rights and Freedoms, compare and contrast the basic rights of citizens in each nation.

▶ Develop a diagram showing how laws are made in Canada.

▶ Conduct a model parliamentary question period or debate on one of the contested issues in Canada today.

CHAPTER THREE

Canadian Society: The North American Other

By Martin N. Marger
Michigan State University

AFTER SPENDING MOST OF THE 1980S in Canada, Jan Morris, the noted British journalist, historian, novelist, and travel writer, concluded that while it "might not be the most thrilling of countries, it did have a genuine claim to be considered the best."[1] In fact, the United Nations has given substance to the claim. Each year, the world body announces its Human Development Index (HDI), in which countries are ranked on a "most livable" scale, based on measures of income, education, and health. Until 2003, Canada had consistently finished number one, ranking ahead of not only the United States but all others among the world's most industrialized and modern countries. Efforts to rank societies, of course, are always plagued by issues of definition and validity, and the UN HDI is no exception. Moreover, the differences between ranks of the most highly developed countries are usually minuscule. Yet, Canada's consistently formidable standing on this and other international measures would seem to indicate that, though hardly Utopia, its quality of life may be as high as can be expected at the outset of the twenty-first century.

What are the unique social features that have given Canada universal recognition as a humane, peaceful, prosperous, and just society? In trying to account for its high regard among the world's developed nations we need to examine at least three aspects: its people, its primary values, and the components of its national identity.

For Americans, the apparent similarities that make them feel so comfortable in Canada disguise the discordant features that separate the two North American societies. Common consumer patterns, norms and traditions, and, except for French Canada, language, do not make Canada a northern microcosm of the U.S. Although there are undeniable elements of shared culture, there are also significant, albeit often subtle, differences—differences that Canadians are more sensitive to than Americans. Through vital economic links and by omnipresent American mass media,

Canadians are constantly reminded of those with whom they share the continent. Americans, on the other hand, have a mostly dim, and often distorted, view of Canada.

Many sociologists and historians have argued that the most daunting perplexity that has confronted Canada throughout its history is its proximity to the U.S. Pierre Elliott Trudeau, Canadian Prime Minister during the 1970s and early 1980s, trenchantly described the curse of Canada's geography when he suggested that living next to the U.S. was "like sleeping with an elephant." "No matter how friendly and even-tempered is the beast," he lamented, "one is affected by every twitch and grunt."[2] Historically, the essential problem for Canada in North America has been maintaining an economic, political, and cultural relationship with the colossus to the south without being swallowed by it. The economic, political, and cultural power of America is constantly on the minds of Canadians. And, not unexpectedly, Canadians' perception of their national identity is, in large measure, formed in comparison with their American neighbors.

In addition to its unavoidable link to the U.S., Canada has been beleaguered from the outset by its dual national character—essentially founded by two heritages, French and English. The upshot of that bi-national endowment has been the dread of all confederations: separation. The estrangement of what the novelist Hugh MacLennan called "two solitudes" has constantly hovered over the Canadian state, threatening to shatter what has often seemed a fragile and uncertain union.

Geographic and Demographic Features

In terms of sheer physical magnitude, Canada's land mass is second only to Russia's. Yet Canada is an underpopulated country, with immense areas thinly settled. Most of the population is compressed within a narrow strip close to the U.S. border. To appreciate the underpopulation of

Canada, consider that, if it were part of the U.S., its almost 31 million inhabitants would not even make it the size of the largest state, California.

Along with its relatively limited population, Canada is handicapped geographically by a serious imbalance between its east and west regions. The overwhelming majority of the population lives in the east (Ontario and Québec together contain more than half the total), resulting in disproportionate economic and political power. This regional disparity has caused much resentment among westerners, who often see themselves as playing second fiddle to the more powerful eastern provinces, in particular, Ontario.

Most Canadians live in urban areas. Canada, in fact, is one of the most highly urbanized societies in the world, more so even than the U.S. But it is massively dominated by only three urban areas; over one-third of the entire population resides in the metropolitan areas of Toronto, Montréal, and Vancouver.

In addition to urbanization, ethnic heterogeneity is today one of Canada's most striking socio-demographic features. Basically, three dimensions embody this society's rich ethnic diversity: French and English founding groups; new immigrants from various regions of the world; and native groups.

Most obvious to the rest of the world is Canada's major ethnic breach: the French-English schism, created by the English conquest of 1757. Essentially this ethnic division stems from language and cultural differences created by the confrontation of what are essentially two nations within a single Canadian state. The vast majority of French-speaking Canadians (Francophones) reside in the province of Québec and see themselves as not only linguistically but culturally different from the rest of Canada.

Because the past and current issues of Québec in Canada are described in detail in another article in this volume, there is no need to recapitulate them here. A few vital points, however, need to be iterated in order to better understand the sociological bases of this ethnic divide. Until the 1960s, Québec was essentially a backward, rural society, ill-prepared for the challenges of the modern world. Although a numerical majority, Francophones in Québec were a sociological minority in their own province, occupying primarily low-status jobs and lagging behind all other Canadian ethnic groups on various measures of socioeconomic status.

With the Quiet Revolution of the 1960s, Québec society underwent a radical transformation. A progressive provincial government replaced the Catholic Church as the overseer of education and social welfare. French was now established officially as the language of education and work, and the school curriculum was revised to promote commercial and technical skills.

The Quiet Revolution produced a strong French-Canadian nationalism that held out the promise of a fundamentally changed place for Québec in the Canadian confederation: No longer would it be a second-class partner in the national pact. For Francophones, Québécois replaced "French Canadian" as the preferred term of identification. Some, however, desired to go further, giving birth to a separatist movement whose threats to take Québec out of Canada consumed domestic politics for the next four decades.

In essence, Québec has sought recognition as a "distinct society," different from other provinces. Francophone Quebeckers do not see themselves as simply one ethnic group among Canada's many, but as one of Canada's two founding peoples, thereby entitled to special status within the confederation. This has been resisted by the rest of Canada, however, and there the issue remains. Despite the fact that the class differential between French and English Canadians has today virtually disappeared, that the dominance of the French language in all provincial institutions is unchallenged, and that a Francophone business elite has largely replaced the old Anglophone elite, the issue of Québec's place in Canada remains unresolved.

While it remains the key ethnic issue, the traditional Franco-Anglo division has been overshadowed in the past four decades by the increasingly multiethnic nature of Canadian society. Issues concerning non-English, non-French groups—often referred to as a "third force"—have begun to take center stage in Canada's ethnic drama. Put simply, Canada's population has evolved into one of the most ethnically diverse in the world, a significant change from past eras. As a result, multiculturalism and ethnic integration have emerged as major policy concerns and points of societal debate.

Although immigrants from various parts of Europe entered Canada almost from the outset of European settlement, for about one hundred years following the British conquest, most immigrants came from England, Scotland, and Ireland. In the late 19th and early 20th centuries, non-British Europeans, as well as some Americans attracted by the promise of farmland, settled in the prairie provinces. Immigration of southern and eastern Europeans to Canada's large cities also occurred during this period. But until the end of World War II, immigration to Canada remained mostly British and almost exclusively European. This was not a random occurrence but was determined by design. Canadian immigration policy, like that of the other major immigrant-receiving societies—the U.S. and Australia—was driven by the dictum of "whites only."

Starting in the 1950s a dramatic re-composition of the Canadian population commenced with the onset of the modern period of immigration. In the 1950s and early 1960s, immigrants from southern and eastern Europe—Italians, Greeks, Poles, Portuguese—rather than the British Isles, now made up the largest component of the newcomers. The most radical change was set in motion in the 1970s, however, as large numbers began arriving from south and east Asia, as well as the Caribbean. The predominance of non-European immigrants—almost 60 percent from Asia alone—continues to characterize current Canadian immigration patterns.

Immigration to the U.S. surpasses Canada's in total numbers by many times, but the foreign-born constitute 18 percent of the Canadian population, compared to 11 percent of the United States. Canada continues to accept more legal immigrants in proportion to its total population than any other country.

Although the immigration flow of recent decades has transformed the Canadian population, it is important to consider that immigrants have settled mostly in the country's largest urban areas (over half of Toronto's population is foreign-born, a higher percentage than in any North American city) and overwhelmingly in the province of Ontario. Other regions of Canada have been less radically impacted by the new immigration. Nonetheless, the diversity of its population has become one of Canada's distinguishing marks and has led to a changed national concept. In a recent poll of Canadians, when asked what distinguished their country from others, its multicultural makeup was among the most frequent responses.

Historical and contemporary reliance on immigration has led to the formation of a varied ethnic population in both Canada and the U.S., but the expectations of ethnic integration and, therefore, ethnic policy, have taken different forms in the two societies. The popular terms of comparison are melting pot, characterizing the U.S., and mosaic, descriptive of Canada.

The American idea of the melting pot—the fusing of many immigrant groups into an American hybrid culture—has dominated public opinion and policy since the early part of the 20th century and, despite multicultural rhetoric in recent years, continues to do so. The mosaic, in contrast, is a notion favoring a more pluralistic outcome of the massing of various ethnic groups. A commonly understood meaning is "unity in diversity." In this view, Canadian society is a mosaic, the various pieces of which fit together within a common political and economic framework. Ethnic groups, therefore, are not pressured to assimilate to a dominant culture. At the risk of oversimplification, it might be said that the tolerance of ethnic differences, both in public policy and attitude, is more pronounced in Canada.

Despite this ideological distinction (one that both native-born and foreign-born Canadians are very conscious of), the reality of ethnic incorporation—in both societies—lies somewhere between these two ideals. Moreover, a wealth of sociological evidence shows that most ethnic groups in both Canada and the U.S. assimilate quite thoroughly to the mainstream culture by the third generation.

To acknowledge that the outcome of ethnic relations in Canada is not radically different than in the U.S. should not lead to the belief that the symbolic importance of the mosaic ideology is unimportant. In fact, ethnic pluralism is today a fundamental part of the Canadian national identity. Moreover, Canada proclaims itself officially a multicultural society. Multiculturalism is a firmly established doctrine and is manifested in public policies that recognize, protect, and support the retention of ethnic communities within the larger society. Canada celebrates its ethnic diversity and encourages the expression of unique ethnic cultures. As the political commentator Richard Gwyn has put it, "Tolerance towards diversity and the acceptance of pluralism have become the defining characteristic of the country and its citizens."[3]

Native—or as they are referred to in Canada, Aboriginal—groups constitute a third dimension of ethnicity clearly apart from the others. The Aboriginal population consists of three components: North American Indians (called First Nations); Métis, a unique mixed racial/ethnic group whose members derive historically from the relations between French trappers and Indians; and Inuit, groups that populate the far north. Together, Aboriginals comprise about 4 percent of total population—four times greater than the proportion in the U.S.—and are settled in all provinces.

The social condition of native peoples in Canada parallels the experience of Native Americans, with abnormally high rates of disease, crime, homelessness, alcoholism, and other social afflictions. Relatively generous funding for native social supports has not seemed to significantly alleviate these conditions. Moreover, successful land claims in recent years and new self-governing arrangements have failed to raise the socioeconomic status of Aboriginal groups. Clearly the integration of the native population into the mainstream society constitutes Canada's most urgent and confounding ethnic issue.

Social Values and National Identity

All societies live by a set of beliefs and values that usually blend into a coherent ideology. The dictum of "life, liberty, and the pursuit of happiness" has given a popular meaning to the liberal individualism that so strongly characterizes American society. The Canadian counterpart is "peace, order, and good government." Although equally simplified, this maxim does serve as a convenient contrast in understanding how Canadians view their society and its major institutions, and how, in particular, they distinguish themselves from their southern neighbors. One must keep in mind that national ideologies, no matter their content, are ideals to which societies rarely conform in full and may, in fact, remain in large part myths that only slightly resemble reality.

In examining Canadian cultural and political values we might begin by considering a thesis suggested by the sociologist Seymour Martin Lipset, a keen observer of both North American societies for many years. Lipset has argued that the U.S. and Canada are unquestionably different and their distinctions are the product of historical forces, namely that America was born of revolution, while Canada was born of counter-revolution. The latter, of course, is Lipset's reference to the settlement of late 18th century "refuseniks" from the thirteen American colonies who chose not to participate in the revolutionary movement against Britain. These so-called United Empire Loyalists became the core of English-speaking Canada and can be seen as a founding, or charter, group. The revolution/counter-revolution peculiarity, Lipset maintains, is key to understanding the subsequent development of different value systems and national characters. Out of the loyalist establishment came a population that, by comparison with the U.S., was more

class conscious, more elitist, more law-abiding, more collectivity-oriented, more particularistic, and more inclined to accept a strong and active state. These societal values seemed to be validated in large measure by most historians and sociologists well into the twentieth century. Only after World War II, when Canada underwent a fundamental demographic, political, and ethnic reformulation, did serious challenges to this description arise. Lipset's thesis is controversial and has been hotly debated among Canadian sociologists for many years. But almost all agree today that the striking social and political changes that have occurred over the past half century dictate a more contemporary accounting of the value differences that separate Canada and the U.S.

While Canadians certainly subscribe to notions of individual achievement, self-reliance, and trust in the marketplace, in the U.S. these are taken as sacrosanct principles, manifested in virtually every institution from education to government. Following these principles, Americans are insistent on meritocracy and assumptions of equality of opportunity in the distribution of societal rewards. Inequality in income and wealth as well as other forms of social stratification are tolerated so long as all citizens are, presumably, assured an equal place at the starting line in the race for the society's goodies. Canada, by contrast, is more concerned with equality of results, that is, assuring that the race ends with the runners as close to each other as possible at the finish line. There is no expectation that everyone will be wealthy and successful, of course, but the objective is to reduce socioeconomic extremes of wealth and poverty. All democracies must strike a balance between liberty and equity. In the U.S., the balance is weighted strongly toward liberty; in Canada, it leans toward equity.

The inclination toward equity as a societal goal has produced a class system that is more compressed than that of the U.S., one that corresponds closely with those of western European countries. While in the U.S. the income ratio of the top quintile of families to the bottom quintile is about 11 to 1 (that is, the richest 20 percent of families earns eleven times more than the poorest 20 percent), in Canada the ratio is about 7 to 1. This is comparable to countries like Germany, the Netherlands, and Italy. Compared to the U.S., then, the gap between top and bottom—rich and poor—is less extreme in Canada. The more compressed Canadian class system is reflected as well in markedly lower poverty rates.

It has sometimes been remarked that "it is better to be rich in America but poor in Canada." What is implied is that opportunities for the accumulation of wealth are much greater in the U.S., while the social safety net protecting those who fall to the bottom is more comprehensive and generous in Canada. Indeed, Canadians themselves commonly see this as a salient point of contrast with their American neighbors. The U.S. relies mostly on market driven mechanisms in the distribution of national wealth, and therefore, unlike other liberal democracies, maintains a minimal welfare state. This relates to the comparatively lower marginal taxes paid by Americans. The Canadian welfare state and the tax structure that supports it are, by contrast, more clearly in line with those of western European nations.

Canada's universal health care system, called Medicare, is today the most fundamental and revered part of the Canadian welfare state. Its structure and method of delivery create a degree of equity that exceeds even western European health care programs. This single payer system (plainly not what American detractors often like to refer to as "socialized medicine") provides a common quality of health care to all Canadians, regardless of social class, at a cost that falls well below that of the U.S.

The more liberal Canadian welfare state is in large measure a product of the stronger expectations of—and greater trust in—an activist government. The state in Canada is not seen as a necessary evil, but as a vital benefactor. Canadians do not instinctively view government with suspicion, as Americans are prone to do, but understand that it is critical in performing functions that the private sector cannot or will not perform. The state, in the Canadian view, has a responsibility to act to ensure economic security, but also physical security. It is in the latter sense that Canadians have commonly been portrayed as more law-abiding and more inclined to acquiesce to authority. Gun controls, for example, are far more stringent than in the U.S., and the issue simply does not resonate with the same degree of controversy.

In addition to its strong collectivist values and preference for a proactive government, Canada today is a society that exhibits a high level of social tolerance. This is reflected in the generally strong propensity of Canadians to accept changes in traditional family structures. Consider the highly contentious issue of same-sex marriage. Surveys conducted in 2002 and 2003 revealed that 53 percent of Canadians, compared to 38 percent of Americans, supported

gay marriage. In 2003, judicial decisions in Ontario, British Columbia, and Québec rendered gay and lesbian couples the same marital rights as opposite-sex partners. Although Canadian public opinion on the issue is evenly split, it is likely to be resolved with relatively minimal social disruption.

But can Canadian values really be secure, it might be demurred, in light of powerful and seemingly irresistible American cultural influences? To be sure, the flow of culture in North America moves overwhelmingly from South to North, making for a steady Canadian diet of U.S. media: television, movies, music, books, and magazines. English Canada's efforts to stanch this flow and thus to preserve its cultural integrity are, therefore, a constant struggle. Ironically, however, the dominance of American culture in North America has, in effect, helped to define the Canadian national identity. Canadians often are described as being uncertain of who they are, but certain of who they are not—Americans. Moreover, one of the more surprising sociological findings of recent years refutes the generally held view that Canadians, like it or not, are culturally drifting ever closer to their American neighbors, and the societal values of the two societies, as a result, are unavoidably converging. The Canadian sociologist and pollster Michael Adams has recently issued the most convincing evidence that in fact the opposite seems to be the case. In both countries, individualism has been a growing trend in the past half century, but the nature of that individualism in Canada is more responsible than rugged, and more egalitarian than competitive. What is most astonishing, however, is the apparent shift of Canadian and American values during the past several decades. Put simply, Canadians and Americans seem to be moving in opposite directions. Thus, for example, whereas obeisance to traditional authority has been historically attributed to Canadians—as opposed to the freer and less deferential attitudes of Americans—the very opposite trends are evolving in the two countries.

It is perhaps in the realm of religion that the value divergence of the two societies has become most apparent. While the U.S. is drifting toward greater religiosity and faith, Canada—in the past, a more religiously observant society—seems to be moving in a counter direction. A recent national study, for example, showed that only 30 percent of Canadians claim that religion is "very important" to them, compared to almost 60 percent of Americans. Similarly, double the percentage of Americans say they attend religious services regularly. Canada's pattern of sectarian beliefs and observances is today closely in line with western European nations, where religion plays a relatively minor social role.

Canadians are less inclined to see religion as the source of morality and consequently religion in Canada does not enter the public discourse as it so commonly does in the U.S. Issues like abortion, pornography, religious displays, and prayer in schools, therefore, simply do not resonate with the general public as they do in the U.S., nor do they carry much political potency. The failure of the rightist Canadian Alliance party (recently merged into a new Conservative Party) to attract much support beyond its narrow western Canadian base is attributed largely to its religiously-grounded position on most social issues. Canadians often are bemused by the vigor with which religious overtones suffuse American political matters. Rare is the American politician, for example, who does not feel obligated to declare his religious affiliation (the particular denomination is unimportant); a candidate's admission to being a non-believer would be an almost certain kiss of political death. Canadian politicians, by contrast, do not routinely identify their religious preferences, nor do people expect them to. Pierre Trudeau, arguably the most prominent and admired Canadian of his time, was a devoutly observant Catholic, but that fact was not publicly known until his death. The thought of political leaders calling upon God to bless Canada would be seen as improper and certainly presumptuous.

The value differences between Canada and the U.S., it should be emphasized, are not polar opposites. Indeed, the adoption of the Canadian Charter of Rights and Freedoms in 1982, as part of constitutional reform, seemed to signal a move further in the direction of individual rights and liberty, that is closer to the American model. Also, the content of social values is strongly affected by regional and generational disparities in each society. Yet the general distinctions remain evident. Moreover, Canadians themselves perceive these differences quite decidedly. In a recent national survey, 67 percent disagreed with the statement that "Canadians and Americans basically have the same values." Moreover, only 10 percent thought that Canada should become more like the U.S.

The Current and Future Climate: Canadian Attitudes Toward the U.S.

As was noted earlier, the U.S. factor has, perhaps more than any other, helped define the Canadian nation. For Canadians, the experience of having to share the continent with the U.S. has created a kind of love-hate relationship. While they have admired and, perhaps unwittingly, at times envied Americans, they have sought to distance themselves from American ways, understanding that only by doing so could they maintain a national identity of their own. This schizoid affair has manifested itself in recent years in calls either for further continental integration or for a more vibrant Canadian nationalism, fueled by mild anti-Americanism. At the present historical juncture, the debate has flourished in the press and among scholars.

A palpable unease characterizes the current state of U.S.-Canada relations. Conflicting perceptions of security and military threats are the major wellsprings of these strained relations, though diverging views on controversial social issues are an additional source of apprehensiveness. Canada's decision not to participate in the U.S.-led military action against Iraq created greater distance and distrust between the two societies and their governments than in many decades. In contrast to the genuine affinity enjoyed by Jean Chrétien and Bill Clinton, the Chrétien/Bush relationship following the Iraq decision turned into a rancorous affair, with acrimony forthcoming from both sides. How the current Prime Minister chooses to deal with pressures to adapt to U.S. security concerns will probably set the tone of U.S.-Canada relations for the next several years. For Canada, the Iraq affair crystallized more clearly than ever the internal debate over its proper military role: either an international peacekeeper or a combatant inextricably allied with the U.S. in defending (U.S.-defined) North American interests.

The U.S. war on terrorism and its invasion of Iraq have produced other, integrally-related, points of discord. Chief among these are border and immigration issues. For generations, nothing celebrated the North American alliance better than the ease of movement back-and-forth across the elongated U.S.-Canada border. But as the U.S. has imposed tighter security measures, the trans-border flow has become problematic for both people and goods. Moreover, U.S. zealousness in pursing terrorists has led to a number of high-profile incidents in which Canadian citizens have been detained in the U.S. without charges and even deported to third countries against their will. Political officials have found that to ensure the American tie, they continue to have to persuade U.S. authorities that Canada is not part of their security problem.

Another related issue concerns trade. Because the U.S. is, by a wide margin, Canada's largest trading partner—more than 85 percent of its exports go to the U.S.—virtually no economic decision, and few political decisions, can be made without considering the potential impact on trade. Indeed, many have long felt that the trade imbalance has created a relationship of dependency. Moreover, despite the implementation of the North American Free Trade Agreement (NAFTA), trade disputes arise quite frequently. Recent surveys indicate that most Canadians not only are well aware of the U.S. trade dependency, but believe that trade relations almost always favor American interests. In 2002, only 10 percent of Canadians believed that Canada rather than the U.S. benefited more in their trade relationship. Along with the heavy investment of American corporations in Canada, the trade imbalance has given fresh ammunition to economic nationalists.

All of these issues have caused Canadians to debate and reevaluate perceptions of their American neighbors. The current rupture and the antagonistic posturing of the past few years may, of course, be only an episodic lapse in what has been, by global standards, an exceedingly concordant relationship with only occasional bumps. Moreover, an undercurrent of anti-Americanism has a long tradition in Canada, so it should not be thought that the present rift has broken new ground. Furthermore, disaffection with the U.S. today extends well beyond the Canada-U.S. border. Indeed, as numerous world surveys have shown, anti-U.S. sentiment has reached new heights throughout Western Europe and much of the developing world.

There is no question that in terms of political ideology, the two countries today are as far apart as they have ever been. While the U.S. is led by an administration and congress more conservative and ideologically driven than any of the past century, Canada has continued to move in a more liberal direction. Despite the breach, however, for Canadians, the relationship has hardly reached a breaking point. In an Ipsos-Reid bi-national poll taken in 2002, Canadians were asked to pick the one country they personally considered Canada's closest friend and ally; 60 percent chose the U.S. Whether Americans are in a reciprocally tolerant mood, though, is debatable; in response to the same question, 56 percent chose the UK, while Canada finished a distant second at 18 percent.

Although Canadians evince a strong preference for intercontinental cooperation, this should not be interpreted as a desire for policy harmonization, let alone integration. They do not see the likelihood of a continental union anytime soon, nor do they seek it. By almost 2 to 1, Canadians in 2002 rejected the idea that a political union between Canada and the U.S. was inevitable. More important, by a far wider majority they expressed the belief that Canada provided a better quality of life than the U.S. To reiterate my earlier admonition regarding mutual perceptions of Canadians and Americans: Acknowledging similarities that cannot be seriously debated should not obscure differences—some quite fundamental—that mark off the people, institutions, and values of these two adjacent, but only loosely coupled, societies. Ironically, despite the forces of globalization and the shadow of American power, Canadians today appear to recognize their uniqueness more strongly than at any time in the past.

Notes

1. Jan Morris, *The World: Travels 1950-2000* (New York: W. W. Norton, 2003), 367.
2. Andrew H. Malcom, *The Canadians* (Markham, Ontario: Fitzhenry and Whiteside, 1985), 165.
3. Richard Gwyn, *Nationalism Without Walls: The Unbearable Lightness of Being Canadian* (Toronto: McClelland & Stewart, 1996), 206.

Canadian Society: The North American Other

By Dean V. June

❶ CULTURE
- ▶ Conduct a survey on U.S. perceptions of Canada and its people.

❸ PEOPLE, PLACES AND ENVIRONMENTS
- ▶ Compare a political map of Russia with that of Canada. Be sure to locate areas of population. What conclusions can be drawn?
- ▶ Discuss the problems that arise with conducting business in Canada due to its size.

❹ INDIVIDUAL DEVELOPMENT AND IDENTITY
- ▶ List major cultural differences between English and French Canada.
- ▶ Describe life in Québec before and after the Quiet Revolution of the 1960s.

❺ INDIVIDUALS, GROUPS AND INSTITUTIONS
- ▶ Prepare a bar graph illustrating the country of origins of immigrants coming to Canada during the 19th and 20th centuries.
- ▶ Produce a collage that best demonstrates the cultural "melting pot" of the US, and the "mosaic" of Canada.

❻ POWER, AUTHORITY AND GOVERNANCE
- ▶ Discuss the pros and cons of Canada's multicultural policy.
- ▶ Compare and contrast the Canadian ideals of "peace, order, and good government", with the American ideals of "life, liberty, and the pursuit of happiness."

❽ SCIENCE, TECHNOLOGY AND SOCIETY
- ▶ Using Lipset's *Continental Divide* (Routledge, Chapman, and Hall, 1990), develop a chart supporting his statement "…that the U.S. and Canada are unquestionably different, and their distinctions are the product of historical forces."
- ▶ Discuss what it means to be "…better rich in America but poor in Canada."

❾ GLOBAL CONNECTIONS
- ▶ Design a bulletin board of recent news events involving U.S./Canadian border security problems.
- ▶ Design a political cartoon illustrating Canada's dependence on U.S. trade.

❿ CIVIC IDEALS AND PRACTICES
- ▶ Create arguments for/against Canada staying with NAFTA.
- ▶ Present examples that support this statement: "…the U.S. is led by an administration and Congress more conservative and ideologically driven… Canada has continued to move in a more liberal direction."

CHAPTER FOUR

Canadian Cultural Life

By David McKnight
McGill University

Canada is a dynamic, social democratic, bilingual nation located on the northern half of the North American continent. Canada co-exists on the continent with the United States of America and México. Historically, the United States and Canada share, in part, a common origin and language and many shared values and attitudes. Apart from co-existing along the world's longest undefended border, Canada and the United States share close economic ties expressed under the terms of the North American Free Trade Agreement (NAFTA) which also includes México. Despite the many commonalities between the United States and Canada, most Canadians are adamant that Canada possesses a separate identity and a distinct culture. In many respects this is true. The following chapter will provide an outline for the discussion of the broad contexts and the key issues related to Canadian culture.

Contexts

When attempting to discuss the manifestation of culture in Canada the immediate problem is one of definition. This problem not only relates to the noun culture but also Canada or Canadian, as well. First consider the term *culture*. In the view of the British literary critic Raymond Williams "culture" is one of most complex words in the English language.[1] However difficult it may be to define culture, the classic definition of culture and the one that will be adopted here is taken from anthropologist Edward Tyler. In 1871, Tyler proposed the following definition in his classic study *Primitive Culture*:

> Culture . . . is that complex whole which includes knowledge, belief, art, morals, law, custom, and any other capabilities and habits acquired by man as a member of society.[2]

I will use the term culture in this broad sense. However it is important to add that the concept of culture is commonly used to refer narrowly to the "arts": literature, film, painting, music and the performing arts, etc. Increasingly, the definition of culture embraces not only the arts but also "life culture," which includes sports and recreation as part of the total cultural expression of a region or a country.

Within the context of broad cultural expression, the term culture also carries social and economic connotations which are expressed in terms of high or elite culture; these are, in turn, pitted against notions of popular or mass culture. However, the notion of high and low culture largely dissolved in the twentieth century.

To understand Canadian culture then is to be familiar with the "ideas" that have been generated and made manifest in Canada since 1867 and form the basis of English Canada's cultural life, which is an ever evolving project defined by the absorption of wide ranging models and influences that have shaped Canadian identity and values and which form part of Canada's broad history.

What is "Canadian?"

As problematic as it is to define culture, a similar problem exists in defining the term "Canadian." What is Canadian? Who is a Canadian? From the perspective of the twenty-first century the answers might seem obvious; however, as John Ralston Saul has suggested, Canadians tend to define themselves in terms of negative myths.[3] For example, Francophones residing in Québec often define themselves as Québécois first and Canadians second. English-speaking Canadians maintain loudly that they are not Americans. To add to the problem, regional loyalties take precedent over an all encompassing national identity. Thus it becomes problematic to define what precisely "Canadian" means and more particularly what Canadian culture is.

Historically, the term "Canadian" referred to the tribes of the First Nations who occupied the land prior to the arrival of the French settlers who established the French

Colony of Nouvelle France along the banks of the St. Lawrence River. As the French regime in 1759 drew to a close, "Canadian" referred generally to the French-speaking inhabitants of what is modern day Québec. However after the fall of Québec, the French Monarchy ceded control of New France to the British, and the term "Canadian" began to acquire its modern meaning referring to all the inhabitants dwelling in British North America.

There were several important consequences of the fall of Québec. First, there was a steady influx of immigrants from the British Isles (England, Scotland, Ireland and Wales) who settled in what is now the Atlantic region of Canada first in Halifax and later Montréal and Québec City. Second, there was an influx of Empire Loyalists, dissenters, who fled the Thirteen Colonies after the outbreak of the War of Independence. Together the British, French and American Loyalists serve as the foundation upon which Canadians draw the historical parameters of their national identity which was consolidated and forged at the time of Confederation in 1867 and entrenched in the British North America Act (BNA Act), which served as the constitutional and legal framework for the governance of the newly created Dominion of Canada.

As a defining moment in North American history, Canada was, at the time of its inception, as it continues to be today, a great political and cultural experiment. In particular, the BNA Act carefully entrenches the rights of Canada's French speaking minority living within Canada as a whole and especially in Québec. Within Québec, the French speaking population is in the majority. One of the legacies of Canadian history is the fractious state of English-French relations, which has been played out on both the political and cultural stage.

From the perspective of constructing a Canadian pan "ethnic" national identity the result has been a failure within Canada as whole. This can be explained in two important ways. First, Canada was created within the context of the British Empire and there was deeply expressed loyalty to the Empire and its ideals. (Though Canada has gained its constitutional independence from England, this nation remains loyal to the English Monarchy and is an active member of the British Commonwealth.)

Second, relations between the Province of Québec and English Canada (often referred to today as the "ROC," i.e., the Rest of Canada) can be characterized as complex and at times fractious, especially in light of the growth of the Québec nationalist movement in the 20th century and made manifest in two referendums on the future of Québec within Canada. A public opinion poll published in January 2004 revealed that 47% of French speaking Quebeckers support some form of political independence.[4]

At the same time as the English-French debate gained momentum in the 1960s with the rise of the Québec nationalist movement, new forces were coming into play in terms of redefining the nature of Canada and what "Canadian" means in terms of both acknowledging and embracing the numerous multicultural communities of Canada within the political and cultural fabric of the nation, which is commonly referred to as the "Canadian Mosaic." During the same period, there was a growing awareness that Canada's Aboriginal peoples, long forsaken and marginalized, had been absent from the debate upon what it means to be Canadian.

To compound matters, Canada's relations with the United States were and have been at times complex and ambiguous. Although we share a common language, origins and values and mutually claim each other as closest friends and neighbors, Canada views the United States suspiciously as the elephant ready to crush the Canadian mouse. Given the discrepancy in the comparative size of populations—a 10 to 1 ratio—and the fact that the United States emerged in the 20th century as the world's largest exporter of cultural products, one Canadian view is that the U.S. has posed, whether real or imagined, a threat to the much smaller Canadian cultural market place.

This held especially true in the age of mass communications. In particular, Canadian Nationalists have felt threatened by the influx of American cultural products, i.e., magazines, music, films and television programs which dominate the Canadian cultural space and have led to measures and policies to protect, perhaps futilely, Canadian indigenous cultural forms and over exposure to American attitudes and values transmitted via the mass media.

At the heart of the debate is a fundamental disagreement regarding the nature of American cultural exports as a commodity as opposed to the Canadian view that cultural artifacts are containers which mirror a nation's vision, values and identity. Concern over cultural sovereignty is writ large within the terms of the North American Free Trade Agreement and many of Canada's apprehensions regarding the protection of Canadian culture are now shared by many smaller nations who have joined in the debate on the question of globalization.

Canadian Culture or Culture in Canada?

How can one discuss precisely what makes a work of art "Canadian" or define more broadly what Canadian Culture is? The appellation "Canadian" can be as simple as "Made in Canada," which associates a manufactured product like a book printed in Canada as Canadian. But what happens when a Canadian authored book is published in Canada, but printed in the United States? Few modern countries have troubled over the nature of their national identity more than Canadians. In fact this was, until recently, the famous Canadian identity problem. If you don't have an identity, then how can you possibly translate this state of non-being into a sense of community, values, an identity or a work of art?

Historically, Canada like other former colonies has in reality developed its identity through a long standing pattern of the transmission of ideas, values and cultural forms from elsewhere and adapting and transforming them to the new environment. In the case of Canada we draw heavily upon English, French and American influences. But this pattern is changing as the term "Canadian" has come to mean less where one is from and reflects who, what and where you are in the present.

One of the other issues which posses a fundamental problem in defining Canadian Culture is the fact that Canada has strong competing regional interests. Canada possesses the second largest land mass in the world. Its small population of thirty million is concentrated in regions as diverse as Newfoundland, the Maritimes, Québec, Southern and Northern Ontario, the Prairies and the mountainous Pacific West Coast. Though Canadians have been linked for over a century by the railroad and today long distances are dissolved through the mass media and the Internet, regional loyalties are strong. Are you a Maritimer or a Canadian? Well that depends.

Cultural Forms

Despite many challenges and problems, Canadians have developed over the past 130 years a vigorous culture. This holds particularly true for the arts: painting, sculpture, literature, music, film, media and the performing arts. Today Canadian-born artists are achieving unprecedented success both at home, in the United States and internationally. Within the field of popular music, alone, such performers

as Céline Dion, Shania Twain, Alannis Morrisette, Avril Levigne, and Bryan Adams have sold millions of records and achieved a level of market penetration that is unprecedented.

As remarkable as the recent successes of a select group of Canadian popular musicians has been, the reality is that cultural activity in Canada is directed towards three goals: first, facilitate opportunities for Canadian artists to display, perform, publish or record their works within Canada; second, develop the economic conditions for indigenous cultural industries to flourish; and thirdly, continue to cultivate audiences for Canadian cultural forms within Canada, and abroad.

In the field of Canadian literature, the climate and opportunities for Canadian authors have improved largely because Canadian authors and readers are no longer dependent upon publishing their work abroad or with a handful of commercial publishers with conflicting interests and agendas. During the 1960s, the Canadian publishing industry was transformed with the appearance of a number of small publishers like Oberon, Coach House Press, House of Anansi and Talonbooks to name several of the most important ones served as a model for others who followed. Today there is a strong network of small publishers across Canada. These publishers represent strong regional interests and provide outlets for many writers who would other wise find it difficult to be published. The small press launched the careers of such writers as Margaret Atwood, David Adams Richards, Anne Michaels, Michael Ondaatje, Yann Martel and many more.

At the same time as the small presses were emerging, Jack McClelland was transforming the commercial publishing business in Canada. The firm he inherited from his father, McClelland and Stewart, under Jack's direction became known as the Canadian Publisher and synonymous with a generation of Canadian writers, many of whom were instrumental in transforming Canadian literature. Such writers as Pierre Berton, Leonard Cohen, Irving Layton, Margaret Laurence, Farley Mowat, and Mordecai Richler, to name some of the most celebrated, have explored a wide array of Canadian based subjects and themes in poetry, fiction and non-fiction.

The visual arts are flourishing in Canada and, yet, there is continued fascination with the work of the Group of Seven, whose impact on the visual imagination of Canada is unprecedented. The original members of the Group of

Seven, Frank Carmichael, Lawren Harris, Frank Johnston, A.Y. Jackson, Arthur Lismer, J.E.H. MacDonald, and F.H. Varley captured in their landscape paintings, in particular, the direct emotional impact of Canada's vast unpopulated Northern wilderness terrain. Assimilating and adapting techniques from the Impressionists and early modernist European painters, the Group of Seven have provided subsequent generations of Canadians with a visual vocabulary which resonates with a Canadian passion for the outdoors and the marvels of the North. Although the Group of Seven's work received a mixed reception from the critics when it was first exhibited in 1920, it is their vision and their works which subsequent generations of Canadians responded to and thus serves as a cultural paradigm for those who succeeded them.

Unlike literary works or paintings which can be imbued with cultural identifiers which link a work to a locale, region or country, music does not easily lend itself to a national attribution. Across the musical genres from folk, classical and popular music in its many forms—rock, jazz, and country and western—many Canadians have made their mark both at home and internationally. Among the most notable artists to achieve wide fame include the great interpreter of J.S. Bach, the late Glenn Gould who emerged at the outset of his recording career in the 1950s as not only a Canadian icon, but an international star. Or consider Oscar Peterson, the Montréal born jazz pianist who was "discovered" by influential jazz producer Norman Granz, who persuaded Peterson to follow him to New York in 1949. During the Sixties a number of Canadian pop artists, for lack of opportunities, migrated to the United States where they embarked on successful and influential musical careers. The notables include Joni Mitchell, Neil Young, and members of the rock group, the Band. Interestingly, many Canadians follow the annual Grammy awards to see how many Canadian artists have been nominated. In recent years popular performers such as Shania Twain, Bryan Adams, Sarah McLachlan, Alanis Morrisette, Diana Krall and Avril Levigne have made a major impact on the U.S. charts. Success abroad improves record sales at home.

Yet there are certain performers and groups who remain for a number of reasons uniquely Canadian. Certain performers like Country singer Stompin' Tom Connors, whose passion for Canada is evoked in almost every song he has recorded, refuses to perform in the United States. He is a passionate cultural and political nationalist intent upon singing his popular songs for Canadians. Consider The Tragically Hip, the Kingston, Ontario band which can fill large arenas performing their modulating innovative pop songs, but are unable to break into the American market. The stock answer has been that American audiences can't penetrate the idiosyncratic heavily Canadian referenced lyrics. Other musicians who express a unique Canadian perspective range from the urban irony of the Bare Naked Ladies, folk artist Garnet Rogers, and Celtic-influenced performers Natalie McMaster, and Great Big Sea.

If Canadians have enjoyed success in the field of literature, art and music, film provides an important lesson which points to a cultural industry that for a number of complex reasons which date back to the 1920s have made it almost impossible for a true English-Canadian film industry to exist. Within English Canada, the reality is that three percent of the films screened in commercial movie theatres are Canadian. The dominant film genre in English Canada was and remains the documentary form. There is a small feature film industry and more recently film directors like James Cameron, David Cronenberg, Atom Egoyan, and Norman Jewison have demonstrated that Canadians can compete with Hollywood. But this is not a problem unique to Canada. Hollywood is the world capital for film and television. It is difficult for small countries like Canada to compete with Hollywood. It has not been uncommon for Canadian actors and directors from the beginnings of the film era to the present to seek their fortunes in Hollywood. Within the past generation the number of Canadians who have achieved success in the United States is a who's who: Dan Ackroyd, John Candy, Martin Short, Eugene Levy, Andrea Martin, and Catherine O'Hara, among others.

Like culture, sports and recreation are integral to defining Canada's complex cultural mosaic. Until recently sports and recreation were not strictly speaking considered part of culture in the sense of the arts. However, it is evident that they play an important part in defining who Canadians are, and their relationship, especially to the outdoors. Following the rhythm of the seasons, from spring, summer, fall and winter, Canadians have for over two centuries popularized many sports which were adapted from the First Nations, for example, snow shoeing, tobogganing and lacrosse. Scottish immigrants brought to Canada curling and golf, both of which remain popular today.

In the 1870s new sports were invented in Canada, such as football and basketball, and the American national game, baseball, surprisingly, was popular in Canada. The national sport at the end of the 19th century was Lacrosse; however, at the beginning of the 20th century ice hockey emerged as a widely popular sport. Today, hockey is acknowledged as the national game of Canada and it has a wide following. Hockey's success can be traced in part to the 1930s when the Canadian Broadcasting Corporation began broadcasting "Hockey Night in Canada" on the radio; it was for many Canadians a Saturday night ritual. Like baseball, hockey has become deeply entrenched in the Canadian psyche. It transcends low and high culture and one can trace the game's influence and impact on Canadian identity and culture through works of art, poetry, fiction and film. Indeed, the producers of Hockey Night in Canada have recently inaugurated Hockey Day in Canada in recognition of Canadians' passion for the game and in recognition of the sport which many Canadians believe is their national game and reflects the country's northern, rugged character.

Commissions, Institutions and Policies

Central to an understanding of contemporary Canadian cultural life since the 1950s is the fact that Canada, like the United Kingdom, Australia, and European countries, has placed high value on culture as a social good and it has become deeply woven into the political fabric of the country. The Government of Canada plays a central role in the regulation, protection and funding of the arts. The Government has achieved this through four key instruments.

The first is through Royal Commissions, which often have broad mandates to investigate such broad questions as the state of broadcasting, newspapers, bilingualism, and the arts, in general. Royal Commissions, though not invested with legislative power, make recommendations which are tabled for the governments of the day to either act upon or lie fallow.

Second, the Canadian government has been very active in creating cultural policies and regulations since the 1960s. With rising nationalist sentiments during the years leading up to Centennial celebrations in 1967, there were increased concerns on the part of Canadian nationalists who argued that there was a strong need for the Government to insure the survival of Canadian culture and identity in the wake of Canadian's exposure to American mass culture across the 49th parallel. In response to nationalist concerns, the Liberal Government of Pierre Trudeau created the Canadian Radio-Television and Telecommunications Commission

(CRTC) in 1968.

The CRTC is responsible for managing and regulating Canadian broadcasting space. In 1971, the CRTC introduced Canadian Content (Can-Con) regulations which required radio and television stations to program thirty per cent Canadian music content into their weekly rotations (now thirty-five per cent). While the effects of the Can-Con regulations were not immediately felt, it is unquestionable that over the course of the past thirty years, the music industry in Canada has flourished. The same cannot be said for television, especially in the digital age; the task is, arguably, self-defeating.

Third, the Canadian government, along with Provincial and Municipal governments, have through a variety of departments and agencies provided funding for a wide range of cultural activities from libraries to individual artists. In the fiscal year 2001-2002 the three levels of government spent $6.2 billion dollars on culture in Canada.

Fourth, the Department of Canadian Heritage sets cultural policy and oversees a number of national cultural institutions which include the National Gallery of Art, Library and Archives Canada, and the National Arts Centre to name several.

From a historical perspective, the turning point for Canadian culture was the publication of a Royal Commission on the Arts, Letters, and Sciences in 1951.[5] Commonly referred to as the Massey Report in honor of the Commission's Chair, Vincent Massey, the Commission examined in depth the state of Canada's arts, culture, sciences and universities. For students of Canadian culture, the Massey Report represents a watershed event.

The most important recommendation put forward by the Commission was the creation of the Canada Council for the Arts. Today Canada Council is the country's single most important cultural funding agency. In spite of criticisms, the Council has transformed the arts in Canada from a nation of amateurs into professionals. The mandate of the Council is "to foster and promote the study and enjoyment of, and the production of works in, the arts." In 2002-2003 the Canada Council awarded $142 million dollars to individual artists, institutions and organizations.

A nation's cultural life is expressed in many ways and among the most important manifestations in Canada are the many cultural institutions which play a number of key functions. One of the most significant in Canada is the Canadian Broadcasting Corporation (CBC).

Broadcasting in English, French and Native languages, the CBC has been an integral part of the Canadian cultural life since its first broadcasts were aired in 1936. According to the CBC's mandate it "should provide radio and television services incorporating a wide range of programming that informs, enlightens and entertains." In addition, the CBC "tells Canadian stories reflecting the reality and diversity of our country; informs Canadians about news and issues of relevance and interest; supports Canadian arts and culture; builds bridges among Canadians, between regions and the two linguistic communities of Canada."

Until the 1950s, the CBC dominated and regulated the air waves in Canada. However, with the advent of television and pressures from private industry, the CBC's control over broadcasting eventually was transferred to the CRTC in 1968. Today the CBC is subject to the terms of the Broadcasting Act. Despite its success, the CBC has vocal critics who do not simply criticize programming choices—which are often considered irrelevant or of poor quality—but argue that the CBC is irrelevant and costly to Canadians. Despite the critics, the CBC has many allies not only within government, but beyond in such groups as the Friends of the CBC which defends the role of the CBC with passion.

Conclusion

Canadians are often viewed as nice, a people who respect authority, listen when they are spoken to, say "eh," live in a cold country and love hockey. Canadians continue to question their identity, wonder if they have a history, search for their future in the past and live both in awe and trepidation of the United States. Since the founding of Canada with the act of Confederation in 1867, Canada like other former colonies has slowly absorbed the traditions of the peoples who settled the country and with creativity, intelligence and will evolved into a mature nation at the beginning of the 21st century. The fruits of this labor are reflected in the works produced by Canadian artists, a diverse cultural life and many institutions which express a unique Canadian identity.

Notes

1. Raymond Williams, *Keywords: A Vocabulary for Culture and Society* (London: Fontana, 1976).
2. "Culture," *Encyclopedia Britannica* (Encyclopedia Britannica Online, 2004), www.search.eb.com/eb/article?eu=118246 [accessed 21 Feb. 2004].
3. John Ralston Saul, *Reflections of a Siamese Twin: Canada at the End of the Twentieth Century* (Toronto: Viking, 1997).
4. Rhéal Séguin, "Voter Dismay Fuels Sovereignty Support," *The Globe and Mail* 23 (January 2004): A8.
5. Royal Commission, *National Development in the Arts, Letters and Sciences*, Canada (Ottawa: Queen's Printer, 1951).

Canadian Cultural Life Activities

By Dean V. June and Ruth Writer

❶ CULTURE
- ▶ Create a collage of contemporary artifacts representative of the Canadian culture.

❷ TIME, CONTINUITY AND CHANGE
- ▶ Describe the major areas of disagreement likely to occur when American and Canadian students discuss the merits of current pop culture in the two nations.

❸ PEOPLE, PLACES AND ENVIRONMENTS
- ▶ Create and defend your personal list of the ten most important Canadian cultural icons.

❹ INDIVIDUAL DEVELOPMENT AND IDENTITY
- ▶ Justify the adoption of the Canadian Content (CanCon) rule.
- ▶ Mcknight claims "that most Canadians are adamant that Canada possesses a separate identity and a distinct culture." Assess the accuracy of this statement.

❺ INDIVIDUALS, GROUPS AND INSTITUTIONS
- ▶ Compare and contrast the history of the CBC with the history of PBS.
- ▶ Compare the ways in which a newsworthy event is covered by the Canadian press/media and the U.S. press media.

❻ POWER, AUTHORITY AND GOVERNANCE
- ▶ Create a timeline depicting stages in governmental support of Canadian culture.

❼ PRODUCTION, DISTRIBUTION AND CONSUMPTION
- ▶ In light of global technology, develop a plan to protect the Canadian identity.

❽ SCIENCE, TECHNOLOGY AND SOCIETY
- ▶ Predict the future development of a distinct Canadian culture without a Canadian content rule.

❾ GLOBAL CONNECTIONS
- ▶ Using a world map or timeline of Canada's history, create a visual of the impact of the founding nations as well as more recent waves of immigration on the current Canadian culture.

❿ CIVIC IDEALS AND PRACTICES
- ▶ Justify or reject the current Canadian fear of the "invasion of the American culture."

CHAPTER FIVE

The 2003 Election in Québec: Another Chance for Federalism?

By Philip J. Handrick
Canadian Studies Centre, Michigan State University

FOR OVER A CENTURY, Québec had been dominated by the Catholic Church and an inward-looking, conservative government that worked closely with the English-speaking business elite to maintain a stable social arrangement in which English-speaking business interests dominated the economy, and the Catholic Church dominated the social life of Québec. This changed in the 1960s when the provincial government challenged the power of the Catholic Church and launched a series of reforms, many of which involved legislation to protect the French language and expand the use of French in the business life of the Province. Legal challenges and resistance to these reforms within English Canada led many in Québec to conclude that the French language and culture could only be protected in an independent Québec. By 1980, however, efforts to protect the French language were proving successful and Quebecers overwhelmingly rejected a referendum to separate from Canada.

In 1982 Prime Minister Trudeau precipitated a new crisis by repatriating the Canadian constitution. Québec, fearing the loss of British Parliamentary oversight, which had been consistently sympathetic to their minority status within Canada, and concerned that its declining population would make it a permanent minority within Canada, refused to sign. In the decade that followed, two initiatives negotiated between Québec, the other provinces and the federal government to resolve the crisis were defeated. The cost of failure was high: the federal and provincial parties that had invested their effort in seeking a solution were roundly defeated in the subsequent elections. Sympathy for separation within Québec and resentment towards Québec in the "Rest of Canada" reached its climax in 1995 when Québec held a second referendum that was defeated by less than half a percentage point.

Had the vote gone the other way, the Québec government would have demanded independence from Canada, splitting the country politically, demographically and in a deeper sense, morally. For if Canada, with its long tradition of tolerance and compromise could not come to terms with Québec, what hope would there be for less stable federations around the world? But this larger question was not the issue in April 2003. Canadians and Quebecers were exhausted from decades of constitutional wrangling and even the separatist Parti Québécois was not talking about third referendum. So the stage was set for the first televised debate in the provincial election campaign.

The Election Debate

Early in April 2003, three candidates stood in the blue and white decorated television studio to put their party's position before the voters of Québec. The issues and players would be familiar to voters anywhere in Canada and in much of the United States: improving health care while controlling costs, reform of education and social services, and, of course, cutting taxes. The three men standing before the cameras represented three distinct visions of Québec's future and perhaps the future of Canada as well.

The decidedly younger face was that of 32-year-old Mario Dumont, the leader of Action Démocratique du Québec (ADQ). In the 1998 election, the neo-conservative ADQ won 11.7% of the vote but Dumont held their only seat in the National Assembly. The ADQ argued that an activist government had served Québec well for forty years but it was time to reexamine that role. It claimed the support of a youthful constituency. However, Premier Bernard Landry, the leader of the separatist Parti Québécois (PQ), was not about to concede the youth vote. There were, he argued, many young people among the 26% of the population who were unwavering in their support for the PQ and Québec independence. For Landry who was fighting his first election as party leader, the real threat was Jean Charest.

Charest, a staunch federalist, was first elected a Member of Parliament from Sherbrooke, Québec for the

Progressive Conservative Party in 1984 when at age 26 he became the youngest person ever to serve in the Cabinet. He was one of only two Conservative candidates elected to the House of Commons in the crushing defeat of Brian Mulroney and the Progressive Conservatives in the 1993 election and became party leader in 1995. He was reelected in 1997 but he resigned the following year to become the leader of the Québec Liberal Party. Even with less than a year to prepare for the election, Charest and the Liberals won 43.7% of the popular vote in the 1998—one percent more than the PQ—but only 48 seats. To win in 2003, Charest could depend on the support of the strong federalists who make up 22% of the electorate, but would need support in rural Québec that had given the PQ much of its 75 seat majority in 1998. Since the last election, the Liberal Party had rebuilt its base, carefully selecting candidates across the province. Now Charest had to reach the uncommitted voters.

A survey was commissioned by the Québec news magazine, *L'Actualité*, and *Le Point* in early 2003. The results, presented in a rather whimsical set of descriptive categories we will explore in detail later, were published in April and showed a divided electorate.[1] The ADQ found a natural constituency among 11% of voters, "les chevaliers-de-la-table-rase" ("the knights of the empty table"), who were disillusioned with separatism and with government. In addition to the staunch federalists, dubbed "Les Ö-Canada," the Liberals could find support among the "Orphelins-de-Boubou" ("Bobby's orphans"), traditional liberals who identify with Canada but who remain unimpressed with the current Liberal leadership and long nostalgically for the unifying leadership of Robert Bourassa. The Parti Québécois could count on the support of the Purzédurs and could find support among the "Purzémous" ("pure but soft"), another 24% of voters who identify strongly with Québec but are uncertain about separation. What is most interesting about the survey is it that it defined the electorate in terms of values and lifestyle, not in the traditional categories of language and ethnicity. Nevertheless, it may have been the old question of Québec's place in Canada that in the end determined the outcome of the election.

Background to the Election

French Canadians have always been proud of their role in the founding of Canada and aware of a shared language, religion and history that set them apart from the rest of Canada. Events like the Conquest, the defeat on the Plains of Abraham and Papineau's Rebellion[2] that are captured in the motto "Je me souviens" ("I remember"), stamped on every Québec license plate, inform a sense of common history and grievance among French Canadians. There is also a sense of belonging to a nation, to a group of people with a shared heritage, that was reinforced by the Catholic Church in the 19th century when Canadiens were by definition French-speaking, rural and Catholic. Even as the French-speaking or francophone population of Québec was becoming increasingly urbanized in the early 20th century, the Catholic Church remained the preeminent institution. Catholic rituals and the icons of an agricultural society, such as the annual St. Jean Baptiste parades celebrating the patron saint of Québec, provided the symbolic and ideological basis for a type of conservative nationalism that sustained Maurice Duplessis and his Union Nationale party for nearly four decades. However, by 1950s, Québec had become an urbanized, industrial society and the hegemony of church and conservatism was beginning to crumble.

The decision by the Duplessis government and the Catholic Church to side with management against the workers during the Asbestos Strike in 1949 was viewed widely as a betrayal of the common interest. Pierre Trudeau was one of the young intellectuals who supported the miners and who began *Cité libre*, a humanistic, progressive journal that challenged the reactionary and inward looking nationalism of the Union Nationale and the clergy. A growing awareness of deficiencies in the educational system and of limited employment prospects for French-speaking Quebecers fueled a reform movement that was led by Jean Lesage, the leader of the Québec Liberal Party. *Rattrapage* ("catching up") was the motto and the agenda during the 1960s and few societies have ever reinvented themselves as rapidly or as radically as Québec. In this "Quiet Revolution," the provincial government became the mechanism for change with the teachers and technocrats the missionaries. As the society become more secular, church attendance among Catholics dropped from 88% in 1950 to 40% in 1970 and fell to 20% in 2000. The Total Fertility Rate dropped from nearly 4.0 births per woman in 1956 to 2.0 births in 1966 falling to 1.5 in 2004. As an urbanized secular Québec turned its back on its rural Catholic past, a new mission presented itself—the preservation of the French language and culture. Language replaced religion in the emerging Québécois identity and no one realized the political implications of that better than

René Lévesque.

René Lévesque was a journalist who in the late 1950s became well known in Québec as the host of a weekly television talk show, Point de mire ("Focus"). He and Trudeau were allies during the miner's strike but came to hold radically different views of Québec and Canada and became intense rivals. Rarely in Canadian politics have two such charismatic figures confronted one another. Lévesque was elected to the National Assembly in 1960 as a member of the Liberal Party and held several key positions in the Lesage government. But for Lévesque and many of his generation demographic changes were threatening to weaken the French-speaking majority and with it control of the only government they believed could ensure the survival of the French language and culture in North America.

During the late 19th and early 20th century, the Canadian economy was dominated by an English-speaking elite that lived in Montréal. English was the language of business and most of the immigrants to Québec during this period were from the British Isles. The non-British ethnic communities in Montréal date to the late 19th century when immigrants began to arrive from Western, then Eastern Europe. In Québec, people whose first language or "mother tongue" is neither English nor French are called allophones and their choice of language was becoming important. Immigrant children tend to raise their children in the language they were educated in and immigrants viewed the curriculum offered by the English-language public schools as better suited to life in North America. By 1960, 90% of allophone children attended English-language school. The "English" community was no longer an ethnically British enclave but a multiethnic, multicultural community that shared a common language. And, it was also growing faster than the French-speaking population in the rest of Québec. Equally worrisome for the nationalists was that 15% of anglophones, people whose first language was English, were of French Canadian origin. If the French were to become "mâitres chez nous" ("masters of our own house"), they would have to stem the tide of assimilation and linguistic transfers.

The 1960s were marked by confrontations over parents' right to choose the language of instruction for their children. Language legislation passed by successive Liberal governments failed to satisfy either the English-speaking community or the nationalists. Following their defeat in 1968, René Lévesque left the Liberal Party and began to build a new coalition from disparate political parties, socialist and conservative, that shared a common goal—the independence of Québec. In 1976, Lévesque's Parti Québécois (PQ) won the election and the following year passed Bill 101, the Charter of the French Language. Bill 101 had two prime objectives. The first was to integrate French fully into the Québec economy and thus improve the economic prospects for French-speaking Quebecers. The second was to reshape the educational system to protect the demographic position of the French-speaking community in Montréal by restricting access to English-language schools. In essence, only children whose parents or older siblings had been educated in English in Canada or who were themselves receiving instruction in English could attend "English" schools. Bill 101 was not well received in the English-speaking community and contributed to the decision by many anglophones to leave Québec in the decade that followed. Having addressed the language issue, Lévesque and the Parti Québécois moved to their main objective – independence for Québec. This agenda would determine the course of Canadian politics for decades and the course of the 2003 election.

The Constitutional "Crisis"

The 1980 Referendum was a softly worded proposal asking Quebecers to permit the government to negotiate a new relationship or sovereignty-association with Canada. The ensuing debate was acrimonious and in the end 60% of voters voted "Non," rejecting separation. Although this "Non" vote included over half of Québec's francophones, a disappointed Lévesque underscored the ethnic division in Québec between those of French origin and the immigrant and English communities declaring that "once again the others have denied Québec its independence." Following the defeat of the referendum, Trudeau realized his nationalist dream to repatriate the British North America Act of 1867, severing constitutional and legislative ties with the United Kingdom and enshrining his deeply held liberal principles of individual rights in the Charter of Rights and Freedoms. Repatriation under the Constitution Act of 1982 was more than a symbolic gesture of sovereignty. It also meant the Canadian provinces could amend the Constitution without the largely pro forma assent of the British Parliament.

The Lévesque government feared that the other provinces might use the amending formula to change the fundamental arrangements that govern federal-provincial relations in a manner indifferent or inimical to the needs and desires of the French-speaking majority in Québec. Even with the inclusion of the "notwithstanding" clause that allowed provinces to pass laws that violated the constitution provided they acknowledged it was in violation, Lévesque believed the new arrangement would disadvantage Québec and refused to ratify the act. Lévesque resigned as leader of the Parti Québécois in October 1985 and left it to his successor, Pierre-Marc Johnson to fight the general election in December. The 1985 election returned the Liberal Party to power under the leadership of Robert ("les Orphelins-de-Boubou") Bourassa who quickly found himself invoking the "notwithstanding" clause to defend Bill 101 even as he worked to resolve the constitutional impasse.

Working with the Conservative Prime Minister, Brian Mulroney, the Bourassa government began a series of consultations with the provincial premiers to win recognition of Québec as a "distinct society" and to gain acceptance of the minimum of institutional and political duality that even the Liberal government felt was essential to ensure the long term survival of the French language and culture in Québec. The proposed constitutional amendment acknowledged the role of the provincial legislature "to preserve and promote the distinct identity of Québec," acknowledged its right to control immigration policy, and ensured continued representation for Québec in the Senate and in the Supreme Court. Known as the Meech Lake Accord, this amendment was passed in 1987 but collapsed when two provinces failed to ratify it in 1992. Undeterred, Mulroney and Bourassa, in consultation with provincial premiers, drafted a second set of amendments, known as the Charlottetown Accord. This accord again recognized Québec as a distinct society and addressed a broader range of issues in federal-provincial relations that had been identified in the Meech Lake debacle. The Accord was presented in a national referendum in 1992 but with only 46% of Canadians in support, it was defeated in all but three provinces and one territory.[3] This was the last time the Canadians would have an opportunity to vote on the fate of their country.

Alienated from the "Rest of Canada," Quebecers returned the Parti Québécois to power in 1994 under the leadership of Jacques Parizeau, who immediately set about preparations for a second referendum the following year. The separatist campaign for the "Yes" vote, the "OUI," was off to a weak start. Polls showed no more than 40% supporting separation until Lucien Bouchard, the leader of

the Bloc Québécois—a coalition of conservative and liberal Members of Parliament formed after the defeat of Meech Lake—entered the fray. Bouchard was popular in Québec and provided a less "tribal" and more inclusive face to the separatist cause. Bouchard reached out to the English and immigrant communities whose marginal support he needed to win. The referendum, presented once again as a vote to permit the government to renegotiate confederation, was held in October 1995. Canadians watching the results that evening feared for the future of their country and took small consolation in final tally: 50.58% Non to 49.42% Oui. This time 60% of francophones had voted Oui. Tired and angry, Parizeau lashed out, declaring on national television that the Oui side had again been "beaten by money and the ethnic vote." Broadly criticized for his remark, Parizeau resigned as party leader and Bouchard, who had effectively taken leadership during the campaign, became Premier in 1996. For the second time in fifteen years, Québec had taken Canada to the brink of a constitutional crisis and relented. And after a quarter century of conflict neither Canada nor Québec had much energy for constitutional reform or for separation.

Bouchard endured continued sniping from Parizeau, who had been famously exiled to his vineyards in France after the Referendum, and from members of his own party for failing to advance the separatist agenda. The conflict came to a head in December 2000 when Yves Michaud, a veteran of the Québec sovereignty movement, was seeking to run as a by-election candidate to fill a vacated seat in the National Assembly. Michaud appeared as a witness before a commission on language and in an appeal to garner support among old-style nationalists, noted that non-French ethnic groups, particularly Jews, did not support Québec independence and observed that Jews were "not the only victims of genocide." Angered by his remark, Bouchard refused to accept Michaud as a candidate and had him condemned by the National Assembly. For Bouchard the condemnation of Michaud by the National Assembly was a vindication of his belief that racism was no longer part of the PQ agenda. But although he won, the controversy took its toll on his Bouchard and his family and he retired from politics in 2001. Bernard Landry became Premier and faced the challenge of winning the support of Québec's non-francophone populations. L'Affaire Michaud had served to remind many in the minority community of the comments made during and after the 1980 and 1995 referenda. Landry had to present an inclusive vision of a multicultural Québec if the PQ was to garner the non-francophone, ethnic vote needed to win the 2003 election, much less pass a referendum on sovereignty.

The 2003 Election

Surveys had consistently shown that the support for separatism had returned to its pre-1995 level of about 40%. A more nuanced look at this forty percent suggests that only half of the hardcore Purzédurs would be certain to vote for separation. The "soft" nationalists, the Purzémous, could be expected to support the Parti Québécois and might, if provoked, vote for separation. To win, Landry had to expand his base and to his credit he had made progress. He had negotiated an agreement with the Cree in northern Québec ending decades of confrontation over the James Bay project that had blocked and diverted several rivers flooding their traditional hunting grounds. The resulting controversy had been a source of considerable embarrassment to the government for nearly three decades and in 1995 the Cree voted to separate from Québec if Québec voted to separate from Canada. But sovereignty was not the only issue in the campaign and Landry had been careful not to make his party's plans for sovereignty an issue in the election even if it meant alienating his core constituency. Charest, however, would not let it rest.

During the debate Charest informed Landry that Parizeau, who had returned to Québec to campaign for the PQ, had once again repeated his analysis of the 1995 Referendum and his remark about the role of the "ethnic community" in its defeat. To be fair, Parizeau had gone on to say that the trend was changing and that the children of immigrants were voting "like us." But political debates are not fair and the damage was done. Charest had reminded wavering liberal voters, the Orphelins-de-Boubou and the chevaliers-de-la-table-rase, that a vote for the PQ, or even a vote for the ADQ, could mean another PQ government and yet another referendum. It worked. Charest and the Liberals won the election, taking 76 of the 125 seats in the National Assembly with 46% of the vote. Action Démocratique du Québec strengthened their position as a political party with 18% of the vote and four seats. The Parti Québécois received 33% of the vote winning 45 seats. Québec voted for change, but what kind of change remains to be seen for no one, it seems, wants to run the risk of addressing the constitutional issue.

The Road Ahead

The popularity of Brian Mulroney and the Progressive Conservative Party plummeted following the collapse of the Charlottetown Accord. His Liberal successor, Prime Minister Jean Chrétien, showed no inclination to engage in a constitutional debate even during the 1995 Referendum. It was Charest who argued the case for Canada across Québec during the referendum and it was his passion for Canada that brought him to the leadership of the Québec Liberal Party. On the day following the election, two different images of Charest appeared in *The Globe and Mail*. Geoffrey Simpson predicted that in time Charest would follow the pattern of other provincial Liberals in Québec and while he might not threaten separation, he would demand more money and power from Ottawa. The new Prime Minister, Paul Martin, the former Finance Minister who succeeded Chrétien as leader of the Liberal Party in December 2003, might be tight fisted but more open to discussion with the provinces. André Pratt, a journalist with *La Presse*, who wrote a biography of Charest, offered a slightly different interpretation.

Charest, he argues, is a federalist but not one to take the current constitutional arrangement for granted and it is possible that the new Liberal government may start to take incremental steps towards resolving the constitutional crisis. Pratt suggests that Charest and his team will not put forward Québec's traditional demands but rather ask: How can the Canadian federation accommodate the different needs of all the provinces? The Québec Liberal Party has indeed proposed a "council of the federation," a new structure in which the provinces and Ottawa work together to resolve concrete social and economic issues through "consultation, and joint-management and decision-making." And Charest may have had a more willing partner in Paul Martin. But none of this was guaranteed. The ideological differences between the Québécois who contend that Canada is comprised of two founding peoples and the multicultural vision of Canada widely held outside Québec cannot be easily resolved. Pratt suggests that this issue is a sleeping dog best left undisturbed. But, Pratt observes that Charest believes in a nuts-and-bolts approach to solving provincial-federal issues, which in time just might provide the confidence needed for a much needed round of constitutional talks. Before he can get to the nuts and bolts, Charest must deal with his problems at home.

Charest faces the challenge of improving health care

and education while cutting taxes and dealing with the provincial debt. The voters in Québec will judge him on these issues first. No one believes that separatism is dead and it is clear that Charest will have his hands full as he tries to renegotiate contracts with Québec's public service unions. Both came into play when Charest, hoping to get the nasty business over quickly, moved to reform the labor code to allow out-sourcing and to streamline collective bargaining by introducing a bill to curtail parliamentary debate. The public perceived this as high-handed and the unions dusted off their PQ membership cards as support for separation rose to 47%. The unions, however, are not wed to the PQ. The unions contributed to the defeat of the PQ and Pierre-Marc Johnson in 1985 by withholding their support because he and the Parti Québécois had reduced union pay and benefits in their effort to control public sector spending. But Charest is less dependent on union support and he has time to win back support.

Even if the Parti Québécois were to win in the next election in 2008, the federal landscape has changed. Following the defeat of the PQ in the 1995 Referendum, then Prime Minister Jean Chrétien introduced a motion "Respecting the Recognition of Québec as a Distinct Society." Though far from a constitutional amendment, the motion calls on the House of Commons to recognize that Québec is a distinct society within Canada; that this distinct society includes its French-speaking majority, unique culture and civil law tradition; and that the legislative and judicial branches of government should guide their conduct accordingly. The motion, which did not give any new powers to the Québec government nor the National Assembly, was seen as symbolic at best by most people in Québec. The majority outside Québec disapproved of any formal recognition of a "distinct society," fearing it might be used in a future separatist referendum but Bill C-20, known as the Clarity Act, defines the rules governing any future referendum.

The year after the 1995 Referendum, a suit was filed against the Québec government challenging the legality of the referendum process. Lawyers represented in the Canadian government eventually presented the suit to the Supreme Court of Canada asking whether Québec or any province had the right under Canadian or international law to unilaterally secede from Canada. In 1998, the Court ruled that Québec did not have the right to secede unilaterally but if a clear majority of Québec's population voted in favor of secession, then the other provinces had an obligation to negotiate separation. Based on this ruling, the House of Commons passed Bill C-20 in June 2000. The Bill requires that the question put to the voters in any future referendum must clearly state the outcome of the referendum—complete and total separation from Canada—and not as a soft option like the "permission to negotiate" new arrangements with Canada as was the case in 1980 and 1995. The House reserved the right to determine if a question was clear prior to the vote and could override the outcome if it felt the referendum violated the Clarity Act. Critics of the Clarity Act have dismissed it as ineffective, arguing that a separatist government with a strong referendum mandate would simply ignore it. So where does this leave Canada?

When asked to comment on the statement by one of his own cabinet ministers that the Clarity Act is "useless," Paul Martin replied that it is nevertheless the law but that he did not expect that it would be an issue while he was Prime Minister because in his words "we're going to have the kind of country where Quebecers will want to build a stronger Canada." How Québec and the rest of Canada use this opportunity remains to be seen.

Notes

1. Pierre Cayouerre, "Enquetê sur l'Homoelectus," *L'Actualité*, (April 15, 2003): 24-39.
2. The British government faced simultaneous rebellions in the late 1830s, in what was then Lower Canada (Québec) and Upper Canada (Ontario). While they differed in their specific demands, rebels led by Papineau in Lower Canada and by William Lyon MacKenzie in Upper Canada demanded representative government, and the breakup of the unelected British-dominated ruling elite known in Québec as the Chateau Clique and in Ontario as the Family Compact. Although defeated militarily, Canadians were granted self government under the British North American Act, which is also known as the Constitution Act of 1867 that Pierre Trudeau would bring home ("patriate") in 1982.
3. Procedures for amending the Constitution of Canada require that the amending legislation be approved by at least 2/3 of the provinces that have, in the aggregate, at least fifty per cent of the population of all the provinces. The provinces of Newfoundland, Prince Edward Island, New Brunswick and Ontario, the Northwest Territories, and only 46% of Canadians voted in favor of the Accord.

The 2003 Election in Québec: Another Chance for Federalism?

By Dean V. June and Ruth Writer

❶ CULTURE
- ▶ Research the changing role of the Catholic Church in Québec Society.
- ▶ Create a map of an independent Québec without including the areas of native revolt from the separatist movement.

❷ TIME, CONTINUITY AND CHANGE
- ▶ Critique the arguments over the "Québec Question" in 1980 and 1995.
- ▶ Create a time line in the history of separatism issues beginning with the British defeat on the Plains of Abraham to the election of 2003.

❸ PEOPLE, PLACES AND ENVIRONMENTS
- ▶ Create a letter to the editor written by an allophone and/or anglophone in response to passage of Bill 101.

❹ INDIVIDUAL DEVELOPMENT AND IDENTITY
- ▶ Compare major political achievements of Trudeau and Lévesque.

❺ INDIVIDUALS, GROUPS AND INSTITUTIONS
- ▶ Compare and contrast Canada's Charter of Rights and the Freedoms with the U.S. Bill of Rights.

❻ POWER, AUTHORITY AND GOVERNANCE
- ▶ Prepare and defend an argument for or against Québec separation in the world today.
- ▶ Create a chart showing the political philosophies of the three candidates in the 2003 election.
- ▶ Create a circle graph depicting the results of the survey by the Québec news magazine in early 2003 reported in this chapter.

❼ PRODUCTION, DISTRIBUTION AND CONSUMPTION
- ▶ Describe the role of labor unions in Québec.

❽ SCIENCE, TECHNOLOGY AND SOCIETY
- ▶ Summarize the author's major conclusions about social change in Québec via a poem, song, Powerpoint presentation or dance.

❾ GLOBAL CONNECTIONS
- ▶ List the dilemmas that could have confronted the U.S. government if Québec had voted yes in the 1995 referendum and had demanded its independence from Canada.

❿ CIVIC IDEALS AND PRACTICES
- ▶ Prepare a hypothetical conversation between Jean Charest and Paul Martin on the future of Québec.

México

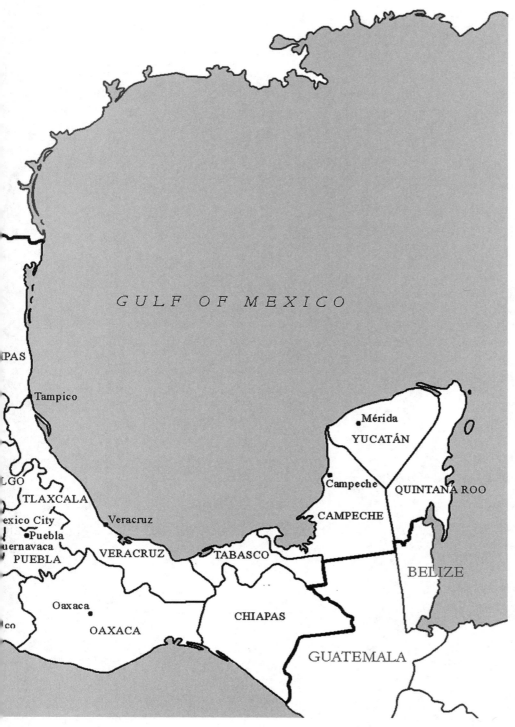

Modern México

GULF OF MEXICO

IPAS

Tampico

Mérida
YUCATÁN

LGO

TLAXCALA

Campeche   QUINTANA ROO

exico City   Veracruz

CAMPECHE

Puebla

uernavaca

VERACRUZ   TABASCO

PUEBLA

BELIZE

Oaxaca

co

OAXACA

CHIAPAS

GUATEMALA

CHAPTER SIX

Before Cortés: Pre-Hispanic México

By Amy J. Hirshman
Michigan State University

TEOTIHUACÁN. THE MAYA. THE AZTECS. These names evoke a grandeur and romance from another place and time. Ancient Mesoamerica is known in the popular imagination as a land of strange customs and magnificent temples. Yet it was also a place not unlike our modern world—with cities and statesmen, rural communities and farmers. Within the ruins of ancient Mesoamerica lies a dynamic cultural tradition in which real people lived and died. This ancient Mesoamerican world continues to be a testament to the ability and creativity of the people who lived there. In this varied and diverse landscape, a number of civilizations rose and fell, leaving the people of Mesoamerica with a long, rich cultural tradition of nearly 4,000 years.

Defining Mesoamerica

The civilizations of Mesoamerica (literally "Middle America") occupied what is today the southern portion of México, Belize, Guatemala, Nicaragua, Honduras, and Costa Rica (map 1). This region contained considerable environmental diversity: mountains, valleys, rivers, lakes, forests, jungles, and coast. The environmental mix was matched linguistically and culturally as well. However, the people living within what has been called "Mesoamerica" shared more cultural similarities than they did with the people to the north or south.

The northern boundary (Map 1, p. 64) was marked by the limit of consistent rainfall sufficient for agricultural production. This was an environmental boundary, and it fluctuated back and forth with changes in rainfall patterns. As a result, the whole northern edge of Mesoamerica was permeable; it was open to cultural influences moving both north and south. We know from archaeological evidence that there was trade both north and south between the people of this arid area and Mesoamerica. Trade included Macaw feathers (and perhaps the birds themselves) and semi-precious stones.

However, in the north of Mesoamerica there was often insufficient rainfall for intense agricultural production. As a result, the people living in what is now northern México actually had more in common with and lived a lifestyle closer to that of the people of what is now the American Southwest than with the people of Mesoamerica. Archaeological work in Northern and Western México and the Southwestern United States demonstrates that people lived there throughout prehistoric and historic time periods.

Mountains defined the southern boundary. Again, this was not an absolute boundary, but the mountains did provide southern Mesoamerica with relative isolation from the cultures of what are now Panama and the rest of South America. As with the north, there is evidence for trade with these southern cultures and for consistent maritime contact up and down the Pacific Coast. Some of this contact included the introduction of plant cultivars from South America into Mesoamerica, such as the peanut.

Within Mesoamerica one can find a rich landscape, with high plateaus and mountains, flowing rivers, lakes, valleys and ocean coastlines. Several features dominate the Mesoamerican landscape: the temperate central highlands and the tropical lowlands. The central highlands are situated on a plateau to the north, nestled between the Sierra Madre Oriental and Sierra Madre Occidental mountain ranges. The topography of the plateau was formed by volcanic action, and is still volcanically active (as evidenced by the eruption of Parícutin, in the state of Michocán in the 1940's, and the continued rumblings of Popocateptl to the southeast of México City). The highlands include many large valleys, most famously the Valley of México and the Valley of Oaxaca. This plateau falls off to the southwest into the large Balsas Depression and river system and to the southeast into the Tabasco-Veracruz Gulf Coast lowland plain. The tropical lowlands are located further south and include the Petén Jungle, which is situated on the

Map 1

MESOAMERICA

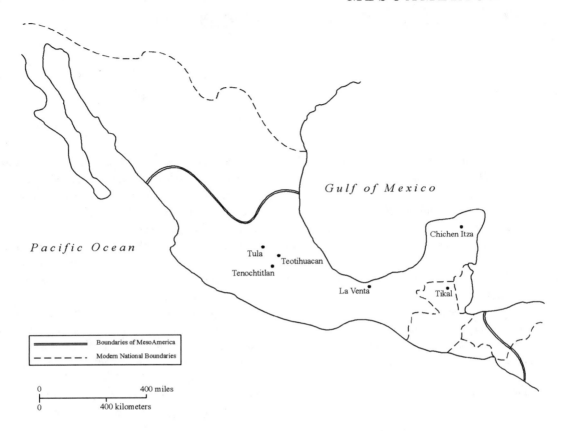

border between México, Belize, and Guatemala. The Petén is a dense and swampy jungle. To the north of the Petén is the Yucatán Peninsula, a relatively low-lying region situated on top of limestone, jutting north into the Gulf of México. Within this landscape there are a number of large river systems, which facilitated communication and trade, but no one river system dominates the entire landscape as in other regions of the world where ancient civilizations emerged (such as ancient Sumer and the Tigris-Euphrates Rivers or Ancient Egypt with the mighty Nile River.)

The diversity of this landscape provided the people living there with many resources and with opportunities for trade for any resources that may not have been near at hand. The natural resources of Mesoamerica include a wide variety of plants for food, spices, fibers for cloth and rope, for basketry, and for construction of houses. Abundant animal and insect species provided food and bones for tools. Other natural resources included salt, metal ores, stones (for both building and for making tools), semi-precious stones,

marine shells, and feathers (for making ornate capes and decorating warriors' shields). What one smaller area of Mesoamerica lacked, another region typically had in abundance. Long-distance trade facilitates the exchange of these regionally available, but locally scarce, resources. Kings and elites, especially for rarer items such as gold, apparently controlled some of this trade. However, almost everyone could find at least the basics in markets. Eventually, markets in Mesoamerica became extremely important to local economies; city dwellers could sell their specialized craft products in exchange for the agricultural produce of rural farmers. Though most exchanges were conducted in a barter manner, some exchanges were mediated by certain exchange mediums, such as cotton blankets and cacao seed. Cacao is a seed that grows in pods on a tropical tree. It was used both as an exchange medium and as the core ingredient of drinks made for kings and other members of the elite classes. Today we know cacao as chocolate.

The natural landscape provided everything necessary to

meet the needs of the Mesoamerican people as they built their great cities and as their populations grew. It is interesting to note that Mesoamericans never domesticated animals larger than the dog and the turkey; they could not because there were no horses, cows, sheep or goats living wild in Mesoamerica. Though a few wheels are known from several archaeological contexts in Mesoamerica, they were on small objects resembling pull-toys rather than from larger carts. Without larger animals to domesticate, and with the variety and difficulty of the Mesoamerican landscape, all long-distance transport utilized either waterways or human carriers.

Arguably the most important plant in Mesoamerica was maize (corn), the domesticated form of a wild grass. Maize formed the basis for the diet of every culture in Mesoamerica, providing a reliable and high caloric food source. Coupled with beans (such as runner beans), maize provides a complete dietary protein. Maize can be also be a high protein source when prepared after soaking in water with lime or ashes (in a process called nixtamalization). Maize can be ground into flour and prepared a number of ways, such as in tortillas (flat, round cakes usually toasted on flat griddles), tamales (plump dough cakes, often stuffed with other foods, that can be boiled, steamed, or roasted), or in beverages (notably atole, a corn meal drink). Maize can also be eaten off the cob or cooked as whole kernels in soup. Maize was so important to the ancient Mesoamericans that most of the cultures had a maize god. The Mayan myth of creation indicated that the gods made people from maize meal.

Another important plant in Mesoamerica was maguey (Agave, sometimes called the century plant). Though it has an austere appearance and broad leaves ending in long sharp spines, the maguey is not a cactus. But like a cactus, it also thrives in marginal soils with minimal rainfall. The maguey is useful in a number of ways. The flesh of the plant is nutritious and can be easily cooked. The spines are long and sharp and can be used as awls or tacks. The leaves can be processed for fibers, which can be spun into thread and woven into cloth for clothing or made into rope. From the sap, collected when the mature plant is ready to send up its once-in-a-lifetime shoot, a syrup, sugar, vinegar, and an alcoholic beverage called pulque can be made. Though many other plants could provide substitutes for the many maguey products, maguey was an economically important plant both prehispanically and during the colonial period. Even

today, maguey is used to stabilize erosion in marginal soils.

One more natural resource worthy of special note is obsidian. Obsidian is a volcanic glass, formed when lava cools very quickly. It is typically black, but can also be other colors, such as red or green. Obsidian is an extremely useful stone in that it fractures easily and someone skilled at handling obsidian can make tools and jewelry of many sorts: scraping tools, projectile points, and long, thin blades, to name a few types of tools. Of these, the blades were particularly important: hundreds of prismatic blades (so-called because of their shape in cross-section) could be made from one large obsidian nodule and these blades were used alone as knives, or were hafted into handles to make other tools. Obsidian has an extremely sharp edge—even sharper than metal. However, if a blade became dull, you didn't need a sharpener; instead you simply made a series of delicate chippings on the cutting edge until you exhausted the material. Most of the obsidian in Mesoamerica is available in the central Mexican highlands, and it was traded over all of Mesoamerica from very early times.

In general, the varied topography of Mesoamerica was rich in natural resources—an often-lush environment that provided the raw resources and dietary items necessary for sustaining large numbers of people. Within this context we find continuous human habitation and cultural change, from prehistoric time to first contact with Europeans.

The Archaic Period (ca. 7000 B.C. to 2500/2000 B.C.)

By 9,000 years ago, people were living throughout Mesoamerica as they were everywhere in the New World. The early Mesoamericans lived in small nomadic groups that were really multi-generation families. They were very mobile, carrying with them everything they needed. As different plants and animals became more abundant in different places and in different seasons, these small family groups would travel to collect the resources they needed to eat and make their tools and clothes. It is likely that these families were integrated into larger social groups through extended family ties, marriage, and trade connections. It may be possible that these small bands gathered annually for feasting and renewal of social ties, but we do not know that for sure. Most of our archaeological evidence for the archaic populations consists of projectile points, other stone tools, and small campsites.

After 7,000 B.C., there is evidence that people in some areas learned how to grow various plants for food and for

CURRICULⁱ
UM-DEARBUⁱⁱ

making useful resources, such as chili peppers, avocados, and bottle gourds (used to make durable, lightweight storage containers). Maize seems to have been domesticated between 5000 and 3400 B.C. Evidence for domestication comes from plant remains found in archaeological contexts and from the addition of certain artifacts like grinding stones used for preparing maize. At first these domesticated plants were simply added to the resources that the nomadic people were using. However, permanent villages were eventually established as people settled down near their agricultural fields as they became more reliant on domesticated plants. By 2500 B.C., most people in Mesoamerica lived in small villages and grew maize, beans, and squash—a trio of plants that grow well together and form the basis of a balanced diet. Other important domesticated plants included avocados, chili peppers, cotton (for fibers, not food), husk tomato, jícama, manioc, and prickly pear. A wide range of tropical fruits and non-domesticated plants were also consumed.

As noted before, there were no large animal domesticates. However, the ancient Mesoamericans were able to domesticate smaller animals, such as the turkey, Muscovy duck, the honeybee, and a hairless dog (but not the Chihuahua). Wild protein sources continued to be utilized throughout the prehistoric cultural sequence (and still are in some rural regions), from game animals like deer, peccary, and rabbits, to lacustrine resources like fish, shellfish, turtles, and frogs, to more interesting alternatives, like insects and even the iguana.

With the domestication of plants and animals, and with people living together in small villages, the stage was set for major social changes in Mesoamerica.

The Preclassic Period (2500/2000 B.C. to A.D. 300)

The Preclassic period (also called the "Formative" in central Mexican archaeology) was dominated by small agricultural villages of upwards of 100 people. These villages shared many similarities despite their dispersion throughout different environmental and cultural regions of Mesoamerica. These villagers used pottery (too heavy and breakable for their nomadic ancestors). Tools such as bone needles, spindle whorls, bone chisels, and obsidian scrapers have been recovered from household contexts, indicating a variety of tasks took place within and adjacent to houses. Construction of early houses must have varied somewhat by region, but they generally were one-roomed with stamped clay floors and a marked use of inside and outside space for different activities. Early houses were generally constructed of wattle (slender reeds lashed together) and clay daub, with more houses of later time periods constructed of adobe. They were generally one room and were large enough for a nuclear family. Often 1-3 houses were grouped together around a central, shared patio space. Storage pits are typically found by archaeologists adjacent to the houses.

The household and small village is a persistent theme in Mesoamerican history, continuing still today. Throughout prehistory, these houses usually contained no furniture, though sometimes low benches were built within them. People slept on woven mats, which could be rolled up and put out of the way during the day. Food was usually cooked over a hearth containing three stones. On the stones a large stew pot or griddle could be balanced over the fire. Other common ways of cooking included roasting pits and small spits. Every household would also need a metate, a grinding stone for maize, and a range of agricultural and building tools, such as a fire-hardened digging stick and axes made of stone and wood. Though the earliest households in Mesoamerican villages were socially equal, with distinctions in social structure made mostly on the basis of age and gender, it did not take long for some households to demonstrate relative wealth differences exhibited in the artifacts found by archaeologists in household and burial contexts. These wealth differences point to the development of social differences and the emergence of social rank and social classes.

Some of the small farming villages in many areas of Mesoamerica started to build one or two houses larger than all of the others. These villages also started to grow in size early in the Preclassic period. They grew into regional centers and became more important than their neighbors. One of the best-known examples of the growth of larger centers is to be found within Olmec society. The Olmec built large ceremonial centers with pyramids, plazas, and houses full of elaborate and distinctive art. Perhaps best known are the colossal heads, carved from a single piece of basalt stone standing nearly nine feet tall. The Olmec lived in what is today the Tabasco-Veracruz region of México, along the Gulf of México. It is hot, humid and tropical. One of the earliest Olmec sites is La Venta, located in modern Tabasco (map 1).

People were planting maize and living in a small village in a swamp at La Venta as early as 2250BC. Positioned advantageously on a large salt deposit and on a river, La Venta easily interacted with a wide region. The community began to grow, and by 800BC, it had reached the height of its power and population. The center of La Venta was marked by an earthen pyramid (all stone had to be imported, as there were no naturally occurring stone deposits in the immediate area) along with a large number of altars, platforms, public buildings, monuments and other examples of public religious and political art. Among the more amazing finds were four colossal heads and buried mosaics and offerings of jade figurines. The population was stratified, that is, people lived in different social and economic classes within the society. Commoners in Olmec society lived in and around the ceremonial centers and in small villages. They grew maize on levees constructed above the flood stage of the rivers and swamps, though they also consumed a diverse diet consisting of plants and animals collected in their lowland, swampy context.

Though we do not exactly understand the nature of politics in the Olmec region, we know that the political rulers (kings, though they probably exerted political power over only a small area) used religious themes to justify their power. Artifacts found at La Venta made of materials not found in the area, such as obsidian, jade and iron ore, demonstrate that the Olmec were involved in long-distance trade with other cultures in Mesoamerica. The exact reason for the Olmec's political decline is not completely clear, but the society as a whole began to decline in power and prestige and its large centers began to be abandoned after 700BC.

The Olmec have often been called the "mother culture" of Mesoamerica because Olmec or Olmec-influenced art and architecture have been found throughout Preclassic Mesoamerican cultural contexts. The Olmec are well known for certain motifs such as the importance of caves, early glyphs, the "were-jaguar" (a male half human/half jaguar creature with everted lips, jaguar fangs, and cleft foreheads), and large hollow ceramic doll-like figures. However, we now know that the Olmec were but one of many cultures experiencing the growth of regional centers during the Preclassic era. Such centers are known throughout Preclassic Mesoamerica, such as San José Mogote in the Valley of Oaxaca, and Chalcatzingo in the modern Mexican state of Morelos. The Maya also built urban centers in the Preclassic era. While each reflected their own unique culture, these centers also shared similarities with Olmec sites, including the importance of monumental architecture,

public art displays, ball game courts, and shared ideological themes as demonstrated in artistic themes. The urbanism exhibited at Olmec and other contemporary sites became an important trend in Mesoamerican civilizations, as was the notion of divine kingship. Additionally, the fact that Olmec motifs occur elsewhere is a testimony to the open trade and communication lines between the gulf coast, the southern lowlands, and the central highlands.

The Classic Period (300AD to 900AD)

Called the "Classic" period because 19th Century European explorers felt the ruins and monuments were as impressive as that of Classic Greece, this is the period of the emergence of the first great civilizations of Mesoamerica—Teotihuacán and the Classic Maya.

Teotihuacán, located in the northwest arm of the Valley of México (Map 2, p. 68), is known today for its massive Pyramid of the Moon and Pyramid of the Sun, both built along what is today called the Avenue of the Dead. In fact, it was a huge city, covering an area of eight square miles, with a population of perhaps 150,000-200,000 people.

The main axis for the city was the Avenue of the Dead, oriented 15½ degrees east of North (an orientation also applied to all other Teotihuacán-dominated centers) and along which a large number of pyramids, temples, and elite residences were built. The planned civic and ceremonial center of Teotihuacán held many ideological messages for those who lived there. The large temples were built over caves, thought to be sacred. The magnificent scale and grandeur of the religious and political edifices in the center of the city were designed to inspire awe and reverence in the beholder. Even today, the Pyramid of the Sun and the Pyramid of the Moon excite and impress visitors to the ruins of the city.

Elite rulers lived in far more splendor than the bulk of the population, with rich personal adornments and palaces in the center of the city. These rulers of Teotihuacán not only ruled the city, but also most of the Valley of México, and even points beyond, including what is now the modern states of Puebla and Morelos. The city was the primary settlement in the Valley of México and included approximately 90% of the Valley population. The other 10% was lightly dispersed across the rest of Valley.

Most Teotihuacános lived in large one-story "apartment" compounds. The apartments were large square buildings and they were built all over the city. Up to 100 people could

Map 2

PREHISPANIC VALLEY OF MEXICO

• Tula (outside Valley)

Lake Xaltocan

Lake Zumpango

•Teotihuacán

Lake Texcoco

Tenochititlán

Lake Xochimilco

Lake Chalco

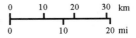

live in one of these compounds, approximately 15-20 nuclear families. The apartments had many rooms and small patios within them, often designed to provide a little privacy to smaller nuclear family units within the larger compound. They also tended to have a larger, central courtyard where a small altar for family religious activity could take place. The apartment compounds probably housed large, multi-generational and extended families that were all engaged in a single craft, such as jewelry making and lapidary work, pottery production, or feather working. Obsidian stone tool manufacturing seems to have been an especially important industry in Teotihuacán. Not everyone lived in apartments, however, as archaeologists have identified "slums," smaller room complexes constructed of inferior construction materials (adobe as opposed to stone), as well as palaces in the city.

Physical anthropologist Rebecca Storey[1] studied skeletal remains from one such apartment compound, called Tlajinga 33. Tlajinga was a smaller, poorer compound constructed of stone and adobe located near the southwestern edge of the city. It was continuously occupied for approximately 450-500 years and was remodeled many times. The inhabitants were lapidary specialists, though by the time the compound was abandoned, they were also producing ceramics as an additional economic strategy. As some individuals were buried within the compound, it is possible to study the health of people who actually lived in the compound. Storey determined that the population at Tlajinga 33 suffered from poor nutrition, which affected the overall health of all the people living in the compound. It was particularly bad for infants and children: over half of the individuals represented by skeletal material were under the age of 15. While higher status people living in Teotihuacán probably were healthier, this is a sobering reminder that with large cities come large problems for the provisioning and care of the people living within them. This is a problem most cities continue to struggle with.

While most Teotihuacénos engaged in agriculture or craft production, the rulers of the city exerted far-ranging influence through long-distance trade. Teotihuacán strongly influenced art and architecture throughout most of Mesoamerica during the Classic period. Exotic trade items occur within multiple contexts in Teotihuacán. There is also evidence for foreigners, non-native Teotihuacános, living in the city, notably in the famous "Oaxaca Barrio," in which the pottery and other art suggests people from Oaxaca lived there.

From approximately AD 650 on, the population in Teotihuacán began to decline. Craft production quality began to suffer and the building of public architecture dropped off. There was an increase in military motifs in the art. Teotihuacán's reign ended violently, probably caused by internal strife, with evidence of burning in the temples in the city center as well as other temples scattered throughout the city, dated to around AD 750. Though small remnant populations continued to live in and around the city, it was largely abandoned soon after the burning. Less than 700 years later, at the beginning of the Aztec Empire, Teotihuacán was largely mythologized and the details of its existence forgotten.

At about the same time that Teotihuacán dominated the highlands, the Maya, with a population in the millions, controlled directly or indirectly the southern portion of Mesoamerica. Instead of being ruled by one city, as with Teotihuacán, the Classic Maya had a number of cities in the highlands and the lowlands of what are now Southern México, Guatemala and Belize. The elite rulers of individual Mayan cites, like Tikal (in contemporary Guatemala), Palenque, and Copan, competed with one another for power and prestige within the Mayan region. Long-distance trade was important to the Mayan economy; it was especially important to the elites who used exotic, imported goods to demonstrate their political and religious importance. Meanwhile, the poorer people were mostly farmers, using slash and burn agriculture practices to produce the food that fed and fueled the Mayan cities of the jungle.

The Maya are well known for their achievements in science, art and architecture. Their architectural achievements include the corbelled arch and large stone temples. The Maya are also known for their astronomical observations and their calendar. Mesoamerican civilizations generally used a 365-day solar calendar to track the year and a 260-day ritual calendar to track important feasts and celebrations. These two calendars coincided every 52 years, the Calendar Round, a sacred year and a period of uncertainty as to whether or not the 52-year cycle would repeat. The Mayans also used the "Long Count" calendar, which tracked every year chronologically from the time they reckoned the beginning of the earth. Scholars were able to line the Long Count dates (using Short Count dates from the calendar in use by the Postclassic Maya at the time of Spanish contact) with the Western calendar, thus helping scholars unravel the Mayan chronology. Mayan mathematicians also discovered the zero and used a counting system in base 20 (the Western decimal system uses base 10).

The Mayans also developed an elaborate writing system based on glyphs rather than an alphabet. The glyphs were memory devices, signs that stood for complex ideas. Glyphs also stood for city names and names of rulers. Monuments carried this information, carved into stone, as displayed publicly for all to see (though only a few could actually read.)

These achievements led early explorers and archaeologists to think of the Maya as a peaceful people ruled by priests; this idea persists in the popular imagination even today. However, research since the 1960s clearly demonstrates that the various Mayan cities warred with one another. The public art of the Classic Maya depicts conquering kings and bound captives; the writing tells of cycles of conquest of neighboring cities; and, most interesting of all, several Mayan sites exhibit defensive architecture, such as deep ditches and earthen parapets.

An important example of a Mayan city is Tikal, located in what is today Guatemala. At its height, Tikal was a city of approximately 72,000 people, situated in a hilly, tropical forest area (Map 1). The city center was composed of numerous buildings, plazas, pyramids, monuments, causeways, and ball courts. The layout of the center was according to typical Mayan tradition, with different architectural elements exhibited in different cardinal directions according to Mayan cosmological belief. Interestingly, some of the artistic motifs at Tikal demonstrate Teotihuacán influence, though everything is strongly Mayan in origin and execution. The kings and religious elite lived in the center, while the majority of the people lived outside the center of the city, in scattered households. The population density of Mayan cities never rivaled the density of Teotihuacán.

Most people lived in houses dispersed outside of the city center. Their houses were spread out around the city and were built on low stone platforms. Typically, a house was composed of a group of rooms, each separately built around a patio, with foundations of stone and walls of wood poles with a thatch roof. Each room was large enough for at least a nuclear family, and often multi-generational and extended families lived together. Some of these house platforms were in use for hundreds of years. There is some evidence that not all households lived at the same wealth level. In order to make a living, many people were craftspeople, making ceramics, stone tools, or working with wood, or they were farmers. Interestingly, the dispersed houses of Tikal tended to cluster around smaller temple/ritual complexes. This clustering, along with the planning and execution of the city centers, indicates that the Maya were as interested in city planning as the Teotihuacános. Mayan cities tend to be more irregularly organized, but that may be due more to the topography of the land in the jungle than lack of desire on the part of the Mayan rulers.

From Mayan hieroglyphs, we know that Tikal was an important Mayan center with few rivals from about AD 300 to AD 530. After a period of about 100 years, in which other centers were more powerful, Tikal once again became the most prestigious of the Mayan centers until around AD 700. After AD 700, most of the population of the Classic Mayan centers, including Tikal, left the cities, moving far into the jungle or to the north. There was no "Maya Collapse": rather, most of the population and the political power shifted north in search of new agricultural and trade opportunities. This population shift allowed new centers to rise; the pattern of rival, competing powers continued in the north.

The Postclassic Period (900-1522AD)

After the fall of Teotihuacán and the Classic Maya, a period of conflict among small competing states followed. Several states, however, were able to exert control for short periods of time, such as the Toltecs and the Postclassic Maya.

The Maya did not "vanish" at the end of the Classic period. There is no evidence for invaders or mass destruction. Rather, it seems as though the great Classic Mayan cities became too populous for agriculture to support; people moved away to where food was more plentiful. They tended

to move north, into the Yucatan, and there they built new cities, though much smaller than the ones before. One of the last major Mayan centers was Chichen Itza, now a well-known tourist destination in northern Yucatan.

Chichen Itza (map 1) is a large, sprawling site with a ballcourt, many large pyramids, temples, and public buildings. It is unknown how large an area the Itza directly controlled; however, we do know that they were involved in a far-flung trading network. Their influence was felt over a large region, including all of the Yucatan, and points north and south along the coast. The basis for this economic and political power was salt. Salt is a necessary staple for any human diet, and the Itza controlled the finest salt sources in the region. The Itza also seemed to have some diplomatic contact with a great culture far to the north, the Toltecs.

The Toltecs filled the political void left by the dramatic decline of Teotihuacán. Tula, their capital, was less than 20 miles north of the Valley of México. Most of what we "know" of the Toltecs is in fact rooted in myth and stories told long after the Toltecs themselves ceased to be politically important. Tula, their capital, was a vibrant center full of skilled artisans and craftsmen (map 2). First settled in the Classic Period, Tula was situated near limestone deposits and was a lime production site for Teotihuacán. But it wasn't until after the decline of Teotihuacán that Tula grew into a regional power. At its height (ca. AD 950-1150), Tula was a city of 5 square miles with 30,000-60,000 people living in it. The city center was well planned, with two ball courts, two pyramids, council halls and a colonnaded hall or gallery. Most of this central complex was on a large platform, 30-50 feet tall. The great warrior sculptures are famous. They stood over 12 feet tall and served as supports for a roof, on top of a pyramid. While the elite lived in palaces, most people lived in groups of houses of four to eight rooms built around interior courtyards. While the Toltecs were a dominant power for over 200 years, they cannot be considered as having an "empire." Rather, they engaged in a far-flung trade and diplomatic network, including the Valley of México, and points to the west and south, perhaps including areas as far removed at the Yucatan. As a result, the Toltecs are thought of as being rather multi-ethnic and peaceful. But by AD 1200, Tula had fallen, having been sacked and burned by as yet unknown intruders.

Meanwhile, the Valley of México experienced a long period of warfare and competition between centers, with no one center dominating the basin or even parts of the basin for long periods of time. This changed, though, with the appearance of the Mexica, a rag-tag migrant group from the north.

The Mexica, in their legendary history, claimed their god Huitzilopochtli told them to seek out a new home. The sign of this new home was to be an eagle perched on a prickly pear cactus. This sign forms the basis of the modern flag of the country of México. Settling on an island in Lake Texcoco in the early AD 1300s (in part because no one wanted them nearby), they named their new settlement Tenochtitlán. The Mexica were but one of many Nahua-speaking groups to immigrate to the central highlands, including the Valley of México, in the Late Postclassic period. The term Aztec properly refers to these Nahua-speaking people.

At first the Mexica became mercenaries for hire. In AD 1428, through a combination of warfare, diplomacy, and deception, they became co-leaders of the powerful Triple Alliance Empire along with two other city-states in the Valley of México. The Mexica dominated the Triple Alliance (commonly called Aztec), and from their capital Tenochtitlán, they eventually conquered most of Mesoamerica, leaving a legacy of language and culture that persists today.

The Aztec capital of Tenochtitlán (map 2) grew to be a wonder, with temples, causeways, housing, and a great market at Tlatelolco full of farmers, craftsmen and merchants with their wares. It is estimated that over 200,000 people lived in this city. Large causeways connected the island city to lakeshore. The most famous temple, the Templo Mayor, dominated the large central civic-ceremonial complex in the heart of Tenochtitlán. The Templo Mayor was a twin-pyramid, built up and remodeled many times. Each time they included many offerings; archaeologists have found more than 85 of them. These offerings included items of obsidian, shell, jade, pottery, and stone. The Templo Mayor was dedicated to Huitzilopochtli, the patron deity of the Aztecs and a god of war, sacrifice, and the sun, and Tlaloc, the god of rain and associated with maize fertility.

At the Templo Mayor, as well as at many other temples in Tenochtitlán and throughout the empire, the Aztecs practiced human sacrifice. They believed the gods had sacrificed themselves for the creation of the world and it was the Aztec duty to please and sustain the gods through a reciprocal sacrifice of human life. Though conducted in several different ways, most noteworthy was the ritual killing of sacrifices by cutting open their chests and removing their hearts. Being a sacrifice was an honor; these individuals were regarded as taking the place of the gods in a reenactment of the mythic sacrifice. Most (but not all) of the individuals sacrificed were warriors captured in battle.

Military themes dominated Aztec ideology. Military ability contributed to the political ascent of the Mexica and placed them at the head of the largest empire in North and Central America. Moreover, the Aztec leaders ruled by threat of war and by terror and military conquests increased the power of the leaders and of the empire. Conquests also financed the Aztec economy, bringing food and wealth to Tenochtitlán. One way a man, whether a noble or a commoner, could earn social prestige was through bravery and success in battle. When not engaged in wars of conquest, the Aztecs sometimes participated in "flower wars" with Tlaxcalla, an independent kingdom entirely surrounded by the Aztec Empire to the southeast. These wars were conducted in a highly ritualistic manner, for "practice" according to the Aztecs, and contributed captives for sacrifices. However, the Aztecs never conquered the Tlaxcallans, who were later willing allies to the Spanish in their assault on the Aztecs.

Aztec society had many classes, from the king and nobility to priests, merchants and craftsmen, to farmers, and finally, to slaves. One could not become part of the nobility, no matter how wealthy, if one was born a commoner. The Aztec king, or tlantoani, and the nobility lived in palaces near the city center while commoners lived in smaller houses throughout the city. Most of these houses were apparently not much different from houses in the rural countryside: small one to three room houses with an open patio. The population density of Tenochtitlán was not as great as Teotihuacán's, and houses were usually interspersed with gardens. Gardens provided households with a variety of foodstuffs, such as chili peppers, while the agricultural fields outside of the city provided the bulk of the maize for the city.

The intensive production of maize was made possible by using different ways to reclaim land for cultivation throughout the Valley: terraces, irrigation, and an ingenious technology called chinampas. Chinampas are often called "floating gardens," but in actuality they were attached to the shallow floor of the southern lake in the Valley. As the canals around were dredged, they were heaped with rich muck and decaying vegetation. The chinampas were extremely fertile.

Unlike the situation with Teotihuacán, where the city so dominated the political landscape that nearly everyone in the Valley of México lived within the city, the Valley was full of medium to small settlements, though none became as large as Tenochtitlán. Many of the people living in the countryside were farmers, but many were also craft specialists, making the items demanded in the market system and in the city. Craft specialists also lived in the city. These goods and excess agricultural produce were exchanged in the markets, of which the Tlatelolco market was the largest. According to Spanish eyewitness accounts, every conceivable food and item was available in the market. The wares of long-distance professional merchants, called pochteca, augmented locally available goods.

Aztec children were taught from a young age how to take care of their chores and learned the jobs that they would be doing for the rest of their lives. Girls were taught to spin, weave, and cook, while boys were taught to fetch wood, fish with nets, and, if their family were craftsmen, they learned a trade. Children, especially boys, went to school, even commoner children. All were given religious instruction and taught music, but boys were also taught how to become warriors. Girls tended to marry young, but boys often waited until about 20 to marry. One's family arranged the marriage.

We know more about Aztec society, especially these details about everyday life, because the Aztecs left records about themselves. The first Spanish, coming in AD 1519, encountered an empire at the height of its power. They too wrote about what they saw and experienced.

Summary

By the time the Spanish arrived and "discovered" Mesoamerica, the people of Mesoamerica had already participated in the rise and demise of great states and empires for millennia. The Aztecs were but one in a long line of complex societies. The legacy of the ancient Mesoamericans persists today in the myths, identity, and culture of modern México.

Notes

1. Rebecca Storey, *Life and Death in the Ancient City of Teotihuacán: A Modern Paleodemographic Synthesis* (Tuscaloosa: The University of Alabama Press, 1992).

Before Cortés: Pre-Hispanic México

By Kristin Janka Millar

❶ CULTURE
▶ Compare and contrast the structure of Mesoamerican household and village life with yours in the U.S.
▶ Research the Olmec civilization and explain why the Olmecs are considered by some to be the "mother culture" of Mesoamerica.

❷ TIME, CONTINUITY AND CHANGE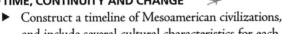
▶ Construct a timeline of Mesoamerican civilizations, and include several cultural characteristics for each period. Select one time period to compare with your experience in today's world.

❸ PEOPLE, PLACES AND ENVIRONMENTS
▶ Create a chart describing the environmental diversity of Mesoamerica. Use this chart to explain the impact of the environment on Mesoamerican language and culture.

❹ INDIVIDUAL DEVELOPMENT AND IDENTITY
▶ Write a journal entry describing the roles and responsibilities of a Mesoamerican child for a typical day. Discuss how these roles and responsibilities compare with your own.

❺ INDIVIDUALS, GROUPS AND INSTITUTIONS
▶ Research the decline of Teotihuacán and provide possible explanations for its demise.

❻ POWER, AUTHORITY AND GOVERNANCE
▶ Investigate the Triple Alliance Empire (A.D. 1428) and the role of the military in expanding its power.

❼ PRODUCTION, DISTRIBUTION AND CONSUMPTION
▶ In Mesoamerica the barter system was an important form of exchange. Using one product as an example, explain how this system worked (examples might include maize, maguey, obsidian, and cacao).

❽ SCIENCE, TECHNOLOGY AND SOCIETY
▶ Describe Mayan mathematical achievements and explain the significance of the Mayan discovery of "zero."

❾ GLOBAL CONNECTIONS
▶ Maize is considered to be the most important plant in Mesoamerica. Debate the pros and cons of genetically modified corn in Mesoamerica and its implications for global food security.
▶ The peanut originated in South America and was introduced into Mesoamerica through maritime contact. Research the origin of other Mesoamerican agricultural products and create a map illustrating their origin.

❿ CIVIC IDEALS AND PRACTICES
▶ Using the internet, find an image of the Mexican flag and explain its origin and symbolism.

CHAPTER SEVEN

From Conquest to Modernity: México 1519-1946

By Dina M. Berger and John F. Bratzel
Loyola University, Chicago   Michigan State University

México has a complex and fascinating history. Its rich pre-Columbian past, the arrival and colonization by the Spanish, and México's independence and development as a modern nation-state offer historians and teachers a full source of concepts and teaching potential. While this essay offers a quick gloss, further reading and study will reveal fascinating stories of multiple cultures and histories.

The Conquest

The story of the conquest of México is clearly one of the most dramatic in human history. When Hernán Cortés first landed on the continent, he brought with him more than just horses and weapons; he also brought the culture of Spain. And this culture had been defined by seven centuries of conflict over control of Spain between the Islamic Moors and the Roman Catholic Spanish. While religion cannot be underestimated as a driving force for the Spanish, the desire for wealth and position was also a powerful stimulant for the conquistadors. The goal of many Spaniards was to gain title to newly captured land and to supervise and draw support from the people who worked the land. The usual phrase to describe the motives of the conquistadors is "God, Gold, and Glory," and while it is an oversimplification, it is also a reasonable generalization.

Cortés, who ultimately led the Spanish invaders of México, was a bright and a resourceful individual and this coupled with his well-established Spanish family helped him gain early success in Cuba, then the frontier of the Spanish conquest. Indeed, he could have easily spent his whole life in Cuba and lived well. Instead, he accepted the offer of the Governor of Cuba, Diego Velásquez, to lead an expedition to the west to gain information about the area. Velásquez, however, at the last moment grew fearful that Cortés would not willingly remain under his control and decided to replace him. Getting wind of the removal order, Cortés quickly ordered the departure of his squadron for what was ultimately to become México.

Fortune shone on the expedition, particularly when Cortés encountered Pedro de Aguilar, a shipwrecked Spaniard who had lived with the Maya and who had learned their language. Later, he garnered further help in his journey by finding Mariana (Malinche) who spoke both Maya and Náhuatl, the latter being the language of the Aztecs. This was particularly helpful because it allowed Cortés to communicate with the Aztecs, albeit through two translators, and to gain an appreciation for the political situation in México.

What Cortés discovered was that the Aztecs ruled an empire by might, demanding tribute in the form of goods and people to sacrifice. Cortés was able to take advantage of the antipathy of the indigenous groups that had been subjugated by the Aztecs to gain their support. This help probably would not have been enough if the Aztecs had moved immediately and decisively to block Cortés. Moctezuma II, the leader of the Aztecs, however, vacillated and instead of rallying his people against the intruders, he temporized and tried to discourage Cortés from coming to the Aztec capital, Tenochtitlán (contemporary México City). Despite Moctezuma's efforts, Cortés, along with thousands of Indian allies, arrived in Tenochtitlán. Distressed by their leader's lack of resolve as well as aggressiveness against the invaders, the Aztecs killed Moctezuma and drove the Spanish from the city. Undaunted, Cortés did not give up, and with his Indian allies, returned and destroyed Tenochtitlán. Aiding Cortés was an outbreak of smallpox among the Indian population that took a terrible toll on the defenders.

México as a Spanish Colony

As the Spaniards established themselves, they understood that control of Indian labor was the key to wealth. This was true whether it was farming, crafts, or mining. The Spanish crown wanted to reward the conquistadors with Indian labor, but the crown, along with the Catholic clergy, also wanted to convert the Indians to Roman Catholicism.

Furthermore, the crown feared any individual in the New World gaining sufficient power to challenge Spain. The outcome of these conflicting interests was continuing turmoil as a struggle developed between the Spanish living in México and the Roman Catholic clergy there. The Spanish crown both mediated this dispute and used it to fulfill its goal of total control over Latin America. Spain also achieved this goal by appointing only Spaniards born in Spain to significant governmental positions such as Viceroy or to the Audiencia (a legislative and judicial body). Even then, those chosen to serve could only serve for a short time.

But Spain could not control the effects of disease and the indigenous population plummeted. While estimates vary, in 1519, when Cortés arrived, the indigenous population was probably around twenty million people. By the start of the seventeenth century, most experts agree that the indigenous population had fallen to about two million people. It would be well into the twentieth century before the total population of México returned to its pre-Columbian levels.

Offering some stability in colonial México was the Catholic Church. In a remarkable display of faith and fortitude, the Spanish converted virtually the entire indigenous population of México to Catholicism in one generation. Undoubtedly, some of these conversions were not complete. The subsequent religious structure was ultimately more of a blending of indigenous religion and Catholicism than pure Catholicism, still the Church's effort represents one of the great mass conversions in history. It also must be pointed out that the Church was instrumental in maintaining Spanish control.

The Spanish desire for laborers coupled with the decline of the indigenous population caused the Spanish to import African slaves into México. In particular, the Spanish used slaves in the shipping and hauling industry: from unloading ships in the port of Vera Cruz to transportation of goods to México City. Escaped slave attacks were a continuing problem in colonial México, particularly raids on freight wagons bound for México City. At one point, the problem was so bad that México paid protection money to escaped-slave communities to stop this activity.

Independence

By the beginning of the nineteenth century, the ideas of the enlightenment, the specters of the American and French Revolutions, and the decline of the power of Spain all con-tributed to the possibility of independence for México. In most of Latin America, the Creole elite, the wealthy Spaniards born in the New World, led the independence revolts. This was not initially the case, however, in México.

In 1803, the Catholic Church exiled Father Miguel Hidalgo y Castilla to the small town of Dolores, Guanajuato. The Spanish assumed that the freethinking priest, who talked about dangerous ideas such as liberty and equality, would slip into obscurity. He didn't, and as a result, the civil administration decided to arrest him. Hearing this, on September 16, 1810, Hidalgo brought his Indian and mestizo followers together and called on them to end bad government. His followers, who quickly became a mob of 25,000, sacked Guanajuato and slaughtered the Spanish. His following grew to 100,000 people and other cities decided not to fight. It appeared that he would capture México City, but perhaps because he wanted no more bloodshed, he withdrew. The Spanish eventually defeated him near Guadalajara. Hidalgo was promptly tried, found guilty, and executed.

His revolution was not, however, at an end. José María Morelos and Vicente Guerrero, both lieutenants of Hidalgo, continued to fight. During the next five years, Morelos gave definition and depth to the original call of Hidalgo, but he too was eventually captured and shot. Later, the Spanish government sent an army under the command of Augustín Iturbide to destroy Guerrero. Realizing that the Mexican creole elite was losing faith in Spain and the Spanish King, Iturbide decided to join with Guerrero and call for independence with himself as Emperor of México. Iturbide was successful, but his reign was short. He had no money and no strong base of support. He was quickly ousted by the individual who would dominate Mexican politics for the next thirty years, Antonio López de Santa Anna.

The Era of Santa Anna

With the end of Iturbide's reign, a constitutional convention was called that clearly revealed the lines of disagreement concerning the structure of a new Mexican government. On the one hand were the conservatives who favored a strong central government, and on the other were the liberals who supported more power for the states. Ultimately, a basically liberal constitution with some conservative components was adopted. In 1824, Guadalupe Victoria, an officer in Morelos' army, was chosen as the first president of México. He survived his presidency, but he was the exception.

What followed was continuing political dispute between liberals and conservatives. This source of disagreement was itself overlaid by the actions of Santa Anna who made a mockery of any kind of systematic process of government. The result was chaos. Santa Anna was elected or chosen president on a number of occasions; sometimes he accepted the presidency, but on other occasions he refused to serve. In 1835, for example, Santa Anna decided not to serve as president even after being chosen, but subsequently decided to overthrow his own liberal vice-president who had ruled in his stead. Moreover, at the same time, Santa Anna changed his position and supported a conservative-centralist government. When liberal states opposed his sudden shift, Santa Anna decided to march on the Mexican state of Tejas (Texas) because, among other reasons, it had refused allegiance to the conservative government.

Santa Anna's choice of Texas was logical, because in the years since independence, more and more Americans had moved into Texas and English, rather than Spanish, was becoming the dominant language. Striking a blow against the northern state would have wide public support in México. Initially successful, Santa Anna was eventually defeated. Texas was lost and it appeared as if Santa Anna's tenure in politics was over. But he reestablished his position with an attack on French troops in Vera Cruz. Known as the "Pastry War," this action, in which Santa Anna lost a leg, gave him back his leadership position in México.

When Texas became part of the United States, the exact borders of the state were unclear. Under President James K. Polk, the United States provoked a battle and ultimately a war over the disputed land. México, although unready for war, was anxious to fight to establish itself as a strong power. Moreover, many European observers believed México could win. México, however, did not win and the United States occupied México City. Ultimately a peace treaty was signed and México surrendered one-third of its territory to the United States.

This debacle, however, did not lead to good government in México. More confusion followed until the conservatives took over once more. To help them in their cause, they brought in Santa Anna to attract followers, but the general could not be controlled and he established a virtual monarchy. To fund his spending, he sold the Mesilla Valley to the United States (the Gadsden Purchase).

La Reforma

Santa Anna's excesses were so extreme that in 1855, without a shot being fired, a new group of liberals drove the general into exile. Led by such people as Benito Juárez, Melchor Ocampo, and Miguel and Sebastián Lerdo de Tejada, this movement known as La Reforma wanted to put an end to governmental chaos, create modern institutions, and end the special rights of the army and the clergy. Their attempt to do this brought about strong opposition from the groups affected. When the reformers announced that the Church had to divest itself of all property not used in worship (Ley Lerdo, 1856), the split between the liberals and conservatives became unbreachable. Ironically, Church property was bought by the wealthy, which tended to concentrate ownership rather than create the independent farmers sought by the leaders of La Reforma.

The election of 1857 ultimately resulted in two governments, two presidents, and civil war. By 1860, the liberals had won and Benito Juárez became President of México. But the México of which he became president was in very poor condition. Fifty years of strife had seriously weakened the country and it was vulnerable to foreign adventurers. Emperor Napoleon III of France decided to try to take advantage of the situation to increase his country's power by gaining control of México. As a pretext, he used the collection of debt, on which Juárez had suspended payment, to send in French troops. Other nations also invaded, but it was only the French who remained when the other European nations withdrew. The Conservatives, realizing that this was their chance to regain power, at the urging of Napoleon III, agreed to invite the Archduke Maximilian of Austria and his wife Carlota to accept the newly created and French-supported throne of México.

Maximilian accepted and with the support of French troops, in 1864 he became Emperor Maximilian I. Early in his reign, Maximilian upset his conservative supporters by confirming the laws of La Reforma. The Catholic Church would not regain title to its lost land. Conservative support dwindled. So did French support. Napoleon III discovered that sustaining Maximilian was very expensive and that there did not seem to be any indication that the drain on the French treasury would stop in the near future. Moreover, France itself was growing fearful of German power. And in the United States the Civil War, which had lessened the United States' ability to influence developments in México, was over. The U.S. was not the slightest bit subtle in its opposition to Maximilian. As French support dwindled, Maximilian's situation became increasingly perilous. The Mexican emperor could probably have escaped, but he chose to stay. He was captured, and on June 19, 1867 he was shot.

Modern México (1876-1946)

The defeat of the French and the death of Maximilian mark the beginning of modern México. Led by Benito Juárez, the restoration of Liberals to political power in 1867 ushered in a new era of modernization and nation building. Despite interruptions and reinterpretations these two goals remained top priority for México's political leaders from 1876-1946.

Leaders agreed that national progress depended on expanded transportation and communication, improved sanitary conditions (potable water and drainage systems), industrial growth, increased literacy rates, and a strong, stable political system. But, they often disagreed about which path their nation should take to realize these goals. This discord, rooted in regionalism, secularism, and elitism, not only shaped México's fractured revolution and revolutionary state but also gave rise to religious rebellion and political violence. Nonetheless, because modernization and nation building remained hallmarks of political administrations, México emerged as an industrialized, united, and stable nation by 1946.

Porfirian México (1876-1911)

General Porfirio Díaz rose to presidential power in 1876 with a campaign that condemned, among other things, presidential reelection. Ironically, (even more so than Antonio López de Santa Anna), Díaz became México's most relentless head-of-state, who despite a brief interregnum by his colleague, Manuel González (from 1880-1884) ruled for over thirty years. During Díaz's enduring presidency, called the Porfiriato, México underwent rapid development: railroads were constructed, agribusiness boomed, industry in Monterrey flourished, Puebla's textile industry grew, and mining advanced. And, México City became an urban center. With impressive population growth, wealthier Mexicans and foreign residents moved to the suburbs; some 30,000 houses received electricity and a streetcar system connected the wealthier areas.[1]

México City also became a showcase for pomp. The Paseo de la Reforma, a boulevard with grand monuments and circles (glorietas), became the avenue for the city's parades and ceremonies. One of the most famous was the parade in which Mexicans rode bicycles (all the rage by the 1890s) decorated with flowers. And, whereas Díaz prohibited bullfighting because it was offensive, wealthier residents who belonged to the Jockey Club inaugurated México's first racetrack and introduced horse racing and polo. Supporting the wealthy, and keeping order among his poorer citizens, was the Díaz-created gendarmerí, a modern police force.

Yet, despite these developments, which were based on Díaz's four tenets: property, profits, peace, and progress, only a few benefited and it was at the cost of the many. Justification for Díaz's support for a strong, elitist state came from the views of the philosopher, August Comte, who argued that a society could only enjoy progress once order was maintained. To ensure México's path toward modernity, Díaz made concessions to foreign investors who soon owned nearly 70% of the nation's industries. His treasury minister sold railroad construction bonds to German and British investors in order to consolidate México's foreign debt, and the government relinquished its subsoil rights to foreign land surveyors. In so doing, Díaz disaffected the urban and rural poor as policies excluded them from staking a claim to their nation's economic growth. Opposition groups emerged. In particular, two began to rally support against Díaz and his 30-year regime: one led by Francisco Madero, a conservative landowner from Coahuila, and the other led by the Flores Magón brothers, anarchists who formed an opposition political party while in exile in St. Louis, Missouri. By 1910, as Díaz and his supporters attended extravagant ceremonies commemorating 100 years of México's independence,[2] Madero proclaimed a revolution based on suffrage and no reelection as the only means for unseating "Díaz-potism."[3]

México's Revolution

There were many revolutions within México's larger revolution that, as a whole, succeeded in unseating Porfirio Díaz by 1911. Factional leaders of the revolution represented diverse groups and diverse interests: Francisco Madero (assassinated 1913) represented regional landowning elites who sought to regain control over agribusiness from foreign investors; Emiliano Zapata (assassinated 1919) represented peasants from Central México who sought land redistribution; Pancho Villa (assassinated 1923) represented a transient population that included railroad workers and miners who sought reformed labor laws; Venustiano Carranza (assassinated 1920) represented urban interests who sought Constitutional reform; and Álvaro Obregón (assassinated 1929) from Sonora represented a mix of shopkeepers, schoolteachers and businessmen who sought renewed social order.[4] For the next decade, these revolutionary leaders vied for political power, often resorting to violent means—assassinations and coup d'états—to realize their revolutionary vision. Out of the disorder of the revolution emerged its great accomplishment: the Constitution of 1917.

Putting the Revolution into Practice

The revolutionary elite, under the leadership of Venustiano Carranza, wrote the 1917 Constitution with five critical provisions, rooted in the first liberal Constitution of 1857, that addressed the church, land, labor, education, and monopolies. Its authors believed that secularization of society would bring about modernization in México. Therefore, the Constitution removed the church from public life: all church property was nationalized and priests had to be Mexican, were regulated by the government, were forbidden to organize public processions, were not allowed to vote or discuss politics, and were prohibited from wearing religious garb in public. The constitution also provided that landholdings, which had fallen into the hands of a few after the Ley Lerdo (1856), were to be returned to Indian villages, and be redistributed by the government to those who would tend them, and it forbade foreign ownership unless the landholders became naturalized Mexican citizens. For labor, the constitution provided workers with a minimum wage and a standard 40-hour workweek. It offered protection in the workplace, regulated child and female labor, gave workers the right to unionize, mandatory arbitration, and profit sharing. Education was made secular, mandatory, and free. And, monopolies that threatened the public's well-being were prohibited.

Between 1920-1929, leaders such as Álvaro Obregón and Plutarco Elías Calles made the revolution work. In their own way, they began to implement the articles written in the Constitution of 1917. Both redistributed land in the form of ejidos (communal land-holdings in which each member of the community received a lot on which to practice subsistence agriculture). Minister of Education José Vasconcelos devised an education program to reach the rural poor, especially Indians. The program resettled peasants into villages where teachers, en masse, taught adults and children to read and write as well as introduced

the cornerstones of a hygienic lifestyle. Teachers sought to reeducate the rural poor by introducing modern cooking and health care, and even introduced modern sports such as basketball and soccer to pull men away from alcohol and the pulquería (a traditional bar for the poor where men drank pulque made from maguey cactus).

A cultural revolution was also underway during these years. In an effort to celebrate the new "cosmic race," or mestizo,[5] revolutionary leaders commissioned México's greatest muralists—Diego Rivera, José Orozco and David Siqueiros—to adorn the walls of government buildings with the history of México ending with the glorious revolution that sought to incorporate all racial types in the nation's future. On the wall of the National Palace and Ministry of Education, for example, Diego Rivera's murals contrasted images of Porfirian elites and foreign investors as hoarding, capitalist pigs with images of the hardworking Indian peasant and industrial laborer who represented México's future. Through art, revolutionary leaders sought to redefine México's national identity in the hope of building national unity.

However, not all Mexicans agreed on the path leaders took toward progress. When Calles became president in 1924, he passed a series of harsh anti-church laws because he believed, more fervently than other leaders, that religion impeded progress. State governors were forced to limit the number of priests and priests were required to register with the government. In the state of Tabasco, for example, Governor Tomás Garrido Canibal organized the "red shirts" that devoted themselves to burning idols and to confiscating religious images in churches and homes. As a result, a lay Catholic religious uprising took place in Western México between 1926-29, known as the Cristero Rebellion. Because México's government had replaced the Catholic religion with teachings of the revolution, rural Catholics took up arms to shouts of "¡Viva Cristo Rey!" (Long Live Christ the King!). Church leaders fled to Europe and the U.S. as their congregations fought a bitter 3-year civil war against the revolutionary administration. By 1929, the U.S. Ambassador to México, Dwight D. Morrow, brought about a peaceful accord between the cristeros and the government, and the era of violence, revolution, and rebellion ended.

As president between 1924-1928 and as the head-of-state behind México's rotating presidential administrations between 1929-1934, Calles succeeded in consolidating political power into one party, the National Revolutionary

Party (PNR),[6] and in implementing important development programs like his massive road-building project and his inauguration of the Bank of México, the nation's first central bank. But, his ability to coalesce political power under the PNR and bring together the military, state governors, labor organizers, and mobilized peasants, was indeed a great accomplishment. It, too, ushered in a new era of relative political stability that lasted until well after 1946.

Nationalism and Cardenismo

Lázaro Cárdenas, México's president between 1934-1940, is revered as the ideal revolutionary. In the first four years of his six-year term, he undermined regional bosses to tighten executive power, he redistributed land to peasants and met with them to discuss their concerns, he expanded earlier education programs and, above all, he nationalized México's railroads and oil. In so doing, he won a wide base of support and some even likened him to Jesus Christ. His direct attacks on foreign-owned railway and oil companies may have disrupted, at least for a short time, relations with the U.S., but it boosted pride in México as nationals took control over their own industrial development.

Cárdenas also evoked pride in things Mexican through the mass media: radio, music, film, and even comic books. He was the first president to address the nation through a radio broadcast. He pumped money into México's film industry, creating a government company called the Cinematográfica Latino Americana (CLASA) that produced the famous film entitled *Vámanos con Pancho Villa*, that mythologized Villa into a revolutionary hero. He created the government's first official propaganda department, the Department of Press and Publicity that developed radio programs, newspaper articles, tourist brochures, and school events in support of his administration.[7] And, he created the first official radio station, XEFO, in an effort to reach a wider audience.

Through these measures, Cárdenas unified a once-fissured Mexican nation. He also moved México into the international limelight when he took railroads and oil away from British and U.S. hands and offered México as a safe haven for controversial figures like Leon Trotsky and for Spaniards fleeing Franco's regime. On the eve of impending world war, Cárdenas walked a tightrope between his loyalty to México and the sovereignty of México.

World War II and Pan-Americanism

When the U.S. declared war on the Axis powers in 1941 after the bombing of Pearl Harbor, President Avila Camacho could no longer uphold México's neutrality and declared war on the Axis. He sent one air force troop, Squadron 201, to the Philippines in 1942. Even before México joined World War II, the president continued earlier efforts to foster nationalism through culture. He continued sponsorship of the national film industry and funded a national ballet and national symphony. Mexican icons such as singer Jorge Negrete and comedian Cantinflas emerged as part of a broader boom in popular culture known as "The Golden Age." Expressions of *lo mexicanidad* (Mexican-ness) through film, music, art, and literature symbolized Mexican modernity.

Once México entered into World War II, it gained a powerful ally; the US offered financial and technological assistance that México used to continue development. To promote hemispheric solidarity efforts, Rockefeller's Office of the Coordinator of Inter-American Affairs and the Pan-American Union promoted tourism to México, cooperated in film making, and produced promotional literature, as well as introducing new crops and farming techniques. And a labor program for Mexican contract workers, called braceros, offered short-term work to Mexicans on U.S. railroads and in agriculture during the war.

By 1946, México transformed into a modern nation. Development programs before 1946 paved the way for México's economic "miracle" and its era of political stability. New challenges would face México in the ensuing years, but the basis for growth had been established.

Notes

1. Colin M. MacLachlan and William H. Beezley, *El gran pueblo: A History of Greater México*, 2nd ed. (New Jersey: Prentice Hall, 1999), 106.
2. México's Independence Day was celebrated on two different occasions: September 16, 1810, when Miguel Hidalgo declared his famous Grito de Dolores, at which time the Wars for Independence began; and September 27, 1824, when the royalist, Agustin de Iturbide, declared México's independence from Spain and named himself emperor of México. For a series of essays on Independence Day celebrations in México, see William H. Beezley and David E. Lore, *Viva México! Viva Independencia! Celebrations of September 16* (Wilmington, DE: SR Books, 2001).
3. MacLachlan and Beezley, 224.
4. *Ibid.*, 243.
5. A mestizo is a person of mixed Spanish and Indian blood. The majority of the Mexican population is mestizo.
6. The PNR was the predecessor to México's official party, the Party of the Institutionalized Revolution (PRI) that was in power until the 2000 election, when Vicente Fox won as a member of the Party of National Action (PAN).
7. MacLachlan and Beezley, 346-348.

From Conquest to Modernity: México 1519-1946

By Kristin Janka Millar

❶ CULTURE

▶ Compare and contrast how the culture of the Aztecs and contemporary Mexican society are similar and/or different.

▶ Contrast Jose Vasconsuelo's conception of race in Mexican society with those of the United States.

❷ TIME, CONTINUITY AND CHANGE

▶ Create a timeline illustrating the influence of foreign cultures on indigenous Mexican culture/s throughout history.

▶ Compare and contrast issues and events leading to the Mexican Revolution and U.S. Civil War and explain similarities and differences.

❸ PEOPLE, PLACES AND ENVIRONMENTS

▶ Describe the role of disease and control over human and natural resources in the conquest of México.

❹ INDIVIDUAL DEVELOPMENT AND IDENTITY

▶ Research Father Miguel Hidalgo y Castilla and explain how his ideas may have seemed threatening to the Spanish. Who benefited?

▶ Write a diary entry describing the people and experiences that shaped you as a child during the pre-conquest, conquest, revolution or contemporary period in México.

❺ INDIVIDUALS, GROUPS AND INSTITUTIONS

▶ Describe and explain the historical role that the Catholic Church has played in shaping Mexican society.

❻ POWER, AUTHORITY AND GOVERNANCE

▶ Compare and contrast, then debate, the views of General Porfirio Díaz and Francisco Madero.

❼ PRODUCTION, DISTRIBUTION AND CONSUMPTION

▶ Research the *Ley Lerdo* and describe the difference between the original aims of the *Ley Lerdo* and its practical applications.

❽ SCIENCE, TECHNOLOGY AND SOCIETY

▶ Describe and provide examples of historical interpretations of what counted as progress over the years.

▶ Investigate and explain how technology has impacted Mexican society historically.

❾ GLOBAL CONNECTIONS

▶ Create a diagram describing how historical events in other countries have influenced México.

▶ Consider México's history of conquest and current events in the world and then compare and contrast how contemporary society might respond to a foreign invasion.

❿ CIVIC IDEALS AND PRACTICES

▶ Describe and explain nationalism and its advantages and disadvantages.

▶ Investigate the Cristero Rebellion and present a debate between Catholics and the Mexican government.

CHAPTER EIGHT

México's Political System: 1929-2004

By Paloma Bauer de la Isla
Michigan State University

MÉXICO'S RICH HISTORY and its resulting complexities are reflected in every aspect of its social, economic, cultural, and political spheres. An exploration of this nation's politics is, by nature, all encompassing, which makes any analysis incredibly challenging, as each area easily deserves multiple volumes. This piece, however, will focus on the last seventy years and the dominant political regime that on the one hand has remained virtually untouched, and on the other has adapted to changing circumstances in many—but not all—cases.

Following a discussion of the beginning of the modern Mexican political party structure at the end of the Revolution, this essay will examine two themes, the contemporary structure of the Mexican government and the rise of Mexican opposition parties and its significance. The last section will look into the near term and suggest future directions.

Revolutionary Political Legacies

Without a doubt, the Mexican Revolution of 1910 introduced significant changes as it touched all social classes to different degrees. Whether or not it was truly a revolution, that is, whether it truly transformed the social structure, as was the case in the Chinese or Russian Revolution, has been debated for a long time, but the Mexican Revolution did convulse the country in its own way and had lasting consequences that shaped post-revolutionary politics in México. Thus, in order to better understand Mexican political developments in the 20th century, it is necessary to explore both the ideology of the revolution and the political actors and structures that emerged in the immediate post revolutionary era.

Violence did not end with the end of the revolution. In 1917, the country was left exhausted and in disarray, a political and social wreck. In the local and national elections that were held, corruption was obvious, and violence marked numerous regional rebellions. The private sector was also weak and politically fragmented. Clearly, the nation was in need of some kind of peaceful mechanism to create order and to bring unity. Taking advantage of these conditions, Plutarco Elías Calles, president from 1924 to 1928, became the major architect of what was to become México's official state political party. He envisioned a party that would encompass all power factions into a strong central authority which would in turn control the distribution of power among the numerous power holders. It was relatively easy for Calles to persuade regional strongmen to support the creation of a central party. He presented party membership as the only way to retain political power and attain economic benefits.

Soon, regional leaders realized they had more to lose if they did not join. Therefore, groups either joined or were marginalized if they posed a threat to the state. In 1929, the National Revolutionary Party or Partido Nacional Revolucionario (PNR) was officially created as an inclusive official party with the main objective of building a strong state. The goal of the party was not electoral politics but to administer power without sharing it. The PNR was the antecedent of the Institutional Revolutionary Party or Partido Revolucionario Institucional (PRI), renamed under Avila Camacho's administration (1940-1946). The creation of the official party marked the start of a regime in which the state was equivalent to the official party, thus the reference to the government as the "PRI-state regime." Among the sectors the PRI recruited were the peasants, business, the Catholic Church, organized labor, intellectuals, the military, the media, and nongovernmental organizations.

Soon after the establishment of the party, the government reached out to incorporate peasants and workers. Within this sphere, the presidency of Lázaro Cárdenas (1934-1940) undertook an ambitious land reform. The government appropriated land and gave it to peasants on *ejidos* or communally held village-owned lands. In this way, thousands of rural villages obtained use rights, but not legal title to land. By this means, the government institutionalized the ancient indigenous communal land-holding system. Local peasant leagues were organized into an official agrarian sector. On the labor side, worker groups were incorporated into a giant central labor union, the Confederation of Mexican Workers, Confederación de Trabajadores de México (CTM). Organized labor became an ideal, traditional corporatist group. President Cárdenas and his successors maintained a close relationship with union leaders that amounted to government control. Among the methods used by the party to control the labor movement were: co-optation of labor leadership; governmental regulation, such as legal recognition of unions and strikes; and sweetheart contracts. Furthermore, the party's control over organized labor was sealed by incorporating the CTM as the foundation of one of the three pillars of the PRI. In this way, unlike business, the church, or the military, labor grew within the PRI developing a prominent role. For instance, between 1979 and 1988, approximately 25 percent of the PRI's congressional candidates were labor leaders, mainly from the CTM. Thus, by including peasants and workers in the formal political structure, the regime clearly hindered their independent development. The state was very careful in preventing workers and peasants from unifying, however, and building large-scale opposition. It would take many decades before the state-labor and state-peasant alliances began to disintegrate.

Starting with President Lázaro Cárdenas, a force that has historically threatened many other Mexican regimes and has threatened many Latin American countries, the military, was brought under the control of the government. Although the military's loss of power was not sudden, it was clear and definitive. No longer would the military play a dominant and direct role in politics. In fact, the subordination of the military to civilian rule has been an outstanding feature of the Mexican political system. To many observers, México's military appears unique. Unlike much of Latin America, where civilians officially rule, but must, in reality, share considerable power with the military, in México, the military serves and protects the civilian system's interests. This relationship can be seen, as with other groups, as a contract in which the military was given benefits, job opportunities, and control over its internal budget. In return, the regime enjoyed an important source of support and legitimacy. Furthermore, the military's loyalty to the system

guards it from any civilian groups that might want to violently oppose the political system.

The institutionalization of the Catholic Church is another essential component in the creation of the regime. The church had immense privileges and power during the pre-Columbian and colonial periods. The 1917, post-Revolution Constitution severely restricted the power of the Catholic Church. Among other provisions, the Constitution denied the church legal standing, prohibited property ownership, forbade its participation in politics, denied voting rights to the clergy, and limited its participation in education. Many of these constitutional restrictions would not be lifted until the 1990s. As part of his attempt to centralize political power, Calles launched a violent anti-church fight in which many Catholics (including a force willing to fight for Catholic rights called the cristeros) engaged in a civil war that lasted three years (Guerra Cristera). Again, a "contract-like" agreement was finally reached in 1929 between the hierarchy of the Church and Calles; the Church retreated from politics and its demands, and the government eased its restrictions. Church-state relations would normalize even more with Avila Camacho and his successors.

Institutionalization, as seen with the prior cases, was the regime's principal tool to centralize power in México City. Institutionalization can be seen as a huge strategic success, as Levy and Bruhn argue: "…the genius of institutionalization lay in how the regime attained such extensive control without more blatant and brutal repression."[1] From being in a state of complete disorder and instability in which numerous social forces were fighting for power after a revolution that lasted 10 years, the PRI transformed a weakened political system into an organized apparatus through a number of pact-like relationships.

México's hegemonic political party, the PRI, was clearly a corporatist-type intermediary between the state and the interest associations of the popular classes, especially the organized working class and the peasantry. Corporatism was the PRI's device to channel the most influential groups' demands (the labor, agrarian, and popular sectors), enabling the government to monitor the demands and mediate among them. This arrangement remained largely intact until the 1990s. The government managed in this way to act as the ultimate decision-maker and to prevent any group from dominating the others.

Corporatism served as a mechanism through which the government allowed some form of dissent, but successfully controlled its level. Thus, through a series of contract-like relationships, in which the regime gave either autonomy to run their own affairs or resources, or both, the regime managed to develop an almost incontestable control. This dynamic had serious consequences for the further development of contemporary México. While some institutions were left out and others were included, this approach seriously weakened competitive and democratic participation. Through this give-and-take approach, the regime also almost fully controlled public policy making. Thus, in retrospect, the two major weaknesses of post revolutionary México were the lack of democracy and increasing economic inequality, and the two successes were political stability and economic growth.

The New Ruling Class

The new ruling class that took over the governance of México following the Revolution is often referred to as the "Revolutionary Family." It is usually defined as being comprised of former presidents, powerful regional and national leaders, as well as leaders of México's major interest groups. These interest groups cross-cut the entire political spectrum from left to right, but still fit within the ideologically flexible "catch all" Revolutionary Family. The structure of this group was maintained through loyal ties to the president, fear of political defeat, and self-interest in retaining power, prestige, and wealth. The resulting consensus, headed by the president, drove México's political and economic development and stemmed directly from the PRI-structure.

Since its founding, the PRI portrayed itself as the party that represented the "Principles of the Mexican Revolution." While there is no exact definition, over time, these principles can be defined as: a) nationalism and anti-imperialism, b) commitment to social justice, c) state responsibility to defend the rights of labor against (particularly foreign) capital, d) commitment to a mixed property rights system, e) anti-clericalism and an emphasis on public, secular education, and f) state commitment to promote sustained growth (through Import Substitution Industrialization). Any other alternative was pictured as "counterrevolutionary" or anti-nationalistic. Based primarily on loyalty ties, the process of political recruitment became a crucial element in the formation and maintenance of this political elite. To gain access to the top positions in the PRI, those in important government and bureaucratic positions were selected for the most part by the president; significantly, their personal loyalty was the most important consideration in their recruitment. Upper level functionaries in turn chose lower level functionaries, based also on personal loyalty. In any case, loyalty to the president was always assured. Thus, a successful political career depended upon establishing a patron-client relationship with a successful political superior. In fact, this clientalist structure extended from the president all the way to the lower ranks of local government. In México, a form of "authoritarian clientelism" developed, where uneven bargaining relations required the enduring political subordination of clients which were reinforced by the threat of coercion. This asymmetrical (but reciprocal) exchange of favors for political support guarded the political system for decades. This system sustained the new ruling class and succeeded in maintaining tight control of México, but this tight control was always situated around the president of the country.

Presidentialism

Perhaps the PRI's major accomplishment—in terms of maintaining political stability—was to institutionalize the process of presidential succession. Although the Mexican federalist system is formally enshrined in the 1917 Constitution, political power has been concentrated at the central level, particularly in the hands of the president. The powerful nature of the presidency is well known. Besides exercising constitutional powers, up until recently, the Mexican president has also maintained a series of extra-constitutional powers. These powers refer to the unwritten norms of the Mexican political system. The Mexican president has traditionally had the authority to amend the Constitution, to act as chief legislator, to establish himself as the ultimate authority in electoral matters (the most important case being the designation of his own successor), to assume jurisdiction in judicial matters, and to remove governors, municipal presidents, and legislators at the federal and state levels. The mix of constitutional and extra-constitutional powers made the Mexican president one of the most powerful chief executives in any democracy.

The great degree of centralization at the federal level, particularly in the hands of the president, dramatically reduced the ability of the separation of powers to act as a system of checks and balances. Although in theory a system of checks and balances existed in México, in practice it was overridden by an overpowering presidency, which was based on unified government, high party discipline, and the president as head of the party.

The Executive, Legislative, and Judicial Branches

The Constitution of 1917 defines the Mexican government as representative, federal, and democratic. The nation is divided into thirty-one states and the Federal District (México City), the latter being the seat of the federal government. The government of the Mexican State is based on the principle of division of powers among the executive, legislative, and judicial branches, delegating a certain amount of power to state and local governments. In practice, however, the Mexican system has been dominated by the executive branch, which did not share power with another branch from the 1920s until the 1990s, and has allocated few powers to state and local governments.

The President as well as the governors of the states all serve a single six-year term (popularly known as *sexenio*) and may not be re-elected. During the period of PRI-dominance (1929-2000), the executive branch generally, and the presidency specifically, were the primary voice in the decision-making process. As noted, much of this power was derived extra-constitutionally from being the head of the PRI.

México's national legislature is bicameral, vested upon the Union Congress, which is divided into the upper (or Senate) and the lower (or Chamber of Deputies) bodies. The legislative branch of the 32 federal entities is single chambered. It is called Local Congress in the 31 states, and Legislative Assembly in the Federal District. All legislators serve a three-year term, except for the Senate members, who serve a six-year term. There is no consecutive reelection in both chambers.

Five hundred representatives constitute the Chamber of Deputies. Deputies are elected on the basis of roughly equally populated districts. They may only be re-elected after an intermediate term. Three hundred of these representatives are elected by relative majority in single-member districts, and the other 200 are elected by proportional representation through the system of party lists in five multi-member districts. As a result of the constitutional reforms approved in 1996, the majority party cannot hold more than 300 seats.

One hundred and twenty eight members constitute the Senate. Three senators are elected in each of the 31 states and the Federal District. For this purpose, political parties must register a list with two formulas for their candidates. Two of the seats are allocated through the relative majority principle, that is, they belong to the party that obtained the largest number of votes. The third one is appointed through the first minority principle, that is, to the party that obtained the second largest number of votes. The remaining 32 seats are appointed by means of the proportional representation system according to voter rolls in one single national multi-member district.

The legislative branch was long controlled by the PRI, whose members accounted for more than 90 percent of the district seats in the Chamber of Deputies and, until 1988, all Senate seats. Until 1997, the president appointed a congressional leader who headed all the state delegations. The legislative branch traditionally had little say in the decision-making process because whoever was a member of the PRI depended on his or her higher authority, and indirectly on the president, for both his or her current position and future public career. Traditionally, the legislative branch served to legitimize, rather than debate executive legislation. Mexican presidents and the executive branch used constitutional amendments to give major, controversial legislation an extra measure of legitimacy. One consequence of the elections since 1988, when opposition parties began obtaining significant representation in the Chamber of Deputies, was that the government lost its ability to amend the constitution; the PRI did not have two-thirds of the seats in the lower chamber, the number necessary to do so. Furthermore, since the opposition won control of the Chamber of Deputies in 1997, for the first time deputies elected their own leader and opposition members chaired and served on the various committees. Committee chairs play a significant role in the legislative process.

The Senate also has a leader, and the senior senators from each state form the internal governing body. The Senate has taken on a more plural character since 1994, when both major opposition parties, the National Action Party or Partido Acción Nacional (PAN) and the Party of the Democratic Revolution or Partido de la Revolución Democrática (PRD) obtained 25 percent of the total seat share, a figure they increased in the 2000 elections to 53 percent.

Overall, the role of the legislative branch in the Mexican decision-making process has changed dramatically since late 1997. In the past, congress members blindly supported presidential legislative initiatives and made only symbolic recommendations to the executive branch for alterations. Theoretically they could have rejected a presidential initiative, but most presidential legislation was approved, usually overwhelmingly. However, the new presence of opposition parties in the legislative branch led to important changes. At present, legislators have significantly altered bills proposed by the executive before their approval. Indeed, the legislative branch either modified or rejected all of President Vicente Fox's (2000-2006) major bills. Opposition legislators have created a much more contentious environment for debates, and they have also increased attention to bills that originate from within congress. Given their importance, members of the Fox cabinet have sought to lobby them in ways resembling the competitive relationship between the executive and legislative branches in the United States.

The Mexican judicial system maintains courts on the local, state, and national levels. Presently, the Supreme Court consists of eleven justices who may serve terms of up to fifteen years. Traditionally, they were appointed by the president, a practice that developed a "compliant" image of the legal system as being highly dependent upon the legislative and executive branches. The lower levels of the legal system were known for breeding corruption and being subject to outside political manipulation. A lack of respect for the law and the legal system in general has been a damaging result of these circumstances. Under President Ernesto Zedillo's administration (1994-2000), however, important changes were introduced in an effort to empower and legitimize the judicial branch's role. For instance, the court was empowered to determine constitutional issues, rather than ruling only on specific questions of limited scope. Furthermore, President Fox has made significant efforts to increase the autonomy of the legal system and encourage a more activist role.

Opposition in México

Until the 1980s México's political system remained highly authoritarian. Opposition political parties were closely controlled or outlawed altogether. In fact, until 1979 only those parties that did not threatened the PRI-regime were permitted to take part in elections. Competition for political power took place only within the PRI itself, where rivalries were intense among organized groups or camarillas. Nonetheless, ideological differences were often minor in these intraparty conflicts and they did not pose any real threat to the regime until 1986, when some former *priistas* (PRI members) split from the party and eventually formed México's third major political party, the Party of the Democratic Revolution (PRD).

By 1970, México's political stability began to shake as a result of the 1968 social unrests, as well as increasing economic difficulties. This dissatisfaction with the ruling party provided opportunities for opposition parties and civic organizations to challenge the regime. Political opposition groups started to seriously push for wider participation in the system. In response to these demands, President Luis Echeverría Álvarez (1970-1976) offered a so-called "political opening" (apertura política) strategy in 1973. Political parties were allowed to legally exist and for the first time were given what seemed a realistic opportunity to gain seats in the congress. Furthermore, in the late 1980s and 1990s, this political opening expanded to include recognition by the PRI of opposition-party electoral victories in races for municipal governments and even state governorships. It is important to mention, however, that at least in its early stages, this reallocation-of-power strategy was never intended to give up central control. Pluralism might be demonstrated, but control was never intended to be sacrificed. However, although the PRI continued to dominate, it no longer held a monopolistic control over national politics as in the past, and its internal crisis continued to increase.

Beginning in 1982, a significant number of city governments were won by opposition parties. In 1983, the administration of Miguel de la Madrid Hurtado (1982-1988) recognized several opposition victories at the municipal level, including some in major cities. At least five of these were state capitals (Chihuahua, Durango, Hermosillo, Guanajuato, and San Luis Potosí) and another one was in a large border city (Ciudad Juárez). Following the highly questionable election of 1988 in which voter fraud was apparently widespread, in every subsequent election opposition victories multiplied. At the state level, the first major breakthrough was the PAN's victory in the gubernatorial elections in Baja California in 1989, followed by Chihuahua in 1992 and then by Jalisco, Guanajuato and Baja California (again) in 1995. Mexican politics in the mid 1990s included areas where the PRI continued to exercise the same old monopolistic control it had in the past, but now there were also regions and localities where genuine pluralism and intense competition between parties existed.

Electoral Reforms: Impacts at the Federal Level

In order to undertake the revitalization required to sustain the PRI's credibility and legitimacy, electoral reform initiatives were undertaken beginning in 1963, extended in

1973 and 1977, again in 1986, and most recently, in 1993, 1994, and 1996. From the mid-1960s to the mid-1970s, the opposition held less than 20 percent of the seats in the lower house, the Chamber of Deputies. The 1973 reform allowed for a wider range of political parties, particularly those on the left. Most important of all was the 1977 Law of Political Organizations and Electoral Processes (Ley de Organizaciones Políticas y Procesos Electorales, LOPPE). This law required that one quarter of all seats in the lower house had to be divided among the opposition parties on the basis of proportional representation. The objective of the reforms was to indirectly strengthen the PRI by encouraging a more credible (but carefully constrained) opposition. Indeed, although the initiation of a plurinominal deputy system encouraged opposition parties, their representation proportion between 1979 and 1985 remained roughly the same.

As noted before, however, both the amount and the quality of debate in the Chamber of Deputies slowly improved, and representatives no longer unconditionally supported legislation initiated by the PRI or the president.

Under President de la Madrid (1982-1988), a law was passed that prevented the winning or majority party from holding more than 70 percent of the seats in the Chamber of Deputies. It increased the number of seats in Congress to 500, with 300 of those reserved for those elected by relative majority in their congressional districts, and 200 for proportional representation. The party winning the greatest number of the 300 majority seats received some additional proportional representation seats, which still allowed one political party to gain an overall majority in Congress. Thus, while the opposition's representation was raised to a minimum 30 percent of the now-enlarged legislature (150 of the 500 seats), the PRI managed virtually to guarantee its hold on Congress by extending plurinominal seats to any party receiving fewer than 50 percent of the legislative seats. Once again, the increased power given to the opposition was carefully allocated by the PRI to give voice but not power to their opponents. The PRI was willing to make space for the opposition only to the extent that its own majority position in the Chamber of Deputies would not threatened.

The PRI, however, miscalculated. The 1988 elections were historic because for the first time opposition parties acquired enough seats in the lower house to shape the policy process, particularly when a two-thirds majority vote

to change the Constitution was required. By 1989 opposition parties acquired close to 50 percent of the seats in the Chamber of Deputies, causing the first true alteration in the PRI's power in the Congress. With PRI representation dropping to a bare majority, and well below the 66 percent majority required for constitutional changes, the party had to seek coalition partners for any constitutional amendments.

Major changes followed in electoral matters. In 1989 the Federal Electoral Institute (Instituto Federal Electoral, IFE) was also created as a completely autonomous institution in order to conduct the entire electoral process in a professional manner. The previous institution for monitoring elections, the Federal Electoral Commission, was run directly by the interior secretary as a part of the executive branch. Largely unchanged since its creation in 1946, this institution was notorious for directing elections toward outcomes dictated by the president and his party, rather than for its accountability to the voting public. The Federal Electoral Tribunal was also created in 1989 as an autonomous body capable of challenging IFE decisions. The 1993 and 1994 electoral reforms extended the autonomy and jurisdiction of the IFE, further scaled back PRI overrepresentation—this time in both houses of the national Congress—and codified a role for electoral observers. In order to win *panista* support to be able to undertake major economic reforms, the Carlos Salinas de Gortari administration (1988-1994) offered major political concessions. The most important of these was that after 1994 each state would have four senators, three of whom would be elected directly and the fourth allocated to the party coming in second.

The 1996 reforms resulted from a different intraparty bargaining dynamic than the pre-1991 and pre-1994 reforms. Having been elected by the smallest margin ever, Ernesto Zedillo found himself needing to reach consensus between the right and left, so his administration sponsored dialogues for reforming government in which PRD and PAN demands were taken seriously. The result was a set of highly controversial electoral reforms that even disrupted the traditional party discipline among PRI congress members when many of them voted against these reforms. Such reforms further distanced the IFE from the executive and legislative branches by finally allowing the supervising body of citizen counselors to select their own director, rather than rely on executive nomination, and by giving citizen counselors the autonomy to monitor their own affairs. In the most significant reform to the electoral court, it was placed in 1996 directly under the jurisdiction of the Supreme Court, with magistrates nominated by the judiciary rather than by the executive with legislative confirmation. Perhaps the most important aspect of the 1996 reform was granting the electoral court jurisdiction to resolve election-related constitutional conflicts arising at the local level, where great disparities still exist. Other significant changes prior to the 1997 midterm elections included the first congressional redistricting in twenty years and the tightening of IFE control over public funds used by political parties. The 1997 elections were a watershed in México's democratizing efforts; the PRI lost its long-standing monopoly on power in the legislature.

Conclusion

Over the last decade, México evolved from a 71-year old, one-party regime to a multiparty electoral democracy. The transition process has been gradual, and it is not complete yet. The nation is still finding its way in the new redefined political system.

The victory of Vicente Fox Quesada, a non-PRI candidate, in the Presidential election of 2000 represented a major watershed in Mexican politics. It is important to note, however, that this could not have taken place without the tacit approval of President Ernesto Zedillo. Historians will need to recognize that without his support, institutions to insure free and open elections would not have worked. Moreover, he ordered restraint by the PRI militants who

were willing to use any mechanisms to maintain the hegemonic control of their party in the national politics. President Zedillo's commitment to transparency resulted in a historic election that he honored and respected. Moreover, his cooperative transfer of power to a member of another party gives historical credibility and legitimacy to democratic politics in México.

President Fox promised during his campaign to respect the Constitution and to end the era of presidentialism and authoritarianism. He also promised the end of manipulation and fraud, an independent legislature and judiciary, and the consolidation of political reform. However, after being in office for three years, the achievement of these goals seemed much more elusive than originally imagined in the midst of the excitement of his election in 2000. Ironically, exactly those political reforms that brought Fox into office represented his major obstacles; divided government and electoral competition are finally working as real limits to political power. This new era of negotiation is still alien to Mexican politics. Issues of accountability, transparency, and empowerment are at the core of what is required. Without doubt, México's path toward democratization has been a long and a complex one, but the climate in México has indeed changed and it will continue to change.

Notes
1. Daniel C. Levy, and Kathleen Bruhn, with Emilio Zebadúa, *México: The Struggle for Democratic Development* (Berkeley, CA: University of California Press, 2001) 59.

México's Political System: 1929-2004

By Kristin Janka Millar

❶ CULTURE

▶ Investigate the Mexican Revolution of 1910 and discuss its impact on Mexican society and culture.
▶ Describe and explain the role of the ejido communal land-holding system in México and Mexican politics.

❷ TIME, CONTINUITY AND CHANGE

▶ Create a timeline of historical changes in Mexican politics.

❹ INDIVIDUAL DEVELOPMENT AND IDENTITY

▶ Research Plutarco Elías Calles (1924-1928) and describe his vision for the first official Mexican state political party.

❺ INDIVIDUALS, GROUPS AND INSTITUTIONS

▶ Choose one of the following groups/institutions: Catholic church, military, labor unions. Trace its historical role in Mexican politics. How does the role of this group/institution in Mexican politics compare with its role in the U.S.?

❻ POWER, AUTHORITY AND GOVERNANCE

▶ Compare and contrast individual rights under the Mexican constitution with those under the U.S. constitution.
▶ Describe the structure of the "Revolutionary Family" after the Mexican Revolution and the "Principles of the Mexican Revolution." How have these changed over time?

❼ PRODUCTION, DISTRIBUTION AND CONSUMPTION

▶ Compare and contrast changes in the role of the Mexican government in economic policymaking under the Cárdenas presidency and Fox presidency.

❾ GLOBAL CONNECTIONS

▶ Compare and contrast the role of the military in politics in México and another country.
▶ Discuss how Mexican-U.S. relations have changed through history and provide possible explanations.

❿ CIVIC IDEALS AND PRACTICES

▶ Compare and contrast the constitutional and extra-constitutional powers of the Mexican presidency and U.S. presidency.

CHAPTER NINE

Mexican Literature, Cinema and Television

By Daniel J. Nappo

University of Tennessee, Martin

THE GOAL OF THIS ESSAY is to offer a general overview of Mexican literature, cinema and television with the aim of providing the base from which individuals will be able to learn more about the important contributions México has made to these fields of expression. The emphasis of this essay will be on the last one hundred years, not only because cinema and television have really only come into existence in this period, but because many of the most important literary developments in México have also occurred within the twentieth century.

Mexican Literature

Mexican literature is as old as the earliest pre-Columbian text and as new as the latest bestseller by Carlos Fuentes. But in spite of its richness and vitality, the tradition remains relatively unknown outside Latin America. In a recent keynote speech, the critic Daniel Sada explained that books by Mexican authors sell poorly in Europe, and that many universities there and in the United States do not offer courses about Mexican literature. Furthermore, the Spanish language literary market is controlled largely by a handful of publishers in Spain. The result is that only a select number of Mexican authors are promoted and marketed on an international level in spite of México City's enormous publishing output.

Because of its pre-Columbian roots, any study of Mexican literature should begin before the arrival of the Spanish in 1518. The literature of pre-Hispanic México encompasses untold centuries. The Mayan and Aztec civilizations, located in the Yucatan peninsula and the central México region respectively, have left us the most significant collections of texts. From the Mayan civilization, which saw its peak from about 300 to 900 AD, we have the *Popul vul* (The Book of Counsel) and the *Libros de Chilam Balam* (The Books of Chilam Balam). The *Popul vul*, written in the Maya-Quiché language, describes the creation of mankind and the deeds of Mayan gods and kings. Francisco Ximénez, a parish priest in Guatemala, discovered this fundamental text in the early 1700s. The *Chilam Balam* is a fascinating work of multiple authorship with sections devoted to science, calendrical information, prophecies, and medical lore. The extant literature from Tenochtitlán, the Aztec capital, is almost exclusively poetry written in Náhuatl. The most accomplished poet was Nezahualcóyotl (1402-72), a statesman and legendary promoter of the arts. Although Náhuatl poetry is thematically sophisticated, it employs a fixed repertoire of metaphors and images—the most recurring being semi-precious stones, blood, brightly plumed birds, and flowers. The absence of amorous or erotic subject matter is notable, suggesting that for the Aztecs poetry was a highly imaginative chronicle or medium for philosophical reflection. The work of scholar José Luis Martínez is a requisite reference for any investigation of Náhuatl literature.

The colonial period (1519-1810) offers a literature rich in questions of authority, censorship and identity, particularly since the imposition of Spanish civilization was not merely from above but from without. It is worth noting that for nearly four centuries the geographical area now known as México was called Nueva España (New Spain). The *criollos* (American-born Spaniards) were the initial factor in the gradual movement toward independence for, as a result of geography and the highly stratified nature of colonial society, they were not permitted the privileges of the peninsular Spaniards who came to make their fortunes. The *mestizos* (people of European and Native American descent) would follow the *criollos'* insurgent example and come to represent the Mexican national identity in the twentieth century. Spanish authorities struggled to control printed materials after the first press arrived in México City in 1537, but the physical distance that made such regulation necessary permitted a certain laxity in the implementation of laws intended to control what was printed.

The novel developed slowly in México, perhaps as a result of censorship (for example, the Spanish picaresque novel *Lazarillo de Tormes* [1554] was banned in the colonies) and the preeminence of the historical chronicle. Indeed, the first such chronicles—the *Cartas de relación* (*Five Letters*, 1519-26), written by Hernán Cortés (1485-1547), and the *Verdadera historia de la conquista de Nueva España* (*The True History of the Conquest of New Spain*, 1632), written by one of Cortés' soldiers, Bernal Díaz de Castillo (1492-1580?), were enormously popular in Europe. In neither account was there any pretension to polished style or a sophisticated lexicon. In his correspondence with the Spanish throne, Cortés admits his failures and expresses admiration for the Mexicans' valor and organization. Díaz de Castillo's narrative masterpiece was originally written to address the inaccuracies of other accounts and to soften the negative image of the Conquest throughout Europe. The work that was most responsible for the so-called "Black Legend" of the Conquest was the *Brevísima relación de la destrucción de las Indias* (*Brief History of the Destruction of the Indies*, 1552), written by the great humanitarian Fray Bartolomé de las Casas (1474-1566).

In the colonial era, theatrical productions were originally performed under the auspices of the Catholic Church to facilitate the conversion of the native populations. By the seventeenth century a theatre for the emerging *criollo* class had appeared, offering a more refined language and versification, as well as secular themes. The most notable playwright was Juan Ruiz de Alarcón (1581-1639?), author of such plays as *La verdad sospechosa* and *Las paredes oyen* (*The Suspicious Truth* and *The Walls Have Ears*, 1634). Ruiz de Alarcón was born in Taxco but immigrated to Spain so that his work would be staged in the corrales of Madrid. Although he was ridiculed mercilessly by Spanish contemporaries for his *criollo* status and physical deformities, it is a testament to his considerable talent that his plays are usually read alongside those of Lope and Calderón in Golden Age anthologies. Poetry does not appear in colonial México with the same vigor of the chronicle and theatre, suggesting the functional nature of those genres and the more ornamental and personal nature of verse. The first Mexican-born poet of some renown was Francisco de Terrazas (1525?-1600?). Bernardo de Balbuena (1561?-1627?) is best remembered for his carefully constructed *Grandeza mexicana* (1604), which praises the grandeur of México City and the achievements of the Spanish empire.

Colonial México produced two outstanding cultural figures in the seventeenth century: the polymath Carlos Sigüenza y Góngora (1645-1700), and Sor Juana Inés de la Cruz (1651-95?), a nun who lived most of her life in the San Jerónimo convent of México City. Sigüenza's *Primavera indiana* (Indian Spring, 1668) is a poetic hymn to the Virgin of Guadalupe, the patron saint of México and an important symbol of Mexican national identity. Sigüenza's most influential work is a narrative entitled *Los infortunios de Alonso Ramírez* (*The Misfortunes of Alonso Ramírez*, 1690), which is viewed by some as a precursor of the novel. *Infortunios* is Ramírez' first-person account of his life in Puebla, failures at various jobs, torture at the hands of English pirates and eventual release. The text shows many similarities to the *Lazarillo*, and Sigüenza reorders Ramírez' straightforward, chronological account in a more novelistic manner.

Sor Juana Inés de la Cruz (born Juana Ramírez de Asbaje) is the single greatest literary figure México has produced. A voracious reader even as a child, she became a nun for her unwavering faith and the opportunity to continue her literary pursuits behind convent walls. A public figure despite her vocation, Sor Juana was hailed in Spain as the "Tenth Muse" (among a pantheon that included the classical authors), but the small-minded colonial authorities were only willing to tolerate her achievement as long as she remained an entertaining curiosity. Nevertheless, Sor Juana's precocity and rebelliousness are evident in her finest works: the long, metaphysical poem *Primer sueño* (*First Dream*, 1692), her emotionally charged sonnets, her plays *El divino Narciso* and *Los empeños de una casa* (*The Divine Narcissus* and *Household Intrigues*, 1692), and her semi-autobiographical *Respuesta a Sor Filotea* (*Answer to Sister Filotea*, 1691). The *Respuesta* was Sor Juana's apology for having written a controversial reinterpretation of a prevailing church doctrine. In the *Respuesta* she makes several concessions to orthodox conventions but also marshals her unrivaled knowledge of the Bible and classical literature to assert that women have a right to exercise their God-given intellectual capacity. Following Sor Juana's death, few notable figures appeared in the eighteenth century, which was dominated by imported Neoclassic tendencies. The unfinished *Biblioteca Mexicana* (Mexican Library, 1755) suggests the nascent nationalism of the late colonial period.

The nineteenth century not only brought independence but the emergence of the novel as the preeminent genre in Mexican literature. In this regard, the work of José Joaquín

Fernández de Lizardi (1776-1827) is truly revolutionary. His hilarious picaresque work, *El periquillo sarniento* (*The Itching Parrot*, 1816, 1830-31), has been judged by many to be Latin America's first novel. A journalist by trade, Fernández de Lizardi served a role in the context of national independence not unlike that of Benjamin Franklin in the United States, galvanizing public opinion in favor of independence by publicly demanding it and by sketching a vivid portrait of the Mexican people and their values.

Although México gained political independence from Spain in 1821, two movements imported from Europe, Neoclassicism and Romanticism, were the dominant tendencies in literature. Representative Neoclassicists include the poets Manuel Carpio (1791-1860) and José Joaquín Pesado (1801-61). One of the outstanding Romantics was Ignacio Rodríguez Galván (1816-42), who is best known for his patriotic poem "Profecía de Guatimoc" ("Cuauhtemoc's Prophecy", 1851). *Costumbrismo*, a literary style featuring detailed descriptions of rural life with a nationalistic flavor, emerged by mid-century and is best exemplified by the novel *Astucia* (*The Shrewd One*, 1865) by Luis G. Inclán (1816-75).

If the long dictatorship of Porfirio Díaz (1876-1910) did not permit complete intellectual freedom, it did at least provide the necessary stability for Mexican letters to flourish, as evidenced by the dozens of literary journals and best-selling novels that appeared in the period. Ignacio M. Altamirano (1834-93) founded the journal *El renacimiento* (*The Renaissance*) and wrote popular, well-crafted novels such as *Clemencia* (1869) and *El Zarco* (*El Zarco, The Blue-Eyed Bandit*, 1901). Among the representative authors who had their work serialized in major periodicals are José López Portillo y Rojas (1850-1923) and Rafael Delgado (1853-1914). Emilio Rabasa (1856-1930), a distinguished lawyer, published the tetralogy *Novelas mexicanas* (*Mexican Novels*, 1887-88), providing the most detailed depiction of Mexican society since Fernández de Lizardi. An important precursor of the Revolutionary novel was *Tomóchic* (1893-95), written by the journalist Heriberto Frías (1870-1923). Frías had served as a junior officer in a military expedition ordered by Díaz to destroy Tomóchic, a small community in Chihuahua state that was the site of a bizarre millennial cult. Frías' novel highlighted the injustice and brutality of the incident, forcing the novelist into hiding for several years.

Although the Mexican Revolution (1910-20) claimed the lives or forced the emigration of nearly a million Mexicans, it revitalized the national literature. But by 1909 there had already been signs of change, as evidenced by the intellectual group known as the *Ateneo de la Juventud* (*Athenaeum of the Youth*). Ateneo members included José Vasconcelos (1882-1959), Martín Luis Guzmán (1887-1976) and Alfonso Reyes (1889-1959). Following the Revolution, Vasconcelos became the Minister of Education, a position from which he acted as patron for a new generation of writers. In the late 1920s Guzmán would produce two of the three fundamental novels of the Mexican Revolution: *El águila y la serpiente* (1928) and *La sombra del caudillo* (1929)—a *roman à clef* portraying the corruption of post-Revolutionary leaders. Reyes, one of the major figures of Mexican literature, was an extremely imaginative classicist who excelled in drama, poetry, short fiction and essays.

The essential novel of the Revolution is *Los de abajo* (*The Underdogs*, 1915), written by a humble doctor from Jalisco named Mariano Azuela (1873-1952). Its frenetic pace, concision, vivid descriptions and powerful conclusion make it one of the classics of world literature. Although the novel was virtually unknown before 1925, it inspired hundreds of revolutionary novels during the next twenty years. In general, the novels, which appeared in the second decade of this trajectory, tend to feature more social criticism (rather than straightforward accounts of military conflicts) and more sophisticated narrative techniques such as stream of consciousness, interior monologue and flashback. Among the most accomplished revolutionary novels are *Cartucho* (*Cartridge*, 1931) by Nellie Campobello (1909-1986), *Campamento* (*The Encampment*, 1931) by Gregorio López y Fuentes (1897-1966) and *El resplandor* (*Sunburst*, 1937) by Mauricio Magdaleno (1906-86).

José Revueltas (1914-76) was a dissident intellectual who was incarcerated for much of his life. His second novel, *El luto humano* (*Human Sadness*, 1943), combines imaginative narrative techniques with allusions to pre-Hispanic mythology in order to describe Mexican identity and to criticize post-revolutionary programs. Other important works of Revueltas include the novels *Los muros de agua* (*The Walls of Water*, 1940), *Los errores* (*The Errors*, 1964), and *El apando* (*The Punishment Cell*, 1971); the short story collections *Dios en la tierra* (*God in the Earth*, 1944) and *Dormir en tierra* (*To Sleep in the Earth*, 1960); and the theatrical productions *La otra* (*The Other Woman*, 1949) and *El cuadrante de la soledad* (*The Quadrant of Solitude*, 1950). Revueltas was also a prolific essayist and screenwriter, as well as a leader of the student demonstrations of 1968.

In the 1940s Mexican literature found itself in a period of stagnation. The revolutionary novel had ceased to be innovative because it was proving difficult to combine the increasingly predictable nationalistic sentiments with more sophisticated literary techniques. The work that most clearly signaled a new direction in Mexican fiction was the novel *Al filo del agua* (*The Edge of the Storm*, 1947) by Agustín Yáñez (1904-80). With this landmark novel Yáñez provides stream of consciousness, interior monologue and flashback narrative sequences and weaves them flawlessly into a narrative of several levels. Absolutely no action occurs in the first hundred pages of *Al filo del agua*, and the "Acto Prepatorio" ("Preparatory Act") is deservedly admired for the manner in which it establishes the novel's oppressive setting.

Juan Rulfo (1914-86) followed Yáñez in developing the so-called "Modern Mexican Novel" with Pedro Páramo (1955), a mysterious work about the life and death of a revolutionary boss who dominates a ghost town called Comala. Rulfo's *El llano en llamas* (*The Burning Plain*, 1953) remains the most influential collection of short stories yet produced in México. Carlos Fuentes (1928), the best-known Mexican novelist, has enjoyed a long career producing innovative novels such as *La región más transparente* (*Where the Air is Clear*, 1958), *La muerte de Artemio Cruz* (*The Death of Artemio Cruz*, 1962), *Terra nostra* (1975), and *Inez* (2002).

The commanding figure in Mexican literature of the twentieth century is Octavio Paz (1914-98). As a poet and essayist, he is unmatched in versatility and production by any other Latin American writer. Although Paz had already established himself by the late 1930s, the essential elements of his poetics—the Mexican cultural tradition, the Western literary canon, Surrealism, and Eastern philosophy—would not become fully developed and integrated until *El arco y la lira* (*The Arch and the Lyre*, 1956). The same decade also saw the publication of his enormously influential essay on Mexican identity, *El laberinto de la soledad* (*The Labyrinth of Solitude*, 1950, 1959). Paz remained active editing his poetry, writing, and directing the journal *Vuelta* until his death. In 1990 Paz was awarded the Nobel Prize for Literature; to this day he is the only Mexican who has received the award.

Rodolfo Usigli (1905-79) stands as the most professional and most often anthologized of Mexican dramatists of the twentieth century. A master of establishing scene, Usigli's dramas feature many political, social, and psychological themes. Usigli's most famous works include *El gesticulador*

(*The Impersonator*, 1937), *El niño y la niebla* (*The Child and the Mist*, 1936) and *Corona de sombra* (*Crown of Shadow*, 1943). Carlos Monsiváis (1938), a prolific essayist, critic and journalist, is credited with almost single-handedly revitalizing the genre of the crónica (chronicle), where many ideas and events are explored using slang, a colloquial tone and much irony. Other important Mexican writers during the second half of the twentieth century include the novelists Elena Garro (1916-98), Elena Poniatowska (1933), Gustavo Sainz (1940), José Agustín (1944), Emilio Pachecho (1939), Luis Zapata (1951), and Carmen Boullosa (1954).

This overview of Mexican literature would be even sketchier if it failed to mention the Mexican popular ballad known as the *corrido*. The *corrido* is a lyrical narrative genre derived from the Spanish romance tradition; almost all *corridos* can be performed by a single singer and guitar. Some scholars place the genre's origin in central México, especially Michoacán State, although the eminent folklore scholar Américo Paredes believed that the *corrido* originated in the northern border regions once known as Nuevo Santander. The *corrido* saw its apogee during the Revolution of 1910, where hundreds depicting battles and political upheavals were composed in situ, offering a popular perspective of historical events. New *corridos* continue to be written and performed throughout México and the United States. *Los Tigres del Norte* (*The Tigers of the North*) are perhaps the most well known musicians who continue to compose and perform *corridos*.

Mexican Cinema

Mexican cinema is a magnificent tradition that is generally unknown among critics, most of whom have tended to look to Europe for serious films. Indeed, many critics dismiss Mexican cinema as nothing more than low-budget productions featuring masked wrestlers. However, in México and throughout much of Latin America, stars such as Pedro Infante, Cantinflas, and María Félix shine even more brightly than Clark Gable, Charlie Chaplin or Elizabeth Taylor ever did in the United States. The success of the Mexican movie industry, especially in the so-called "Golden Age" from the late 1930s to the late 50s, had repercussions on the popular culture of all Latin America and Spain.

Mexican cinema began in 1896 with the introduction of US and European projection technology. Unfortunately, the silent film era (lasting up to the 1920s) is difficult to research given that most of the films have been lost and newspapers are the only reliable source of information. The beginnings of Mexican film are normally linked with the name of Salvador Toscano Barragán (1872-1947), an engineering student who opened the first movie salon in México City. Using primitive equipment, Toscano Barragán began showing Lumière films and reels of prizefights in the late 1890s. As the scholar Carlos Mora explains, Mexican filmmaking was limited in the pre-revolutionary period to largely propagandistic features intended to enhance the glory of the Díaz dictatorship. When the Revolution swept México (1910-20), audiences were treated to footage of revolutionary forces sweeping through the northern states and European soldiers fighting on the Western Front. But entertainment films were also introduced during this tumultuous period. For example, in 1919 the first Charlie Chaplin shorts were shown. *1810 o los libertadores de México* (*1810 or the Liberators of México*, 1916), the first full-length (one hour) feature film produced in México, was premiered during the Revolution, as well as the first film to be produced in México City, *La luz* (*The Light*, 1918). Modest film studios, such as Aztec Films and México-Lux, were also established. In sum, the essential elements were in place for the steady growth that was to occur in the 1920s.

Following the Revolution, the new government undertook an ambitious program to promote a national culture built upon a re-interpretation of Mexican identity. No longer a divided nation of European elites and millions of poor laborers of indigenous heritage, Mexicans were now seen as *mestizo*. Pioneering initiatives, largely originating from José Vasconcelos' Ministry of Public Education, helped to finance the artistic movement known as Muralism (c. 1921-40). The leading figures of this movement were the artists Diego Rivera (1886-1957), José Clemente Orozco (1883-1949), and David Alfaro Siqueiros (1896-1974). Their panoramic depictions of pre-Hispanic civilization, the Conquest, Independence, and of course the Revolution gave Mexicans a sense of their unique cultural and ethnic heritage. Unfortunately, this same patronage was not provided as energetically to the nascent film industry, although many of the same monumental visualizations of national identity would be incorporated into that medium.

In this period, many of the biggest Mexican film stars went to Hollywood to develop their careers, most notably Ramón Novarro (1899-1968) and Dolores del Río (1906-83). Del Río was the first Mexican actress to attain icon status, and before her return to Mexican cinema in 1943, she

starred in such US films as *All the Town is Talking* (1925), *Resurrection* (1927), and *Evangeline* (1929). In the silent period, importation of films to México was a cost-effective means of earning money in the first salons and theatres; one did not need to know English to enjoy Chaplin's comedy. However, the advent of sound was to provoke profound changes in México because it provided an added incentive to produce homemade films. México would begin to find its voice, however fitfully, in the films of the 1930s.

For most students of Mexican cinema, the first essential national film was *Santa* (1932), which was filmed in southern México City by director Antonio Moreno and with the stars Lupita Tovar and Donald Reed (Ernesto Guillén). All three of these artists had been earning a living in Hollywood but returned to México to work on the project. The film, which reworks a Federico Gamboa novel about a humble country girl who is forced into prostitution, is not a classic by any stretch of the imagination. However, *Santa* was the first Mexican film with sound that compared favorably to a Hollywood production.

While the film industry did not enjoy much initial support from the government, it did benefit from the presence and cooperation of innovative foreigners. In the early 1930s, the great Soviet director, Sergei Eisenstein, visited México to produce a film called *¡Que viva México!* Although the project was eventually aborted, Eisenstein's techniques had a profound influence on several fledgling Mexican directors, most notably Emilio "El Indio" Fernández (1904-86). Fernández, who would go on to produce some of México's finest films, was also indebted to his close friend, the artist Dr. Atl (Gerardo Murillo, 1875-1964). Dr. Atl's non-traditional manner of presenting almost surrealistic clouds and landscapes, as well as arranging scenes with dual vanishing points, would be adopted and modified in Fernández's major films. Gabriel Figueroa (1908-97), Fernández's cameraman for twenty-three of his films, worked in Hollywood in the 1930s with the celebrated cameraman Gregg Toland, who would go on to film such classics as *The Grapes of Wrath* (1940) and *Citizen Kane* (1941). The Fernández-Figueroa team would produce a series of classic, sophisticated films such as *Flor silvestre* (*Wildflower*, 1943), *La perla* (*The Pearl*, 1944), and *Salón México* (1948). Their 1943 collaboration, *María Candelaria*, won the Golden Palm Award at the first Cannes film festival in 1946. In 1947, the Fernández-Figueroa team scored another critical and commercial hit with *Río Escondido* (*Hidden River*), featuring the most beloved Mexican actress of all time, María Félix (1914-2002). María Félix is so famous in her native country that she is more commonly known as "la bonita" (The Pretty One) or "la Mexicana" (The Mexican Woman).

It was during this crucial decade of the 1930s that the government, led by the new Secretary of Public Education Narciso Bassols, decided to lend significant financial support to the industry. The first successful production was *Redes* (*Nets*, 1934), a film directed by American photographer Paul Strand. Director Fernando de Fuentes (1894-1958) put the popular revolutionary novel *¡Vámonos con Pancho Villa!* (*Let's go with Pancho Villa*, 1935) on the silver screen to much critical and commercial acclaim. However, the landmark Mexican film would be de Fuentes' *Allá en el rancho grande* (*Over on the Big Ranch*, 1936), which is comparable to the Hollywood classic *Gone With the Wind* (1937) for its popular appeal and international success. It was this film, more than any other, which established the Mexican film industry as the most profitable, prolific and influential south of Hollywood. *Allá en el rancho grande* also established something of a Mexican style in popular films: singing *charros* (cowboys), beautiful señoritas with braided hair, and popular music sung by actors. It would be into this mold—sometimes called the *comedia ranchera* (country comedy)—that two of the greatest Mexican actors-musicians would carve out their legendary careers.

Pedro Infante (1917-57) began his career as a successful recording artist. However, when his movie career began with *La feria de las flores* (*The Fair of Flowers*, 1942), it was clear that his charisma and musical talent was even better suited to film. Infante starred in nearly fifty films, with the most famous including *Nosotros los pobres* (*We the Poor*, 1948), *Ustedes los ricos* (*You the Rich*, 1948), and Ismael Rodríguez's *Tizoc* (1956), where he worked alongside María Félix. Although Infante was an accomplished comedic actor, usually demonstrating much chivalry and good-natured machismo, he was also a competent serious actor. Infante died in a plane accident and to this day Mexicans observe the day of his death, April 15, 1957, with the same mixture of sadness and enthusiasm that many Americans demonstrate when they commemorate the death of Elvis Presley. The other great singing *charro* of Mexican cinema was Jorge Negrete (1911-53). After his first starring role in *Ay, Jalisco, ¡no te rajes!* (*Jalisco, Don't Be Scared!*, 1941), Negrete became a huge celebrity throughout Latin America and later married María Félix. Sadly, Negrete died during a publicity

tour in California from liver complications. The two premature deaths of Infante and Negrete signaled the end of the Golden Age of Mexican cinema.

However, this rich period also produced one of the world's greatest comedians. Cantinflas (born Mario Moreno, 1911-93) was also a writer, producer and a generous contributor to many charitable causes. Chaplin once called Cantinflas the greatest comic alive. In his forty-nine films, he usually played a wise-cracking peasant or regular guy who managed to get out of trouble with authorities by overwhelming them with pompous, rapid-fire monologues that, while sounding gloriously informed, signified absolutely nothing. So profound was his influence on Mexican culture that his career introduced a new verb in the Spanish language: cantinflear, which means to say a great deal without saying anything at all. Cantinflas was a master improviser, and made many of his films without the help (or perhaps hindrance) of a script. He was also a master of *albur*, a Mexican style of double entendre with sexual connotation. Some of Cantinflas' finest films include *Ahí está el detalle* (*There's the Detail*, 1940) and *Ni sangre ni arena* (*Neither Blood nor Sand*, 1941), a hilarious parody of Blasco Ibáñez's bullfighting novel *Sangre y arena*. Cantinflas is perhaps best known among American audiences for his role in *Around the World in Eighty Days* (1956). Another comedic actor who enjoyed much success was Tin Tan (born Germán Valdés, 1919-73), who combined music and dance with his imaginative comedy. Tin Tan's classic film *El rey del barrio* (*The King of the Neighborhood*, 1949) has enjoyed much popularity among U.S. Chicanos because of his character's *pochismos*: slangy, fast-paced dialogue laced with an English word here and there.

The economic expansion and security that México enjoyed during the 1940s slowly gave way to more precarious times. By the 1950s, the major studios were not producing nearly as many films as they had over the previous two decades, and the government no longer provided the same level of financial support. Furthermore, the national cinemas of Argentina and the U.S. began to reassert themselves in the Mexican market. While many talented directors, such as Alejandro Galindo (1906-99) and the Spaniard Luis Buñuel (1900-83), continued to produce films in the 1950s, an era of collective creativity and inspiration had clearly passed. The decadent trend continued into the 1960s and 70s, with only a few important films being produced: Arturo Ripstein's *Tiempo de morir* (*Time to Die*, 1965) and *El lugar sin límites* (*The Place Without Limits*, 1977, based on a novel by the Chilean writer José Donoso); and *Pedro Páramo* (1966, based on the novel by Juan Rulfo).

In spite of the relative lack of high quality films, many filmmakers directed their attention to social and political issues that never would have been attempted during the Golden Age. For example, Felipe Cazals' *El apando* (*The Punishment Cell*, 1975), based on the short novel by José Revueltas, provoked such a public outcry over the scenes of inmates being tortured that it helped to finally close the enormous prison, Lecumberri, where the dissident author had been imprisoned during the end of his life. María Novaro's *Lola* (1989) deals with a young woman who raises her five-year-old daughter and tries to make a living selling clothes on the streets of México City. Lola's ambivalence about motherhood stands in sharp contrast to the standard depiction of mothers—as nurturing, self-sacrificing saints—provided by Mexican cinema.

Perhaps the most unforgettable Mexican film of the past forty years is Jorge Fons' *Rojo amanecer* (*Red Dawn*, 1990), which takes place on the day and night of the student massacres at Tlatelolco Plaza (October 2, 1968). All the action of the film takes place in a middle-class family's apartment. Gradually, and despite the warnings of the politically active young people, the building savagery in the plaza forces its way into the apartment with tragic consequences. *Rojo amanecer* was the first major film to treat what was an unmentionable topic in the national media: the government's murder of several hundred of its citizens. The film has done as much to commemorate the student massacre as writer Elena Poniatowska's powerful work, *La noche de Tlatelolco* (1971). To this day countless Mexicans watch broadcasts of *Rojo amanecer* every October 2.

Since the 1990s, Mexican cinema has enjoyed a renaissance both within its national boundaries and in the international market. The first success of this renaissance—sometimes called *el nuevo cine mexicano* (the New Mexican Cinema)—was Alfonso Arau's *Como agua para chocolate* (*Like Water for Chocolate*, 1992), based on the bestselling novel of Laura Esquivel. In this film, several scenes feature magical realism: a technique of contemporary Latin American literature where a seemingly normal situation suddenly becomes more fantastic and surreal. México has had three especially successful films in the past four years: *Amores perros* (*Love that Betrays*, 2000), which like the American film *Pulp Fiction* (1994) features interwoven stories, a circu-

lar plot and much violence; *Y tu mamá también* (*And Your Mother, Too*, 2001), a raucous yet poignant coming-of-age, road movie; and *El crimen de Padre Amaro* (*The Crime of Father Amaro*, 2002), which is about a young and charismatic parish priest who becomes corrupt after satisfying his sexual desire for one of his parishioners. With these recent critical and commercial successes, Mexican cinema is clearly poised for yet more success and acclaim in the future.

Mexican Television

The history of Mexican television begins as early as the 1930s, but in an unsuccessful manner. The first TV system was installed in June 1935, as a project of the PNR (the National Revolutionary Party, later to be known as the PRI, the Party of the Institutional Revolution), which had just become the ruling political party. The purpose of this initial television system was essentially to disseminate political propaganda. The project quickly failed, first because the electro-mechanical equipment acquired by the PNR became obsolete due to the invention of a new electronic model. Secondly, political conflicts between Plutarco Elías Calles (Mexican president, 1924-28, de-facto president 1928-34) and Lázaro Cárdenas (president 1934-1940) occasioned significant changes in party leadership. When Cárdenas' rule was firmly established, the television project was neglected until the late 1940s.

Latin America was the first region to witness the development of television outside of industrialized nations such as the U.S., Great Britain and France. In México, the question was not so much selling the concept of television (cities sharing the border with the U.S., for example, had enjoyed television broadcasts for several years), as it was establishing it as a commercial enterprise in the capital. The first Latin American station was México City's XH-TV, which began broadcasting in August 1950. Although its audience was small, financiers quickly understood its potential and within a year XH-TV had two competitor networks. The result, according to Wilson P. Dizard, was a state of over-competition that nearly bankrupted all three networks. In 1955, the three networks decided to merge to form the nucleus of México's first national commercial network, Telesistema Mexicano. Mexican television began to expand rapidly and soon there were over twenty programming stations in operation, many of which were controlled by Telesistema. By 1961, México had a million receivers and television sets were being produced nationally. By the end of the 1960s, television was nearly as much of a fixture in the urban Mexican household as it was in similar areas of more highly-industrialized countries.

In 1973, Telesistema Mexicano and Televisión Independiente de México (established 1965) merged to form Televisa, the country's largest television network. Televisa dedicated itself largely to producing telenovelas (programs similar to soap operas, but broadcast during the hora estelar, or prime time, in addition to daytime slots), specials, talk shows, children's programming and made-for-TV movies. Televisa also shows boxing and wrestling programs, but its most lucrative sports programming is soccer. Televisa has often been accused of being a tool of the PRI, the political party that ruled México for over seventy years. Under the leadership of Emilio Azcárraga Milmo (1930-97), who was Televisa owner and president from 1972-97, the network's fortunes were closely linked to those of the national government. In exchange for imposing a strict self-censorship, smothering dissident voices (for example, there were no news reports of the Tlatelolco student massacre in October 1968) and providing a national propaganda outlet for the Priísta presidents and their hand-chosen successors, Televisa under Azcárraga Milmo was allowed to enjoy more than forty years of monopolistic media domination and preferential treatment by government agencies. Azcárraga Milmo turned over the reins of Televisa to his son who, while only in his twenties, has managed to provide the network a more contemporary perspective. Today Televisa's most formidable competitor is TV Azteca, which was established in 1994. Most Mexicans see TV Azteca as being more popular, and the network is often credited with helping to elect Vicente Fox Quesada, the PAN (Party of National Action) candidate, to the presidency in 2000. Televisa and TV Azteca, in terms of their stations and numbers of viewers, are the two largest Spanish-language television networks in the world. In addition to these meganetworks, which control several channels each, México has its own equivalent of PBS: Channel 11, which is broadcast from the National Polytechnic Institute.

By and large, Mexican television programs have not enjoyed the longevity of their American counterparts such as 60 Minutes, M*A*S*H, or All My Children. However, a number of Mexican programs have survived long enough to become something of a cultural phenomenon if not an institution. In the late 1970s, Azcárraga Milmo launched the telenovelas Los ricos también lloran (The Rich Also Cry) and Yesenia I, which proved enormously popular and made television celebrities of the actors Verónica Castro, Rogelio Guerra and Fanny Cano. A more recent and highly successful telenovela is TV Azteca's La mirada de mujer (The Look of a Woman), which premiered in the early 1990s as a new variety of telenovela where the actors looked and behaved like real people. No doubt capitalizing on the sudden popularity of reality television programs (which in a real sense it helped to create) La mirada de mujer was reintroduced to television in 2003 (with most of the original actors) to much commercial success. A popular sub-genre of the telenovela is the historical telenovela, often using the Reform Wars or the Mexican Revolution as backdrop. Some outstanding examples of the historical telenovela are El carruaje (1972) and Televisa's Corazón salvaje (1993). A Sunday afternoon entertainment extravaganza was Siempre en domingo, hosted by Raúl Velasco, which resembled the Ed Sullivan Show and was on the air for over thirty years. Some of the most challenging and racy material on Mexican television has appeared courtesy of comedians. Albur is regularly employed by many comics such as Adalberto Martínez ("Resorte" the Spring, 1916-2003), Brozo, el Payaso Tenebroso (Brozo, the Sinister Clown) and Eugenio Derbez. The comedy program La parodia offers highly developed imitations of famous people and programs rich with albur and satire.

Contemporary Mexican television offers a wide variety of programming. As in the U.S., there are several different sports channels featuring soccer, baseball and U.S. sports such as basketball and football. The Simpsons are an extremely popular television comedy in México. Many U.S. programs that have left the air have enjoyed prolonged runs in México; for example, the sitcom La niñera (The Nanny), starring Fran Drescher, is still seen in México. México has always offered some of the best programming available for children. For example, Mexican television featured one of the most beloved Bozos in José Manuel Várgas Martínez (1930-2001), who performed as the famous clown from January 1961 to shortly before his death. Evening programming in México often features talk shows and news discussion programs, many of which are recorded at major Mexican universities.

Mexican Literature, Cinema and Television

By Kristin Janka Millar

❶ CULTURE

▶ Analyze a Náhuatl poem or literature and describe how Aztec culture is reflected in its metaphor and imagery.

❷ TIME, CONTINUITY AND CHANGE

▶ Construct a timeline of the development of Mexican literature and politics since the pre-Columbian period.

▶ Compare and contrast the subject matter of films from the "Golden Age" and contemporary period.

❸ PEOPLE, PLACES AND ENVIRONMENTS

▶ Analyze a *corrido* and explain the purpose of *corridos* and the historical event/s reflected in this particular *corrido*.

❹ INDIVIDUAL DEVELOPMENT AND IDENTITY

▶ Compare and contrast how Mexican identity was re-interpreted through film before and after the Revolution, and the role of US film industry in shaping Mexican identity in film.

❺ INDIVIDUALS, GROUPS AND INSTITUTIONS

▶ Describe how shifts in national identity during the colonial and contemporary periods influenced literature.

❻ POWER, AUTHORITY AND GOVERNANCE

▶ Select one period in Mexican history and describe how political events have influenced Mexican literature and how literature has influenced politics.

❼ PRODUCTION, DISTRIBUTION AND CONSUMPTION

▶ Create a graph providing an historical overview of the Mexican television industry.

▶ Nappo suggests that Televisa may have been used as a "tool of the PRI." Explain what he means by this comment.

❽ SCIENCE, TECHNOLOGY AND SOCIETY

▶ Compare and contrast the connection between media and politics in México using the examples of TV Azteca and Televisa.

❾ GLOBAL CONNECTIONS

▶ Describe how having control over a particular market can help/hinder local producers, as with the publishing industry in Spain.

❿ CIVIC IDEALS AND PRACTICES

▶ Examine *Respuesta a Sor Filotea* by Sor Juana, and describe its implications for women in society.

▶ Explore work by José Vasconsuelos, Martín Luis Guzmán or Alfonso Reyes and describe how national identity and social change are/are not reflected in the work.

CHAPTER TEN

United States Images in México

By Manuel Chavez
Michigan State University

COUNTRIES AND THEIR SOCIETIES develop perceptions of one another on the basis of the information available to individuals. In some cases the information is based in social research with scientific standards of validity and reliability. More frequently, information is passed by informal conversations and anecdotes influenced by the mass media. Entire countries and their people do not escape superficial stereotyping and representations shown by the media. This has been especially true since the expansion of electronic media—radio and TV. Europe before World War II was the best example of how the mass media distorted the images of other countries, societies, and their cultures. Many Germans believed the messages broadcast by the Nazis that included the concept of themselves as the supreme race.

While some messages are created to show or distort reality, others are created to build or enhance markets. The U.S. and other countries with powerful media industries create perceptions on the basis of information and content provided by producers. So, the main creator of U.S. images of other countries is the American entertainment industry. American TV shows and films have created a constant and pervasive image of the American way-of-life that many times is not based upon truth or fact.

In the case of North America, perceptions of neighbors are very important because they may influence public decision making in each country. Being part of one of the largest trade blocs in the world has allowed Mexicans, Americans and Canadians to become closer by trying to know each other better, given the important elements of proximity and interdependence. This chapter shows the images of the United States in México and examines the different implications of those images. First, the nature of historical construction of images of the U.S. is explored. Then, the current forms of Mexican interaction with the U.S. are placed in an analytical context based on an analysis of survey data and original research data. Also, this chapter illustrates the differences in Mexican perceptions about Americans as people and about the U.S. as a country.

It is commonly accepted in the social sciences, that societies create their images about others by direct or indirect interaction and by information acquired. Direct interaction is the one that is experienced when someone travels frequently or lives—for long stays—in other society. Under this last category people who live for more than 6 months in a completely different place have a direct, informed perception of that society and its people. This is the case of business travelers, academics, and students who tend to have a more rounded experience of the society they are visiting.

Under direct interaction is the experience of those who frequent a place for work or business purposes, including every workday, but which is not their place of residence. This is the case of thousands of commuters who work in the U.S. but live in México and who cross the border every weekday. While this experience is ample and intense the experience can be either positive or negative; that depends on the nature of the experience itself. Yet, the more time a person spends in a place interactively, the more likely that person will develop a more informed perception or image of a place. Under this category, literally millions of Mexicans have a defined perception of the U.S.

Indirect interaction is the one that is generated by short, social encounters which are trivial, occasional, and non recurrent. This is the case of tourists or consumers who have short stays in a country or consume products or services from an ethnic provider. In other words, eating at a Mexican restaurant such as Tio Pepe or Rio Bravo does not create a deep understanding of the culture and society of México. Likewise, for Mexicans in México City, Puebla or Guadalajara, eating in a McDonald's or TGIFriday's is not a full exposure to the United States either. Even for Mexicans who visit Walt Disney World for four days, the experience does not constitute a complete experience of what the U.S. is all about.

The United States in the Mexican Mind

The relationship of the United States and México has been built around mistrust, misconceptions, misunderstandings, and misinformation. Historically, the two countries started their relationship with an incorrect set of assumptions. The Anglo-Protestant ideology that has been the main force in the creation of the U.S. collided very early with the Latin-Catholic ideology entrenched in the Spanish colonies, especially in México.

The perceptions built about each other are extremely complex because both countries are different in their origins, legal systems, governmental functioning, culture, and language. Today, the two countries have come to the realization that regardless of the differences they are very interdependent neighbors with a relationship that is extremely critical for each other, especially for their government. Here lies the importance of perceptions about each other.

The images created of each other are based on political bias needed to justify political decisions. While historians in both countries still disagree about how the expansion of the U.S. under the banner of Manifest Destiny provoked the Mexican-American War, the scars of the confrontation have not disappeared in some segments of Mexican society. During the 1830s the central idea in Washington about México and its territories was that Catholicism and the legacy of Spanish centralization kept the country in serious backwardness. Interestingly, those perceptions and images were built at a time when the American ambassador did not speak the local language and did not know the local culture. The impressions were based on preconceived notions that had little or no contribution from systematic and educated observations. The same problem emerged when the Mexican ambassador in Washington perceived only an imperialistic and antagonistic sentiment in the American administration, but he had no significant knowledge of the workings, formalities, mechanisms and fundamentals of the U.S. society.

The Mexican-American War happened more than a century and half ago, but for some Mexicans the issue is that the U.S. unjustifiably took half of the land of their new nation. This sentiment about the power of the U.S. is evident when Mexicans are asked if México would be better off, if President Santa Anna (at the time of the war) had sold all México to the U.S. In a recent survey, a significant majority (78%) disagrees with that idea, a little less than one fifth (17%) agree, and a small minority (3%) does not care

one way or the other. These responses illustrate that most Mexicans identify their land with their cultural and historical origins, even when time has mitigated the old scars.[1]

During the middle part of the 1900s, the knowledge of each other was based on conflict and not on collaboration. The beginning of the serious understanding of México and the U.S. started with the termination of the Bracero Program (Farm Guest Worker Program 1939-1964) that led the initiation of binational economic/trade programs. This in turn caused the strengthening of labor interdependence between the two countries, one as a supplier of labor and the other as a "demander" of it, a labor condition that has not changed for the last 40 years, and which has had inevitable social consequences for individuals and their families in México. These programs unintentionally caused the separation of members of a family at many stages of their lives, based on the location and term of employment that each obtained.

Lately, with the 1993 creation of the North American Free Trade Agreement (NAFTA), social, economic, cultural, and political interactions have grown significantly. Again as a consequence of economic forces, individuals of México and the United States have increased their interaction across the border. While the free trade agreement facilitated the ongoing economic integration, social actors are ultimately the final implementors of the process. Every year thousands of Mexican professionals (mostly engineers and business people) working for U.S. corporations move to different places in the U.S. as part of their assignment. This is also true for U.S. professionals who work for the North American division of their companies; they move to México. Particularly in the last 20 years, this interchange has facilitated a closer relationship that is helping to generate direct experience and information about México and the U.S.

In the case of neighboring countries, perceptions may be built on a daily basis. That is the case of the intense and daily relationship of México and the U.S. that takes place at the border between the two countries. The population living in the conurbated areas of the border by 2005 is expected to reach 13.5 million people, divided roughly in half on each side of the border. These cities are permanently interacting in a wide array of issues such as: environmental and tourist protection, family reunions, trade, municipal services, security and law enforcement, education, health, and economic development.

The amount of interaction is staggering. No other border in the world has the cross-border traffic of México and the United States. For instance, in 2002, roughly 200 million people crossed the border to the U.S. in a passenger vehicle. The same year, more than 50 million people crossed as pedestrians. Within these numbers are commuters, tourists, and family members as mentioned before.

Despite the knowledge gained by these daily visits, the reality is that contrary to general opinion in the U.S., not many Mexicans want to move to the U.S. Only two in ten would if they could. In fact, in a survey conducted in April of 2003, more than three fourths of the Mexican respondents (77.7%) said that they would not move to the U.S. while less than a fifth (17.3%) said they would if they had an opportunity.[2]

A source of information that also influences the construction of perceptions is the governmental information generated by one country about another. While intended to serve the public interest, this information contains within it a whole series of assumptions and perceptions about the other country and its culture that may expose residents to a biased view. Good examples are the U.S. Central Intelligence Agency (CIA) Fact Books and the travel advisories generated by the U.S. Department of State. In México, the same is true of the documents and public campaigns generated by the Interior Department Secretaría de Gobernación that informs and advises people about travel to the U.S. Lately, for example, it has offered life-saving information for those crossing the border illegally.

The Images of the U.S.A. in México

Like most countries, México is not unique in creating images of other countries through its media, whether electronic or printed. However, the long border with the United States, the degree of economic integration, and the movement of people back and forth between the two nations directly impacts the Mexican perception of the United States. But the factors mentioned above become less intense as one moves south from the northern border of México. As a result, perceptions and images are not the same for those who live in México City, which is more than 1,500 miles from the border, as for those who live in Mexican cities just across the border with the U.S. There is a clear segmentation in the perception and image that Mexicans have of their neighbor depending on where they live in México.

For those living in cities across the U.S. border the general image of America is a confusing one. On the one hand, many residents in the Mexican border cities who live across from the U.S. cities feel as if they are living next to a gated suburban community in which they are not altogether welcome. Yet, many of the Mexican border residents do see the U.S. side as a place to shop, visit family, and a convenient locale to run errands and do business. Residents on Mexican border cities are always influenced by the messages diffused by the mass media, especially TV and radio. The distance is so short that airwaves are received with no problem of reception. Since World War II, Mexicans living on the Mexican side of the border have grown up with the same United States TV images as their counterparts in the U.S. Even in the local newspapers of McAllen, El Paso, and Laredo, it is very common to have ads and news that cover local issues across the border in cities such as Reynosa, Juarez, and Nuevo Laredo.

For the border resident group that is exposed 24 hours a day to the American media, it is not surprising that most images are created by the media whether positive or negative. Later when a member of this group actually crosses the border in a direct interaction with Americans this has a more significant impact on their perceptions, again depending on the degree of positive or negative experiences. An interesting fact about the border area and its impact on the images Mexicans have of the U.S. is that the American border cities provide only a narrow slice of the American way of life. This is in part because residents on the U.S. border cities in the Southwest are mostly of Mexican descent. So, it is an area with a unique combination of American and Mexican styles that produced a culture in itself. Little data exists to illustrate how the perceptions are made by border residents about the U.S. since what constitutes the true society and culture of the region is still debated.

On the other hand, many residents on the Mexican side are so-called daily commuters who work legally in the U.S and who embark everyday in an international journey. Every morning, lines of vehicles and people cross the border creating traffic jams that last more than four hours (Tijuana-San Diego and Juarez-El Paso are the worst). These workers have mixed images of the U.S. First, they know first hand the functioning of American organizations, employers, and culture. But, they also know first hand some of the negative features such as discrimination, harassment, and alienation. This group also has a daily interaction with U.S. officers at the border stations that may not be a positive or pleasant experience everyday, not to mention the long delays to cross the border that create images of exclusion. This group is part of the 50 million pedestrians who crossed the U.S. border in 2002.

The Importance of Class

One predictor of how Mexicans view the United States is their location in the social structure. Working class and lower class Mexicans have a less favorable view of the U.S. than their counterparts in the middle and upper classes. This is explained by two facts. First, working class Mexicans have reduced possibilities to travel to the U.S. not only due to U.S. visa requirements but also due to financial constraints. For the lower classes, especially in rural areas of the central region of México, their attitude involves negative experiences related to illegal crossings to the U.S. In addition, the language barrier limits the opportunities for a positive exchange with the American society and compounds the initial negative experience.

Lower class Mexicans tend to view the U.S. as exploitative of their labor. This group bases its images on the direct experience of working in the U.S. and seeing the relationship in a contractual-business context. It is not uncommon for this group to think that wages and working conditions are adverse because the employer wants to increasingly benefit from the marginal cost of Mexican labor. This group also tends to have more contact with the U.S. and State bureaucracy of social and labor agencies that also can serve to compound a negative attitude.

For the middle and upper classes the experience is completely different. Most urban middle and upper class enroll their children in schools that have intensive instruction of English as a second language. Many of them send their children to summer camps, military academies, and special sport-academic programs in the U.S. as early as elementary education age. For the upper classes, undergraduate education will take place, without a doubt, at elite American higher education institutions. These experiences have a different impact on the perception of the United States and its people, since the relationship is not subordinated but one of equals.

In addition to the school experience, this group comes to vacation and shop in the U.S. very frequently. In Northern Mexican cities such as Monterrey, Chihuahua, and Hermosillo, located less than 150 miles from the border, families in the middle class travel during the weekends to shop and to be entertained regularly. It is also very common that these families take their annual vacation in destinations in the U.S. Members of this group have a consumer experience that is typically a positive one, making it a completely different experience from the others. Part of this class is the professional group who travel regularly for business to the U.S. This last group is also more likely to develop a positive image of the U.S.

Media Influence

Interestingly, one image that remains constant among Mexicans is the tendency towards violence in American society. This is the result of not only of constant programming of violence in TV and films, but of the news media coverage of the U.S. for Mexican audiences. In a recent content analysis study by the author in mainstream Mexican newspapers, almost 80% of the content about the U.S. was related to urban violent events, drugs and human trafficking, youth-gun related violence, and organized crime incidents.[4] Other news related to the U.S. military position on world affairs, attacks on Mexicans crossing the border illegally, and the glorification of a gun culture. All of this published or broadcast news perpetuates an image of pervasive violence in the United States towards Mexicans.

Commercial TV in México broadcasts almost half of its daily programming with U.S. content. Typical programs include: *Friends, Survival, Law and Order, CSI, Alias, Las Vegas, The Sopranos*, etc. While most programs are dubbed in Spanish, many of them are simply subtitled; the content is totally unchanged and some references are simply contextualized so that the audience recognizes them more easily. However, with the arrival of satellite and cable television, the Mexican market offers all of the channels available in any city in the U.S. This market receives commercial non-premium cable channels such as A&E, Fox, CNN, USA Network, ABC Family, Spike, VH1, MTV, and Disney Channel undubbed and unsubtitled.

The exposure of Mexican audiences to American programs has created a distorted image of the U.S. society. Many sociological and cultural studies have explained the constant tension between what programs present and the portrait of characters that are essentially fictional. The characters in general have little connection with the realities of their environment or their culture; however, that is not necessarily known in other countries. So, for many Mexicans this massive onslaught of media programs creates a second image, one that contradicts the direct perception of American society.

Films featured in México are fundamentally produced and marketed by U.S. companies. Almost 8 out of 10 films being shown in México are made in the U.S. with themes and topics that portray Americans similarly to TV. The impact here is less dramatic than in the daily bombardment of television programming, but it serves as a more general cultural spread given its massive and inexpensive reach. For those audiences who are not within cable or satellite access, cinema offers a reachable vehicle. In a review of programming of movie theaters during the third week of May (2004) in México City, Monterrey and Guadalajara, three of the largest cities of the country, the titles were: *Legally Blonde II, Scary Movie 3, Kill Bill II, Mean Girls, The Incredibles, Shrek 2,* and *Spiderman 2,* which again reproduce a stereotypical view of the U.S.

The volume and penetration of the American film industry in México is so enormous that little is left to other sources. Regardless of the social strata to which a person is attached, the pervasive portrait of American society, through the American film industry has caused ultimately more distortion than any other source. In asking Mexicans how they formed their images about the U.S. and its people, the most common response relates to the mass media, especially films. This response is also true for other countries.

But regardless of the stereotypes portrayed by the media, Mexicans on the overall have a positive image of the U.S. Recently, in one of the most comprehensive Mexican opinion surveys about the U.S, more than half or 55% of the respondents felt that even when the American media induces the creation of similar tastes and patterns, that was okay or positive for México.[5] Other studies are consistent with these findings, such as the Pew Global Attitudes Project that shows that a little less than two thirds of Mexicans (60%) like the American popular culture as presented by the U.S. media.[6]

Surveyed Opinion of Mexicans

An important question that is being explored by academics in México and in the United States is whether the massive influence of TV and film is changing the images of the U.S. in México. While there is not a comprehensive and conclusive study of how U.S. images are formed by Mexicans, there is evidence that most Mexicans have a positive opinion and image of the U.S. In a survey conducted in October 2001 and referenced below,[7] a little less than three in four Mexicans (72.3%) had a fair or positive view of the United States. In the same survey other countries had a more favorable view of the U.S., including Canada and France with an almost 80% favorable responses.

The cited survey conducted by Mitofsky in October of 2001 reflects an interesting perspective where more than half of the respondents (54.2%) said that they have a sympathetic opinion of the U.S while less than a quarter (23%) had no opinion, and only less than one fifth (19%) had a negative opinion of the U.S. This is consistent with most studies that show that Mexicans generally have a positive image of the United States.

In the same survey, Mexicans were asked about how they feel about the proximity of living next to the U.S.; the results showed mixed responses. In a question phrased as how comfortable the respondents were about being a neighbor of the U.S., a majority (58.3%) said that it was okay or very much okay. In the same survey, 40% expressed little or no comfort at all about being a neighbor of the U.S. This question was intended to gain a little more understanding in the mode of thinking and feelings of Mexicans in their relationship with the U.S. The results presented above reflect that most Mexicans are comfortable with the reality of being neighbors with the most powerful nation of the world.

But when the question was asked about how close Mexican respondents are to "being" an American, almost half (49%) said they are far from it, while a little less than a third (31%) said they felt very close, and 18% felt neutral about being close to the American-way-of-life. This shows that Mexicans feel that they have some connection with the Americans, but they are far from ready to identify with them.

Regardless of the sense of similarity with Americans, Mexicans do feel that a neighbor is a neighbor and that when something wrong or bad happens, proximity requires sympathy, compassion, and support. Right after the attacks of September 11, 2001, an overwhelming majority of Mexicans said that the U.S. did not deserve the terrorist attacks. More than 85% said that the U.S. did not cause or deserve the attacks. Only, a small minority believed the opposite (11%) with 3% having no opinion. The same survey also indicated that most Mexicans agree (53.5%) that after September 11, the relationship with the U.S. should be maintained as equal or increased; only a third believe (34%)

that the relationship should be decreased.[8]

One point that is clear in the periodic study of attitudes of Mexicans is that they respond closely to the opinions and attitudes of other countries. It is also clear that Mexicans also respond to events that affect them directly or indirectly. That is the case of the decline in positive opinion of the U.S. in the last three years after the attacks on Afghanistan and the recent war against Iraq. The responses are similar to other nations switching from favorable to unfavorable. The results show that in October 2001, more than half (55%) of the respondents had a good opinion of the U.S. but, by February 2003 that number declined to 42% and by March 2003, the original half was reduced to only 26.3%. This is an indication that information and knowledge caused a shift in Mexican opinions based on the circumstances and characteristics of U.S. actions. Another example is that the overall positive image that Mexicans had of the U.S. in October 2001 changed negatively during the initial military intervention in Iraq. Surveys indicate that the positive image declined from 54.2% to just 34% in a poll taken in March of 2003, a clear loss of 20 percent points.[9]

Additional factors have an impact on the creation of images of the U.S. especially for Mexicans. Binational issues between México and the U.S. also have an impact on the creation of images of each other. For instance, the small decline of positive images of the U.S. in México from 68% in 2000 to 64% represents the tension in the water conflict at the U.S.-México border. The conflict was a long contested water delivery from the Northeastern Mexican border states to Texas, in which México argued it lacked water due to drought, while the U.S. demands were considered as unreasonable in those circumstances. Also, this is the time in which a panel of the WTO declared the American government decision to deny entry of Mexican trucks into the U.S. was illegal based on the previous negotiations of NAFTA. So, very specific binational problems had an impact on the formation of images of the United States.

Also, México is not much different from other countries in the general opinion of the U.S. held by its public. In fact, in the Pew Global Attitudes Project 2002, México was very close to Canada and Italy in terms of positive opinion about the U.S. with more than 2/3 of Mexicans with a favorable opinion. This response, contrary to general opinion, offers a notion that regardless of the common problems of living next to each other, Mexicans have a generally good perception of the U.S. Also, this indicates that regardless of border or trade related binational disagreements and the fact of living next to the richest and powerful country of the world, the U.S. has a general positive image in México.

However, attitudes about the acceptance of ideas and customs spread by the U.S.—what it is called as Americanization—are a different matter. In the same 2002 Pew Global Attitudes Survey, a significant majority of less than two thirds of Mexicans (65%) said that the spread of American ideas and customs was bad. México was close to the European countries such as Germany and France with similar rates of negative perception about American intrusion on local values and culture. This indicates that even while there is a general positive sense of respect and admiration for American science, business and technology, there is a general negative sentiment towards cultural or political influence.

While national polls give us a general view of the opinion and attitudes of a population, they don't provide a secure way to generalize to specific groups, cities, or states. The variation could be significant to the point that makes the analysis inconclusive. So, in the next section, a small data set provides more local insights into the Mexican perceptions and images.

A Set of Images in North Central México

In the city of Ramos Arizpe, there is one of the largest plants of General Motors' North American division. The city is a suburb of the capital of the state of Coahuila, called Saltillo. The metro area is less than 60 miles from the industrial city of Monterrey. Both cities are located less than 150 miles from the Texas border. The GM plant manufactures essentially for the U.S. market small vehicles, pick up trucks, and multiple auto parts. Workers are mainly from the region, and supervisors are from different cities in México, including México City and Guadalajara. Upper level position managers are a combination of American and Mexican professionals with college degrees. GM Corporation was interested in improving the relationship of Mexican and American managers and supervisors; to that end it contracted a set of training seminars with one of the providers of cross-cultural management.

A group of Mexican managers (90) at the upper and supervisory level received in the fall of 2000 a training seminar on cross cultural management offered by a GM private consultant group from Southfield, Michigan. The author assisted the consultant in the formulation, conduction and analysis of a pre and post-testing instrument to evaluate the impact of the training. During the two-day seminar, the total group was divided into two, so the groups would be more manageable.

Each group during the training faced the same questions about perceptions of Americans and the U.S. They also were asked to rank the attributes and characterizations that better described the U.S. and Americans. The questions tried to emphasize the difference between formal corporate relations and more familiar informal relations.

The group of managers and participating supervisors were all college educated and were mostly middle or upper middle class. An interesting finding is that most of the perceptions did not surprise the trainers and supported earlier studies. In fact, there was a clear validation of what national opinion survey data reveals. Mexicans perceive a clear difference between the United States on one hand, and the American people on the other.

The following list shows the top 10 rankings of how Mexicans perceived the U.S. in general. The ranks illustrate the frequency of votes by both groups.

Perception Ranks of the United States (American Society)

1 Rich
2 Powerful (Imperialistic)
3 Consumerist
4 Disciplined
5 Liberal
6 Racist
7 Ethnocentric
8 Low priority for the family
9 Pragmatic
10 Socially in decay

The list shows what most people know about American society, which is always portrayed in the media. The initial rankings show the image of a powerful neighbor who likes to consume, is very much concentrated on himself, dedicates little attention to what others consider important, such as the family itself, and one that lives in contradiction. It seems a fair representation of the negative. On the positive side, Mexicans ranked wealthy, disciplined, and pragmatic as traits of the country as a whole.

When the Mexican staff, however, was asked about Americans as people they know or work with, the ranking had interesting variations. Mexicans ranked very high independency and hard working attributes. Also among the positive traits the rankings showed that Americans demonstrate degrees of loyalty. The negative traits are no surprise: highly technical but not very culturally educated, high concentration on the local (place of living, origin, school, etc.), superficial, and unable to speak another language.

Perception Ranks of Americans as Individuals

1 Independent
2 Hard working
3 Informed but not educated
4 Localist (as opposed to globalist)
5 Superficial
6 Informal (as opposed to rigid)
7 Distrustful
8 Monolingual
9 Stingy
10 Loyal

So, it is clear that even when national surveys tend to generalize trends to the general population, small sample findings and opinions are consistent with the overall survey. The findings in the case of the Mexican automobile employees show a conciliation of positive and negative traits that balance the images of the United States and of Americans. In other words, what media and experience creates seems to match a general perception of those with more interactive experience with the U.S. and its people.

Conclusions

United States images in México have been created over time, as part of a historical process, media influence, and personal experiences. The range of images and perceptions depend on the intensity and on the degrees of interaction that Mexicans have with the American society.

Different areas in México and their people have different experiences of the U.S. Those living in cities on the Mexican border with the U.S. have an experience that is constant, permanent, and highly interactive. For cities and areas far from the U.S. border, the experience is based on periodic exchanges and on the media. It seems that the closer a Mexican is to the U.S. the more positive the images are.

Socio-demographic characteristics also tend to have an impact on the images created by Mexicans. More educated Mexicans have better opinions given the frequent interactions with the U.S. Most individuals in the middle and upper classes tend to have direct positive images and opinions due to the fact that most of the children in these classes attend higher education institutions in the U.S. Clearly, the role played by information and knowledge cannot be ignored. Professionals and their families who typically are part of the middle class seek printed information that is produced by informed, educated and critical sources that in theory try to present an objective perspective.

Another important characteristic in the formation of images in México is the condition of the relationship of the United States with México in a given time. As discussed previously, the recent tensions derived from the water conflict between the two nations, and the unresolved issue of the entry into the U.S. of Mexican trucks have caused more significant damage than any other factor.

Also it is clear that Mexicans, like people from other countries, changed their images and opinions based on the nature of the question, depending on whether it was about the U.S. or about Americans. In other words, most international opinions about Americans tend to be more favorable than opinions about the United States. In the particular case of México, if the U.S. were interested in changing these images, an investment in public diplomacy and public image with its neighbor would be in order. The problem is that the United States is so powerful that it is taking the neighbors for granted, and that is not a good long-term policy.

Notes

1. Mitofsky Consulta. "Sentimientos hacia Estados Unidos despues de los atentados a Nueva York y del bombardeo a Afganistám," National phone survey s=400 (México D.F. México: Consulta Mitofsky. October 9, 2001), 6.
2. Mitofsky Consulta, "La Guerra en Irak," National Phone Survey s=400 (México D.F. México: Consulta Mitofsky. April 8, 2003), 4.
3. This department in the Mexican government is very powerful, and is often described as the equivalent of the United States Department of the Interior, but it is much more all encompassing, having functions similar to the Department of State and the Justice Department.
4. Manuel Chavez, "New Focus and New Images of México and the U.S.: The Importance of National Security" (Paper presented at the Center for North American Studies, UNAM, México D.F. México, September 2003).
5. Mitofsky Consulta, 2001, 6.
6. The Pew Global Attitudes Project, "Global Publics View the United States," What the World Thinks in 2002 (Washington, DC: Pew Research Center for the People & the Press, 2003), 66.
7. Mitofsky Consulta, 2001, 2.
8. Mitofsky Consulta. 2001, 9.
9. Mitofsky Consulta. "Mexicanos ante la Guerra en Irak." National phone survey s=400 (México D.F. México: Consulta Mitofsky. March, 2003), 3.

United States Images in México

BY KRISTIN JANKA MILLAR

❶ CULTURE

▶ Compare and contrast perceptions of the U.S. from México and the U.S.-Mexican border. Explain these differences.

❷ TIME, CONTINUITY AND CHANGE

▶ Compare and contrast Mexican and U.S. perceptions of each other during the Mexican-American War. How have these perceptions changed or remained the same over time?

▶ Create a time line of key events that have influenced perceptions of México and the U.S. throughout history.

❸ PEOPLE, PLACES AND ENVIRONMENTS

▶ Describe stereotypes about the U.S. and México and analyze the purpose of these stereotypes. How might these stereotypes differ depending on location, class, and politics?

❹ INDIVIDUAL DEVELOPMENT AND IDENTITY

▶ Analyze examples from the U.S. media (films, T.V. shows, advertisements) and discuss what perceptions and images of the U.S. are promoted. Compare and contrast your findings with your own personal experiences.

❺ INDIVIDUALS, GROUPS AND INSTITUTIONS

▶ Describe the impact of programs such as the Bracero Program (1939-1964) and NAFTA (North American Free Trade Agreement) on Mexican family structure.

❻ POWER, AUTHORITY AND GOVERNANCE

▶ Describe the impact that location and social class have on attitudes towards México and the U.S. Provide examples from the article "United States Images in México."

❼ PRODUCTION, DISTRIBUTION AND CONSUMPTION

▶ Describe how the U.S. film industry influences images of the U.S. in México and México in the U.S.

❽ SCIENCE, TECHNOLOGY AND SOCIETY

▶ Research NAFTA and present pros and cons of the agreement from the perspectives of México and the U.S.

❾ GLOBAL CONNECTIONS

▶ Using a topic such as NAFTA or the September 11 attacks in the U.S., compare and contrast the perceptions of at least 3 countries on the same event.

CHAPTER ELEVEN

México: Contemporary Achievements and Challenges

By Leonardo Curzio

El Centro Investigaciones sobre América del Norte
Universidad Nacional Autónoma de México

MÉXICO IS A COUNTRY OF 120 million inhabitants. A large population does not necessarily mean, however, that the country has a demographic problem. Other countries, such as the United States, have double the Mexican population and China has ten times more people than México. Demographics do become a problem when the population doubles in only 25 years. In the 1970s, México had 48 million inhabitants; in the 1980s the number of inhabitants grew to 67 million and by the year 2005, México had 105 million people living within the Mexican boundaries and up to 15 million people living abroad, mainly in the United States.

Because of this sharp increase in population, México has to confront a variety of issues having their basis in Mexican demographics. These issues concern economics, society, urban development, educational needs, labor issues, and access to quality food. This increase in the population is equivalent to the whole population of Thailand or France. Experts consider that the curve of demographic growth has reached its highest level and that the population growth will slow and become stable by the year 2050; the total number of inhabitants in México will be 132 million. In other words, some of the problems mentioned will tend to diminish but for today, they are very serious issues.

Demographic change affects many sectors of the society. For example, both the Mexican health system and educational system will have to confront another twenty years of demographic growth; this is a very serious challenge for any health or educational structure. It is also a challenge for the country's economy because it is very difficult to absorb the employment demands of such a vertiginous growth of population. These facts help to explain the migration of millions of Mexicans abroad and to understand that there is no simple solution to the migration problem. The rapid population growth has generated structural problems of great significance that will be discussed below. This chapter will also consider the changes and reforms México has un-dertaken. Let us look at some historical facts.

The Mexican Peso Crisis

1982 is the referent year in understanding the structural changes in México's economy and politics. That year was the last year that President José Lopez Portillo was in office. He was a frivolous President who managed public finances in a capricious manner. The wealth created by the oil sector was squandered as spending increased on sumptuary programs. The country became indebted as never before. All of these bad decisions caused the Mexican economy to collapse. By the end of his term, President Lopez Portillo's legacy was an empty treasury and international insolvency.

Exacerbating a bad situation was Portillo's decision to nationalize the banks and subsequently to convert all U.S. dollar accounts in México to pesos. This decision generated a total lack of trust between the private sector and the Mexican government. The ruling Partido Revolucionario Institucional (PRI) party, which had dominated the Mexican government for the previous seventy years, was severely injured.

After Lopez Portillo left office, the new administration headed by President Miguel de la Madrid had to confront a country with an economic crisis of huge proportions and a crisis of credibility inside and outside the country as well. México didn't have many options and the President had to implement a series of reforms to stabilize the economy. These changes were created by technocrats and followed the policies of the International Monetary Fund (IMF). In general terms, this package of reforms was based on five criteria formulated by the "Washington Consensus," which were:

1. The privatization of the public companies
2. Deregulate the economy and allow the market to work.
3. Open the frontiers and lower tariffs to promote free trade.

4. Balance the government budget and not increase foreign debt.
5. Eliminate government subsidies and price controls and allow the marketplace to determine prices.

These changes represented a 180 degree turn from the economic orientation México had adopted since the 1940s. In those times, the economic strategy was based on public ownership of companies, close government regulation of economic activity, and restrictions on foreign investment in many sectors of the economy. The commercial sector was protected by the government; the national industry did not have to confront any international competition.

In summary, the Mexican economy in the 1980s had to transform itself in an adverse context at a time of high levels of inflation and of great mistrust. Despite these problems, it is amazing to see how much México achieved during this period.

As a result of the economic problems, elements within the middle class and a great number of small and middle businessmen, mostly from the north and center parts of the country, became more politicized and started to confront the authoritarian ways of the political system. This political uneasiness drove them to the National Action Party (PAN). This party had existed since 1939, but it had never had sufficient support to seriously challenge the PRI. Vicente Fox, the President of Mexico from 2000-2006, is a member of this party.

As a country in bankruptcy, with a financial system defined by restrictions imposed by the IMF, México was unable to maintain the old forms of political control which were based on an exchange of public services for support for the PRI. A bankrupt state can neither buy any loyalties nor can it give anyone subsidies. For the previous seventy years, the middle classes and the privileged sectors had accepted a pragmatic exchange with the government which traded the maintenance of an authoritarian government (with high levels of corruption) in exchange for economic stability that permitted economic development and social mobility. The Mexican economic crisis broke this pact as the middle class witnessed a sharp drop in its buying power due to rampant inflation. In some years, inflation reached 100%, which brought about the constant devaluations of the Mexican peso. In 1981 one American dollar was exchanged for 23 pesos; in 1990 the exchange was of 3,000 pesos per dollar.

Nevertheless, the poor still received subsidies, free education and other public services that permitted the PRI to use them as their electoral base. This clientele culture, which consisted of vote buying and in the politicization of social policy, is still alive in México, and today it is an obstacle in the consolidation of México's young democracy.

The social disapproval of the government generated by the crisis started to undermine the cohesion of the PRI, and five years after the beginning of the crisis, in 1987, the PRI fractured. Cuauhtémoc Cárdenas, the son of former President Lázaro Cárdenas (President Cárdenas expropriated the oil industry in 1938 and became the symbol of Mexican nationalism) and Porfirio Muñoz Ledo, one of the most important politicians in México, broke with the party leadership of President De la Madrid and founded an alternative political group called National Democratic Front, Frente Democratico Nacional (FDN). One of the group's first actions was to offer Cárdenas as a candidate for President in the next elections that took place in 1988. In that year, the traditional ways that the PRI won election by using the corporate machinery of the party proved insufficient; the party turned to electoral fraud to insure that its candidate, Carlos Salinas de Gortari, would win the election.

The Salinas Dilemma: Perestroika or Glasnost?

Carlos Salinas's ostensible victory in the election had its basis in illegal voting and from then on he had to confront a paradox. On one hand, he was the man who guaranteed the continuity of the economic reforms that were to transform México, and on the other hand, he represented the wall that obstructed Mexican modernization. Moreover, the FDN and a huge sector of the PRI questioned his policies.

Salinas was liberal in his economic strategies and an authoritarian in his political ways. He declared once that the Soviet leader, Mikhail Gorbachev had made a mistake by attempting economic reforms (*perestroika*), at the same time as political reform (*glasnost*) because each was an obstacle to the other. Salinas's government had chosen a sequential strategy: first economic reforms, and afterwards political reform.

At the beginning of his administration, Salinas started to harvest the results of the changes in the Mexican economy enacted by De la Madrid; inflation started to calm down and interest rates went down. Imports from other countries started to appear on the counters of the Mexican supermarkets. The word globalization started to become popular.

Salinas used all the power of the government and the positive economic results to gain political legitimacy. He wanted to convert his image as an illegitimate President to that of a pragmatic president who offered results and a new image for the country.

It is said that fortune doesn't exist in politics, but comparing the De la Madrid administration with the Salinas administration, it is clear that President De la Madrid had to cope with a very difficult time in the bilateral relations between México and the United States because of Ronald Reagan's war against drug traffic. Salinas had to cope with George H. W. Bush, who proclaimed himself to be the winner of the cold war and proposed to the world the famous New World Order, in which the liberal democracy and the market economy would dominate the world.

This end of the cold war brought a new reality to the international relations between the two countries. It brought a new opportunity to improve the bilateral relations between the United States and México. With economic reforms at hand, it was time for both countries to plan a new commercial relationship. Salinas welcomed commercial integration with the United States with great enthusiasm.

The official Mexican government position was that México was preparing itself to enter the First World. This goal created great enthusiasm in certain sectors of public opinion, and using the popularity of this idea, Salinas transformed himself from a villain to a modernizing despot. In spite of mistakes that led México into a deep political crisis in 1994 with the Zapatista struggle in Chiapas and the murder of Luis Donaldo Colosio, PRI's candidate for the next President of México, Salinas still managed to achieve two significant reforms: the privatization of the public sector and the entrance of México into the American commercial market.

México was "hooked" into economic globalization with the signing of the North American Free Trade Agreement (NAFTA) in 1994; however other issues such as national security, foreign policy and México's role in the world remained largely anchored to doctrinaire matrixes of the past. This is due in part to national inertia, and in part because the door has not been opened in the United States to the possibility of thinking of a more generous integration scheme that was politically attractive to the majority of Mexicans.

Strategic debate has been narrowing considerably since 2001. Any topics not resolved at previous moments in time have been removed from the panorama of discussion. However, if changes do not appear to be that significant in the area of international politics, the process of México's integration into the US economy is a tendency that seems to be irreversible.

In 1995, in the beginning of the Ernesto Zedillo administration, México fell once again in a deep crisis. The reasons for this new economic disaster that cost México 7% of its Gross Domestic Product were a lack of transparency in the financial indicators throughout 1994, a year as already noted that was complicated by developments in the political arena; and an increase in short-term bond indebtedness that México used to restore the flow of international capitals. The portfolio investment in these bonds called "tesobonos" reached 40 billion U.S. dollars.

Fortunately for México, U.S. President Bill Clinton understood that the economic collapse of México would have severe consequences for the United States. He made it possible for federal authorities and international organizations to grant almost 50 billion U.S. dollars in credit. This was important for among the likely results of default would have been a diminution in trade, an increase in illegal immigration, increased power for illegal drug cartels, and significant damage to emerging markets in the rest of Latin America. With the United States credit, México was able to repay investors for unwise decisions made by the Salinas administration. Clinton knew that this political decision would face opposition in Congress, but at the end of the day, as Tom Friedman stated, the Mexican loan guarantee was the least popular, least understood, but most important foreign policy decision of the Clinton presidency.[1]

This credit saved México from disaster and allowed President Zedillo both to undertake economic reforms and to begin a genuine process of political reform in order to establish a real democracy in México. With the support of Clinton, Zedillo could continue to foster perestroika and complete glasnost. Today Zedillo enjoys great prestige in México and abroad and his contributions to México will be remembered in the history books. He is a professor at Yale University and an adviser for the U.N. In contrast, Carlos Salinas is one of the most discredited politicians in the country.

What Clinton discovered in 1995 was the significance of the interdependence between the American and Mexican economies. The level is truly astounding. In the 1990s, México defined itself as one of the world's export powers.

The total volume of México's trade in the year 2000 was 2.3 times greater than that of Russia, or to make a comparison with another Latin American economy with a practically identical GDP, México's foreign trade volume was more than five times greater than that of Brazil. In 1993, one year before NAFTA, México's total exports amounted to nearly US $52 billion. Three years later, the figure had reached nearly US $96 billion,[2] and by the year 2000, the total exports rose to just over US $182 billion.

The process of becoming more intertwined internationally was also accompanied by increasing integration into the US economy. In 2003, of México's total exports, US $165.3 billion, approximately US $146.7 was to the United States. On the other side of the coin, imports were less concentrated. In 1992, 71.2% of México's imports came from the United States, and in 1999, the percentage increased to 74.2%. In 2002, of a total of US $168.6 billion, imports from the United States had increased to US $111 billion.[3] In other words, what México purchases from the United States—which supports competitiveness, jobs and the well-being of the United States—is greater than the sum of the amount purchased from the United States by several European countries, such as Italy, France, Spain and England.

Other figures are equally revealing. For example, since NAFTA went into effect, the number of commercial vehicles that enter the United States from México has increased by 41%. And in recent years, México has been one of the primary suppliers for the US economy.[4] In 2003, México was in third place after Canada and recently China, providing nearly 11% of all US imports.

The economic connection between the two countries, however, is not the only way to understand the relationship between México and the United States. It is also important to consider demographic dynamics, since they offer a clear basis for analysis. In the thirty years between 1970 and 2000, as noted before, México doubled its population. A significant portion of that growth migrated to the large cities in México or to the United States. The number of Mexicans living in the United States has increased enormously in recent years.

This has caused visible effects in the demographic dynamics. Between 1960 and 1970, 290,000 Mexicans migrated to the United States. This number grew to 1.55 million between 1970 and 1980, and to 2.10 million between 1980 and 1990. These numbers reflect that the annual net migration has multiplied in absolute terms more than 12 times in the last 30 years.

Today, between nine and ten million Mexicans live in the United States, and approximately 40 to 50% of them are undocumented. According to estimates received by México's Federal Electoral Institute, Instituto Federal Electoral (IFE) for its electoral census, the number of Mexican citizens who could vote, if this were to become legal and operational, could be greater than eleven million and could represent as much as 14% of those eligible to vote in presidential elections. In other words, expatriates could have more influence in determining the next president than the inhabitants of México City.

Migration and trade figures demonstrate that the degree of integration currently existing between the two countries is enormous, although many sectors prefer to ignore this. México is a country with approximately 120 million inhabitants, and a fifth of its citizens live in other countries. It is clearly a country that has been transnationalized in economic and demographic terms.

For the Mexican economy, the flow of remittances has been growing in the last five years. In 2004 the amount transferred by Mexican workers to their families in México was about 16.6 billion dollars, which is an increase of 23% over 2003. It is important to remember that this amount is equal to the foreign investment in the whole Mexican economy (16.2 billion in 2004).

As shown in the next table, the significance of remittances is becoming more and more considerable for México's economic stability. In short, for an emerging economy such as México's, worker remittances are as important as the General Motors or Ford Motor Company. Remittances play a significant strategic role in México's economy and account for 2.5% of the GDP.

Worker's Remittances 1996-2004 (in millions of US dollars)

1996	4,223.8	2001	8,895.3
1997	4,864.9	2002	9,814.4
1998	4,743.7	2003	13,396.2
1999	5,909.5	2004	16,612.8
2000	6,572.8		

Source: Banco de México

North American Integration: A Pipe Dream?

Despite growing integration as demonstrated by trade and demographic trends, and even with the demonstrated political will of the Vicente Fox administration to redefine bilateral relations concerning migration and NAFTA, the foundations for deepening bilateral relations have not been established.

Because of this failure, many years have been lost to México, which has been unable to find a meeting point between, on the one hand, its economic and demographic reality, and on the other, a nationalist discourse on foreign policy that continues to be deeply rooted in the nation's political class. México has a great degree of confusion as to its place in the world. The revolutionary nationalism that holds together the PRI and the PRD political parties is anachronistic for one of the world's export powers; however this continues to be the dominant focus of the discourse used by these two political parties. It is their generalized opinion that the United States does not consider México as a real partner. The predominance of nationalism has had an important reactive component and has methodologically hindered any progress in reformulating national interests. Few dare to state clearly that a North American focus is—by geographic, economic and demographic definition—of the highest priority for México, and to a significant degree, for the United States as well.

In this context, the region is experiencing a period of great ambiguity. México defines its trade and economic interests separate from and sometimes in opposition to its foreign policy. And the United States defines its foreign and security policies as if México were a country with which it has only insignificant exchanges and as if it were a potentially dangerous country.

Thus, we have an ongoing problem that provokes heated patriotic discussions on both sides of the border. The rhetoric does not seem to prevent the integration of the North American region from moving forward; however, it does create mistrust and reinforce prejudices. Nor does patriotic propaganda endanger the bilateral relation, which is handled with a great deal of pragmatism; however what we have is far from an ideal situation. It is worth asking seriously and directly whether the United States is interested in developing a different relationship with México.

One year before NAFTA was approved, Samuel Huntington, in his article on the clash of civilizations, proposed the concept of "torn countries," and referred to three cases: Turkey, Russia and México. He stated that México is the closest country to the United States, and is a country that debates whether it will remain part of Latin America or be-come part of North America. At the end of his article, he stated that in order to define to which civilization a "torn country" belongs, it must satisfy three requirements. The first is that its economic and political elites support the transformation. The second is that its people are in agreement with the redefinition, and the third is that the dominant groups in the civilization of destination are willing to receive the new convert. It is important to point out that in the text cited here, Huntington indicated that "all three requirements, for the most part, exist with respect to México."[5]

If this were true in 1993, and if structural data for 2005 points toward even greater convergence between México and the United States, the two countries should, in the coming years, find a point of collaboration and cooperation within security issues that, in turn, should generate greater trust. Jorge Montaño, former Mexican ambassador in Washington, phrased it well when he said: "There is no way to ignore that we are neighbors."

The possibility of México and the United States becoming further distanced from each other in the coming years seems unthinkable in the context of new threats and the configuration of a new international order. To the contrary, and without lapsing into voluntarism, we can assume that we are condemned in the long term to develop a better understanding of each other due to the converging interests we share.

If México is politically stable, it can generate the conditions for sustainable development that not only offers prosperity but also well-paid jobs that do not force people to migrate. If México is demographically stable, as predicted by experts for the coming decades, this will imply fewer tensions with its neighbor, and we will have a safer border. If México benefits from infrastructure and investment, it will enhance the region's global competitiveness and strengthen the relative power of the United States in the world economic context. It seems evident to me that if both countries have the political will to overcome the prejudices that each side has toward the other, United States security will inevitably be formulated from a perspective that unquestionably includes México.

The Fox Administration and the Issues that México Must Confront in the Future

President Fox has been a victim of three main paradoxes. The first paradox is that while Fox has been a popular president, he has lacked the legislative backing needed to move forward his program. Despite enjoying a broad and comfortable approval rating among the public, Vicente Fox was not able to translate that political capital into sufficient votes to give his party a majority that would allow him to govern effectively. In May 2003, before the federal elections, Fox enjoyed a 63.5 percent approval rating. Based on this, some of his party's strategists thought that this high approval rating would mechanically be transformed into legislative support. Those who based their decisions on this supposition had their mistake demonstrated to them. The electoral results for the National Action Party (PAN) were very negative.

The president's party had a first warning of what would happen in July 6, 2003 during the local elections in the strategic State of México, which has the largest voter registration in the country. In that balloting, despite the president's visible support for his party's candidates, the PAN made no significant advance. The PAN's seats in the lower chamber plummeted from 206 to 151, a calamity whose political dimension has yet to be clearly weighed. The man who threw the PRI out of the presidency now had to govern by making pacts with a PRI opposition that controlled the two chambers of Congress. The PAN had only 36 percent of the Senate, in addition to having 25 opposition governors out of 32; the majority of governors were from the PRI.

With the new make-up of the Chamber of Deputies, in addition to his own party's votes, the president needed almost 100 deputies from other political parties to pass the federal budget and other bills. Changing the Constitution in some manner that would help Fox was effectively impossible, because he would need the support of more than 180 legislators from other parties. Never has parliamentary arithmetic been so adverse for a chief executive.

With this balance of forces against him, Fox realized that his popularity was not as high as in the first half of his term, even though he could not be said to be unpopular. After the federal elections, different polls said the president continued to enjoy the support of almost 60 percent of the population. The situation of a popular president without the ability to pass bills in Congress is likely to recur if México does not change its electoral system in order to facilitate the construction of majorities within the Congress.

The second contradiction is linked to the economy. The majority of economic indicators, looked at from any angle, are positive and should foster optimism. The peso-dol-

lar exchange rate, for example, has been stable over recent years. Interest rates are hovering at their lowest levels in decades, and the Mexican financial system has recovered after the severe crisis it suffered in the last decade.

One achievement of the Fox government has been its success in improving the economy at a much higher level than some of the other countries in the region. Proof of this success is México's achievement of investment grade status for its financial instruments from prestigious evaluating houses such as Moody's, Fitch, and Standard and Poor's. In addition México is in a privileged position, third after China and the United States, on the list made up by A.T. Kearney that classifies the destinations of preferred investments for large companies.

A few years ago, the figures and data attesting to the stability of the economy would have been a delight for a majority of investors. It is ironic that in a country that went through two decades of economic turbulence, the public now sees these successes as just another piece of data. According to the surveys, almost two-thirds of the population (65.5 percent) does not view the economic situation with optimism. The fact is that while the macroeconomic indicators have been positive, prosperity has not been achieved by a majority of the population. This concern is reflected in the polls. People's main concerns today are unemployment (27 percent) and the economic state of México (26 percent). It is significant that these two items rate much higher than traditional concerns such as insecurity, corruption and poverty.

Recapitulating, Vicente Fox has not managed to transmit either to the broad public or the business community that the success the country has today is due fundamentally to the fact that his administration has not attempted (like former President Salinas did, for example) to use policy for political ends. This great achievement by Fox has not been adequately communicated.

The lack of high growth rates and insufficient job creation has undermined the optimism of many sectors of society. The country is in a state of uncertainty about the future of its economy due to external factors (such as U.S. economic performance) and internal ones such as the frustration created by the impossibility of advancing structural reforms and a climate of helplessness fed by the president himself through his idealization of the reforms.

Almost all the significant actors in the economy agree on one central paradigm: that macroeconomic stability is a necessary precondition, but it is not sufficient to foster economic growth, income and employment. For that, increased productivity and competitiveness in the Mexican economy are required. The structural reforms and, in general, measures that increase the flexibility and capability of responding to the changing conditions of the world economy must be the goals of any reform.

There is also consensus that the reforms cannot be postponed. In his last report to the nation the president reduced them to five: labor policy, fiscal policy, telecommunications reform, energy reforms and an overall restructuring of the state. The passage of any changes, as has already been noted, depends, to a great extent, on the PRI's willingness to cooperate in the legislature. The PRI holds the key to the reforms, and therefore, their success depends on complicated political negotiations. One fear is that any changes will become watered down in the legislative process. For many national political observers, the question is no longer whether there will be reforms but how profound they will be. Fox's problem has been that despite all his success in the macro-economy, the reforms have not materialized.

Fiscal reform, for example, is necessary. What is more, it is absolutely indispensable. But by no means is it a panacea for solving all country's woes. One should not minimize its effects, but it is clear that the reform that is politically possible, even in the best of cases, is no more than a prologue to real change. When Fox proposed his first fiscal reform program in 2001, the administration calculated that it could increase tax revenues by two percent of the gross domestic product, or about U.S. $12 billion, by applying the value added tax (VAT) to food and drugs. Revenues would increase to 13 to 14 percent of GDP. This is still a low standard when compared with other economies in the Organization for Economic Cooperation and Development (OECD).

Even if tax revenues rise, México has made a series of prior commitments. Rebates would flow to lower income families and educational spending would increase to eight percent of GDP by 2006. The reform will give the administration sufficient revenues to deal with the country's problems and qualitatively change the economic situation.

President Fox's third great contradiction has been that his administration's success in the political arena and in the normalization of democracy is no longer deemed to be a singular achievement. This substantial success has been overshadowed by the tendency to look down the road at new problems rather than to consider the success achieved to date.

The Fox administration has had numerous successes. But it is not the aim of this essay to review advances in education by reciting the number of schools dubbed "quality schools" or the numbers of scholarships given out in the five years of this administration. Neither is it its aim to look at the successful housing program that has benefited thousands of families. Nor will it discuss the Fox administration's other achievements, such as the fight against drug trafficking and kidnapping. Indeed, success in this later arena has been recognized by the Bush government, which is known to be sparing in its praise.

The administration's most important success was to maintain political control of the country at a time when presidential power was decreasing. With all its problems, the system of checks and balances is functioning; the relationships, with some friction, have been relatively smooth. The country is experiencing a democratic life and regimen of freedoms as though it has always been the norm.

Other matters of great importance such as the passage of the Law of Transparency and the early efforts of the Federal Institute of Access to Public Information, Instituto Federal de Acceso a la Información Pública (IFAI), as well as the Law of Public Functioning coming into effect have not been sufficient to demonstrate to the public that the country has changed.

This ultimately is Fox's last paradox: the country has changed but it does not seem to have changed.

Notes

1. Bill Clinton, *My Life* (New York: Alfred Knopf, 2004), 642-634.
2. See http://www.naftaworks.org.
3. The data corresponding to 2002 has been taken from the *Anexo Estadístico del Tercer Informe de Gobierno*. (México: Executive Federal Branch, 2003), 328-329.
4. Lourdes Dieck, *China: Reto y Oportunidad para México* (Mexican Foreign Relations Ministry, Assistant Minister's Office of Economic Relations and International Cooperation, 2004).
5. Samuel Huntington, "The Clash of Civilizations?," *Foreign Affairs* (summer 1993): 44.

México: Contemporary Achievements and Challenges

By Kristin Janka Millar

❶ CULTURE

- ▶ Think about ways that your family preserves cultural traditions. How are these similar and different from those of other families you know?
- ▶ Describe ways that people who migrate to the U.S. from México may try to preserve their culture.

❷ TIME, CONTINUITY AND CHANGE

- ▶ Identify key demographic shifts in México within the last 30 years and construct a chart or timeline.
- ▶ Describe how these demographic shifts have impacted society in México and the U.S.

❸ PEOPLE, PLACES AND ENVIRONMENTS

- ▶ Compare and contrast ways that migration from México to the U.S. has had economic and political effects in México and the U.S.

❹ INDIVIDUAL DEVELOPMENT AND IDENTITY

- ▶ Think about and discuss ways that your identity is shaped by your community, and you shape your community.
- ▶ There are many Mexicans living in the U.S. Read a story or talk to someone who has lived in México and describe how these two countries have influenced their identity.

❺ INDIVIDUALS, GROUPS AND INSTITUTIONS

- ▶ Describe ways that the Mexican peso crisis of the 1980s shaped the role of political parties in Mexican politics.
- ▶ Research the Zapatista movement in Chiapas, and compare and contrast the Zapatista goals with those of the Mexican government.

❻ POWER, AUTHORITY AND GOVERNANCE

- ▶ Many Mexicans live in the U.S., 40-50% of whom are undocumented. Compare and contrast the impact (and potential impact) of these groups on politics in México and the U.S.
- ▶ Discuss the pros and cons of economic structural adjustment policies, using the example of México during the 1980s.

❼ PRODUCTION, DISTRIBUTION AND CONSUMPTION

- ▶ The flow of remittances to México has increased within the last 5 years. Investigate how remittances impact the local and national economies in México.

❽ GLOBAL CONNECTIONS

- ▶ Describe some of the connections between México and the U.S.
- ▶ Describe the role of international organizations such as the International Monetary Fund, and its impact on national and local economies.

❿ CIVIC IDEALS AND PRACTICES

- ▶ Compare and contrast the contemporary Mexican political party system with that of the U.S.
- ▶ Explain why Curzio described the poor as a "clientele culture" and how they are seen as an obstacle in the consolidation of México's democracy.

México Snapshot[1]

Recent Population
106,202,903

1970-71 Population
62,600,000

Age distribution of population (2005)
0-14 years: 31.1% (male 16,844,400/female 16,159,511)
15-64 years: 63.3% (male 32,521,043/female 34,704,093)
65 years and over: 5.6% (male 2,715,010/female 3,258,846) (2005 est.)

Longevity
Total population: 75.19 years
Male: 72.42 years
Female: 78.1 years (2005 est.)

Rural/Urban distribution of population
25% rural
74% urban (2005 est.)[2]

Proportion of population aged 15 and over who can read and write
Total population: 92.2%
Male: 94%
Female: 90.5% (2003 est.)

Per capita income
$9,600 (2004 est.)

Distribution of labor force among economic sectors (2003) [3]
Agriculture 18%
Industry 24%
Services 58%

Comparison: Distribution of labor force among economic sectors (1965) [4]
Agriculture 50%
Industry 22%
Services: 29%

1. All statistics come from *CIA World Factbook* unless indicated otherwise.
2. http://www.inegi.gob.mx/est/contenidos/espanol/rutinas/ept.asp?t=mpob12&c=3189
3. Figures come from *CIA World Factbook*.
4. 1965 figures. Sources from *Statistical Abstract of Latin America* volumes 28 and 38

North America

Building an Integrated Continental Economy: The Emergence of North American Free Trade

By Dimitry Anastakis
Trent University

Linking nearly 400 million citizens in a single economic unit producing more than us$11 trillion worth of goods and services, the 1993 North American Free Trade Agreement (and its predecessor, the 1989 Canada-U.S. Free Trade Agreement) is among the most pivotal agreements in the social, political and economic evolution of an integrated North American polity. Today it remains a central theme in Canada-U.S.-México relations. Within the North American context, free trade has been related to privatization, deregulation, environmental concerns, and the erosion of the sovereignty of national governments. It has also been credited with boosting economic productivity, creating greater employment opportunities, and reducing the costs of business. Yet the question of whether free trade has generated new wealth or merely further enriched corporations at the expense of citizens still remains to be answered.

This chapter will discuss the creation of this new North American trade regime, the NAFTA agreement and its impact on the continuing economic integration of the three countries, and speculate on what the future may hold as continental trade and economic issues become increasingly important.

Creating the North American Free Trade Agreement (NAFTA)

Before 1989, there had been a number of efforts to create a free trade agreement between Canada and the United States, though all had failed. While some steps had been taken toward free trade such as the 1965 Canada-U.S. auto pact, many Canadians believed the free trade option would threaten Canada's political and economic independence. Yet from the 1960s onwards, supporters called for the dismantling of costly trade barriers between Canada and the U.S. (and to a lesser extent México), and used the auto pact as an example of the benefits of free trade. North American advocates of free trade also took note of the creation of the

European Economic Community, and by the early 1980s when the U.S. and Canadian experienced economic difficulties, there were renewed calls for fresh approaches to the organization of the North American economic space.

U.S. president Ronald Reagan was a prominent advocate of North American free trade. He led a new conservative wave that embraced free trade as part of an ideology that espoused loosening governmental regulation on businesses and the primacy of the free market in society. In Canada, where the Liberal party had historically been the party of free trade after the 1984 federal election, it was Conservative Prime Minister Brian Mulroney who staked his fortunes on free trade. Mulroney was willing to turn his back on more than a century of Conservative policy to embrace this most difficult of Canadian choices. Increased American protectionism, a result of massive trade deficits with Japan and a restructuring economy, prompted fears that Canada would be shut out of its most important market (by the mid-1980s over 70% of Canada's exports headed to the U.S.), and convinced Mulroney that free trade was Canada's best bet. Reagan visited Mulroney in Québec City in 1985, where the two held exploratory meetings capped off by a gala event that played up both leaders' Irish roots. Mulroney instructed Canadian officials to begin negotiations. American representatives, who understood the significance for Canadians of embarking on such a proposal, nonetheless remained hard bargainers. After years of spirited but often acrimonious negotiations, an agreement was reached in 1988.

In the U.S., the agreement was met with little interest. In Canada, however, Mulroney was forced to contest an extremely bitter 1988 election campaign which was essentially a referendum on free trade. Mulroney emerged victorious, and the agreement went into effect following its passage in Congress and in the Canadian Parliament. Mulroney's victory was the most significant achievement of his political career, while Reagan, on the other hand, quietly signed the agreement into law with little fanfare.

Reagan's successor, George H.W. Bush, was also an advocate of free trade. Keen to build upon the Canada-U.S. agreement, the U.S. government began working on an identical deal with México. In México, President Carlos Salinas of the Institutional Revolutionary Party (PRI) had, like Brian Mulroney in Canada, turned his back on decades of PRI policy: Mexican industry had been greatly protected by tariffs, but advocates of free trade argued that México would benefit immensely from access to the U.S. market. Salinas believed that México could use its low cost labor advantage to lure American business to México, particularly to specially created industrial zones called *maquiladoras*, where companies were provided incentives to locate in special economic development zones. Not wishing to be left out of any new developments, Canada joined in the US-México negotiations, and in 1992, an agreement was reached between the three countries which largely echoed the earlier Canada-U.S. Free Trade agreement. The North American Free Trade Agreement became a reality.

This time, free trade was much more contentious in the United States. Similar to the Canadian fears of loss of sovereignty to the U.S. during the Free Trade Agreement (FTA) debate, Americans feared that joining with México would cause economic hardship as U.S. jobs and production shifted southward. Although President Bush was defeated in the 1992 election, his successor, Bill Clinton, was also an advocate of free trade and the agreement was signed into law in the U.S. Congress. Similarly, while Jean Chrétien, Mulroney's Liberal successor following the 1993 federal election in Canada, had promised the shelve the agreement, he too eventually agreed to it and it passed in the Canadian Parliament. In México, President Salinas, the only leader who had originally argued for the agreement, also saw the new deal passed by the Mexican government, though he was out of office by 1995.

Prior to NAFTA, the three countries did not give any special treatment to each other when it came to international trade and investment, and there were many areas where tariffs and rules were not consistent with each other. With the signing of the NAFTA, the main elements of the agreement were the reduction of tariff and non-tariff barriers in virtually all areas of goods and services, the establishment of "national treatment" and "rules of origin" to allow goods from one country to enter the other two duty-free, rules regarding investment and services such as financial services, dispute resolution over trade problems between the three NAFTA partners, and provisions for temporary workers and customs procedures for all three countries.

The reduction of tariff barriers is the main reason for free trade. Under NAFTA, almost all tariffs between the three countries were eliminated by January 1, 2003. The agreement covers a host of sectors, including energy, agriculture, and manufactured goods. Mexican tariffs on U.S. goods, which averaged 10%, were to be phased out over 10 years, allowing the Mexican economy time to adjust to the new competition that its entry into the North American market represented. After all, México's economy represented less than 5% of the U.S. economy. A number of tariff exceptions remain, however. Canada's dairy and poultry industries are exempted from the agreement. Similarly, the sugar, dairy, peanuts and cotton sectors are exempted in the United States. In México, tariffs will remain on corn, beans and powdered milk until 2008, fifteen years after NAFTA's enactment.

"Rules-of-origin" establish whether products are made in a NAFTA country, and thus can enter into member countries duty-free: Each NAFTA partner maintains its own external tariffs which govern goods coming from non-NAFTA countries. These rules of origin are particularly important in certain sectors including the auto industry, where cars and parts must have 62.5% North American content (that is, made in one of the three countries) in order to enter the other two NAFTA partners duty-free. Nonetheless, over 90% of trade between the three countries is duty-free.

Investment is a second key component. The well-known "Chapter 11" section of NAFTA, which governs investment, makes rules on how investors should be protected by the NAFTA member governments. These rules state that governments in each of the NAFTA countries cannot treat companies which set-up or invest in any of the NAFTA countries any differently. In a high-profile case in 1997, the Canadian government banned the importation of MMT, a fuel additive produced by the American chemical company Ethyl Corporation. The government felt that the use of this fuel additive may be environmentally damaging, while the company believed that this was not the case, since the product was not banned in the US. In response, the Ethyl Corporation sued the federal government of Canada based on the NAFTA Chapter 11 rules, and won the case, forcing the Canadian government to pay the company $20 million in damages. This has led to some severe criticism of the investment clauses of NAFTA: critics claim that Chapter 11 creates a "bill of rights" for corporations which allow them to conduct business even at the expense of environmental or health standards, and that corporate rights supersede national laws.

Dispute settlement between the member countries is another central element of the NAFTA agreement: Although most of the Canada-U.S.-México trade is problem free, there have been instances where governments have disagreed and imposed penalties, such as countervailing duties, which apply tariffs on products which are coming from one of their NAFTA partners. The dispute settlement mechanism also governs anti-dumping: when one country claims that another country is selling its goods for a price that is below its actual value, i.e., "dumping" goods into a country. In cases of countervailing duties or dumping, countries will go to an arbitration panel made up of members of the two disputing countries and a chair who is picked by both countries to decide on whether these penalties should apply, or whether they should be lifted and restitution should be paid. However, dispute resolution under NAFTA is not always effective: For example, the U.S. has recently attached a 27% duty on softwood lumber from Canada. Canada claims this is unfair, and sought recourse under the NAFTA dispute resolution provisions. When the panel found in Canada's favor, the U.S. ignored the decision. This long-running lumber dispute between Canada and the U.S. illustrates that NAFTA dispute resolution decisions are not necessarily binding on signatories to this agreement.

NAFTA also allows citizens of each country to move across borders for work, outside of the regular immigration channels, through special visas for specialized workers, intra-company transfers, business people, and traders. This facilitates the flow of cross-border professionals and business people to meet economic needs in member countries and expands the pool of labor and job opportunities. These measures have been criticized by some labor groups as allowing employers to lower labor costs, hurting workers in all three countries.

NAFTA also contains special side agreements on the environment and labor. These agreements were added during the negotiations to ensure that each country enforced proper labor laws and environmental standards in an effort to maintain a certain level of consistency from country to country, and so that none of the countries would weaken these areas in order to attract investment. Some observers have criticized these agreements as not being effective in maintaining proper standards in either the environment or in the workplace. Many critics point to the Mexican maquiladoras (special work zones near the U.S. border) as examples where lower wages and poorer working conditions have hurt workers and their communities.

The Impact of the 1989 and 1993 Free Trade Agreements

The economic impact of NAFTA on the economies of the three countries since 1993 has been significant, and has resulted in changing political relations between the continental partners. Trade growth is by far the most telling statistic of the impact of the FTA and NAFTA.

In 1994, the total trade between Canada, the U.S. and México amounted to US$297 billion. By 2000, that figure had reached US$676 billion, an increase of 128%. Every day, NAFTA partners trade US$1.8 billion in goods across the continent. By 2001, México had overtaken Japan as the U.S.'s second largest trading partner (12.4% of U.S. trade), after Canada (20.4%). The key sectors for trade in NAFTA region include transportation equipment, electronics and communications equipment, and textiles.

The impact of free trade on each of the three countries has been impressive: Canada, as the most trade-dependent of the three NAFTA partners, attributes 40% of its Gross Domestic Product to external trade. Every day more than $1 billion of goods crosses the Canada-U.S. border, with the Windsor-Detroit border crossing serving as the most important trade corridor on the planet. Canada's merchandise trade with the U.S. and México has risen from US$112 billion in 1993 to US$235 billion in 2000. Canadian trade with NAFTA countries has more than doubled, while trade with the rest of the world has grown only by 29%. Of particular significance in Canada's NAFTA trade is the auto sector, and more than $100 billion in autos and parts crosses the U.S.-Canada border every year. Along with the auto trade, lumber, agricultural products, and energy (oil and gas) exports constitute the primary trade for Canada. Since 1993 employment in Canada has grown by 2.1 million jobs, or 16%. While this growth may not be directly attributable to trade growth, there is no doubt that Canada's trade related growth has been vital to its overall economy.

The U.S., by far the largest economy of the three partners, has also witnessed a significant growth in its NAFTA trade. Between 1993 and 2000, U.S. merchandise exports to its NAFTA partners more than doubled, and was well ahead of the 52% growth in exports to the rest of the world. Trade growth with México has been particularly robust. In 1993, total U.S.-México trade amounted to US$150 billion. By 1999, that figure had grown to US$320 billion. Exports to México from the United States increased by 133% in that period, primarily in electronic and electrical equipment, industrial machinery, transportation equipment, and chemical and metal products. U.S. trade with Canada has also increased significantly since the NAFTA agreement, although Canada-U.S. trade had been increasing since the 1989 FTA: U.S. exports northwards increased 35% between 1993 and 2001, while imports from Canada increased 69%. Overall employment in the U.S. increased by 12%, or 15 million jobs during that period.

The growth in Mexican trade since joining the NAFTA has been equally significant. By 1996, México's third year in the NAFTA agreement, México-U.S. trade reached US$148 billion, a 65% increase over the 1993 pre-NAFTA level of US$85 billion. Canada-U.S. trade had already increased 43% by 1996 over pre-NAFTA levels, and positioned Canada as México's third largest trading partner, while México is now Canada's sixth largest trading partner. More than the other two NAFTA nations, which were largely industrialized and already integrated due to the 1965 auto pact and 1993 FTA, Mexican industry has been transformed since 1993. For example, México has become a key player in the North American auto industry: In 1993 México produced just over 1 million cars and trucks, but by 2001 the country was producing nearly 2 million vehicles, and the sector had attracted considerable investment from U.S. firms (Chrysler builds the PT Cruiser in México), and Canadian and overseas auto companies (Volkswagen builds the new Beetle in México, as well). Many maquiladoras producing a host of industrial and consumer products have sprung up in México, not only in the traditional U.S.-México border areas, but across the country.

Although all of these statistics point to a massive growth in trade and investment between the three countries, the human benefits of the NAFTA regime are more difficult to ascertain. Has the quality of life of the three NAFTA countries improved since the trade agreement was signed? Unemployment rates in Canada and the United States have remained relatively stable since 1993. Poverty remains a significant problem in México, and while wages and employment may have increased in some areas, much of México retains the status of a developing country. Many have argued that the true benefits of freer trade have been unevenly distributed to corporations which have taken advantage of the new regime. Critics point out that while there has undoubtedly been a massive growth in trade, there has been no corresponding growth in incomes, or quality of life for workers and average citizens of the three countries.

Further, difficulties in trade relations between the three countries remain. Mexican farmers have argued that NAFTA has been devastating by exposing them to the U.S. agricultural competition which is supported by massive subsidies. Canadian lumber producers have been the victim of U.S. trade penalties which have crippled the industry. American organizations such as the Washington-based Economic Policy Institute claim that NAFTA cost U.S. workers 800,000 jobs in its first ten years, primarily in the manufacturing and agrictultual sectors.

Clearly, the economic impact of the FTA and NAFTA has been tremendous. But has this economic integration also had an impact on the political and social linkages of the three countries? Given the dominance of the United States in the trilateral economic relationship, have the two junior partners—Canada and México—been adversely effected by their new closeness to the U.S.?

Unquestionably, the close economic ties between the three countries have led to political strains, especially because of Canadian and Mexican dependence on the U.S. trade market. In México, the federal government agreed to change the country's environmental and labor standards as part of the price for its entry into the NAFTA. These harmonization efforts have come at no small cost to the Mexican government and Mexican workers, and were put in place in an effort to satisfy U.S. demands that low-wage Mexican workers and looser environmental controls would not result in a wholesale shift of U.S. factories and businesses south of the Rio Grande.

Canadian policy makers have also felt the pressure to ensure that social policy does not diverge from U.S. practices. Canadian efforts to decriminalize marijuana use across the country have prompted a number of condemnations from U.S. drug policy leaders, who believe that such a move would increase drug-usage and perhaps lead to the growth of the illicit Canada-U.S. drug trade. The deputy

U.S. "drug czar," for example, has stated that if Canada relaxes its marijuana laws, the U.S. should slap punitive economic penalties on Canada. Canadians have responded by noting that the U.S. "war on drugs" is seen by many as a failure, and that Canadians could easily call for a tightening of U.S. gun laws— U.S. handguns illegally smuggled across the border make up the vast majority of firearms used in crimes in Canada.

Perhaps the most noteworthy example of the pressures faced in the Canada-U.S.-México relationship emerged when the U.S. decided to invade Iraq in 2003 without United Nations approval to do so. After both Canada and México decided not to join the American operation, significant pressure from within and without both nations was exerted on these governments to reconsider and join the U.S. effort. Even the U.S. ambassador to Canada stated that Canada might face the economic displeasure of the U.S. for its refusal to join the invasion. México, which held a temporary seat on the UN Security Council during the debate preceding the invasion, faced similar internal and external pressures. In the end, however, neither country joined the U.S. war effort, and neither country faced economic penalties for refusing to do so. Nonetheless, the case provides a good example of the political pressures that can accompany closer economic ties.

Challenges to North American Free Trade

Free trade in North America has not been without its challenges, many of which originated in Canada, the U.S., and México. In Canada, free trade has historically been linked to national identity and sovereignty, and opposition to the 1989 FTA was particularly intense. During the 1988 Canadian free trade election, for instance, debate over the issue was at times extremely bitter with anti-free trade nationalists claiming that the agreement would mean the end of Canadian sovereignty, and the wholesale abandonment of Canadian independence. The 1988 electoral results indicated that not all Canadians were enamored of the free trade deal. When the ballots were counted, only 43% of Canadians had voted in favor of Conservative leader Brian Mulroney's free trade plan, while 57% of the electorate had voted for the opposition Liberal and New Democratic (NDP) parties, who had both campaigned against free trade. Owing to the particularities of Canada's electoral system (a "first-past-the-post" system, where a party only needs to get the most votes in a riding as opposed to a majority, and win the most

ridings), the two opposition parties effectively split the anti-free trade vote, and the Conservatives won 170 seats, with the Liberals and the NDP winning 82 and 43 seats respectively.

While the signing of the 1989 Canada-U.S. Free Trade Agreement was met with barely a ripple of attention in the United States, the 1993 North American Free Trade Agreement was an entirely different story. During the 1992 presidential election campaign, free trade was among the most divisive issues, and the depth of feeling of Americans towards free trade was most visibly exhibited by the stunning electoral story of H. Ross Perot, the anti-free trade Texan famous for his warning that Americans would inevitably hear the "giant sucking sound" of U.S. jobs being drained southward by the Mexican low-cost labor advantage. During the election, free trade with México was criticized by some as an attack on U.S. workers, and by others as unnecessarily ceding U.S. power, and a weakening of U.S. industrial might. Indeed, Perot's performance, gathering 17% of the votes and playing spoiler to George H.W. Bush, was pivotal to the president's defeat. Clearly, a very strong constituency in the U.S. was mobilized by the anti-free trade rhetoric employed by Perot and others.

However, it was in México that the most pointed challenges to the creation of NAFTA emerged. During the NAFTA negotiations, many Mexicans felt that the agreement would hurt the country. Industrialists feared that exposure to U.S. goods would adversely affect them, while nationalists argued (in the same way many Canadians had) about the political and cultural domination of "El Norte." The PRI party, led by Carlos Salinas, was able to overcome these objections to the agreement by offering a vision of México as a modern nation able to compete with the U.S., and to provide jobs and investment which would boost the average Mexican's quality of life. The influence of the PRI, which had been in power for over 60 years by the time the NAFTA issue came to the fore, was also pivotal.

Yet the most riveting opposition to NAFTA in México emerged on January 1, 1994, when the Zapatista Army of National Liberation, Ejército Zapatista de Liberación Nacional (EZLN) led by "Subcomandante Marcos," forcibly took over a number of villages in the southern México province of Chiapas. The Zapitistas, as they came to be known announced in their Declaration that NAFTA was a "death sentence" for the indigenous peoples of México, and claimed that they were officially declaring a state of war against the Mexican federal government. Although the Zapatista uprising was eventually quelled by the government, the Zapatista legacy is strong, and there remains a consistent anti-NAFTA organization in México uniting labor, academic, aboriginal, and nationalist groups.

Indeed, since the initial outburst of protest against the agreement in the early 1990s, opposition to North American free trade has remained significant. In the late 1990s, with the emergence of rules-based trade bodies such as the World Trade Organization (the successor to GATT, the General Agreement on Tariffs and Trade), many groups and organizations have argued that the pro-business agenda inherent in free trade has made tariff reduction only one aspect of broader corporate friendly government polices such as deregulation and privatization, which attack labor rights and the environment, and add significantly to the problems of developing countries. These "civil society" groups believe that governments have ceded too much sovereignty to corporations and pro-trade bodies such as NAFTA and the WTO, and the globalization represented by "free trade" has given anti-free trade forces significant traction. The high-profile protests against the WTO and the proposed Free Trade Area of the Americas (FTAA) have given anti-free trade groups significant publicity. Students have also joined with labor and minority groups to protest WTO meetings at Seattle (the famous "Battle of Seattle" that marked the beginning of widespread anti-free trade protest), Québec City and Washington. Students on many campuses across Canada and the U.S. have also banded together to ensure that collegiate clothing was not made in Third World sweatshops.

But it is not just "civil society" groups that have continued to challenge free trade. Mainstream opposition to NAFTA has been seen as recently as the 2000 presidential election, when Ralph Nader, the anti-free trade Green Party presidential candidate won enough support from normally Democratic-leaning voters to hurt Democratic candidate Al Gore, and swing a number of close state races to George W. Bush. The U.S. government has also come under attack from the members of the international community who argue that while it espouses free trade, it acts in a protectionist manner. Battles over U.S. steel tariffs, increased farming subsidies and longstanding disagreements over Canadian lumber imports point to certain contradictions in U.S. policy towards freeing trade from tariff and non-tariff barriers. For example, the U.S. has supported American-based pharmaceutical companies in their efforts to maintain patent and pricing regulations which keep drugs expensive and out of the reach of many developing nations, although the WTO recently agreed to ensure that developing nations would have access to medications at reasonable prices.

The Canadian NDP also maintains an anti-free trade position, even as key backers of the party, such as the Canadian Auto Workers Union, enjoy the benefits of an integrated auto industry. Canadian critics of free trade also note the massive privatization of public services which corporate interests see as important to the successful operation of the NAFTA agreement. Canadian challenges to free trade remain central to political discourse even fifteen years after the issue was debated during the 1988 free trade election.

In México, the Anti-Free Trade Network has taken up where the Zapatistas have left off. Annually, Mexican protestors launch anti-NAFTA initiatives to bring the agreement's problems to the public eye. As recently as December, 2002, anti-free trade protesters on horseback stormed the Mexican Congress, demanding changes to the latest phase of tariff cuts on agricultural products. All of these cases show that while free trade has become a central component of public policy for all three NAFTA members, there remains a spirited debate over the benefits and challenges associated with free trade.

The Future of Free Trade in North America

What does the future hold for free trade in North America? Many argue that North American free trade in its current form has been a success, and is only a stepping stone to further continental economic integration. Some even advocate closer political ties between the three countries. Others argue that free trade has only enriched corporations, unfairly hurt workers and the environment, and should be rolled back.

The terrorist attacks on September 11, 2001 provoked a new round of discussions on the future of North American trade, particularly from the Canada-U.S. perspective. September 11 saw the Canadian-U.S. border clogged because of security fears following the attacks, and millions lost because of the slow down as trucks idled for days at border crossings. U.S. ambassador to Canada Paul Cellucci's comments that "security trumps trade," encouraged some Canadians to feel that only by becoming closer to the U.S.

could Canada protect its economic interests. In response, many trade advocates promoted a deeper level of integration between the two countries that would see the end to border security problems and other issues related to cross-border trade.

Variously called "deep integration," a customs union, or a "zone of confidence," these plans call for a virtual economic union between Canada and the United States, resulting in a common policy towards all external trade and a total harmonization of goods and services. Such a plan would render the internal Canada-U.S. border needless, ending fears that the annual US$300 billion cross-border trade would be threatened by security concerns.

Along with complete economic integration, some have even called for a monetary union of the two countries, with Canada adopting the U.S. dollar as its official currency. Advocates of this position argue that such a move would save millions in exchange and transaction costs, and boost Canadian productivity significantly, as Canadian manufacturers would no longer be able to use an inexpensive Canadian dollar as a competitive crutch.

The ideas of "deep integration," a customs union or even monetary union, while interesting to speculate upon, pose serious problems. Most obvious is the question of México, which is already a part of NAFTA. It is unlikely that México would be willing to be left out of any consideration of a next stage of economic integration, but many trade experts believe that the Mexican economy is not developed enough to be part of a full-blown customs union. The 10-year phase-in of tariff reductions under the NAFTA agreement points to the delicate position of the Mexican economy; the Peso crisis of 1995 further indicates that México may not be economically developed enough to be an equal partner in total economic integration of the three countries. Then, there is also the question of Mexican immigration. A customs union would necessarily include the free movement of people across the border, a question which concerns U.S. policy makers, given the estimated 10-15 million illegal immigrants

from México currently residing in the U.S. A monetary union would also face difficulties: If Canada were to adopt the U.S. greenback, would the U.S. allow Canada a voice in fiscal and monetary policy? Most likely not.

On the other side of the debate, many advocate abolition of the NAFTA regime, and a return to more nationalist economic policies. Anti-free trade advocates seek "fair trade" which would alleviate what they see as the many problems associated with NAFTA: job dislocation, challenges to labor and environmental standards, erosion of national policies, and a general attack by corporations upon the state and its ability to intervene in the market-place. But is this realistic? With the integration of the three economies, it seems unlikely that ending the NAFTA agreement would be anything but disruptive. As the world develops into defined trading blocs (the European Union, the Asian bloc), the North American free trade zone remains a counterbalance to other economic zones.

But the debate is not over. As North America continues its economic, social and political evolution, the question of whether the NAFTA was merely a stepping stone to greater integration, or simply an end of the official process, will remain to be seen. No matter what their views on the impact of free trade, citizens of all three countries will be a part of this process, along with the millions of other North Americans who have come to see themselves not just as Americans, or Mexicans, or Canadians, but as part of a larger North American entity.

References

Chambers, Ted and Peter Smith, eds. *NAFTA in the New Millennium*. Edmonton, AL: University of Alberta Press, 2003.

Doern, Bruce and Brian W. Tomlin. *Faith and Fear: The Free Trade Story*. Don Mills, Ont.: Stoddart, 1991.

Krenin, Mordechai, ed. *Building a Partnership: The Canada-United States Free Trade Agreement*. East Lansing, MI: Michigan State University Press, 2000.

Ramírez de la O, Rogelio. *México: NAFTA and the Prospects for North American Integration*. Toronto: C.D. How Institute, 2002.

Rockenbach, Leslie. *The Mexican-American Border: NAFTA and Global Linkages*. New York: Routledge, 2001.

Building an Integrated Continental Economy: The FTA, NAFTA, and the Emergence of North American Free Trade

By Dean V. June and Ruth Writer

❶ CULTURE

▶ Investigate the potential impact of free trade agreements on the sovereignty of Canada, México, and the United States.

❷ TIME, CONTINUITY AND CHANGE

▶ Contact several travel and tourism bureaus. Develop a visual depicting how the FTA and NAFTA have affected travel to México, Canada, and the U.S.

❸ PEOPLE, PLACES AND ENVIRONMENTS

▶ Interview local persons regarding the impact of the Free Trade Agreement or NAFTA on their business.

❹ INDIVIDUAL DEVELOPMENT AND IDENTITY

▶ Create a graph of businesses and factories in the U.S. and México in 1992 proving or disproving Ross Perot's thesis of a "giant sucking sound…"

▶ Recommend solutions to controversial issues which may derail free trade such as prescription drugs, gun control, same gender marriages and bulk water withdrawals.

❺ INDIVIDUALS, GROUPS AND INSTITUTIONS

▶ In groups, decide what institutions and qualities best define the quality of life referred to in Anastakis's article.

❻ POWER, AUTHORITY AND GOVERNANCE

▶ Discuss the political impact of NAFTA on recent national elections in Canada, México and the U.S.

❼ PRODUCTION, DISTRIBUTION AND CONSUMPTION

▶ Create a graph showing trade growth as a result of both FTA and NAFTA.

▶ Debate the benefits of the free trade agreements in North America.

❽ SCIENCE, TECHNOLOGY AND SOCIETY

▶ Design a survey to be completed by international companies on the topic: "What role has technology played in the growth or decline of your business because of free trade in North America?"

❾ GLOBAL CONNECTIONS

▶ After September 11, 2001, the U.S. Ambassador to Canada, Paul Cellucci, stated that "security trumps trade." Defend a position, pro or con, on that statement.

▶ Analyze the positive and negative features of a free trade zone for the entire Western Hemisphere.

❿ CIVIC IDEALS AND PRACTICES

▶ Write a letter to the editor of a local newspaper expressing the pros or cons of free trade in North America.

Contributors

DIMITRY ANASTAKIS

Dimitry Anastakis teaches history at Trent University in Peterborough, Canada, and has held postdoctoral fellowships at Michigan State University (Fulbright), Carleton University, and the University of Toronto. His primary research examines Canada's role in the North American auto industry

PALOMA BAUER DE LA ISLA

Paloma Bauer de la Isla has finished her dissertation at Michigan State University on Mexican politics. Her work deals with democratic change and institution building in Mexico.

DINA BERGER

Dina Berger received her doctorate from the University of Arizona, and is a professor at Loyola University, Chicago. A historian of México, Dr. Berger's work has emphasized the historical effects of tourism on Mexico.

JOHN F. BRATZEL

John F. Bratzel, Graduate Coordinator of the Center for Latin American and Caribbean Studies (CLACS) at Michigan State University, is a member of the Executive Board of the Consortium of Latin American Studies and the author of earlier volumes intended to update K-12 teachers. He is also president of the Popular Culture Association.

MANUEL CHAVEZ

Manuel Chavez, Associate Director of the Center for Latin American and Caribbean Studies at Michigan State University, is a professor in the MSU School of Journalism. He is currently studying community participation in editorial decision-making in the Mexican newspaper organization, Groupo Reforma.

LEONARDO CURZIO

A researcher in the El Centro Investigaciones sobre América del Norte (CISAN) at the Universidad Nacional Autónoma de México, Leonardo Curzio has published extensively on Latin American countries, Spain, and the United States. He is currently a well known political analyst on Mexican radio and television.

PHILIP HANDRICK

Philip Handrick is the Acting Director of the Canadian Studies Centre at Michigan State University. He has done extensive research on the English-speaking minorities of the Eastern Townships of Québec; currently, he directs the annual MSU International Freshman Seminar in Québec City, and teaches the introductory course on Canada at MSU.

AMY J. HIRSHMAN

Amy J. Hirshman received her Ph.D. in Anthropology from Michigan State University with a specialization in Mesoamerican civilizations. Her research focuses on the Tarascan people of western México.

WILLIAM W. JOYCE

William W. Joyce is professor of education and former director of the Canadian Studies Centre at Michigan State University. A co-founder of the National Consortium for Teaching Canada, and an author or co-author of eight professional books, including three on Canada, he currently is researching U.S.-Canada efforts to combat terrorism in North America, and Great Lakes issues.

DEAN JUNE

Dean June teaches seventh and eighth grade social studies in the Attica, New York schools. He has given numerous presentations at meetings of National Council for the Social Studies and at state social studies conferences. He has written extensively on the teaching of Canada in U.S. schools. In 2002, he received a Master Teacher award from the National Consortium for Teaching Canada.

MARTIN N. MARGER

Martin N. Marger, Adjunct Professor of Social Science at Michigan State University, has conducted research on Canadian business immigrants for the past ten years. He has also served as a consultant on immigration issues to the Ontario provincial and Canadian federal governments. He has written extensively on issues of ethnic relations, immigration, and social inequality.

TERRY MCDONALD

Terry McDonald recently retired from Southampton Institute, where he was a Senior Lecturer in History and Politics. He is currently editor of the *British Journal of Canadian Studies* and is an Honorary Fellow at Southampton University's Centre for the Study of Britain and its Empire. His research interests center on nineteenth century Anglo-Canadian social history.

DAVID MCKNIGHT

Since 1997, David McKnight has served as the Director of the Digital Collections Program, McGill University Libraries. As Director, he has overseen the production of numerous scholarly digital collections. In addition, he holds an M.A. in Canadian literature and has worked extensively in the area of twentieth century Canadian Print Culture. He is a part-time lecturer in the McGill Institute for the Study of Canada, where he offers an annual undergraduate course on Canadian Culture.

KRISTIN JANKA MILLAR

Kristin Janka Millar left teaching to pursue a Ph.D. in teacher education with a specialty in social studies. Currently, she is finishing her course work at Michigan State University and constructing the Latin American Studies Educational Resources (LASER) web page, a project of the Center for Latin American and Caribbean Studies aimed at supplying teachers with up-to-date Latin American materials.

DESMOND MORTON

Desmond Morton served in the Canadian Army and was active in politics before teaching at a number of universities including Michigan State University. He was the founding director of the McGill Institute for the Study of Canada (MISC). He now holds the Hiram Mills Chair at McGill University and is honorary colonel of 8 Wing of the Canadian Air Force. He is the author of 37 books on Canadian political, military and industrial relations history.

DANIEL J. NAPPO

Daniel J. Nappo teaches Spanish at the University of Tennessee, Martin. Nappo is a specialist on the novels of the Mexican Revolution, particularly the works of Mariano Azuela.

RUTH WRITER

Ruth Writer is a social studies teacher at Buchanan High School in Buchanan, Michigan. She has published in *Teaching Canada* and in the *Michigan Social Studies Journal*. An avid Canadianist, she co-chairs the Teaching Canada special interest group of National Council for the Social Studies, and received the Master Teacher award from the National Consortium for Teaching Canada.

Index